Television Aesthetics and Style

Television Aesthetics and Style

EDITED BY

JASON JACOBS AND STEVEN PEACOCK

B L O O M S B U R Y

LONDON • NEW DELHI • NEW YORK • SYDNEY

Bloomsbury Academic
An imprint of Bloomsbury Publishing Plc

1385 Broadway
New York
NY 10018
USA

50 Bedford Square
London
WC1B 3DP
UK

www.bloomsbury.com

First published 2013

Library of Congress Cataloging-in-Publication Data
Television aesthetics and style / edited by Jason Jacobs and Steven Peacock.
pages cm
Includes bibliographical references and index.
ISBN 978-1-4411-7992-0 (hardcover : alk. paper)– ISBN 978-1-4411-5751-5 (pbk. : alk. paper)
1. Television broadcasting–Aesthetics. 2. Television–Aesthetics. I. Jacobs, Jason editor of compilation. II. Peacock, Steven, 1974- editor of compilation.
PN1992.55.T3865 2013
791.4502–dc23
2013004521

ISBN: HB: 978-1-4411-7992-0
PB: 978-1-4411-5751-5
epdf: 978-1-6235-6903-7
epub: 978-1-6235-6249-6

Typeset by Fakenham Prepress Solutions, Fakenham, Norfolk NR21 8NN
Printed and bound in the United States of America

Contents

Acknowledgements ix
Contributors xi

Introduction 1
Jason Jacobs and Steven Peacock

PART ONE Conceptual debates 21

1 Television aesthetics: Stylistic analysis and beyond 23
Sarah Cardwell

2 The qualities of complexity: Vast versus dense seriality in
contemporary television 45
Jason Mittell

3 What does it mean to call television 'cinematic'? 57
Brett Mills

4 Rescuing television from 'the cinematic': The perils of
dismissing television style 67
Deborah L. Jaramillo

PART TWO Aesthetics and style of television comedy 77

5 Why comedy is at home on television 79
Alex Clayton

6 Situating comedy: Inhabitation and duration in classical American sitcoms 93

Sérgio Dias Branco

7 Arrested developments: Towards an aesthetic of the contemporary US sitcom 103

Timotheus Vermeulen and James Whitfield

8 Better or differently: Style and repetition in *The Trip* 113

James Walters

9 The presentation of detail and the organisation of time in *The Royle Family* 125

James Zborowski

10 The man from ISIS: *Archer* and the animated aesthetics of adult cartoons 135

Holly Randell-Moon and Arthur J. Randell

PART THREE Critical analyzes of television drama 145

11 Don Draper and the promises of life 147

George Toles

12 Justifying *Justified* 175

William Rothman

13 HBO aesthetics, quality television and *Boardwalk Empire* 185

Janet McCabe

14 Storytelling in song: Television music, narrative and allusion in *The O.C.* 199

Faye Woods

15 Camera and performer: Energetic engagement with
The Shield 209
Lucy Fife Donaldson

16 Flashforwards in *Breaking Bad*: Openness, closure and
possibility 219
Elliott Logan

17 The fantastic style of *Shameless* 227
Beth Johnson

PART FOUR Non-fiction and history 239

18 'Let's just watch it for a few minutes': *This is Your Life* in
1958 241
Charles Barr

19 Gaudy nights: Dance and reality television's display of
talent 251
Frances Bonner

20 Television sublime: The experimental television of Lithuanian
CAC TV 269
Linus Andersson

21 Closer to the action: Post-war American television and the
zoom shot 277
Nick Hall

22 Think-tape: The aesthetics of montage in the post-war
television documentary 289
Ieuan Franklin

23 What FUIs can do: The promises of computing in contemporary television series 309

Cormac Deane

Index 323

Acknowledgements

Thank you first and foremost to the contributors Linus Andersson, Charles Barr, Frances Bonner, Sérgio Dias Branco, Sarah Cardwell, Alex Clayton, Cormac Deane, Lucy Fife Donaldson, Ieuan Franklin, Nick Hall, Deborah L. Jaramillo, Beth Johnson, Elliott Logan, Janet McCabe, Brett Mills, Jason Mittell, Holly Randell-Moon, Arthur J. Randell, William Rothman, George Toles, Timotheus Vermeulen, James Walters, James Whitfield, Faye Woods and James Zborowski. Equally heartfelt thanks to Katie Gallof at Bloomsbury for her support, guidance and enthusiasm for the project. Parts of the Introduction appeared in guest blogs by Jason Jacobs and Steven Peacock for *CST Online*, and in *Critical Studies in Television* 3:1 (2008) and 4:2 (2009). We are grateful to the editors for permission to reprint. Steven would like to thank his colleagues at the University of Hertfordshire for their enthusiastic backing. Jason is grateful for the support of the Cultural History Project funded by the Faculty of Arts at the University of Queensland.

This book is dedicated to Leigh and Val.

Contributors

Linus Andersson recently completed a PhD in Media and Communication Studies at Södertörn University, Sweden. His thesis, Alternative Television: Forms of Critique in Artistic TV-Production explores concepts of aesthetic and social critique in artist's interventions in the TV-medium.

Charles Barr taught for many years at the University of East Anglia, and subsequently in America and Ireland; he is currently Professorial Research Fellow at St Mary's University College, Twickenham. His publications include books on *Ealing Studios, English Hitchcock*, and, in the BFI Classics series, *Vertigo* (new edition, 2012).

Frances Bonner is Reader in Television and Popular Culture in the School of English, Media Studies and Art History at the University of Queensland. Her research focuses on non-fiction television, celebrity, magazines and most recently, adaptation. In addition to many articles and chapters on these topics, she is the author of *Personality Presenters* (Ashgate, 2011), *Ordinary Television* (Sage, 2003), and co-author, with Graeme Turner and David Marshall, of *Fame Games: The Production of Celebrity in Australia* (Cambridge University Press, 2000).

Sérgio Dias Branco is Invited Assistant Professor of Film Studies at the University of Coimbra, where he coordinates the film and image studies in the course in Art Studies. He is researcher in film and philosophy at the Institute of Philosophy of Language at the New University of Lisbon and an invited member of the film analysis group *The Magnifying Class* at the University of Oxford. He co-edits the journals *Cinema: Journal of Philosophy and the Moving Image* and *Conversations: The Journal of Cavellian Studies*. His writings have appeared in refereed publications such as *Refractory* and *Fata Morgana*.

Sarah Cardwell is Honorary Fellow in the School of Arts, University of Kent, and also holds research posts at the University of Glamorgan and Canterbury Christ Church University. She is the author of *Adaptation Revisited* (Manchester University Press, 2002) and *Andrew Davies* (Manchester University Press,

2005), as well as numerous articles and papers on film and television aesthetics, literary adaptation, and British cinema and television: She is a founding editor of 'The Television Series', Manchester University Press.

Alex Clayton is Lecturer in Screen Studies at the University of Bristol, UK. He is the author of *The Body in Hollywood Slapstick* (McFarland, 2007) and co-editor (with Andrew Klevan) of *The Language and Style of Film Criticism* (Routledge, 2011). He has also published essays on performance, colour and music in film.

Cormac Deane is a lecturer in media and cultural studies at the Institute of Art, Design and Technology in Dublin. He is the translator of the final work of Christian Metz, *L'énonciation impersonnelle*, an excerpt of which has appeared in the *New Review of Film and Television Studies*. He is also the author of *The Field Day Archive*, a book-length description of the activities and archives of an Irish theatre and publishing company. His research interests include media theory, systems theory, legal theories of sovereignty and exception, and the depiction of 'terrorism' in contemporary media. He received his PhD from Birkbeck College, University of London, where he was a member of the London Consortium.

Lucy Fife Donaldson is Teaching Fellow in Film Studies at the University of St Andrews. She has published on the materiality of performance in post-studio horror and its relationship to elements of film style in *CineAction* and *Movie: A Journal of Film Criticism*. She is currently writing a book, *Texture in Film*, due to be published by Palgrave Macmillan.

Ieuan Franklin is currently a post-doctoral research assistant at the University of Portsmouth, working on a four-year project funded by the Arts and Humanities Research Council (AHRC) to examine the influence the broad-caster Channel 4 has had on British film culture over the past 30 years. His PhD thesis focused on the uses of oral history in radio documentaries and features. He is also a freelance film archivist and researcher/consultant, with expertise in media archives. He has research interests in low-budget and independent cinema, television documentary, radio documentaries and features, oral history, and vernacular culture.

Nick Hall completed a PhD in Film Studies at the University of Exeter, where he also teaches.

Jason Jacobs is Associate Professor of Film and Television and Reader in Cultural History in the School of English, Media Studies and Art History at the University of Queensland. He has written extensively on television history and aesthetics and is author of *The Intimate Screen* (Oxford University Press, 2000), *Body Trauma TV* (BFI, 2003), *Deadwood* (BFI/Palgrave Macmillan, 2012), and *David Milch* (Manchester University Press, forthcoming in 2014). He is currently researching the history of the BBC's commercial arm.

Deborah L. Jaramillo is an assistant professor in the Department of Film and Television at Boston University. Her first book, *Ugly War Pretty Package* (Indiana University Press, 2009), focuses on the 2003 invasion of Iraq as it was narrativised, aestheticised, marketed and merchandised on CNN and Fox News. Her current research involves the regulation of the US television industry in the 1950s.

Beth Johnson is a Lecturer in Television and Film Studies at the University of Keele. She is the author of various publications in journals such as *Angelaki* and *The Journal of Cultural Research* and her recent book chapters include 'Realism, Real Sex and the Experimental Film: Mediating New Erotics in Georges Bataille's Story of the Eye', in *Realism and the Audiovisual Media* (Palgrave Macmillan, 2009), and 'Sex, Psychoanalysis and Sublimation in Dexter' in *Investigating Dexter: Cutting Edge Television* (I. B. Tauris, 2010). Beth has recently published a co-edited collection entitled *Television, Sex and Society: Analyzing Contemporary Representations* (Continuum, 2012), and has a monograph forthcoming on television auteur 'Paul Abbott' for *The Television Series* (Manchester University Press, 2013).

Elliott Logan is a postgraduate student at the University of Queensland, where he writes about various aspects of film and television aesthetics.

Janet McCabe is Lecturer in Media and Creative Industries at Birkbeck, University of London. She edits *Critical Studies in Television: The International Journal of Television Studies* and has written widely on feminism and television. She has co-edited several collections, including *Quality TV: Contemporary American TV and Beyond* (I. B. Tauris, 2007), and her latest book is *The West Wing*, for the TV Milestone Series.

Brett Mills is Head of the School of Film and Television Studies at the University of East Anglia, and a member of media@uea. He is the author of *The Sitcom* (British Film Institute, 2005) and *Television Sitcom* (Edinburgh University Press, 2009), and co-author of *Reading Media Theory: Thinkers, Approaches, Contexts* (Pearson, 2009, 2012). He is currently undertaking the 3-year AHRC-funded project, 'Make Me Laugh: Creativity in the British Television Comedy Industry'.

Jason Mittell is Associate Professor of American Studies and Film & Media Culture at Middlebury College, Vermont. He is the author of *Genre & Television: From Cop Shows to Cartoons in American Culture* (Routledge, 2004), *Television & American Culture* (Oxford University Press, 2009), numerous essays in journals and anthologies, and the blog Just TV. His next books are *Complex Television: The Poetics of Contemporary Television* Narrative (New York University Press, forthcoming) and *How to Watch TV*, co-edited with Ethan Thompson (New York University Press, forthcoming). In the 2011–12 academic year, he was a visiting fellow at the Lichtenberg-Kolleg Institute for Advanced Study at University of Göttingen, Germany, where he wrote his contribution for this collection.

Steven Peacock is Reader in Film and Television Aesthetics at the University of Hertfordshire. He has written extensively on television aesthetics and style, and is the author of *Swedish Crime Fiction: Novel, Film, Television* (Manchester University Press, 2013), *Hollywood and Intimacy: Style, Moments, Magnificence* (Palgrave Macmillan, 2011), and *Colour* (Manchester University Press, 2010). He is the editor of *Reading 24: TV against the Clock* (I. B. Tauris, 2007) and for 'The Television Series', Manchester University Press.

Arthur J. Randell is an independent scholar who has worked in the television and digital technology industries in Australia for the last ten years. He received his Masters in Media Arts and Communication from the University of Technology, Sydney. His research and writing interests include film and television narrative and representation, visual culture and audience reception studies.

Holly Randell-Moon teaches communication and media studies at the University of Otago, New Zealand. Her publications on popular culture, gender and sexuality have appeared in the edited book collection *Common Sense: Intelligence as Presented on Popular Television* (Lexington Books, 2008) and the journals *Feminist Media Studies* and *Topic: The Washington & Jefferson College Review*. She has also published widely on race, religion and secularism in the journals *Critical Race and Whiteness Studies*, *borderlands* and *Social Semiotics* and in the edited book collections *Religion, Spirituality and the Social Sciences* (The Policy Press, 2008) and *Mediating Faiths* (Ashgate, 2010).

William Rothman received his PhD in Philosophy from Harvard, where he taught for many years. Professor Rothman was Director of the International Honors Program on Film, Television and Social Change in Asia (1986–90). Since 1990, he has been at the University of Miami, where he is Professor of

Motion Pictures and Director of the MA and PhD Programs in Film Studies. He was the founding editor of the 'Harvard Film Studies' series at Harvard University Press, and is currently series editor of the Cambridge University Press 'Studies in Film' series. He has published extensively on many aspects of global cinema. His books include *Hitchcock – The Murderous Gaze* (Harvard University Press 1982; expanded edn, State University of New York Press, 2012), *The "I" of the Camera* (Cambridge University Press, 1988; expanded edn 2004); *Documentary Film Classics* (Cambridge University Press, 1997); *Reading Cavell's The World Viewed: A Philosophical Perspective on Film* (Wayne State University Press, 2000); *Cavell on Film* (State University of New York Press, 2005); *Jean Rouch: A Celebration of Life and Film* (Schena Editore and Presses de l'Université de Paris-Sorbonne, 2007); *Three Documentary Filmmakers* (State University of New York Press, 2009). He recently completed *Must We Kill the Thing We Love? Emersonian Perfectionism and the Films of Alfred Hitchcock*.

George Toles is Distinguished Professor of Film and Literature at the University of Manitoba. He is the author of *A House Made of Light: Essays on the Art of Film* (Wayne State University Press, 2001). For 25 years, he has been the screenwriting collaborator of Canadian film director Guy Maddin. His most recent screenplay has been for Maddin's *Keyhole* (2012). George is currently working on a monograph on the films of Paul Thomas Anderson.

Timotheus Vermeulen is assistant professor in Cultural Theory at the Radboud University Nijmegen, where he is also director of the Centre for New Aesthetics. He is founding editor of the academic arts and culture webzine *Notes on Metamodernism*. Vermeulen has written on contemporary aesthetics, art, film and television for amongst others *The Journal of Aesthetics and Culture*, *Screen*, *Monu*, *Frieze*, and various collections and catalogues. He is currently working on two books on metamodernism.

James Walters is Senior Lecturer in Film and Television Studies at the University of Birmingham. He is the author of *Alternative Worlds in Hollywood Cinema* (Intellect, 2008), *Fantasy Film* (Berg, 2011) and co-editor (with Tom Brown) of *Film Moments: Criticism, History, Theory* (BFI/Palgrave Macmillan, 2010).

James Whitfield is currently completing his AHRC-funded PhD on contemporary found footage media. His research was undertaken at King's College London, where he currently teaches, and his work has appeared in *Screen*.

Faye Woods is Lecturer in Film and Television at the University of Warwick. Her research interests include popular music in film and television, youth representations and television industries. She has published in *Television & New Media* and *Critical Studies in Television*. She is currently writing a monograph on British youth television.

James Zborowski teaches television, media and film studies at the University of Hull.

Introduction

Jason Jacobs and Steven Peacock

Pressing play or finding the series on television, the first, fundamentally eye-catching quality of J. J. Abrams' TV drama *Alias* (2001–6 Touchstone Television) is its supercharged style. Even before the series opens up a Pandora's Box of spy games, generic combinations and narrative twists, it presents cascades of visual pleasures. Soaring landscape shots of exotic locations scud into close-ups of shifty looking agents. The camera roams and skims over the series' glossy décor and day-glo designs before plunging into undercover activity. Jackhammer edits rivet set-pieces and schemes of subterfuge. Poker-faces and tense bluffs suddenly snap into balletic freefalls of hyper-violence. Across shots, sequences and seasons, aspects shift in kaleidoscopic style: costumes, accents, allegiances, hair colour. In the storm's eye, central protagonist Sydney Bristow (Jennifer Garner) remains a tantalisingly ethereal presence: plastically nimble, coldly detached, almost always on the screen but equally constantly on the move: present and at one remove. Flitting across *Alias*' world in outrageous cat-suits and a flame-red mane of hair, Garner-as-Bristow embodies the series' chimerical appeals: an impossibly foolish fancy with visionary flair.

Alias' thrusting visuals, its urgent tone and alluring designs compel us to consider its style, to *think through* its stylistic choices. Yet, such discussions remain curiously absent from many critical appraisals of contemporary television. In 2008, Thalia Baldwin and Steven Peacock noted this odd methodological omission in a review of *Investigating Alias: Secrets and Spies* (eds Stacey Abbott and Simon Brown):

A ... worrying and widespread trend in TV Studies is the lack of attention to style. As the discipline shifts away from the broad overviews often offered in Media and Cultural Studies, a promising focus on the particular has emerged. In this respect, I.B. Tauris's output of books devoted to a sustained scrutiny of individual programmes is at the forefront of the discipline. Yet, for whatever reason, TV style keeps getting missed. This is a particularly curious omission in any study of *Alias*, considering the emphasis the series places on stylistic rhetoric and playfulness. The distinctively slick, cinematic look of *Alias* is at once deceptively superficial and worthy of further attention. Whilst creating a glossy aesthetic akin to the hyper-real cinematic panoramas offered by, for example, McG and Michael Bay, *Alias* uses its sleek surfaces to explore aspects of artifice: in both theme and style the world of the series is rife with artfulness and *shallow designs* ... Yet, the odd allusion aside, a concentration on matters of style in *Alias* remains as elusive as the series' mystical overlord, Rambaldi.[1]

This gap in scholarship is not only evidenced in relation to *Alias*. Despite a resurgence of stylistic criticism in film studies,[2] the related discipline of television studies has not followed suit in earnest. Academic work on television remains, for the most part, entrenched in theoretical frameworks. As noted above, there *has* been a shift from considerations of television in general (as a medium, in terms of 'flow' for instance) to particular programmes (exemplified by I. B. Tauris' *Reading Contemporary Television Series* and BFI's *TV Classics*). Yet, such studies remain, for the most part, informed by approaches through which theory is mapped onto the television 'text' to decipher its so-called coded meanings. Equally, despite many writers' assertions that, within these readings, close textual analysis will be employed, there is a key conflation of terms. Too often, such analysis becomes systematic, determined to 'solve' the text's engagement with a specific subject, rather than employing critical principles to feel through its tensions and complexities, keeping them in play. Further, such work resists a dedicated and sustained scrutiny of television style, attempting to undertake 'close textual analysis' without getting close to the text's integral compositional elements. This despite a call in 2006 by Sarah Cardwell and Steven Peacock in a special issue of the *Journal of British Cinema and Television* entitled 'Good Television?' encouraging debate on the following questions:

> What is good television? Why are appreciation and evaluation so rarely tackled within television studies? How might notions of critical judgement and value enhance television studies? What new approaches or

---

[1] Thalia Baldwin and Steven Peacock, 'Review of *Investigating Alias: Secrets and Spies*, I. B. Tauris, 2007', in *Critical Studies in Television* 3:1 (Spring 2008): 103–6.

[2] See, for instance, John Gibbs and Douglas Pye, 'Introduction', in *Style and Meaning: Studies in the Detailed Analysis of Film*, ed. John Gibbs and Douglas Pye (Manchester: Manchester University Press, 2005), 1–15; Andrew Klevan, *Disclosure of the Everyday: Undramatic Achievement in Narrative Film* (Trowbridge: Flicks Books, 2000); James Walters and Tom Brown, (eds) *Film Moments: Criticism, History, Theory* (London: BFI/Palgrave Macmillan, 2010).

perspectives might aid the critical assessment of television? What might television criticism within television studies look like? What role might interpretation or close analysis play? How useful are criteria for evaluation borrowed from film studies?[3]

A survey of other, more recently published collections and monographs on television affords a revealing view of the current landscape, of the contours of critical debate and the unsettled territory of style. Amongst all these rather strained allusions to mapping, it is fitting to first address a book about an island adrift in space and time: *Reading Lost*, edited by Roberta Pearson. The cult television drama *Lost* notoriously teases its viewers by setting narrative puzzles and withholding information: why did just these people crash on this mysterious island? What are polar bears doing in tropical climes? What is the smoke monster? Not seeking to appease fans by offering solutions to such enigmas, *Reading Lost* responds, primarily, to matters around the programme. The first of three sections presents contextual readings of the series' institutional and technological factors, exploring its place within cross-media platforms, and as a branded television product. The third section follows the more established route of edited collections on particular programmes, offering socio-cultural readings of *Lost*'s representational biases. Having glossed around the series, the middle section of the book focuses in on the text itself. This second set of chapters is commendable in raising the rarely voiced matter of evaluation in television studies. This is especially true of Jason Mittell's chapter in which he states, 'for the readers and writers within this book's core genre of television studies ... an explicit assertion of evaluation and praise probably seems out of place, as evaluation is generally off-limits for television academics'.[4] Citing the intellectual history and academic origins of television studies as reasons for what he terms the 'evacuation of the evaluative', Mittell offers a call to arms:

> It is time to let evaluative criticism out of the closet. It is not enough to use coded signifiers of value like 'sophistication' and 'nuance' in referring to television programming worth studying or teaching – let us admit openly when we think a programme is great. Especially in the context of a book dedicated to exploring a single programme in depth, we must be explicit in acknowledging the roles of evaluation and aesthetic judgement that help

---

[3] Sarah Cardwell and Steven Peacock, 'Introduction' in Sarah Cardwell and Steven Peacock, (eds) 'Good Television?', *Journal of British Cinema and Television* 3:1 (2006): 1.
[4] Jason Mittell, '*Lost* in a Great Story: Evaluation in Narrative Television (and Television Studies)', in *Reading Lost: Perspectives on a Hit Television Show*, ed. Roberta Pearson (London: I. B. Tauris, 2009), 119–38.

to frame our research and drive our field. Many of our scholarly efforts are focused on programmes that we enjoy, value and think are better than others, a forbidden admission that is more often assumed in other fields like film or literary studies, where engaging in close study of an author or text often constitutes an implicit endorsement of its aesthetic merits.[5]

The remainder of Mittell's chapter comprises a persuasive interpretative and evaluative account of *Lost*'s achievements in narrative designs. The other chapters in the section echo Mittell's approach, making claims for the complexity of *Lost*'s plot, generic formulae and character constructions. Yet if one is to follow Mittell's argument, and 'especially in the context of a book dedicated to exploring a single programme in depth', it is even more remarkable to note the omission of any detailed reference to *Lost*'s stylistic elements. Although the book lacks an index, a thorough reading reveals little mention of style, or *mise-en-scène*, or any related terms. We are careful not to conflate or confuse evaluative criticism with stylistic interpretation, though if, as Mittell suggests, there is good reason to follow film studies in a close appraisal of aesthetic merits, then it appears essential to talk not only of meaningful narrative designs but also of points of visual and aural significance. Further, if we *are* to follow film studies in this regard, then all of these methodological strands necessarily intertwine. John Gibbs and Douglas Pye set out such an understanding in their introduction to the edited collection *Style and Meaning: Studies in the Detailed Analysis of Film*:

> We take it that criticism has two basic functions: interpretation (or reading) and evaluation, the two dimensions of the process being inseparably linked ... In viewing most movies we will develop a quite complex grasp of characters and situations and possibly reach towards some sense of their wider resonance. Particular formal and stylistic features – the use of voice-over, extended camera movements, special effects – may strike us as significant. In our tentative, unfocused and often imprecise dialogue with friends after a movie we are all familiar with the mingling of these different responses and ideas as we struggle to articulate ways in which the film has affected us, what we take it to be trying to do, how it relates to other movies, to what we had expected and so on. These are processes of interpretation, and the more systematic and analytical procedures that lead eventually to published interpretative criticism that are tidier, more

---

[5]Mittell, '*Lost* in a Great Story', 122.

considered, selective and reflective versions of the same thing. major part of what we take understanding a film to be.[6]

Calling a series of books 'Reading Contemporary Television' suggests an explicit engagement in similar processes of interpretation. In the case of *Reading Lost*, and especially as the book includes Mittell's rare rallying cry for evaluative criticism, the absence of responsive aesthetic judgements on style is as puzzling as the diegetic presence of the polar bears.

More encouraging is the inclusion of a short section entitled 'Visuals' in Rhonda V. Wilcox and Tanya R. Cochran's edited collection *Investigating Firefly and Serenity*. As the book's blurb explains of its TV and film subjects, 'the 2002 space Western *Firefly* was *Buffy*-creator Joss Whedon's third major work as a television auteur. *Firefly* was cancelled after only three months, but extraordinary interest from fans ("the Browncoats") and the determination of its creators Whedon and Minear resulted in the release of a major motion picture sequel, *Serenity*, in 2005.'

Of the two chapters that make up the section, Barbara Maio's piece provides a useful explanation of how a variety of *Firefly*'s design elements are generically codified for narrative effect. Observing the series' coupling of visual markers from the Western and science fiction, Maio notes how, for example, in costume, 'Captain Malcolm Reynolds is clearly inspired by the character of Han Solo, dressed like a space cowboy. The Solo vest is replaced by a brown coat, but the fascination is the same. The gun becomes a symbol of the character.'[7] Similar categorisations lead to the distinguishing of various thematic dichotomies inherited from the series' generic forms, such as 'wilderness versus civilisation', 'nature against technology', 'East and West'. While holding attention on aspects of set design, such quasi-structuralist exposition risks a move towards reductive analysis of the programme's style, and away from the 'more considered, selective and reflective versions' of our everyday interpretative procedures that Gibbs and Pye delineate.

In order to negotiate the potential complexities and meanings of style, individual moments within television series merit closer study. As Andrew Klevan sets out in his chapter in *Style and Meaning*, scholars might be encouraged to 'involve themselves in the intricacies of a film's style', to show 'how that involvement refines interpretation and enables sensitive evaluation'.[8] Promoting a tradition of expressive criticism favoured by such

---

[6] Gibbs and Pye, 'Introduction', 5.

[7] Barbara Maio, 'Between Past and Future: Hybrid Design Style in *Firefly* and *Serenity*', in *Investigating Firefly and Serenity*, (eds) Rhonda Wilcox and Tanya Cochran (London: I. B. Tauris, 2008), 201–11.

[8] Andrew Klevan, 'Notes on teaching film style', in Gibbs and Pye, 214–27.

figures as V.F. Perkins, George Wilson and William Rothman, Klevan notes how scholars might then also be encouraged 'not to 'solve films by analysis', but rather to be 'responsive to the overlaps, keep in play the balance of meanings'.[9] Encapsulating his approach, an approach which might be equally and fruitfully applied to television, Klevan states that, 'Honing in on moments is a matter of magnification. We can survey the interweaving contours of the drama and better discern the undulating lines without the need to straighten them out.'[10]

The recently published collection *Film Moments: Criticism, History, Theory* (2010) reminds us of the potential critical value inherent in the fact that 'Film endures as a medium made of moments: the brief, temporary and transitory combining to create the whole.'[11] The book provides a series of sustained readings of individual film moments – from works as diverse as *The Night of the Hunter* to *Kill Bill Vol. 2* – all of which develop our understanding of the various constituents of the momentary on screen, and, in turn, of the status and structure of film form. Arguably, the project becomes more complex when applied to television, to the television moment, because of the medium's different relationship to time.

Television is as capable as film of creating expressive richness in moments that are at once fleeting, demonstrative and dramatically declamatory, climactic, or seemingly inconsequential. As with narrative film, and especially genre pieces, TV drama consists of clusters of expected, conventional happenings, such as the moment when characters finally meet, or face-off, or the penny drops and so on. The subversion or recasting of these moments is equally well-trod ground on the small screen, exemplified by a growing trend in TV drama to 'unexpectedly' kill off a main character (see *24*, *American Horror Story* and *Spooks*, for example).

In broad terms, the distinction between film and television is twofold. First, the expansive structure of television fictions – stretching across episodes, seasons, in series capable of running for years and decades – complicates the place of the moment in the whole. A series alert to the possibilities of significant patterning in forms of narrative and narration may rhyme or counterpoint moments from different seasons. To name but a few recent examples, *Breaking Bad*, *Mad Men*, *Sons of Anarchy*, *Misfits* and *Community* are all consummately skilled in this strategy. The series may allude to very early moments in its final stages, even if the mood and tone of the drama

---

[9] Andrew Klevan, 'Notes on teaching film style', 215.
[10] Andrew Klevan, 'Notes on teaching film style', 215.
[11] Tom Brown and James Walters, (eds) *Film Moments: Criticism, History, Theory* (London: BFI/Palgrave Macmillan, 2010), xi.

have transformed fundamentally from within (we are thinking here of *The West Wing*).

At the same time, the fluid consistency of a TV drama with the ability to run on forever makes mischief with the criterion of coherence. How do we judge a television work's unity if it is open-ended, changing and building across episodes, still in flux? How can we make decisive discriminations of a particular moment if its relationship to the (incomplete) whole is as yet undeclared or undecided?[12]

Secondly, the contemporary place of television in the world informs our standing towards its moments. Historically, in Western culture, television has been perceived as a throwaway medium, a provider of information and entertainment, the latter easily devoured and dispensed with by the channel-hopping consumer. This scenario leads to thoughts on traditional forms of television broadcasting, of the image's live-ness, of a fixed schedule of air-dates and times, of groups within nations watching the same drama unfold at the same time. In turn, the ephemeral nature of the TV transmission is ever-present, the moment always disappearing even as it is shown, potentially lost the minute it ends. Of course, the advent of the VCR, DVD and PVR has changed this relationship, allowing repeat viewings of individual series, episodes and moments. So, too, have the online viewing platforms of (myriad incarnations of) the iPlayer and YouTube services. In format, the latter encourages the breakdown and appraisal of television fictions into fragments ('Part 1 of 12', for example) or, in other words, into series of moments.

Yet as the world of social media expands, currently favoured forms of networking show signs of returning us to the 'live' broadcasts of TV drama, to an appreciation of sharing the viewing experience as a collective community. One good recent example comes from the widespread use of Twitter to discuss Steven Moffat and Mark Gatiss's *Sherlock* episode 'The Hounds of Baskerville'. Thousands of tweets accompanied the programme during its UK broadcast on the evening of Sunday 8 January 2012 commenting on its achievements and failings, as it unfolded. At one point in the episode, Sherlock (Benedict Cumberbatch) retreats to his 'mind-palace'; the programme-makers express this act of mental gymnastics as flutters of words and images superimposed on the screen, to be conjured with and wiped away by the detective's hands. As the scene aired, #minorityreport starting trending worldwide on Twitter, as viewers and tweeters recognized the similarity of visual techniques in Spielberg's film. This fact was then instantaneously

---

[12] Jason Jacobs raises this as an issue for criticism in 'Issues of Judgement and Value in Television Studies', *International Journal of Cultural Studies* 4:4 (2001): 436–7.

picked up and propagated in other tweets, feeding the attention being given to one television moment, *just at that moment*.

There are many television moments that strike us as compelling, extraordinary, haunting or distinctive. All provoke both an instantaneous response and linger in the mind, all prompting us to consider what is at stake in the individual moment, and in the individual television fiction. Some of the moments are explicitly designed within and by the TV drama to be appreciated, as high points of an episode or season. Others pass by more quietly or quickly, their expression of meaning – necessarily subtle in the unfolding of that sequence – appreciated through repeat viewing. A rich example, less declamatory than *Sherlock*'s stylistic tricks or *Alias*' shrill aesthetic, comes from *In Treatment*. Dealing with the intricacies and properties of psychiatric conversations between therapist and patient, the series is attuned to the potential significance of individual passing instances, thoughts, gestures and words.

In its third (and final) season, *In Treatment* presents the beguilingly cryptic case of reluctant migrant Sunil (Irrfan Khan). During his weekly sessions with Dr Paul Weston (Gabriel Byrne), Sunil's behaviour and phrasing hint at hostile lusty intentions towards his daughter-in-law. Across episodes, the series builds to the moment when Paul must confront Sunil, articulating his concerns. In 3:9, the dramatically charged instant is met and made eerily complex by the unexpected nature of Sunil's reaction. He finds the idea hysterically funny, tittering and hiccoughing words in fits of giggles. The fact that this is the first time Sunil has demonstratively expressed emotion in any of his sessions heightens the atypical sense of this inappropriate response. That such an unnatural reaction comes out so naturally upsets the usual, formal and cautiously watchful dynamic of the session. A moment of relaxed abandon causes Dr Weston to recoil, uncharacteristically at a loss of what to say or do. His intuitive response is to withdraw, even at the point of revelation. The tensions of the instant play out on his face, as shock, concern and the desire to reaffirm control slide together in a performance of professional composure suddenly and silently unsettled. In the world of the drama, the carefully negotiated roles of these two men's performances in front of one another, developed over weeks, have now become troublingly undefined. Sunil has not acted 'as expected' by therapist and viewer alike, and our gradually advanced understanding of the man is called into question. A few seconds of silence and mumbled words bring the session to a close without satisfactory reconciliation. The effects of Sunil's brief burst of laughter hang in the air and across subsequent episodes.

The intrinsically theatrical (or perhaps tele-visual) nature of the therapeutic set-up – two chairs, primed handkerchiefs, the tea-service – is in place to draw out hidden truths in a safely self-contained environment. However, Sunil's turn tips the balance, highlighting instead the risky fraudulence of such a circumscribed scenario. (This is particularly adroit when one considers the character's own veiled intentions and false enactments during his time with Paul.) Without recourse to point-making, this moment explores the relationship between artifice and reality in the filmed drama. *In Treatment*'s handling of even the most minute emotional, physical and psychological adjustments of its characters, through exact, effortlessly achieved movements of camera, faces and bodies, is without equal on current UK and US television. The moment, too, within *In Treatment*, can be simultaneously momentary and momentous, as a point in which information is contained, revealed and absorbed in precise measures. Without appearing forced or contrived, the series' investment in and engagement with the processes of psychotherapy – in which a casual or accidental comment or gesture, caught and gone in an instant, may hold great significance – points up inherent expressive possibilities of the filmed medium. There is perhaps no better example on the small screen of 'the brief, temporary and transitory combining to create the whole'.

A refined and responsive reading of a television moment in magnification is found in the second chapter on 'Visuals' in the *Firefly* collection, by Matthew Pateman. Over a few paragraphs, Pateman interprets and evaluates the series' singular, unconventional use of stylistic strategies normally associated with moments of melodramatic tension: slow-motion and heightened music. Yet despite the chapter's claimed aim to 'demonstrate the ways in which the *mise-en-scène* of death in the franchise contributes to our affective and moral engagement with the show and its characters', the piece is more concerned with detailing character motivations and plot events than honing in on synthetic arrangements of points of style.[13] Further evidence of the show's 'aesthetic vitality' may stem from more sustained concentrations of interpretative analysis.

If Pateman's dip into detailed stylistic criticism marks a scarce excursion for television studies, it may also represent a pending sea-change. Following examples and interventions by leading figures in the field, certain television scholars are providing significant studies of style in monograph form. Robin Nelson's *State of Play: Contemporary 'High End' TV Drama*, while primarily concerned with contextualising quality television programmes within the global digital culture, provides concise readings of television moments as indicative of series' particularities and TV's possibilities. Sudeep Dasgupta presents a compelling intervention in *NECSUS European Journal of Media*

---

[13] Matthew Pateman, 'Deathly Serious: Mortality, Morality and the *Mise-en-Scène* in *Firefly* and *Serenity*', in Wilcox and Cochran, 212–26.

Studies, thinking through the relationships between television aesthetics, audiences and politics. Jeremy Butler's *Television Style* provides useful examples of formalist analysis. Interestingly though, it is the critical works coming from under the arches of film studies that explicitly and happily acknowledge the necessary bind of style, interpretation and evaluation. In particular, Gibbs and Pye's *Close-Up* series provides a valuable space for the close analysis of film and television, providing sustained studies of sequences and moments. To date, two *Close-Up* monographs have dealt with the meaningful stylistic choices of particular television programmes: Deborah Thomas' *Reading Buffy* and Jonathan Bignell's *The Police Series*.[14]

The latter acknowledges the discipline's predominant reluctance to engage in stylistic criticism, and offers a corrective study of various police dramas. In his introduction, Bignell notes how, 'For a long time television criticism on the US police series [and we may say television criticism in general] has been more interested in methodologies of genre grouping (Buxton, 1990), institutions and authorship (Thompson, 1996) or audiences and ideological representations (D'Acci, 1994).'[15] He continues, 'it is a contention of this study that there is a need for detailed analysis to both question and support theoretical ideas about television as a medium, and the police series specifically, that have been developed without much attention to style'.[16] Following his expressive case studies, of the style of (amongst others) *Miami Vice* and *NYPD Blue*, Bignell concludes in a way that chimes with Mittell's earlier argument:

> Such a process of valuing the popular by analysing relationships between style and meaning motivated the procedures of mise-en-scène criticism in academic film studies from which many of the analytical techniques used in this study derive (see Gibbs and Pye, 2005). Further work about television could benefit from adopting the methodology of detailed analysis which derives from that tradition...[17]

---

[14] Robin Nelson, *State of Play: Contemporary 'High End' TV Drama* (Manchester: Manchester University Press, 2007); Sudeep Dasgupta, 'Policing the people: Television studies and the problem of "quality" ', in *NECSUS European Journal of Media Studies*, http://www.necsus-ejms.org [accessed 4 October 2012]; Jeremy Butler, *Television Style* (London: Routledge, 2010); Deborah Thomas, *Reading Buffy*, in John Gibbs and Douglas Pye (eds) *Close-Up 01* (London: Wallflower Press, 2006), 167–244.

[15] Jonathan Bignell, *The Police Series*, in John Gibbs and Douglas Pye, (eds) *Close-Up 03* (London: Wallflower Press, 2009), 5–66. Internal citations David Buxton, *From The Avengers to Miami Vice: Form and Ideology in Television Series* (Manchester: Manchester University Press, 1990); Robert J. Thompson, *Television's Second Golden Age: From Hill Street Blues to ER* (New York: Syracuse University Press, 1996); Julie D'Acci, *Defining Women: Television in the Case of Cagney and Lacey* (Chapel Hill, NC: North Carolina University Press, 1994).

[16] Jonathan Bignell, *The Police Series*, 5.

[17] Jonathan Bignell, *The Police Series*, 64.

In their stances and statements, both Mittell and Bignell are asking for the formation and activation of a critical community. From different yet converging perspectives, they see an advancement of television scholars engaging in stylistic criticism as both fruitful in refining our understanding of individual programmes and in the development of the discipline. We would like not only to promote such calls, but also, crucially, to encourage more collaborative critical responses to stylistic studies across publications. That is to say, for figures in the field to follow the terribly outmoded yet critically germane appeal of F. R. Leavis to seek, in response to an interpretative claim that 'This is so, isn't it?' the words 'Yes, but...'. This collection forms an invitation then, to talk and think about television aesthetics and style both more widely and more closely, to create not only a wealth of stylistic criticism on television in print, but also to commence a vital conversation across published interpretations.

The structure of the collection is intended to move between close and broad viewpoints, with some contributors exploring the prominent theoretical matters and others focusing on particular shows and their distinctive aesthetic comportment. This reflects an aspect of the medium outlined above, which is its ability to ground the power of its moments in relation to an already established history – call it a tradition – not only one generated by the internal memory of its own past, but anchored, too, to the broader cultural history that we share, debate and disagree with. In this respect 'moments' are always situated; and they often exhibit the inheritance of both their internal and external traditions.

A way of making this clearer is to look at what has become an emblem of stylistic and aesthetic achievement, *Mad Men*. As George Toles's astonishing essay in this collection testifies, that show is able to engage at depth, through the agonised and paradoxical development of its central character, with the problem of human existence as a community of the living and the dead. Which is to say, in a world dominated by 'presentism', the show reminds us that our *now* is a product of a *then* that cannot be dispelled or negated by the blooming, buzzing immediacy of our current circumstances. Many critics have rightly pointed to the way the show exhibits a cinematic rather than a broadcast inheritance (most obviously its Sirkian *mise-en-scène*), but it also utilizes the prominent feature of television serial form, quite distinct from film, in its ability to – moment-by-moment – add layers to the sedimentation that is its own history and its engagement with world history. That this does not decant into a simple reflection or translation of past socio-cultural circumstances we might take as a warning not to be so sure of our present moral and ethical superiority. Toles's account of our experience of Don Draper's Lucky Strike pitch ('Don Draper and the Promises of Life') is instructive in this respect. For Draper, like Gatsby before him, in his attempt to transcend the past ultimately becomes absorbed by it, but, as Toles tracks the moment of his initial failure to convince the tobacco barons, he shows us that our own complicity in wanting Draper to be successful is hostage not to an ethical superiority but a desire to see victorious recovery that only accrues its force in relation to past disaster. Toles is able to make that vivid, not merely because of the force of his exquisite prose, but because he shows how we begin to 'live in' to scenes, characters, moments and series through our fluid responsiveness to the show's careful modulation of its own pitch to us, as it invites and confounds a position of superiority over the past. As William Empson has said of his analysis of a moment from *Macbeth*, the quotations he drills into are there 'to show [how] much work the reader of Shakespeare is prepared to do for him, how one is helped by the rest of his work to put a great deal into any part of it'.[18] To speak of 'living in', then, is to acknowledge the medium's ability to generate a shared history with us, and our willingness to meet its challenges, to work with it in mutual inhabitancy.

To illustrate this point it is instructive to return to Gibbs and Pye's *Style and Meaning*, and their suggestive analogy of artefacts and houses:

> Works of art are not like shipwrecks on the sea bed which inertly form a home for different corals, but significantly organized artefacts which interact with and reflect culture. They are more like a well-designed house: not every occupant will choose to use the rooms in quite the same manner, but the building has been shaped to facilitate certain modes of living, certain ways of moving through it.[19]

True enough of the individual movie or discrete artwork, but the television 'houses' we get to return to again and again want us as long-term tenants, as we become in the offices of Sterling Cooper Draper Pryce. We live into their familiarity and notice the adjustments in décor, light, the way a house absorbs, reflects and shapes the lives of its inhabitants. Only television does this so regularly, with such insistent promotion of familiar spaces, people and objects. And while we may look at the history of architectural design, the provenance and distribution of building materials, in order to place the house within a system and history of construction, it is only by inhabiting the space as a dwelling, a home, that we get to know it intimately and thereby earn the experience from where the first springs of criticism may arise.

But familiarity is not the same as legibility. One of the most pleasing things about editing the collection was the willingness of those contributors,

---

[18] William Empson, *Seven Types of Ambiguity* (London: Chatto and Windus, 1949), 18.
[19] Gibbs and Pye, 'Introduction', 7.

most notably Toles, Rothman and Clayton, who are associated with film style criticism, to turn their attention for the first time in print to television. But characteristically they face the medium with curious humility, rather than critical arrogance, feeling out the beats of conversation, the shadings and gradations of meaning in gestures, moods and looks with tiny fingers of critical illumination, so that in reading their work we feel, as we do with the shows they admire, an unfolding of our experience in all its congealed difficulty rather than an 'unpacking' of neatly demarcated items. This critical comportment seems to us in contrast to the overconfidence of television and cultural studies in the certainty that often accompanies its translation of the content of television into neatly defined socio-cultural objects. To take a final example from *Mad Men*, 'Mystery Men' the fourth episode of its extraordinary fifth season, has a moment when Joan at the breakfast table, tells her husband Greg, an army surgeon who is voluntarily returning to Vietnam, to leave. 'If I walk out that door, that's it', he shouts at her; 'That's it', she replies, effectively ending their marriage. After he slams the door, her mother (who has been living with her and helping with their baby) comes back into the kitchen holding a coffee pot; 'It's over', Joan tells her. The pot is put down: she discards it in one motion, and sits in silence with her daughter, as if in that instant it becomes a quaint irrelevance, once an emblem of servitude now just a raw, gross object. That gesture, the holding with two hands – one on the handle the other protected by a cloth under it, taking its weight in two ways before abandoning it, is marvellous, eloquent. But it is difficult to translate such eloquence into words, hard to be expressive in the face of such expressivity; indeed we might feel haunted by the sheer apparent *obviousness* of what it must be, had we the words to express it. Of course, we might want to say, in that gesture in this arrangement of objects there is something to be said about the domestic labour of women in history, at this time, something that demands a feminist response, or some version or variation of that. But in its discoursing on our recent history, one that seems only an eye-blink from the present, yet sufficiently distant to allow us to be distant too, *Mad Men* is both a temptation to and a warning against this kind of critical hubris. It is doubtful that wanting to tie feminist thinking to this moment could sufficiently capture its expressive *punctum*. Not at least, until there had been the time – for the show and for us – to allow it to settle into the sedimented geology of the cultural imagination.

There are those (admirable) scholars and critics who write about television with the confidence that suggests they can sift and order its complex movement, discourses and resonances with apparent ease; but we should be careful of the kind of approach that exhibits critical, intellectual even imaginative superiority over the objects surveyed, tagged and categorised.

One of the worrying things with writing about very recent television is that one is always aware that one's proximity to the immediacy of its putative aesthetic thrills threatens the reliability of judgement, perhaps because we are forcing the issue before the material has had an opportunity to insinuate its resonances, discourses and achievements into the critical spaces, traditions and debates necessary for it to establish a reliable presence as part of our cultural heritage. This collection offers another layer in what we hope is an emerging tradition of criticism that will cushion the risks of immediate response.

That such responses are often prompted by the delight in particular moments, as noted above, does not negate the need to shift into a critical wide-shot if those compelling particulars are to make any sense more generally. To this end we open the collection with a section that engages with the pressing conceptual issues that a sensible account of television's aesthetics and style must have. Sarah Cardwell's essay fires a blazing arrow at the centre of some recent debates about the appropriateness of juxtaposing 'television' and 'aesthetics', taking us back to some of the central issues in philosophical aesthetics that continue to have relevance to the medium today. While Cardwell notes that the aesthetic attitude is 'attentive and directed' (in contrast to the 'distance' encouraged by formalist analysis), her central plea is for continued debate about the nature of aesthetic criticism in television studies and a deepening of our understanding of some of the philosophical matters at stake when doing so. It is an important reminder that we are near the beginning of a form of critical engagement that, whatever the hostility directed toward it within the academy, needs to be less defensive.

Cardwell was and is a central figure in the resurgence of interest in the study of television aesthetics in the UK (as distinct from earlier work by Charlotte Brunsdon and John Caughie); Jason Mittell occupies a similar position in the US as a pioneer of the study of 'complex' television (as distinct from earlier work on US TV aesthetics by Horace Newcomb and David Thorburn).[20] Like Cardwell, he stresses the importance of engaging 'fully and attentively' with complex works, and is careful to avoid elevating complexity to a prescriptive criterion of value. The caution with which Mittell approaches the necessity of evaluation in tension with the dangers of elitist assertions of value that is not grounded in the work itself, is characteristically expansive, detailed and anchored to a subtle comparison of the realist modes

[20]See, for example, Charlotte Brunsdon, 'Problems with Quality', *Screen* 31:1 (Spring 1990), 67–90; John Caughie, *Television Drama: Realism, Modernism and British Culture* (Oxford University Press, 2000); David Thorburn, 'Television as an Aesthetic Medium', *Critical Studies in Communication* 4 (1987), 161–73; Horace Newcomb, 'Toward a Television Aesthetic', in *Television: The Critical View*, ed. Horace Newcomb (New York: Oxford University Press, 1976), 273–89.

of *The Wire* with that of *Breaking Bad*. These shows become lenses through which Mittell concentrates the light of his critical attention on a diversity of complexities exemplified in each, ultimately 'pointing to the need to evaluate a series on its own aesthetic terms'. If one can hear the echo of New Criticism here it is one leavened by a more open sensitivity to competing voices that is, in Mittell's phrase, 'an invitation to dialogue and debate'.

The necessity of welcoming competing voices is illustrated by the final two essays that complete the section on conceptual debates. If there is one attribute that has been most frequently – both casually and seriously – deployed in relation to the shifting aesthetics and style of recent television it is the notion of 'the cinematic'. In different ways Brett Mills and Deborah Jaramillo seek to ground this, perhaps too vague and contingent, assertion of 'cinematic television'. Mills points to the ways in which the term is deployed to indicate an aspirational drive to promote some kinds of preferred television from a 'lower' broadcast medium to the 'higher' one of cinema, and worries about the complex ways in which this move reinforces a hierarchical contest. Jaramillo also notes the contentiousness of the word and, like Mills, sees in it a problematic conflation with the notoriously difficult idea of 'quality TV'; her historicising of the term is especially useful in pointing to the shifting shadow that cinema has cast over its industrially intertwined companion. Both essays are pitched in speculative and provocative tones that we hope will initiate a deeper and continuing critical grappling with the term.

While the absorption of some television of 'the cinematic' (however we take that) is not merely based on technological convergence (given the historical provenance of a lot of television within a film camera, it cannot be), neither is it the only marker, rightly or wrongly, of distinction and difference. We were surprised to see that one outcome of our original call for papers for the collection was a preponderance of proposals on television comedy. Accordingly we have devoted an entire section to these. One oddity about television comedy is that one might think it would be the one mode most hostage to the time of its making, ossified in the coastal shelf of its present, unable to transcend or speak beyond it. There are moods, fashions and trends in comedy that seem necessarily anchored to their time, and indeed some fine work in television studies has been done (one thinks of Julia Hallam's work on *Butterflies*)[21] where it is addressed though a socio-cultural understanding because of what it says about class, gender and race at the particular time in which it was made. It is used as a matrix or mapping mechanism through

---

[21] Julia Hallam, 'Remembering *Butterflies*: the comic art of housework', in Jonathan Bignell and Stephen Lacey, (eds) *Popular Television Drama: Critical Perspectives* (Manchester: Manchester University Press, 2005), 34–50.

which the writer can get at bigger points. And yet some comedies travel exceedingly well in time and space: one thinks of *The Phil Silvers Show*, *The Munsters* (and in film, *Bringing Up Baby* and *Groundhog Day*); indeed the number of submissions to us about comedy suggests an appetite within the critical community for a different way of approaching television comedy. Comedy, as Alex Clayton suggests, finds a home on television, which is to say there seems to be an organic congruence between its pleasures and the medium. Clayton's essay is a model of critical attentiveness in its eloquent tracking – its close inhabitation and elaboration of – the minute shifts and assertions of comic mood and tone in the original 'Four Yorkshiremen' sketch. Central to his approach and its success is his loyalty to Stanley Cavell's view 'that we understand the conditions and possibilities of a medium… by appreciating the significance of its works – and we can only appreciate the significance of its works by considering their particular qualities, specifically through criticism.' In a similar vein Sérgio Dias Branco's account of the role of the camera in sitcoms such as *Will & Grace* and *Cheers* reveals to us through criticism the centrality of the moment and its relationship to the movement of the generic history in which it participates. Vermeulen and Whitfield are also interested in the expressive dimensions of sitcom, challenging the formalist assertion of the role of audio-visual 'cues' in determining audience involvement by pointing to the way *Arrested Development* encourages 'the audience to always be on the lookout for the most insignificant of details that may or may not come to be influential later on, or hold subtle appeals to significance'. Central to that encouragement in comedy is the role of perfor-mance in shaping our attention; James Walters' account of *The Trip* draws on Andrew Klevan's understanding of the uneventful and undramatic in film in order to explore the ways Steve Coogan and Rob Brydon modulate their self-aware presentation of everyday selves via repeated comic impersonation in repeated settings notably the car interior and restaurant dining table.[22] For Walters 'its achievement lies in its ability to develop those repetitions into points of subdued significance and meaning'. At a different register of the everyday, James Zborowski examines a key moment in *The Royle Family* as emblematic of television's diverse treatment of the time that it occupies and in doing so connects his critical account with some of the standing issues in the philosophical treatment of aesthetics and the everyday. Finally, Holly Randell-Moon and Arthur J. Randell examine the achievement of one of the funniest contemporary adult animated series, *Archer*, paying particular attention to the expressiveness of sound/image relations while locating the show within forms of comic tradition and innovation.

---

[22] Klevan, *Disclosure of the Everyday*.

Walters' invocation of Klevan's work on the everyday points to a shifting emphasis on that topic that this collection wishes to endorse. Television studies has certainly relied on the everyday as a characteristic feature of the broadcast medium, but too often this has been an overly sociological version of it. The opening two essays of third section of the collection, 'Critical Analyzes of Television Drama' are written by veteran film scholars who draw on a different orientation to the ordinary and the everyday. Both George Toles and William Rothman point to the fundamental mysteries at the heart of everyday life, an approach not common in the more cultural studies inflected versions of it we are accustomed to find in television studies. Toles's account of *Mad Men*'s Don Draper, echoing Cavell's writing on the melodrama of the unknown woman, finds a strange yet compelling unknowability in the ways he achieves his versions of success. Rothman argues that *Justified* 'is realized so masterfully that it almost unfailingly achieves what Stanley Cavell calls the "poetry of the ordinary"', and that Raylan Givens 'incarnates, in the way every real human being does, the mystery of human identity: the fact that we are mysteries to each other and to ourselves; that our identities are not fixed, that we are in the process of becoming'. This is a critical comportment that is somewhat alien to the traditional one television studies has adopted and one we welcome as an important extension and expansion of it. Which is not to say we are uninterested in the traditional socio-cultural and industrial accounts of television: far from it. Janet McCabe's account of *Boardwalk Empire* will be familiar to television studies in its tracking and matching of industrial contexts of production with textual content, but it is also one happy to extend its view to more directly aesthetic issues. And each of the four essays that complete the section – Faye Woods on allusion and *The O.C*, Lucy Fife Donaldson on the kinetic rush of *The Shield*, Elliott Logan on the articulation of possibility in *Breaking Bad* and Beth Johnson on the style of *Shameless* – bring to bear a fresh critical perspective that take significant steps outside the traditional approaches to 'reading the text'.

One clear issue is the bias in the collection toward television fiction. Dias Branco refers to Ted Cohen's suggestion that

if philosophy of art devoted attention to television it would concentrate first on dramatic and comedy series. They seem likely to him to be of more interest than other programmes and other aspects of television. That is probably because within the televisual context they are more easily identified as artworks. Fiction television series resemble fiction films in the sense that they are both produced with expressive and narrative ends in sight. This leads us to put them in the same category. This similarity does not exist in regards to quiz shows, for example, which are programmes that present a rewarded competition for entertainment purposes.[23]

While this is no doubt true, we wanted to acknowledge the stunning contribution to television style and aesthetics of non-fiction in the past and present of television, and the collection finishes with five quite different areas of interest. Charles Barr (another veteran film scholar, although one with more form in writing about television) develops an account of the striking continuity of 'empty shots' generated by live television's anticipation of emerging content, where palpable duration sets the tone. His detailed account of an early episode of *This is Your Life* demonstrates the complex ways in which distance, time and technology contribute to our understanding of the ontology of the medium, something once not ordinary and everyday but 'rather miraculous'. Frances Bonner returns us to the nature of non-fiction performance as an aesthetic element, again extending a more traditional discussion of television formats, and the global trade in them, in order to demonstrate, like Barr, the continuing centrality of live television for broadcast television and the ways in which the spectacle and display of performance is seeded with not only conventional and emergent discourses about class and gender, but a 'cheerful vulgarity' that is 'located within the practices and conventions of vaudeville and music hall'. Linus Andersson's chapter reminds us of another bias in the collection, its emphasis on North American and UK television; by contrast Andersson offers a focused history of an experimental Lithuanian television whose innovations in the early part of the century offer a nice contrast to the putative achievements attributed to those more familiar Anglo 'quality' ones. The final three essays of the collection explore the role of technology on and behind the screen, reminding us that television's style and aesthetics absorb a range of technological affordances derived from other media. Nick Hall's fascinating history of the zoom shot in post-war American television, Ieuan Franklin's account of the role of radio and sound in the development of post-war British documentary television and Cormac Deane's account of the usage of computing as a stylistic component in the frame each contributes to our deepening sense that television is the liveliest medium, whose aesthetic agility and stylistic achievement will, we hope, continue to stimulate the kind of criticism that this collection exemplifies.

---

[23] Sérgio Dias Branco, 'Strung Pieces: On the Aesthetics of Television Fiction Series', PhD diss., University of Kent (2010), 5.

Bibliography

Abbott, Stacey and Simon Brown, (eds) *Investigating Alias: Secrets and Spies*. London: I. B. Tauris, 2007.

Baldwin, Thalia and Steven Peacock. 'Review of *Investigating Alias: Secrets and Spies*, I. B.Tauris, 2007.' *Critical Studies in Television* 3:1 (Spring 2008): 103–6.

Bignell, Jonathan. *The Police Series*. In *Close-Up 03*, edited by John Gibbs and Douglas Pye. London: Wallflower Press, 2009.

Branco, Sérgio Dias. 'Strung Pieces: On the Aesthetics of Television Fiction Series.' PhD diss., University of Kent, 2010.

Brunsdon, Charlotte. 'Problems with Quality.' *Screen* 31:1 (Spring 1990), 67–90.

Butler, Jeremy. *Television Style*. London: Routledge, 2010.

Buxton, David. *From The Avengers to Miami Vice: Form and Ideology in Television Series*. Manchester: Manchester University Press, 1990.

Cardwell, Sarah, and Steven Peacock. 'Good Television?' *Journal of British Cinema and Television* 3:1 (2006).

Caughie, John. *Television Drama: Realism, Modernism and British Culture*. Oxford: Oxford University Press, 2000.

D'Acci, Julie. *Defining Women: Television in the Case of Cagney and Lacey*. Chapel Hill, NC: North Carolina University Press, 1994.

Dasgupta, Sudeep. 'Policing the people: Television studies and the problem of "quality".' In *NECSUS European Journal of Media Studies* (October 2012). http://www.necsus-ejms.org [accessed 4 October 2012].

Empson, William. *Seven Types of Ambiguity*. London: Chatto and Windus, 1949.

Gibbs, John and Douglas Pye. 'Introduction.' In *Style and Meaning: Studies in the Detailed Analysis of Film*, edited by John Gibbs and Douglas Pye, 1–15. Manchester: Manchester University Press, 2005.

Hallam, Julia. 'Remembering *Butterflies*: the comic art of housework.' In *Popular Television Drama: Critical Perspectives* edited by Jonathan Bignell and Stephen Lacey, 34–50. Manchester: Manchester University Press, 2005.

Jacobs, Jason. 'Issues of Judgement and Value in Television Studies.' *International Journal of Cultural Studies* 4:4 (2001): 427–47.

Klevan, Andrew. *Disclosure of the Everyday: Undramatic Achievement in Narrative Film*. Trowbridge: Flicks Books, 2000.

Klevan, Andrew. 'Notes on teaching film style.' In *Style and Meaning: Studies in the Detailed Analysis of Film*, edited by John Gibbs and Douglas Pye, 214–27. Manchester: Manchester University Press, 2005.

Maio, Barbara. 'Between Past and Future: Hybrid Design Style in Firefly and Serenity.' In *Investigating Firefly and Serenity*, edited by Rhonda V. Wilcox and Tanya Cochran, 201–11. London: I. B. Tauris, 2008.

Mittell, Jason. '*Lost* in a Great Story: Evaluation in Narrative Television (and Television Studies).' In *Reading* Lost: *Perspectives on a Hit Television Show*, edited by Roberta Pearson, 119–38. London: I. B. Tauris, 2009.

Nelson, Robin. *State of Play: Contemporary 'High-End' TV Drama*. Manchester: Manchester University Press, 2007.

Newcomb, Horace. 'Toward a Television Aesthetic.' In *Television: The Critical*

View, edited by Horace Newcomb, 273–89. New York: Oxford University Press, 1976.

Pateman, Matthew. 'Deathly Serious: Mortality, Morality and the *Mise-en-Scène* in *Firefly* and *Serenity*.' In *Investigating Firefly and Serenity*, edited by Rhonda Wilcox and Tanya R. Cochran, 212–26. London: I. B. Tauris, 2008.

Thomas, Deborah. *Reading Buffy*. In *Close-Up 01*, edited by John Gibbs and Douglas Pye, 169–244. London: Wallflower Press, 2006.

Thompson, Robert J. *Television's Second Golden Age: From Hill Street Blues to ER*. New York: Syracuse University Press, 1996.

Thorburn, David. 'Television as an Aesthetic Medium.' *Critical Studies in Communication* 4 (1987), 161–73.

Walters, James, and Tom Brown, (eds) *Film Moments: Criticism, History, Theory*. London: BFI/Palgrave Macmillan, 2010.

Wilcox, Rhonda V., and Tanya R. Cochran, (eds) *Investigating Firefly and Serenity*. London: I. B. Tauris, 2008.

PART ONE

Conceptual debates

1

Television aesthetics: Stylistic analysis and beyond

Sarah Cardwell

'Television aesthetics': A provocation?

Since the early 2000s, the term 'television aesthetics' has become increasingly conspicuous in television studies.[1] It is used primarily to denote and demarcate both a particular attitude to the televisual medium, and a distinctive approach to the study of television programmes. Generally, those scholars working comfortably under its aegis take the attitude that television has the potential for artistic integrity and achievement, and regard a range of (though not all) television programmes as worthy of the kind of study that closely examines aspects of style. Indeed, to some extent, quite reasonably, 'television aesthetics' has become shorthand for a thoughtful, reflective and respectful consideration of texts' stylistic qualities.

Further, in an important sense, the term functions as a signifier of difference and distinctiveness within the field of television studies, wherein approaches that focus on sociological, ideological and broader cultural matters, but which neglect stylistic analysis and reject aesthetic evaluation, have been historically dominant. To situate one's work within 'television aesthetics' is to distinguish that work from those previous approaches. The term takes on a declarative function.

Thus the combination of 'aesthetics' with 'television' is a potentially provocative one. Moreover, the term itself appears to suggest a synergy

---

[1] For a brief overview of the development of television aesthetics, see Sarah Cardwell, 'Television Aesthetics', *Critical Studies in Television* 1:1 (Spring 2006).

between an ancient, respected branch of academic philosophy and a relatively modern, technological, mass entertainment medium, where one might more reasonably expect (at best) an uneasy, awkward association.

This chapter takes seriously the notion that there are pressing challenges that arise from the alliance of television with aesthetics, whether raised by 'aesthetics sceptics' or our own conceptual interrogations. The essay is, of course, far from comprehensive. It tackles a handful of the most pressing questions for the field of television aesthetics, and raises some possible avenues for future exploration.

Media studies versus television aesthetics

At this time, television aesthetics is undertaken solely within television studies, and has made no incursion into philosophical aesthetics. As the topic gains greater visibility, perhaps we will encounter concern (or objections) from aestheticians regarding the appropriateness of taking such an approach to television, but as it stands the wariest responses to this nascent field come from within television studies itself – especially from those scholars working comfortably within the traditions of media and cultural studies. While an increasing number of scholars embrace the fresh perspective and opportunities inherent within television aesthetics, there is also distrust from some quarters. In a subject area that, generally speaking, exhibits an easy-going, all-embracing pluralism, television aesthetics triggers exceptionally strong objections from its dissenters.

Indeed, a recent essay by Matt Hills, 'Television Aesthetics: A Pre-structuralist Danger',[2] was devoted entirely to the articulation of concerns and anxieties regarding this new line of enquiry, and crystallised many comments we television aestheticians have encountered in more informal interactions. This is the not the place to explore or respond to his arguments in detail, but a necessarily cursory summary highlights some important points.[3] Hills' article aims to expose what he regards as the covert tenets and impulses behind 'television aesthetics'. First, he offers a conceptual proposition: that our work is

---

[2] Matt Hills, 'Television Aesthetics: A Pre-structuralist Danger', *Journal of British Cinema and Television* 8:1 (2011). Hills' article was written in response to a previous, special issue of *JBCTV* 3:1 (2006), edited by Sarah Cardwell and Steven Peacock, which was entitled 'Good Television?', and fell broadly under the aegis of television aesthetics.

[3] Hills' published rebuttal of television aesthetics means that he is 'singled out' in this chapter, but his article echoes many of the views we have heard informally at conferences, in discussions and so on – and thus my arguments here are actually directed towards 'aesthetics sceptics' more generally. This essay does not examine or engage with his argument in detail; it is not a refutation.

'pre-structuralist' – by which he means that we regard value as inherent within particular texts (and not within others). Second, building on this characterisation of television aesthetics, he moves to his overriding argument, which is a widespread ideological concern: that our work is therefore 'regressive'. Finally, he invites scholars to back away from the 'dangerous' approach of television aesthetics as it currently stands and instead undertake 'popular aesthetics', focusing on 'popular' texts and audience's interaction with them. It must be observed that the popular aesthetics he recommends is not so new: it bears a striking resemblance to traditional, established cultural/media studies. It is also noteworthy that when Hills approvingly cites specific philosophers, they are of the continental, rather than analytical (Anglo-American) school: Deleuze is a particular favourite. Just as in philosophy itself, the continental approach is presented as not only alternative but even oppositional, and is characterized as more (post)modern, pluralist and politically correct than the analytic version.

Hills' essay encapsulates the great unease felt by sceptics about the resonances of the term 'aesthetics' and its implications for the study of television. Most fears arise from a misapprehension of 'aesthetics proper', its traditions, scope and central concerns. For instance, aestheticians have spent centuries debating the question 'What is art?', yet Hills uses the term 'television art' as if it is a familiar and agreed category.[4] It is not, and moreover the interrogation of its meaning belongs properly under the aegis of television aesthetics.

More broadly, sceptical scholars fear that aspects of aesthetics are reactionary, harking back to old methods and values that have no place in the study of a popular, mass medium. False anxieties proliferate, perhaps, because of the widespread association of aesthetics with supposedly 'elitist' notions of beauty, value, taste and high art. Consequently, critics suspect that television aesthetics' scholars are old-school elitists concerned with taste, value and canon-building.[5] Media and cultural studies' scholars frequently ally us with historical figures and movements that they perceive as reactionary

---

[4] Hills, 'Television Aesthetics', 112.

[5] Hills, 'Television Aesthetics', 99. Concerns about 'canon building' are amplified when some scholars fail to differentiate 'quality' television' from 'good' television – or fear that others are not capable of making the distinction. 'Quality television' is fundamentally a generic category; 'good television' is an evaluative judgement made by the individual critic. Most television scholars, critics and viewers recognize that, even if one wished to construct a canon, it would have to be based solely on critical evaluation, and therefore no particular 'type' of television (including quality television) would automatically qualify for – or be disqualified from – inclusion. For a fuller examination of quality versus good television, see Sarah Cardwell, 'Is quality television any good? Generic distinctions, evaluations, and the troubling matter of critical judgement', in *Quality TV: Contemporary American Television and Beyond*, (eds) Janet McCabe and Kim Akass (London and New York: I. B. Tauris, 2007).

and old-fashioned: television aestheticians are said to be 'Leavisite', 'Arnoldian' and (worst of all) 'pre-structuralist'.[6] We are guilty of wanting to 'turn back the clock'.[7] There is great concern that our focus on close stylistic analysis means we are labouring under the misapprehension that that the 'pre-audience text' exists.[8]

Misgivings are deepened by the popular use of the term 'aesthetics' to mean simply 'how something looks' e.g. its formal qualities; this suggests that an aesthetic approach is merely out-dated formalism in fashionable new garb. Whether implicitly or explicitly, this accusation of 'formalism' lurks constantly behind critiques of any 'aesthetic' approach. John Corner evokes perfectly the ideologically-committed media studies theorist's enduring cynicism regarding formal analysis and the aesthetic approach:

> Formal analysis suggests a carrying over of concerns from literary and visual arts scholarship, with a tendency towards a finessing of points about aesthetic organisation that might be judged as only of marginal, elaborative interest on an agenda defined by political and sociological investigation, some of it carrying a sense of urgency.[9]

It must also be admitted that those of us who originated and work within television aesthetics have not yet done enough to explain exactly what we mean, and do not mean, by the term – or to clarify the many different areas incorporated within the field, which no one scholar would claim to cover entirely. It was appropriate that the primary (first and main) function of the term 'television aesthetics' was *declarative*, marking out decisively a new field of study, a fresh approach.[10] However, now that the field is becoming

---

[6] Hills, 'Television Aesthetics', 110. Amanda Lotz and Jonathan Gray describe Jacobs's contribution to the special issue of *JBCTV* 3:1 (2006) as a 'rather Arnoldian reinstatement of rhetorics of quality'; *Television Studies* (Polity, 2011), 153n. 60.

[7] Hills, 'Television Aesthetics', 99.

[8] Hills, 'Television Aesthetics', 105–6.

[9] John Corner, *Theorising Media: Power, Form and Subjectivity* (Manchester: Manchester University Press, 2011), 49.

[10] It is hard to pinpoint exactly the first use of the term 'television aesthetics' in its current guise. The term itself was in circulation in the late 1970s, but demarcated a very different object: a formalist, empirical focus on media aesthetics. The approach as we now recognize it was being taught by Jason Jacobs at the University of Warwick from 1994 to 2000, within the context of a film aesthetics course, during which time some initial work was also published by various scholars. (For general historical overviews of early publications in the field, see for instance Cardwell, 'Television Aesthetics' and Jacobs, 'Television Aesthetics: An Infantile Disorder', both in *Journal of British Cinema and Television* 3:1 (2006).)

'Television aesthetics' was taught separately from film aesthetics, as a stand-alone course which I created and convened, at the University of Kent from 2001 to 2007. (Steven Peacock also taught on this course, and continues to teach television aesthetics now, at the University of

more settled, there is too little real engagement with the substantive content of philosophical aesthetics by television scholars, whether they undertake television aesthetics or explicitly condemn it.

Greater familiarity with the abiding concerns of philosophical aesthetics would help to calm sceptics' fears. Within that field, enduring questions about formal analysis, criticism, interpretation and evaluation, including the issue of formalism and its limitations, are explicitly addressed and robustly debated. Aestheticians constantly examine and reconsider the relationship between a text and its reader/viewer. Indeed, if television aesthetics were to take more clearly as its model the robust debate and rigorous pluralism found in philosophical aesthetics, media scholars' fears that 'television aesthetics' signals an unthinking relapse into rusty critical methods and reactionary assumptions would be quickly assuaged.

Thus as television aesthetics develops, and more work is published that draws upon and expands this exciting and thoughtful field, it can be hoped that much of the trepidation and distrust outlined above will dissipate.[11] The project Hills proposes, which he calls 'popular aesthetics',[12] is not an alternative to our approach but a supplement, a different focus. There is no need to supplant one with the other. The study of the television audience that Hills advocates need not – should not – override the aesthetic study of television art (which incorporates the discussion of what 'television art' is). But certainly we television aestheticians must continue to elaborate our aims, and develop and debate our core principles.[13]

Learning from the debate: The value of 'aesthetics sceptics'

One of the most exciting aspects of television aesthetics, then, is its ability to provoke debate amongst 'aesthetics sceptics'. It is rare that an approach in

---

Hertfordshire, in the context of an MA in Film and Television Aesthetics). In each case, the term was/is used to indicate a departure from the traditional media-studies' approach to the televisual medium.

[11] Of course, if some critics of television aesthetics are unhappy with our approach simply because they do not agree that a television programme *ought* to be considered without foregrounding ideological or cultural concerns, that is straightforwardly a difference of opinion or principle, not a conceptual or methodological matter open to reasoned debate.

[12] Hills, 'Television Aesthetics', 113–14.

[13] Several scholars have established and maintained the discussion of principles pertinent to an aesthetic approach to television, whether they overtly consider themselves part of 'television aesthetics' or not. For an overview, see Cardwell, 'Television Aesthetics'.

television studies benefits from sceptical scholars engaging with and critiquing its methods and principles from the outset.[14] Instead, a far-reaching pluralist relativism tends to generate an eclectic profusion of work from a plethora of perspectives, and permits polite dialogue amongst scholars, but admits minimal rigorous debate about the validity of methodologies or the value of its source material. Too rarely do we see lively, considered, passionate argument, challenging another's methodology or core principles. The 'rigorous pluralism' found in analytical philosophy, and in its sub-field of aesthetics, is a far more effective and rejuvenating model for dialogue. Here, the field is repeatedly revitalised, ideas honed, reconsidered, and occasionally abandoned, because of dialogue, disagreement and debate between individual writers.[15]

We should embrace the challenges – and problems – of 'television aesthetics', and in examining them carefully, we will ultimately strengthen our approach. This essay is merely an initial, exploratory incursion into the land that lies between the study of television and aesthetics.

Problems for 'television aesthetics' and close stylistic analysis

How could aesthetics facilitate useful reflection upon the modes and purposes of close analysis in the specific case of television? What other implications arise from the particular association of 'aesthetics' with television? What else might (and should) 'television aesthetics' include, beyond the interpretative activity of close textual/stylistic analysis? Too few scholars have yet attempted to address, or even formulate, such questions.

---

[14] Indeed, it is hard to think of examples. Obviously, there is debate on ideological matters, relating to (for instance) the study of race or gender, which takes place in cultural studies, feminist studies and the like. Those debates can and do impact upon the approaches taken to programmes by television scholars. But there is very little open debate within television studies about 'how one should study television'. Instead, a profusion of different and varied ideas and approaches is regarded as *bonum per se*.

[15] Debate is, of course, even more rigorous in the sciences, but there the nature of 'evidence' is different, and leads to other methods of argument/reasoning. Analytical philosophy is comparable, though, with other humanities, and offers valuable models for argumentation and debate. Many edited collections within the analytical tradition, for instance, proffer side by side essays written by scholars who disagree with each other – sometimes vehemently – on key questions, and who respectfully engage and argue with the other(s)' contribution(s). In comparison, edited collections in media studies *et al.* generally present a range of different perspectives that do not explicitly engage with or disagree with one another, but whose voices form a plural chorus of non-competing ideas. Both models are valuable, but at the moment the latter dominates television studies.

The flourishing of the close analysis of specific television programmes is an entirely positive development – not only for its own sake, but also because the evaluative activity implicit in the choice of particular texts for analysis aids the development of a more thoughtful, considered and lucid television criticism within the academy, by those who are knowledgeable and passionate about the subject. It is true that the criteria being employed by these scholars need, often, to be stated more overtly. Also, we must acknowledge and address the potential problems in taking an 'aesthetic approach' to television programmes.

Philosophical aesthetics has historically been concerned with difficult questions regarding definitions of art; the nature of our engagement with art; questions of taste; and the interrogation of art in terms of beauty, truth and value(s). Aestheticians in the analytical tradition have focused particularly on 'logical, conceptual and epistemological' concerns,[16] but their work has always also addressed ontological, moral and psychological questions. Some of these already-complex issues are complicated even further when considered in relation to television, given its specific forms and function in modern society,[17] and what philosopher Noël Carroll would call its dominant mode of 'junk fiction'.[18]

Very few aestheticians have engaged with the question of television from a philosophical (aesthetic) perspective but many of their ongoing concerns and discussions can be beneficially carried across and considered in relation to the specific instance of television.[19] The configuration of television with aesthetics is not without its challenges; tackling these can only help us to develop a fuller, more coherent aesthetics of television.

Television, entertainment and 'amusement art'

There are philosophical arguments that cast doubts over the reasonableness of taking an aesthetic approach to the televisual medium and its texts.

Television's commercial basis and its social function niggle the scholar committed to an aesthetic approach. R. G. Collingwood, in his classic *The*

---

[16] Cyril Barrett, ed. *Collected Papers on Aesthetics* (Oxford: Basil Blackwell, 1965), viii.
[17] Television is increasingly unclear in its delineation and specificity (especially now that its original broadcast form is only one of many platforms via which it is viewed), but its established commercial and entertainment functions endure.
[18] Noël Carroll, *Theorizing the Moving Image* (Cambridge: Cambridge University Press, 1996).
[19] A handful of philosophical aestheticians write about film, but none focuses specifically on television. However, much of what is written about the 'moving image' is readily applicable to television.

Principles of Art,[20] contrasts art with entertainment, noting that 'art' is a 'courtesy title'[21] that distinguishes it from amusement, magic, puzzle, instruction, advertisement/propaganda and exhortation.[22] The latter are crafts designed to arouse certain responses; although of course 'art proper' can cause these responses, it is not devised in order to do so.[23] 'Amusement art',[24] like other crafts, is constructed to inspire certain, defined emotions;[25] it is a means to an end, rather than being of value in itself. Collingwood argues that when art is thus identified with amusement, aesthetic criticism is impossible.[26]

Though the sway of established cultural theory may make it difficult, it is important to recognize that Collingwood's categorical delineations are not inherently evaluative. 'Amusement art' is not bad art; it is not art at all.[27] According to his persuasive criteria, the medium of television is one of entertainment (or amusement) rather than art proper. However, logically speaking, the acceptance of television as a medium designed primarily for entertainment rather than art does not render untenable the taking of an aesthetic attitude towards specific programmes. There is no ontological or medium-specific reason why a true artwork cannot exist within the medium. Television's commercial and social configuration today suggests that the vast majority of works will fall within the bracket of 'entertainment', but one cannot rule out the logical possibility of the creation of a work of televisual art. We could expect rare exceptions. Note also that Collingwood makes no distinction between genres, types, artists or media. We could find good, bad and non-art (e.g. amusement art) anywhere.

This notion of amusement art is echoed in Noël Carroll's recent work on film and television fictions. Carroll was one of the first philosophers whose work on the moving image helped to showcase the value of aesthetics for approaching conceptual questions within film studies.[28] Yet with regards to

---

[20] R.G. Collingwood, *The Principles of Art* (Oxford: Oxford University Press, 1938).

[21] Collingwood, *The Principles of Art*, 11.

[22] Collingwood, *The Principles of Art*, 32.

[23] Collingwood makes many more distinctions that fall outside the remit of this essay, but that are of potential interest to television scholars. For example, he argues that the artist creating true art is primarily concerned with expressing emotion to himself, rather than arousing emotions in an audience. Thus art proper is (a) expressive and (b) imaginative, and it is concerned with individuals' engagement, not groups'. Collingwood, *The Principles of Art*, 110–18.

[24] Collingwood, *The Principles of Art*, 78.

[25] Collingwood, *The Principles of Art*, 81.

[26] Collingwood, *The Principles of Art*, 90–1.

[27] Collingwood emphasizes the distinction between amusement and bad art. For instance: clichés are not bad art, but amusement (277). Bad art is a failed attempt to express emotion or an unsuccessful attempt to become conscious of an emotion; 'not art' (amusement art) is not an attempt to express emotion, at all (282).

[28] See, for instance, Carroll, *Theorizing the Moving Image*.

television, he appears to undermine the case for close critical attention to individual works, of the kind this volume exemplifies.

Like Collingwood, Carroll avoids categorising entire media in terms of art/ non-art, but instead explores the category of 'junk fictions', which 'include things like Harlequin romances; sci-fi, horror, and mystery magazines; comic books; and broadcast narratives on either the radio or TV, as well as commercial movies'.[29] Carroll notes that this kind of fiction is 'rarely difficult', but that this does not imply passivity on the part of the reader/viewer. Indeed, he emphasizes that 'junk fiction' is very rewarding and encourages strong engagement from the reader/viewer on many levels: cognitive, emotional and even moral. Moreover, though he is aware that the term 'junk fiction' is provocative, Carroll clarifies that this is not a dismissive evaluative stance: the 'value' of junk fiction is 'on a continuum with the value of ambitious fiction'.[30]

However, what Carroll *does* argue is that we engage differently with such fictions, paying less attention, generally, to formal, stylistic and presentational qualities, i.e. aesthetic qualities. Together with Collingwood's work, this suggests problems for the idea that television can offer viewers, critics or scholars an 'aesthetic experience' that justifies an aesthetic approach such as ours to television.

What is an aesthetic situation? Is it in the object or in our experience?

Broadly speaking, there are three key positions on the question of what makes a situation an 'aesthetic' one: objectivist, which pinpoints some feature in the work under scrutiny (beauty, for example); subjectivist, which points to some particular emotion or state of mind experienced by the observer; and the 'balanced' view which understands the aesthetic situation as composed of elements of each. This last is not a fuzzy 'compromise' that solves the problem, for one must still determine the fine balance between the two.

As aesthetician J. O. Urmson argues, 'whatever the criteria of the aesthetic may be, they cannot be found by trying to delimit a special class of objects'.[31] That is, the presence of a particular kind of (art) work is neither

---

[29]Carroll, *Theorizing the Moving Image*, 335.
[30]Carroll, *Theorizing the Moving Image*, 346.
[31]J. O. Urmson, 'What Makes a Situation Aesthetic?', in Joseph Margolis, ed. *Philosophy Looks at the Arts: Contemporary Readings in Aesthetics* (New York: Charles Scribner's Sons, 1962), 15. Urmson goes on to show that the aesthetic is not found, either, in any emotion felt or caused in the onlooker.

necessary nor sufficient to create an aesthetic situation. Perhaps therefore it is more helpful to look to the observer and consider the notion of his/her aesthetic 'experience' or 'attitude'.

The aesthetic experience

John Hospers asks, 'What is it to perceive something aesthetically? Is there a specific way of looking, hearing, and perhaps also feeling and imagining, which can be called aesthetic?'[32] Unsurprisingly, the 'aesthetic experience' has been subjected to sustained debate – and this chapter is not the place to rehearse that debate *per se*. For the moment, we can consider just a few ways in which this unique experience has been defined and conceptualized, and how it might pertain to the case of television.

Clearly, there exist innumerable potential artworks,[33] and an equally vast range and variety of responses to them. Yet especially since the eighteenth century, and Kant's ground-breaking work,[34] scholars have continued to examine whether there can be postulated a unifying 'aesthetic experience'. Perhaps one might begin by considering the aesthetic experience to be a delight in art; certainly there is more often than not an assumption that the aesthetic experience is fundamentally a *positive* one. More specifically, though, and pertinently for television aesthetics, scholars have tried to distinguish aesthetic experience from enjoyment gained from entertainment or other sources of pleasure. Though the topic is contentious, it is possible to outline in a rudimentary fashion some of the key features that have been posited.

First, sense experience and perception are key: 'aesthetic vision' (contrasted with 'ordinary vision') entails a heightened alertness to the formal, sensory and 'design' qualities of the artwork under scrutiny. Second, the observer experiences a specific kind of fulfilling emotional engagement with the work. This engagement has been characterized in different ways. Some scholars have proposed that the contemplation of an artwork results in a suspension of

---

[32] John Hospers, 'The Aesthetic Attitude', in John Hospers, ed. *Introductory Readings in Aesthetics* (New York: The Free Press, 1969), 3.

[33] This is not to imply that the aesthetic attitude requires the presence of an artwork as its object. This section of my essay particularly is painted with broad brushstrokes, offering a general introduction and overview, rather than a detailed analysis (which is a separate project).

[34] Kant examines aesthetic experience, disinterestedness and 'distance' particularly in his *Critique of Judgement* (1790). Accessible explorations of Kant's work can be found in Paul Guyer's *Kant* (London and New York: Routledge, 2006), and in Roger Scruton's concise and informative *Kant: A Very Short Introduction* (Oxford: Oxford University Press, 1982).

will – that we 'lose ourselves'; others that our contemplation is an unusually 'disinterested' pleasure, contrasted with other (e.g. sensuous) pleasures. For Kant, whose work was seminal in this field, the 'experience of art is a practice of contemplation – in it, we need not be slave to our innate proclivities, our passions'.[35] Across such varied characterizations, there is a common thread: a sense of elevated engagement – something removed from and beyond ordinary experience.

These conceptions of aesthetic experience stress a fundamental connection between the observer's response and specific features of the work. Put simply, the observer apprehends formal qualities within the work that give rise to the response. Most explicitly, aestheticians such as Clive Bell consider that 'significant form' gives rise to aesthetic emotion.[36] Note that even within this formalist tradition, there is a great importance placed on the role of the viewer/observer: the formal properties of the artwork are significant because of the 'aesthetic emotion' they trigger in the person who is engaging with it.

The characterisation of aesthetic experience as something that is caused by qualities inherent within the artwork returns us to the problem that television is primarily a medium for 'amusement art' rather than art proper – and frequently prioritizes narrative development (story and plot) over the integration of thematic and stylistic/formal qualities, as per Carroll's junk fiction.[37]

The aesthetic attitude: The 'making' of television aesthetics

But there is an alternative notion of aesthetic experience which serves the television scholar rather better, and which can be detected in Collingwood's remark that aesthetic experience is based on our own 'aesthetic activity'.[38] Many aestheticians write of the 'aesthetic attitude', something consciously sought and assumed by the observer. Hospers, quoted above, answers his own question about aesthetic experience by defining it as the experience we have during periods in which we sustain an aesthetic attitude. This attitude, indeed, is frequently regarded as indissolubly connected with the definition of

---

[35] Denis Dutton, *The Art Instinct: Beauty, Pleasure, and Human Evolution* (Oxford: Oxford University Press, 2009), 162.
[36] Clive Bell, *Art* (London: Chatto and Windus, 1914).
[37] Furthermore, the work of formalist Clive Bell, for example, is hard to apply to the narrative arts, since he refers solely to visual arts. Television clearly crosses the boundaries of both types of art.
[38] Collingwood, *The Principles of Art*, 36.

art itself. As Joseph Margolis notes, '[art] is one of the most basic category-terms in aesthetics, designating *objects that are to be examined from a certain point of view*' (my italics).[39] Here, the emphasis is on the observer approaching the artwork with an appropriate attitude.

The nature of the (appropriate) aesthetic attitude itself is again a matter of contention. The notion of 'disinterested and sympathetic attention' has held strong sway and been much discussed. Jerome Stolnitz, for instance, following Kant, defines the aesthetic attitude as 'disinterested and sympathetic attention to and contemplation of any object of awareness whatever, for its own sake alone'.[40] Such theorists propose that we should seek concordance (sympathy) with the work, combined with critical disinterest or 'aesthetic distance'. The recommended stance of disinterest or distance is not meant to suggest coolness or remoteness, but rather implies an informed approach to the artwork, free from distraction, appreciating it for reasons that are: 'non-practical' (for its own ends alone), 'non-cognitive' (not to gain knowledge, but simply to savour perception) and 'non-personal' (without self-concern).[41] Roger Scruton characterizes Kant's position: 'The observer's desires, aims and ambitions are held in abeyance in the act of contemplation, and the object regarded "apart from any interest".'[42] Importantly, this abstraction of personal or vested interests also means that an aesthetic judgement is not merely a matter of subjective taste, but is instead something that demands universal assent or is, as Hannah Arendt puts it, an 'anticipated communication with others with whom I know I must finally come to some agreement'.[43]

'Under-distancing' is a critical flaw, which can arise from the work, or from the observer who fails to grasp the necessary requirements of aesthetic engagement. The idealisation of 'distance', though, can mislead critics into thinking that what is being proposed is an over-simplified formalism, speciously separating formal from representative qualities, and pretermitting attention to significant elements of 'content' (such as political or moral aspects), and indeed to the viewer's emotional engagement with the work. Perhaps for this reason, most contemporary scholars prefer to avoid the word 'distance', emphasising that an aesthetic attitude is attentive and directed; even the notion of disinterestedness is far from universally accepted.

So details of aesthetic attitude remain up for debate – one which is

---

[39] Joseph Margolis, 'The Work of Art', in Margolis, *Philosophy Looks at the Arts*, 46–7. This is Margolis's second definition of a work of art (the first connects art with value/excellence).

[40] Jerome Stolnitz, 'The Aesthetic Attitude', in Hospers, *Introductory Readings*, 19.

[41] For a fuller explanation, see Hospers, *Introductory Readings*, 3.

[42] Scruton, *Kant: A Very Short Introduction*, 104.

[43] Hannah Arendt, *Between Past and Future* (London: Penguin, 2006), 217.

crucial to those undertaking the interpretation and evaluation of art, including television. However, the most valuable (and potentially reassuring) feature of these accounts of aesthetic attitude is the emphasis they place on the active decision of the observer to take up an appropriate position of engagement. As Michael H. Mitias argues, an aesthetic experience 'requires a creative effort' which is rooted in the 'empathic attention' we bring to the object.[44] Colin Lyas provides a précis: to value something *as* an art is not the same as valuing something that happens to *be* an art; the aesthetic attitude is brought by the viewer.[45] In the case of television, the notion of aesthetic attitude should not be used to sidestep the important question of whether or not television is an 'amusement art', and the implications of that categorisation. However, it does empower us as viewers and critics, and enables us to reflect more fully on our own 'attitude', to what extent we consider it to be assumed by us or suggested by qualities of the work under scrutiny, and thus the nature of the reasoning we can – and cannot – muster in support of our textual analyzes.

The aesthetic attitude: A matter of choice

An awareness of the notion of aesthetic attitude is crucial in understanding the foundations and principles of the aesthetic approach to television. Attention to 'style' is not mere formalism (with all its attendant problems) in disguise. Rather, so long as we understand that 'an aesthetic interest in a [television programme] is properly an interest in the [programme] itself, not some other object', and if we as scholars choose to adopt that interest, then since 'style concepts are aesthetic concepts, the perception of [...] style satisfies an aesthetic interest'.[46]

The question of aesthetic experience and its relation to aesthetic qualities 'can be a significant question only to those who are prepared to take both aesthetic experience and aesthetic qualities seriously'.[47] If one is interested in a television programme *for itself*, as an aesthetic object, such questions are

---

[44] Michael H. Mitias, 'Locus of Aesthetic Quality', in Michael H. Mitias, ed. *Aesthetic Quality and Aesthetic Experience* (Amsterdam and Atlanta: Königshausen & Neumann and Rodopi, 1988), 39, 43.

[45] Colin Lyas, 'The Evaluation of Art', in Oswald Hanfling, ed. *Philosophical Aesthetics: an Introduction* (Milton Keynes: Open University Press, 1992), 350.

[46] Dominic McIver Lopes, 'The Aesthetics of Photographic Transparency', in Noël Carroll and Jinhee Choi, (eds) *Philosophy of Film and Motion Pictures* (Oxford: Blackwell Publishing, 2006), 42. For the sake of clarity, I have taken liberties with the original quotation here, substituting the word 'television' for the word 'photograph'.

[47] John Fisher, 'Experience and Qualities', in Mitias, *Aesthetic Quality*, 1.

pivotal. But this does not mean the exclusion of concerns 'beyond' the formal qualities of the text under scrutiny. Matthew Kieran writes of 'The Aesthetic Triad', the 'subject matter of aesthetics and the Philosophy of Art', which interrelates (a) the aesthetic object, its nature and identity,(b) its creator/ conditions of creation, and (c) our appreciation, and the conditions of that appreciation.[48] Aesthetic appreciation is more than just the contemplation of a work or, as Corner rather dismissively puts it, the study of 'how pleasing things are done'.[49] Rather, aestheticians grant a sense of importance to aesthetic study: 'an artwork is the embodiment of aesthetic purpose, and the actively of aesthetic appreciation is one of both understanding and evaluating that purpose'.[50]

Thus several promising avenues open up from these long-established debates in aesthetics. Reflections on the nature of aesthetic experience, combined with the analyzes of amusement art, entertainment and junk fiction above, raise interesting questions about the kind of criticism found in this volume. The chapters herein function to suggest an aesthetic attitude to television texts is not only possible but valuable. But to what extent are we, as scholars, able to justify the very basis of our work: our 'aesthetic attitude'? Can we point to attributes of the texts, as well as of ourselves as informed viewers/critics? Would we each argue that the text under our scrutiny is one of the 'rare exceptions' to Collingwood's amusement art? If not, with what strength can we persuade others to concur with our approach and analyzes? Given that television seems to mediate against profound aesthetic engagement, are we being deliberately contrary or, worse, self-indulgent in our approach? Such questions need to be admitted and addressed by individual writers.

Viewers, critics, scholars: The function of criticism and evaluation in television aesthetics

Arguments regarding the purposes of close critical analysis and evaluation may have been made and won in other fields, but as television aestheticians

---

[48] Matthew Kieran, *Contemporary Debates in Aesthetics and the Philosophy of Art* (Oxford: Blackwell Publishing, 2006), 6.

[49] Corner, *Theorising Media*, 51. Corner does concede some value in formal analysis, but only in order to understand 'media's sociality'. Like Hills, he also expresses concerns about the notion of the 'text' within formal analysis.

[50] Gordon Graham, 'Aesthetic Empiricism: the Challenge of Fakes and Ready-mades', in Kieran, *Contemporary Debates*, 18.

we should not assume that our purposes are the same or that they are necessarily manifest in our practice. And as we have seen, we must address the philosophical/aesthetic problems raised above, which are particularly germane to television.

The kind of critical work proffered by television aestheticians (and included in volumes such as this one) serve two key purposes in this regard. First, it affirms Carroll's notion that one function of aesthetics/criticism is to illuminate current and future texts, and thus enhance the quality of future aesthetic experiences. As Lyas argues, 'The helpful writer [...] awakens and directs our perception'.[51]

Obviously, the selection of programmes for analysis and criticism within any particular approach, for any specific purposes, including aesthetic ones, is in some sense an *evaluative* action that recommends particular texts to other viewers. And if we choose to look for significance, value will be found in works which reward precisely this kind of appreciation, typically because of their coherence of formal properties, subject matter and thematic vision. Within this critical tradition, 'an artwork is good exactly in proportion to the amount of aesthetic experience it affords'.[52] Texts are selected precisely because they fulfil, for each writer, the functions that their particular approach requires. If the writer is interested in aesthetic concerns, he or she will be by definition drawn to texts that best reward those interests.

Second, through undertaking reflective critical analysis, and engaging in debate about their work, television aestheticians contribute (intentionally or otherwise) to the notion of scholarly criticism as part of an ongoing process of 'aesthetic training'. Frank Sibley famously argued that aesthetic qualities are not felt but perceived, and this requires taste, sensitivity and discrimination.[53] Again, this is not to suggest that there is a plot to indoctrinate future viewers and critics into agreeing on an established canon of 'excellent' texts. Rather, this is a consequence of our understanding that the viewer/observer is indispensable and central to the aesthetic experience (as explored above). As Roman Ingarden argues, 'the work of art is never completely determined in every respect, and [...] its qualities are in fact part the result of its concretizations in the constructive effort of the beholder'.[54] Therefore, given that 'the qualities which make up the aesthetic being of these works are [...] potentialities awaiting actualization on the hands of creative imagination', consequently 'the extent of [a work's] actualization depends upon the

---

[51] Lyas, 'The Evaluation of Art', 366.
[52] As characterized by Noël Carroll in 'Aesthetic Experience: A Question of Content', in Kieran, *Contemporary Debates*.
[53] Frank Sibley, 'Aesthetic concepts', *Philosophical Review* 68 (1959).
[54] Roman Ingarden, *The Literary Work of Art*, (Evanston: Northwestern University Press, 1973), 7.

aesthetic sophistication of the percipient, upon his knowledge, experience, and cultural refinement'.[55]

Marcia Muelder Eaton emphasizes: 'Some tastes must be acquired. They develop as we have more and more experience or change as one becomes more educated.'[56] It is generally accepted that, in television studies as elsewhere, 'to aesthetically appreciate art we have to have knowledge of artistic traditions and style within those traditions'.[57] What is less overtly acknowledged in television studies is that scholarly criticism such as that contained herein may contribute both to the education of its readers/students and also to the development of its writers.

The notion of aesthetic training is valuable in relation even to television. We can encourage our students to develop aesthetic discrimination based in their own, reflective critical practice, and emphasize the importance of engaging in debate and argument, rather than avoiding contentious matters (such as evaluation) as a matter of orthodoxy. We can reassure them that 'the bases of responsible criticism are indeed to be found in the work of art and nowhere else, but this in no ways implies that critical judgements presuppose any canons, rules, standards or criteria applicable to all works of art'.[58]

This entails admitting some possibly unpalatable notions: that some programmes are more likely than others to proffer aesthetic qualities valuable to the television aesthetician; that some pieces of criticism achieve greater levels of aesthetic understanding and sophistication than others; and that the practised scholar is frequently better (though not uniquely) placed to offer such criticism.[59]

This is not an argument for elitism but for meritocracy. The aesthetic attitude depends upon 'commitment to a notion of the real existence of aesthetic qualities'.[60] This means that interpretations and criticisms of any text are up for evaluation, modification and rejection. As Urmson notes, we may need to be trained to use our intellect to appreciate an artwork, but ultimately our appreciation is based on observable aesthetic qualities such as elements of sound and colour, which offer evidential grounds for critical

---

[55] Mitias, 'Locus of Aesthetic Quality', 32.

[56] Marcia Muelder Eaton, 'Beauty and Ugliness In and Out of Context', in Kieran, *Contemporary Debates*, 44.

[57] Ibid., 44.

[58] Barrett, *Collected Papers*, 13.

[59] Here I mean explicitly to counterpoint an argument familiar within television, media and cultural studies, and strongly asserted by Hills ('Television Aesthetics', 100), that evaluative distinctions are best made by television viewers and audiences, rather than by scholars.

[60] Fisher, 'Experience and Qualities', 10.

revisions, disagreements and reappraisals.[61] It is the quality of debate (and disagreement) between scholars and critics that matters.

'Ultimately art criticism aims to produce a community, or communities, of shared aesthetic experience and judgements.'[62] From aesthetic attitude to stylistic analysis, onto critical discussion and debate, we can build a community of critique within television studies.[63]

The integrity of television aesthetics: A *caveat*

How can we be sure that we are writing with integrity in our stylistic analyzes? Can we be confident we are correcting a lack of critical attention to under-valued artworks, rather than importing a framework of values inappropriate to the circumstance and offering unjustly adduced interpretations and evaluations? Ultimately, the crucial principle is that *an aesthetic attitude assumes an object worthy of aesthetic attention*. Following Kant, it is 'a recognition that the object matters'.[64]

Television aestheticians share the tenet that an aesthetic attitude can be taken to programmes, and that it is a valid mode of enquiry to pursue (*contra* Hills). There are other kinds of attention e.g. sociological, ethnographic, anthropological, political, which may be brought to the same and other television works. It is essential to recognize that some television programmes are of primarily sociological, historical, or cultural interest/importance, and some are of primarily aesthetic importance/interest, and to deal with them appropriately.

T. E. Jessop stresses that it is not merely a matter of personal choice to take up an aesthetic attitude towards any object. He criticises the notion that

> anything can be made aesthetic by adapting the aesthetic attitude towards it; some object is needful to provide a focus, but otherwise it is indifferent. This seems to me to be an error of fact. It amounts to saying that an entire

---

61 Urmson, 'What Makes a Situation Aesthetic?', 24–5.

62 Hugh Bredin and Liberato Santoro-Brienza, *Philosophies of Art and Beauty: Introducing Aesthetics* (Edinburgh: Edinburgh University Press, 2000), 4.

63 *Critical Studies in Television* (*CST*), founded by Kim Akass and Janet McCabe, is the best example so far of such a 'community', with its scholarly journal, vibrant website and other activities. *CST* has exhibited a heavy bias towards US programming from the beginning, though there has been increasing critical attention to televisions of other countries recently. British television, however, still appears relatively overlooked.

64 Scruton, *Kant*, 104.

section or function of experiencing consistently lies under no restraint whatever from the objective side.[65]

If we are to persuade sceptics of the validity of an aesthetic approach, we must seek texts rich in aesthetic potential, not only texts that appeal to the individual scholar interested in formal/stylistic analysis.[66] Perhaps the television programmes we examine cannot always 'articulate insights into our deepest human interests', as some aestheticians require of other arts.[67] But philosophical aesthetics can broaden our perspective, and inspire us to seek out moments of beauty, harmony, truth, significance, profundity, transfiguration, defamiliarisation and the sublime.

As this suggests, whilst the stylistic analysis showcased in this collection is a pivotal part of television aesthetics, it is by no means synonymous with it. There is a wider project. Just as aestheticians have learned 'how to advance from art criticism to aesthetic theory',[68] we must develop our work to engage with other pertinent questions in philosophy. Scholarly conceptualisation of television lags far behind that of cinema. Whilst film studies has been revitalised by the now-established crossover with analytical philosophy and cognitive psychology, shedding new light on ontological and epistemological questions, and on the viewer's relations with film, its stories and characters, television aesthetics has mostly focused, till now, on interpretative critical activity. With this volume, that activity takes a leap forward. Yet we should also keep in mind that there is great untapped potential for inspiration in this new relationship between television and philosophical aesthetics – which can be drawn out by returning, finally, to aesthetics itself.

Further pursuits in television aesthetics: Stylistic analysis and beyond

Aesthetics has often been characterized as 'metacriticism', addressing 'the most troublesome feature of evaluative criticism [which is] the justification of its criteria. [... This] is a request for a reason for a reason'.[69] What does this

---

[65] T. E. Jessop, 'The Objectivity of Aesthetic Value', in Hospers, *Introductory Readings*, 273.

[66] Similarly, scholars need to do more than choose to elaborate the appeal and intricacies of a programme from a position of 'fandom', which Hills advocates as a version of 'aesthetic attitude' (my choice of words) with which he is comfortable.

[67] Bredin and Santoro-Brienza, *Philosophies of Art and Beauty*, 13.

[68] Collingwood, *The Principles of Art*, 4.

[69] Morris Weitz, 'Reasons in Criticism', in Barrett, *Collected Papers*, 102.

mean? It means asking of ourselves: if we appreciate, critique and evaluate a text in relation to, for instance, thematic and stylistic coherence, or subtlety, or intricacy, or balance – why are these good or important qualities? Scholars within some traditions of close analysis assume such criteria *prima facie*, but aestheticians engage with their criticism, and pursue the 'reason for a reason'.

Interestingly, the long-standing concern over evaluation in media/television studies is echoed in analytical aesthetics, and has inhibited the fuller integration of aesthetics with art criticism:

> A [...] consequence of an analytical aesthetics' self-construal as a second-order discipline of metacriticism was a strong tendency to avoid evaluative issues, generally by relegating them to the first-order level of criticism itself. The philosopher of art was to analyze the evaluative judgment of critics and to clarify and critically examine their supporting reasons or premises. But it was not his role to contest their expert verdicts.[70]

In television aesthetics we have the opportunity to balance the kind of developed close analysis found herein with (future) meta-critical work in order to attain a reflective self-awareness and closer dialogue between the two strands than is seen now in either television studies or philosophical aesthetics.

Finally, television aesthetics' function as provocateur finds a number of historical parallels within philosophical aesthetics. There, many ideas and theories have served as valuable clarion calls for change. George Dickie, having dismantled a certain theory of 'aesthetic attitude', notes that even if the theory in question 'has turned out to have no theoretical value for aesthetics, it has had practical value for the appreciation of art'.[71] That is, whilst finding fault with the model of aesthetic attitude under scrutiny, he concedes nevertheless that 'no doubt, in recent times people have been encouraged to *take an aesthetic attitude toward a painting* as a way of lowering their preju-dices, say, against abstract and non-objective art'.[72] W. E. Fennick provides an even more striking example: in rejecting Bell's theory of significant form, he nonetheless acknowledges that Bell did discover something – not a truth about how people actually engage with art, but

a new way of looking at pictures. He wanted to share his discovery with

---

[70] Richard Shusterman, ed. *Analytic Aesthetics* (Oxford: Basil Blackwell, 1989), 9.
[71] George Dickie, 'The Myth of the Aesthetic Attitude', in Hospers, *Introductory Readings*, 44.
[72] Dickie, 'The Myth of the Aesthetic Attitude', 44.

others and to reform English taste. *Here* is the point of his dictum; 'Art is Significant Form' is a slogan, the epitome of a platform of aesthetic reform. It has work to do. Not the work which the philosophers assign it, but a work of teaching people a new way of looking at pictures.[73]

Whilst there is nothing yet in television aesthetics that compares to the work of the most established philosophical aestheticians, we have the advantage of standing on the shoulders of giants. We should embrace the provocative quality of 'television aesthetics', and the challenges inherent in an aesthetic approach to television. And in our writing, and the writing of those scholars who work under the aegis of television aesthetics, we can savour that sense of excitement that comes from a fresh analytical approach and a new perspective.

Bibliography

Arendt, Hannah. *Between Past and Future*. London: Penguin, 2006.
Barrett, Cyril, ed. *Collected Papers on Aesthetics*. Oxford: Basil Blackwell, 1965.
Bell, Clive. *Art*. London: Chatto and Windus, 1914.
Bredin, Hugh, and Liberato Santoro-Brienza. *Philosophies of Art and Beauty: Introducing Aesthetics*. Edinburgh: Edinburgh University Press, 2000.
Cardwell, Sarah. 'Is quality television any good? Generic distinctions, evaluations, and the troubling matter of critical judgement.' In *Quality TV: Contemporary American Television and Beyond*, edited by Janet McCabe and Kim Akass, 19–34. London and New York: I. B. Tauris, 2007.
—'Television Aesthetics.' *Critical Studies in Television* 1:1 (Spring 2006): 72–80.
Cardwell, Sarah and Steven Peacock, (eds) 'Good Television?', special issue of *Journal of British Cinema and Television* 3:1 (2006).
Carroll, Noël. *Theorizing the Moving Image*. Cambridge: Cambridge University Press, 1996.
—'Aesthetic Experience: A Question of Content.' In *Contemporary Debates in Aesthetics and the Philosophy of Art*, edited by Matthew Kieran, 69–97. Oxford: Blackwell Publishing, 2006.
Collingwood, R. G. *The Principles of Art*. Oxford: Oxford University Press, 1938.
Corner, John. *Theorising Media: Power, Form and Subjectivity*. Manchester: Manchester University Press, 2011.
Dickie, George. 'The Myth of the Aesthetic Attitude.' In *Introductory Readings in Aesthetics*, edited by John Hospers, 28–44. New York: The Free Press, 1969.
Dutton, Denis. *The Art Instinct: Beauty, Pleasure, and Human Evolution*. Oxford: Oxford University Press, 2009.
Fennick, W. E. 'Does Traditional Aesthetics Rest on a Mistake?' In *Collected*

---

[73]W. E. Fennick, 'Does Traditional Aesthetics Rest on a Mistake?', in Barrett, *Collected Papers*, 10.

Papers on Aesthetics, edited by Cyril Barrett, 1–12. Oxford: Basil Blackwell, 1965.

Fisher, John. 'Experience and Qualities.' In *Aesthetic Quality and Aesthetic Experience*, edited by Michael H. Mitias, 1–10. Amsterdam and Atlanta: Königshausen & Neumann and Rodopi, 1988.

Graham, Gordon. 'Aesthetic Empiricism: the Challenge of Fakes and Readymades.' In *Contemporary Debates in Aesthetics and the Philosophy of Art*, edited by Matthew Kieran, 11–21. Oxford: Blackwell Publishing, 2006.

Guyer, Paul. *Kant*. London and New York: Routledge, 2006.

Hills, Matt. 'Television Aesthetics: A Pre-structuralist Danger.' *Journal of British Cinema and Television* 8:1 (2011): 99–117.

Hospers, John. 'The Aesthetic Attitude.' In *Introductory Readings in Aesthetics*, edited by John Hospers, 1–15. New York: The Free Press, 1969.

Ingarden, Roman. *The Literary Work of Art*. Evanston: Northwestern University Press, 1973.

Jacobs, Jason. 'Television Aesthetics: An Infantile Disorder.' *Journal of British Cinema and Television* 3:1 (2006): 19–33.

Jessop, T. E. 'The Objectivity of Aesthetic Value.' In *Introductory Readings in Aesthetics*, edited by John Hospers, 271–81. New York: The Free Press, 1969.

Kant, Immanuel. *Critique of Judgement* (1790). Translated by James Creed Meredith. Oxford: Oxford University Press, 1952.

Kieran, Matthew, *Contemporary Debates in Aesthetics and the Philosophy of Art*. Oxford: Blackwell Publishing, 2006.

Lotz, Amanda and Jonathan Gray. *Television Studies*. Cambridge and Malden, MA: Polity Press, 2011.

Margolis, Joseph, ed. *Philosophy Looks at the Arts: Contemporary Readings in Aesthetics*. New York: Charles Scribner's Sons, 1962.

McIver Lopes, Dominic. 'The Aesthetics of Photographic Transparency.' In *Philosophy of Film and Motion Pictures*, edited by Noël Carroll and Jinhee Choi, 35–43. Oxford: Blackwell Publishing, 2006.

Mitias, Michael H. 'Locus of Aesthetic Quality.' In *Aesthetic Quality and Aesthetic Experience*, edited by Michael H. Mitias, 25–44. Amsterdam and Atlanta: Königshausen & Neumann and Rodopi, 1988.

Muelder Eaton, Marcia. 'Beauty and Ugliness In and Out of Context.' In *Contemporary Debates in Aesthetics and the Philosophy of Art*, edited by Matthew Kieran, 39–50. Oxford: Blackwell Publishing, 2006.

Lyas, Colin. 'The Evaluation of Art.' In *Philosophical Aesthetics: an Introduction*, edited by Oswald Hanfling, 349–80. Milton Keynes: Open University Press, 1992.

Scruton, Roger. *Kant: A Very Short Introduction*. Oxford: Oxford University Press, 1982.

Shusterman, Richard, ed. *Analytic Aesthetics*. Oxford: Basil Blackwell, 1989.

Sibley, Frank. 'Aesthetic concepts.' *Philosophical Review* 68 (1959): 421–50.

Stolnitz, Jerome. 'The Aesthetic Attitude.' In *Introductory Readings in Aesthetics*, edited by John Hospers, 17–27. New York: The Free Press, 1969.

Urmson, J. O. 'What Makes a Situation Aesthetic?' In *Philosophy Looks at the Arts: Contemporary Readings in Aesthetics*, edited by Joseph Margolis, 13–26. New York: Charles Scribner's Sons, 1962.

Weitz, Morris. 'Reasons in Criticism.' In *Collected Papers on Aesthetics*, edited by Cyril Barrett, 91–106. Oxford: Basil Blackwell, 1965.

2

The qualities of complexity: Vast versus dense seriality in contemporary television

Jason Mittell

I have spent much of the last decade writing about narratively complex American television, exploring the transformations in industrial norms, viewing practices and technologies that have helped give rise to new formal elements of television storytelling.[1] In writing about television form, I believe we should also consider the issue of evaluation, looking at such transformations through the lens of aesthetic judgement. Evaluative criticism can strengthen our understanding of how a television programme works, how viewers and fans invest themselves in a text, and what inspires them (and us) to make television a meaningful part of everyday life.[2] At its best, evaluative

---

[1] See Jason Mittell, *Complex TV: The Poetics of Contemporary Television Storytelling* (New York: New York University Press, forthcoming); Jason Mittell, 'Narrative Complexity in Contemporary American Television', *The Velvet Light Trap* 58 (Fall 2006): 29–40.

[2] I discuss the role of evaluation in television studies more fully in Jason Mittell, '*Lost* in a Great Story: Evaluation in Narrative Television (and Television Studies)', in *Reading Lost: Perspectives on a Hit Television Show*, ed. Roberta Pearson (London: I. B. Tauris, 2009), 119–38. For other examples of the possibilities of evaluative television criticism, see Charlotte Brunsdon, *Screen Tastes: Soap Opera to Satellite Dishes* (London: Routledge, 1997); Sarah Cardwell, 'Is Quality Television Any Good? Generic Distinctions, Evaluations and the Troubling Matter of Critical Judgement', in *Quality TV: Contemporary American Television and Beyond*, ed. Janet McCabe and Kim Akass (London: I. B. Tauris, 2007), 19–34; Christine Geraghty, 'Aesthetics and Quality in Popular Television Drama', *International Journal of Cultural Studies* 6:1 (2003): 25–45; Jason Jacobs, 'Issues of Judgement and Value in Television Studies', *International Journal of Cultural Studies* 4:4 (2001): 427–47; Jason Jacobs, 'Television Aesthetics: An Infantile Disorder', *Journal of British Cinema and Television* 3:1 (May 2006): 19–33; Greg M. Smith, *Beautiful TV: The Art and Argument of* Ally McBeal (Austin: University of Texas Press, 2007).

criticism invites us to see a series differently, providing a glimpse into one viewer's aesthetic experience and inviting readers to try on such vicarious reading positions for themselves. An evaluative critique does not aspire to the status of fact or proof, but makes an argument that I believe to be true that is not asserted as a truth claim – in the terms laid out decades ago by Stanley Fish, evaluation is a discursive act of persuasion rather than demonstration.[3] Even more than other types of analysis, evaluation is an invitation to a dialogue, as debating the merits of cultural works is one of the most enjoyable ways we engage with texts, establish relationships with other cultural consumers and gain respect for other critics and viewers' opinions and insights.

My analysis of complexity focuses primarily on its formal structures that blend serial and episode forms, foreground reflexive storytelling techniques and encourage participatory viewing practices I've called forensic fandom. I do not believe that *complex television* is a synonym for *quality television*, as the latter is a troubling term that shines more light on the assumptions of the speaker than the programmes it labels, while the former is an analytic term that doesn't necessarily imply value judgement. Complexity and value are not mutually guaranteed – personally, I much prefer watching excellent conventional programmes like *The Dick Van Dyke Show* and *Everybody Loves Raymond* to narratively complex, but conceptually muddled and logically maddening series like *24* and *FlashForward*. Nonetheless, we can see complexity as criterion of value, a distinct goal for many contemporary programmes that fits into broader cultural norms. To call something complex is to highlight its sophistication and nuance, suggesting that it presents a vision of the world that avoids being reductive or artificially simplistic, but that grows richer through sustained engagement and consideration. It suggests that the consumer of complexity needs to engage fully and attentively, and such engagement will yield an experience distinct from more casual or partial attention. We teach our students to strive for complexity in their analyzes, as we believe the world to be multifaceted and intricate enough to require a complex account to accurately gain insight, whether the field is biology or media studies. Contrast 'complex' with 'complicated', and the latter seems to suggest both less coherence and more artifice, an attempt to make something appear more nuanced than it really is rather than offering a more intrinsically motivated elaboration or unconventionality that might be found within complex programming. Thus while complexity need not be seen solely

---

[3] Stanley Fish, *Is There A Text in This Class? The Authority of Interpretive Communities* (Cambridge, MA: Harvard University Press, 1980), 365–8.

as an evaluative criterion, it can certainly serve as one that helps shine a light on how serial television can reach aesthetic achievements.

One frequent objection to evaluation is that it inherently creates cultural hierarchies by valorising one cultural practice over another, a mode of distinction that Pierre Bourdieu has convincingly shown can work to reinforce social power relations.[4] However, we must think beyond a reductive binary logic that insists that value is a zero-sum game where lauding any single criterion inherently derides its opposite. Thus while I do believe that complexity is potentially a virtue, that doesn't mean that simplicity is a sin – there are many contexts where simple would trump complex, whether in constructing an effective rhetorical motto or designing a user interface. There is certainly pleasure and value in some forms of simple television, where a straightforward elegance of purpose and execution is a laudable achievement. Likewise, achieving complexity is no inherent marker of value, as a complex narrative that sacrifices coherence or emotional engagement is likely to fall short in any evaluative analysis. In analysing a specific series, we can see the multifaceted qualities of complexity as an evaluative category, avoiding the assumption only complex series are worthwhile or that there is only one formula for successful televisual art.

Complexity is a guiding feature of the two television series that I currently place atop my shifting personal list of best all-time television: *The Wire* and *Breaking Bad*. I am certainly not alone in celebrating these two serial dramas, as both are roundly celebrated by critics and frequently appear in discussions of the best television series of all time – for instance, *New York Magazine* ran a bracket to determine the best television drama of the past twenty-five years, with *The Wire* winning the critics' prize and *Breaking Bad* capturing the fan vote.[5] The parallels and differences between the two series shine a light on complexity as an aesthetic tendency, highlighting how it can function in divergent ways toward similar aesthetic results. In contrasting the two, I'm not interested in attempting to argue that one series is superior to the other, or even validating why I see them as more successful than many other excellent programmes, but instead I want to use the pair to tease out the qualities of complexity and how each manages to succeed in accomplishing its own ambitious aesthetic approach. Like all evaluative claims, my analysis

[4]See Pierre Bourdieu, *Distinction: A Social Critique of the Judgement of Taste* (Cambridge, MA: Harvard University Press, 1987); Michael Z. Newman and Elana Levine, *Legitimating Television: Media Convergence and Cultural Status* (New York: Taylor & Francis, 2011) apply Bourdieu's approach to contemporary television.
[5]See Matt Zoller Seitz, 'The Greatest TV Drama of the Past 25 Years, the Finals: *The Wire* Vs. *The Sopranos*', *Vulture* blog, 26 March 2012, http://www.vulture.com/2012/03/drama-derby-finals-the-wire-vs-the-sopranos.html [accessed 22 October 2012].

is an argument that is not offered as fact, but supported belief – I make my case in the hopes of helping other viewers see the shows in a new light, not to convince the world that these two programmes are the pinnacle of television. Hopefully this evaluative analysis demonstrates the usefulness of academic critics engaging in such discussions and not abdicating questions of judgement solely to journalistic critics and fans.

In many ways, *The Wire* and *Breaking Bad* are strikingly similar. Both were produced for emerging cable channels in the shadow of a critical darling that had immediately established the channel's brand identity (HBO's *The Sopranos* and AMC's *Mad Men* respectively), but both pushed the channel toward new aesthetic directions and slowly grew to match the earlier show in critical reputation. Both came from writers who had established themselves as landmark network innovators in the 1990s (David Simon on *Homicide* and Vince Gilligan on *The X-Files*), but neither producer seemed poised to create programmes as innovative and acclaimed as these follow-ups. Both shows feature five-season runs, ending on their own terms after approximately sixty episodes.[6] And both shows have a somewhat similar focus on drug dealers, crime syndicates, and ongoing battles among police and competing criminal groups, while mixing intense drama along with a vibrant vein of dark comedy to explore contemporary struggles of men attempting to find meaning in their relationship to work and labour.

Yet in other ways, the two series are diametrically opposed, serving as stark contrasts among the range of options within the realm of serialised primetime dramas. *The Wire* is stylistically restrained, following visual norms of naturalistic cinema, eschewing the use of non-diegetic music except for its opening credits and notable season-ending montages, and adhering to typical editing conventions of that we read as 'realistic' storytelling. *Breaking Bad* embraces a wide visual palette, ranging from stylised landscape shots evoking Sergio Leone westerns to exaggerated camera tricks and gimmicks situating our vantage point within a chemical vat or on the end of a shovel, as well as editing devices like time-lapse and sped-up montages. The show's sound design is widely varying, with unusual choices of licensed pop songs, ambient electronic score and even an original composition of a *narcocorrido* ballad (a Mexican genre of songs celebrating drug dealers) about the main character. While *Breaking Bad* embraces atemporal story-telling jumps and subjective sequences much like other examples of complex television that I have discussed elsewhere, *The Wire* is fully linear and conventional in presenting chronology and objective narrative perspective

---

[6]As of this writing, *Breaking Bad* has aired four seasons, with the fifth and final season still to come, putting the show at 62 episodes.

throughout.[7] In short, *The Wire* embraces a 'zero degree style' that strives to render its televisual storytelling techniques invisible, whereas *Breaking Bad* foregrounds a 'maximum degree style' through kinetic visuals, bold sounds and unpredictable storytelling form – it is hard to imagine two programmes within the general norms of crime drama that take such different approaches to narrative, visual and sonic style.[8]

The two series also approach their thematic and storytelling scope in similarly contrasting manners. *The Wire* is nominally about the drug war, especially in its first season, but eventually reveals itself to be more interested in using crime as a window into the larger urban condition of twenty-first century America. As seasons progress, the show's scope expands to include the shipping docks, City Hall, public schools and the newsroom, tracing the interplay between these new dramatic sites and the established police precincts and drug corners. The show begins with an already large scope, as the pilot episode introduces more than two dozen characters who will serve recurring roles, with more to come in subsequent episodes to reach a mass of sixty significant characters in the first season alone. This narrative scope gradually broadens over the course of its run to create a sense that viewers have experienced a full range of people and places comprising the show's fictionalised Baltimore. Moreover, the show not only creates a vast world, but presents a guided tour of the city's political and economic machinery by portraying how each person, place, and institution fits into a broader system of function and dysfunction. No other television series comes close to achieving such a sense of vast breadth as *The Wire*'s storyworld, and, arguably, few examples from other narrative media do either.

The Wire's emphasis on the vastness of Baltimore's interlocking institutions and inhabitants necessitates that it sacrifice character depth to achieve such breadth. Characters on *The Wire* are certainly multi-dimensional and quite nuanced human beings, but they are defined primarily by their relationships to larger institutions, whether the police force, the school system or the drug enterprise – the characters that accomplish their goals are usually those that play the rules of their particular games best, while individualistic rebels fail to escape, change themselves, or transform unjust systems. There is little sense of characters' interior lives, psychological depths or nuanced

---

[7] Mittell, 'Narrative Complexity'.

[8] See Jeremy G. Butler, *Television Style* (New York: Routledge, 2009), for a discussion of zero degree style. I offer the term 'maximum degree style' as its opposite; although maximum degree bears some similarly to John Caldwell's notion of 'televisuality', the highly cinematic influence of *Breaking Bad* makes it far less televisual than Caldwell's video-centred account. See John Thornton Caldwell, *Televisuality: Style, Crisis, and Authority in American Television* (New Brunswick, NJ: Rutgers University Press, 1995).

relationships with each other as a focus of the show's storytelling, as *The Wire* creates a world where people are defined more by what they do than what they think or feel, except as those thoughts and emotions become manifest in their actions. Many individual characters do feel robust and fully realized, but interiority is never the focus of *The Wire*'s representations, as our sense of characters comes from nuanced subtleties in performance and glimpses into how these people do their jobs and live their lives. Depth accrues from the accumulation of numerous characters and their institutional affiliations, as Baltimore itself is constructed as a living entity with its own complex interiority.[9]

Despite its shared focus on drug criminals, *Breaking Bad* has quite different concerns, shifting away from a vast sociological breadth toward an inward-looking psychological depth. The show has little interest in constructing a working model of Albuquerque, forgoing urban verisimilitude in exchange for a tighter focus on a central character and his immediate associates. It has a comparatively small cast for a serialised programme, with an initial core ensemble of six main characters with little expansion over its first four seasons. Every character is defined primarily through his or her relationship to Walter White, and the narrative is focused on how his choices and actions impact each of their relationships. Instead of subsequent seasons spinning outward from the core characters and setting, the show layers itself inward, creating deeper layers of Walt's psychological makeup. If *The Wire* presents a world where characters and institutions are immutably locked into a larger system, *Breaking Bad* is a profile of psychological change as the core character becomes darker and more amoral, pulling everyone around him down on his descent, the journey that creator Gilligan has frequently called the 'transformation from Mr. Chips to Scarface'. Even after four seasons, the programme's spatial universe seems fairly small and non-distinct, but the psychological depth and web of interpersonal history is arguably as complex as the political machinery of *The Wire*'s Baltimore.

These different approaches to style and storytelling highlight distinct modes of realism pursued by each series. Televisual realism is not a marker of accurate representation of the real world, but rather an attempt to render the world in a way that creates the representational illusion of accuracy – a programme is seen as realist when it feels authentic, even though no media text actually comes close to actual accurate representation of the

---

[9] I discuss *The Wire*'s approach to simulating urban systems more in Jason Mittell, 'All in the Game: *The Wire*, Serial Storytelling and Procedural Logic', in *Third Person: Authoring and Exploring Vast Narratives*, ed. Pat Harrigan and Noah Wardrip-Fruin (Cambridge, MA: MIT Press, 2009), 429–38. For other takes on the show's representation of urban America, see Tiffany Potter and C. W. Marshall, *The Wire: Urban Decay and American Television* (New York: Continuum, 2009).

truly complex world.[10] *The Wire* embraces a fairly traditional mode of social realism, with minimal stylisation and strict adherence to norms of accuracy that befit Simon's background as a journalist; we are asked to judge the storyworld, its characters and their actions on the metric of plausibility, with success measured by how much the fiction mirrors society as we know it. The degree to which the show succeeds on this front can be seen by how many sociologists, geographers, and other scholars of urban America have used the show as a teaching tool and research reference point to illustrate social conditions, often denying its fictional frame.[11] The show's realist goals may be conventional, but its techniques for achieving its social realist effects are innovative in their scope and vastness, resulting in a vision of the world with great explanatory and rhetorical power. It is telling that for many fans and critics, *The Wire*'s final season fell short of its earlier heights primarily because it forsook its full commitment to such realist storytelling in exchange for a more reflexive and satirical tone.

Breaking Bad strives for a different mode of realism, privileging the psychological over the social. In its portrayal of a long-term character transformation, the show aims for a nearly unprecedented effect in television: chronicling how a character's core identity and beliefs can drastically change over time in a convincing manner. The Walter White who commits the amoral act of poisoning an innocent child at the end of season four is simply a different person than the broken-down school teacher who begins to 'break bad' in the show's pilot, but his gradual transformation has played out onscreen in such a way that his behaviours never feel untrue to who he is at any given point in the story. The programme's flashy visual style signals that the world seen onscreen is less naturalistic than the thoughts and emotions playing out inside characters' heads, so even something as implausible and anti-realist as the plane crash triggered by Walt's selfish actions is grounded as psychologically plausible and consistent with the show's thematic and tonal approach. *Breaking Bad* is ultimately less invested in creating a realistic representation of its storyworld than in portraying people who feel true, and through this sense of honest representation the show engages with real questions of morality, identity and responsibility.

---

[10] For an influential take on television's realism, see John Fiske, *Television Culture* (New York: Routledge, 1987).

[11] For one of many such instances, see Anmol Chaddha, William Julius Wilson, and Sudhir Venkatesh, 'In Defense of *The Wire*', *Dissent Magazine*, Summer 2008, http://dissentmagazine.org/article/?article=1237 [accessed 22 October 2012], where the authors, including two noted sociologists, write 'Quite simply, *The Wire* – even with its too-modest viewership – has done more to enhance both the popular and the scholarly understanding of the challenges of urban life and the problems of urban inequality than any other program in the media or academic publication we can think of.'

So *The Wire* and *Breaking Bad* are both similar and different – a banal observation probably true for any pair of series. But their storytelling differences point to two distinct modes of narrative complexity, and the fact that two such different shows can be so successful with the same critics (including myself) is instructive for how we evaluate television. The two shows approach serialisation with distinctly different vectors. *The Wire* embraces what we might call **centrifugal complexity**, where the ongoing narrative pushes outward, spreading characters across an expanding storyworld. On a centrifugal programme, there is no clear narrative centre, as the central action is about what happens between characters and institutions as they spread outward. It is not just that the show expands in quantity of characters and settings, but that its richness is found in the complex web of interconnectivity forged across the social system rather than in the depth of any one individual's role in the narrative or psychological layers. For instance, the fourth season's resolution is predicated on how the fate of kids like Randy and Namond are not determined by their own mettle or talents, but by the conjuncture of almost random actions undertaken by agents of the interconnected institutions of the school system, the police, drug gangs and city government. Based on conventional narrative logics, Randy's entrepreneurial spirit and warmth would allow him to rise above his circumstances, while Namond's bitterness and sense of entitlement should doom him to replicating his father's role on the corners – but on *The Wire*, character traits and choices are circumscribed and frequently determined by complex networks of institutions portrayed through the show's vast serial expanses. The series presents a world where character agency is rarely able to make a difference in broader institution systems, and characters at best can hope to escape their fates by happy accident combined with a willingness to make personal sacrifice. Systemic logic trumps character actions or motivations, as when Snoop (quoting Clint Eastwood in *Unforgiven*) answers the question of what a potential victim did to deserve his fate – she justifies an unjustifiable murder by saying, 'Deserve's got nothing to do with it.'

But on *Breaking Bad*, deserve's got everything to do with it. If *The Wire* is all about broad systemic vastness, *Breaking Bad* exemplifies a model of dense television, embracing **centripetal complexity** where the narrative movement pulls the actions and characters inward toward a more cohesive centre, establishing a thickness of backstory and character depth that drives the action. The effect is to create a storyworld with unmatched depth of characterisation, layers of backstory and psychological complexity building upon viewer experiences and memories over its numerous seasons. All narrative expansions connect back to Walter White or his associate Jesse Pinkman, and typically become part of their ongoing interrelated transformations, with nearly every plot event triggered by Walt's choices and behaviours, rather than social systems or conditions. Walt's choices may be circumscribed by his contexts, but they usually present multiple options with divergent outcomes – he could have accepted the generosity of Elliot and Gretchen, walked away from Gus's offers, rescued Jane, or numerous other chances to avoid getting deeper into his criminal lifestyle, yet each time he opts to break bad, triggering spirals of pain and suffering on his community. Additionally, the show frequently revisits moments from the narrative past to fill-in gaps in character histories or relationships, whether through flashbacks to Walt's hyper-confident persona before becoming a teacher or returning to the narrative consequences of Combo's murder, an event that at the time felt marginal but re-emerged to directly trigger a crucial narrative turn at the end of the third season. On *Breaking Bad*, there is always the sense that a past event that seems marginal might get sucked back into the narrative centre and impact Walt's fate in unpredictable but justifiable ways; this centripetal force creates a complex storyworld that seems to always hold its main characters accountable for past misdeeds and refuses to let them (or us) escape these transgressions at the level of story consequences or internal psychology.

A comparison between two similar climactic moments, each coming from the penultimate episodes of their respective seasons, highlights the dual approaches to complexity. *Breaking Bad*'s second season leads Walt to a moment of conflict with his partner Jesse, who is immersed in a heroin habit with his girlfriend Jane; Walt goes to Jesse's house to try to save him, but finds him passed out in bed with Jane. When Jane starts vomiting and choking, Walt reaches out to turn her body to save her life, but hesitates – for the next minute, we watch Walt wordlessly realize that Jane's death provides him an opportunity, and he thus rationalises letting her die in front of him. As Bryan Cranston's stunning performance portrays Walt's thought processes, we watch his character's morality continue to erode through his rationalised selfishness around a choice that might be triggered by his contexts, but is clearly marked as a psychologically motivated action conveyed to viewers through the shared layers of character experience and memories. At the end of *The Wire*'s first season, we also witness the death of character at another's hands, as Bodie and Poot shoot Wallace per Stringer Bell's orders. While there are certainly character resonances between the three friends, and we recognize that this is a point of no return for Bodie and Poot's morality, it is made clear that they have no real choices: their only source of livelihood is as part of a drug crew, and the rules of game demand that they demonstrate their loyalty or end up like Wallace. Ultimately the emotional impact of the scene underlies the social conditions and institutional logics that led inevitably to this moment, not complex moral calculations or psychological developments for the characters – Poot and Bodie undertake an all-too-common action dictated by their institutional marginalisation, while Walt's act is fully unique and individualistic, not standing in for larger social forces. Both deaths are powerful, memorable scenes that resonate emotionally, but *Breaking Bad*'s impact is felt more through Walt's complex psychological characterisation and the lingering shadow it casts on his and relationship with Jesse, while *The Wire* uses Wallace's death to put a memorable human face on the social costs of urban poverty and the drug war.

These two different modes of complexity point to the need to evaluate a series on its own aesthetic terms. Even under the same umbrella of complexity, we can see that their approaches are so different that each would fall short of each other's aesthetic criteria: *The Wire* provides little psychological depth to its characters to suggest how their actions are forged by personal histories and individual tragic choices, while *Breaking Bad* fails to paint a picture of how people are impacted and constrained by interlocking institutions. But their specific modes of complexity function as criteria for their own evaluation, as each demonstrates a relentless commitment to their own storytelling norms and approaches – the failure of each series to achieve the other's model of complexity is not to be viewed as an aesthetic shortcoming, but a facet of its own individual commitments to its particular model of complex storytelling. And it is through these serialised storytelling strategies that each programme speaks to its viewers, and we can see their ongoing attachment to each series through their engagement with such aesthetic facets. Thus I would argue that such models of complexity are not simply embedded in the texts to be rooted out by critics, but emerge through viewers' contextualised engagements with a series – we are the ones who flesh out the models of centripetal and centrifugal complexity by filling in the gaps, making the connections, and investing our emotional energies into these storyworlds, and then discussing those engagements in public fora, both online and in person. By critics and fans publicly reiterating the qualities that they value in their favourite series, the broader cultural understanding of the programme's evaluative terms becomes established and shared.

My goal here is not to prove that these are great shows (although I believe that they are), but to argue that analysing the ways they each achieve aesthetic success is important to understand how they each work as texts and what they say about the world, as well as pointing toward avenues for further research on how they engage viewers, contrast with other series, and fit into trends across media. We could probably analyze such dual models of complexity without considering evaluation, but it would be untrue to cast me as a detached objective observer of these programmes. I find them both tremendously powerful and compelling works of fiction, and I am moved to write about them because I find them both exceptional aesthetically, and exceptionally interesting – two facets that are certainly related. By acknowledging my own personal investments, it allows me to go beyond asking 'How do these programmes work?' to consider 'How do they work *so well*?' By bracketing off that facet of our engagement with media, we are not only being dishonest, but also missing the chance to participate in larger conversations with critics, fans and producers about the very cultural hierarchies that some scholars seem fearful of replicating. What is most important about this analysis is not whether you agree with my take on the evaluative worth of *The Wire* or *Breaking Bad*. Instead, the takeaway should be what these programmes teach us about contemporary television storytelling and the particular qualities of complexity. Through the dual vectors of vast centrifugal and dense centripetal complexity, we can have a better sense of how various series create their storyworlds and characters, and help establish expectations for narrative payoffs and parameters.

I began this piece by highlighting evaluative criticism as an invitation to dialogue rather than attempt to impose a critical judgement onto others. An important part of this dialogic approach is to be upfront about our own self situation, as I write this, and watch these shows, as who I am: an American, white, educated, heterosexual, middle-aged professional man, one with an academic investment and expertise in long-form television narrative that is far from universal. I fully acknowledge that my identity is similar to the class *habitus* that has long policed traditional aesthetic judgements, as well as that of the creators of these two specific programmes – in other words, these shows are speaking my language in my own accent, and I have a vocabulary and voice to respond. But I am not responding with a universalised appeal to transcendent aesthetics outside who I am. I am not asking you to join me in celebrating the complexity of *The Wire* and *Breaking Bad* (although I'm happy if you do), but rather I am inviting you to see the shows how I see them. I have faith that my analysis is solid enough that you would see something interesting if you do, but I also think it's partial enough that there is much more in each show to be explored and discussed – and I welcome the opportunity to read different perspectives that highlight other aspects and evaluations of these and other programmes. What I have done here, and what I think evaluation does more broadly, is to present an argument in order to open a conversation. Making an evaluative claim is not necessarily designed to construct a canon to exclude other possibilities, but rather to posit a contingent perspective on why something matters, both to me and presumably to other viewers who similarly embrace it. It is neither a statement of fact nor a proof, but an invitation to dialogue and debate.

Bibliography

Bourdieu, Pierre. *Distinction: A Social Critique of the Judgement of Taste.* Cambridge, MA: Harvard University Press, 1987.

Brunsdon, Charlotte. *Screen Tastes: Soap Opera to Satellite Dishes.* London: Routledge, 1997.

Butler, Jeremy G. *Television Style.* New York: Routledge, 2009.

Caldwell, John Thornton. *Televisuality: Style, Crisis, and Authority in American Television.* New Brunswick, NJ: Rutgers University Press, 1995.

Cardwell, Sarah. 'Is Quality Television Any Good? Generic Distinctions, Evaluations and the Troubling Matter of Critical Judgement.' In *Quality TV: Contemporary American Television and Beyond*, edited by Janet McCabe and Kim Akass, 19–34. London: I.B. Tauris, 2007.

Chaddha, Anmol, William Julius Wilson, and Sudhir Venkatesh. 'In Defense of *The Wire.' Dissent Magazine*, Summer 2008. http://dissentmagazine.org/article/?article=1237 [accessed 22 October 2012]

Fish, Stanley. *Is There A Text in This Class? The Authority of Interpretive Communities.* Cambridge, MA: Harvard University Press, 1980.

Fiske, John. *Television Culture.* New York: Routledge, 1987.

Geraghty, Christine. 'Aesthetics and Quality in Popular Television Drama.' *International Journal of Cultural Studies* 6:1 (2003): 25–45.

Jacobs, Jason. 'Issues of Judgement and Value in Television Studies.' *International Journal of Cultural Studies* 4:4 (2001): 427–47.

—'Television Aesthetics: An Infantile Disorder.' *Journal of British Cinema and Television* 3:1 (May 2006): 19–33.

Mittell, Jason. 'Narrative Complexity in Contemporary American Television.' *The Velvet Light Trap* 58 (Fall 2006): 29–40.

—'All in the Game: *The Wire*, Serial Storytelling and Procedural Logic.' In *Third Person: Authoring and Exploring Vast Narratives*, edited by Pat Harrigan and Noah Wardrip-Fruin, 429–38. Cambridge, MA: MIT Press, 2009.

—'*Lost* in a Great Story: Evaluation in Narrative Television (and Television Studies).' In *Reading* Lost: *Perspectives on a Hit Television Show*, edited by Roberta Pearson, 119–38. London: I. B. Tauris, 2009.

—*Complex TV: The Poetics of Contemporary Television Storytelling.* New York: New York University Press, forthcoming.

Newman, Michael Z., and Elana Levine. *Legitimating Television: Media Convergence and Cultural Status.* New York: Taylor & Francis, 2011.

Potter, Tiffany, and C. W. Marshall. The Wire: *Urban Decay and American Television.* New York: Continuum, 2009.

Seitz, Matt Zoller. 'The Greatest TV Drama of the Past 25 Years, the Finals: *The Wire* Vs. *The Sopranos.' Vulture*, March 26, 2012. http://www.vulture.com/2012/03/drama-derby-finals-the-wire-vs-the-sopranos.html [accessed 18 March 2013]

Smith, Greg M. *Beautiful TV: The Art and Argument of* Ally McBeal. Austin: University of Texas Press, 2007.

3

What does it mean to call television 'cinematic'?

Brett Mills

Much contemporary writing on television argues that some programmes can be understood as being 'cinematic'. For example, *The Sopranos* (HBO 1999–2007) is referred to as having '*Godfather*-quality montages' and 'superb cinematography',[1] while the *CSI* franchise (CBS 2000–) is seen as having more links to 'sci-fi cinema ... than ... its TV crime drama predecessors'[2] and, as Cohan[3] notes, this is an assumption the *CSI* production crew insist on too. But what does it mean to call television 'cinematic'? What assumptions does such usage draw on, and what does such a definition tell us about its other – the television that is presumed to not be cinematic? And what consequences might the prevalence of the term 'cinematic' have for television studies, and the ways in which television is understood more broadly in cultural terms?

Nelson, perhaps, gives us the clearest outline of what is meant by the cinematic when it is applied to television when he says it 'might best be understood ... as an enhanced visual style, since modern technologies have certainly afforded a denser visual image and more effective soundtrack.'[4] Nelson demonstrates this visual style through analyzes of *Shooting the Past* (BBC2, 1999) and *Carnivàle* (HBO, 2003–5); he sees the former as having a

---

[1] David Lavery, '"Coming Heavy": The Significance of *The Sopranos*', in *This Thing of Ours: Investigating The Sopranos*, ed. David Lavery (New York: Columbia, 2002), xiv.

[2] Deborah Jermyn, 'Body Matters: Realism, Spectacle and the Corpse in *CSI*', in *Reading CSI: Crime TV Under the Microscope*, ed. Michael Allen (London and New York: I. B. Tauris, 2007), 81.

[3] Steven Cohan, *CSI: Crime Scene investigation* (London: BFI, 2007), 56–7.

[4] Robin Nelson, *State of Play: Contemporary 'High-End' TV Drama* (Manchester: Manchester University Press, 2007), 11.

'density of visual texture'[5] which invites the viewer to linger over the meaning of the images in the programme, whereas the latter draws on rapid editing and multiple camera angles to foreground the multiplicity of images the programme has to offer.[6] While Nelson also notes the importance of sound to the 'cinematic',[7] the majority of his analysis focuses on imagery and visual style, and this has parallels to those analyzes of *The Sopranos* and the *CSI* franchise noted above. By these accounts, then, the cinematic can be seen to delineate programming that prioritizes the visual more than what is assumed to be typical for television, offering audiences both narrative meaning and pleasure in the imagery that appears on the screen.

A number of reasons are proffered as to why such television has come into being, and Nelson suggests that a key factor is recent developments in technology which 'afford not only a better quality of image and sound but greater degree of manipulation of that image and sound ... by computer generation (CGI)'.[8] Indeed, Jermyn argues that *CSI*'s 'success cannot be extricated from its spectacular deployment of CGI and special effects' which enables the "gross' display of the body's interior',[9] thereby foregrounding the pleasure of the image assumed to be central to the cinematic. Yet the relationships between television and special effects remain complicated when thought of in terms of the cinematic, not least because the technologies of cinema and television differ. For example, Lury shows how 'good "special effects"'[10] were possible for the series *Walking with Dinosaurs* (BBC, 1999) because, in the words of one of the animators who worked on the programme, 'TV only needs a third of the picture resolution that film does, so you don't need such powerful computers to create the images.'[11] And while developments in HD television technology may problematise such a distinction, these remain marginal technologies; indeed, one of the problems in making sense of television images is the multiple technologies audiences might see them on. Nevertheless, changes in special effects technology (not least their cost) have meant that the idea of the 'cinematic' draws on perceived changes in the relationships between television and manipulated imagery, suggesting that such television offers its audiences access to visuals previously impossible (or, at least, highly problematic).

As Lury also shows, however, it is far too easy to assume equivalence

---

[5] Nelson, *State of Play*, 113.
[6] Nelson, *State of Play*, 113–16.
[7] Nelson, *State of Play*, 118–20.
[8] Nelson, *State of Play*, 109.
[9] Jermyn, 'Body Matters', 80.
[10] Karen Lury, *Interpreting Television* (London: Hodder, 2005), 13.
[11] Mike Milne, quoted in Lury, *Interpreting Television*, 13.

between the technology used to make and communicate an image, and the value of that image.[12] Television's ability to bring events happening right now to viewers who would normally never see such a thing has been one of the selling points of the medium since its inception, and live events remain something audiences turn to television for. Lury argues that many key moments in the history of television – such as the Moon landings – remain remembered not because of their visual qualities but because of a communal experience of a historic event; it is assumptions such as these that support the idea that television has, typically, not expected its audiences to take pleasure from the 'quality' of the images that it presents, and instead requests readings in which images 'dramatize' and 'demonstrate'.[13] This means that 'the audiovisual output of the small screen was considered too transitory, too light, too *small* for the type of critical attention which the cinematic movie had finally been accorded'.[14]

In his foregrounding of technology, Nelson argues that the idea that television might be cinematic has its impetus in the industry itself, for economic ambitions might require broadcasters to reach particular audiences, and those audiences are perceived to be ones with an interest in visual quality and newer forms of technology; McCabe calls this a 'quality demographic'.[15] This can be seen in Pearson and Messenger-Davies's[16] analysis of the promotional material for the *Star Trek* film *First Contact* (Frakes 1996) which was markedly different to that for the *Star Trek* television series – *The Next Generation* (Syndication 1987–94) – with which it was contemporaneous. They show how shots with similar narrative functions are visually different in each media, but, more importantly, that the pleasures foregrounded in the promotion of the film were ones that insisted that the cinema experience was one that would, visually, be something 'you're not going to see … on TV'.[17] The use of the term 'cinematic' to describe contemporary television queries this division, and suggests that one of the ways television might appeal to its audience is through its ability to see those kinds of things you

---

[12] Lury, *Interpreting Television*, 11.

[13] Lury, *Interpreting Television*, 15–21.

[14] Lucy Mazdon, 'Introduction: Histories', in *The Contemporary Television Series*, (eds) Michael Hammond and Lucy Mazdon (Edinburgh: Edinburgh University Press, 2005), 6, italics in original.

[15] Janet McCabe, 'Creating "Quality" Audiences for *ER* on Channel Four', in *The Contemporary Television Series*, (eds) Michael Hammond and Lucy Mazdon (Edinburgh: Edinburgh University Press, 2005), 208.

[16] Roberta E. Pearson and Máire Messenger-Davies, '"You're Not Going to See That on TV"': *Star Trek: The Next Generation* in Film and Television', in *Quality Popular Television*, (eds) Mark Jancovich and James Lyons (London: BFI, 2003).

[17] Jonathan Frakes, quoted in Pearson and Messenger-Davies, '"You're Not Going to See That on TV"', 103.

would not have *previously* seen on TV. This desire to attempt to appeal to a particular audience by offering forms of broadcasting promoted as somehow different to the majority has historical precedents. For example, Feuer shows how the notion that the television production company MTM had a style – which was assumed to mean in terms both of its production ethos and the resultant programming – was important for it to suggest, just like HBO has done since, that it 'is in the business of exchanging "quality TV" for "quality demographics"'.[18]

Yet these changes in technology – which are used as evidence that television is becoming cinematic – might instead query the stability of the assumptions that underpin notions of the norms of cinema that are necessary for such debates. After all, if the cinematic and the televisual are dependent on an idea of different kinds of technology being used in their production, this relies on assuming that television is equated with video, which is seen to have less visual clarity than celluloid. After all, Corner suggests television is 'now the classic instance, of the electronic image'.[19] The discourses that surround cinematic television are ones reliant on knowledge of the kinds of equipment used to make it, and the growth of high-definition television equates technology with expense and quality. But, of course, at the same time as this has been occurring much cinema production has moved towards abandoning celluloid and instead adopting digital technologies, thereby bringing the kinds of technologies used by film and television much closer together.[20] And, of course, television has historically often used film, particularly for location shooting, meaning that watching British television drama in the 1970s and 1980s was an experience of a change in the kind of image presented to you when characters moved from outdoor to indoor locations. In his exploration of televisuality Caldwell notes that, 'Theorists, still bent on pursuing the medium's essential qualities, tend to overlook the fact that television includes a great deal that comes from elsewhere.'[21]

Furthermore, there's difficulty in defining what it is about *cinema* that we can call cinematic, considering that medium encompasses a wide array of visual styles, conventions, genres and aesthetics. In attempting to delineate 'the cinematic' Bordwell refers to 'staging', which he says 'delivers the

---

[18] Jane Feuer, 'The MTM Style', in *MTM: 'Quality Television'*, (eds) Jane Feuer, Paul Kerr, and Tise Vahimagi (London: BFI, 1984), 34.

[19] John Corner, *Critical Ideas in Television Studies* (Oxford: Oxford University Press, 1999), 24.

[20] See Stuart Blake Jones, Richard H. Kallenberger, and George D. Cvjetnicanin, *Film into Video: A Guide to Merging the Technologies*, second edn (Woburn: Focal Press, 2000) for an overview of this history.

[21] John Thornton Caldwell, *Televisuality: Style, Crisis and Authority in American Television* (New Brunswick, NJ: Rutgers University Press, 1995), 110.

dramatic field to our attention, sculpting it for informative, expressive, and sometimes pictorial effect'.[22] Of course, it's hard to see here how this kind of definition is applicable solely – or even primarily – to cinema, for it could easily describe television, websites, video games and any other kind of visual media. Furthermore, Bordwell goes on to critique the notion that cinema remains a high point of visual culture from which television borrows, and acknowledges that, particularly in editing, contemporary cinema's 'prime influences would surely include television techniques (which since the 1960s have relied on fast cutting and camera movement)'.[23] The employment of the term 'cinematic' to describe television might be problematic because it is hard to fully delineate what it is about specific instances of television that render that nomenclature appropriate: it is perhaps even more problematic because such uses of the term draw on unexamined ideas of cinema in the first place.

Indeed, histories of both film and television have often traced their roots to the theatre, even if plenty of critiques of such narratives have queried the simplistic, linear chronologies such statements might imply.[24] For example, early reviews of television urged the medium to 'develop [its] own techniques' for it was assumed it merely combined 'the close-up of the motion picture, the spontaneity of the living stage and the instantaneousness of radio'.[25] But Jacobs has argued against a historical reading of television that sees its imagery as flat and functional, and has shown how early programme-makers were interested in the 'liberation of space'[26] that television technology afforded story-telling. Jacobs does this because of a desire to reject the notion that early television was more than 'photographed stage plays'[27] which implies not only a lack of visual interest, but also the medium's failure to distinguish itself from other, supposedly more legitimate forms. Jacobs asks, 'What counts as "visuality" given that television is *always visual* ... ?'[28] and aims to construct an alternative framework for understanding television imagery that is not dependent on the supposed superiority of other forms. Such an analysis complicates the usefulness of a term such as 'cinematic'

---

22 David Bordwell, *Poetics of Cinema* (New York and London: Routledge, 2008), 8.

23 Bordwell, *Poetics of Cinema*, 30.

24 For an overview of these debates see Ben Brewster and Lea Jacobs, *Theatre to Cinema: Stage Pictorialism and the Early Feature Film* (Oxford: Oxford University Press, 1997), 3–17.

25 Jack Gould, 'Matter of Form: Television Must Develop Its Own Techniques If It Is To Have Artistic Validity', in *Watching Television Come of Age: The New York Times Reviews by Jack Gould*, ed. Lewis L. Gould (Austin: University of Texas Press, 2002 [1948]), 36.

26 Jason Jacobs, *The Intimate Screen: Early British Television Drama* (Oxford: Oxford University Press, 2000), 156.

27 Jacobs, *The Intimate Screen*, 5.

28 Jacobs, *The Intimate Screen*, 6, italics in original.

when applied to television's visuals, for it refutes the notion that television's images were ever simple.

Furthermore, contemporary uses of the term 'cinematic' need to be placed within the context of earlier discussions of television's aesthetics, and the evaluative judgements related to such analyzes. For example, Caldwell's analysis of American broadcasting of the 1980s argues that 'television by 1990 had retheorized its aesthetic and presentational task' and had begun to foreground 'stylization' and 'spectacle'.[29] Caldwell traces these developments partly to technological and industry contexts, but sees them primarily as evidence of changes in broader American culture and therefore the consequence of societal ideological shifts. In his analysis of this development – which he terms 'televisuality' – Caldwell prefigures the specifics of contemporary notions of the cinematic, as he says such televisuality can be seen in 'many variant guises – from opulent cinematic spectacles to graphics-crunching workaday visual effects'.[30] That television style can encompass both the 'opulent' and the 'workaday' is perhaps the key paradigm employed by contemporary theorists of 'cinematic' television', whereby a distinction is upheld between it and what Bonner refers to as 'ordinary television' which is defined by 'the mundanity of its concerns, in the style of presentation and in the people included'[31]. The term 'cinematic' is, therefore, used to describe that which is assumed to be *extra*ordinary, relative to what is perceived to be the norms for the vast majority of television.

These distinctions also apply in terms of genre. It is noteworthy that 'cinematic' is a term, when applied to television, that is used to define drama far more than any other genre. That thinking about drama might be a productive way to think about television as a whole is a recurring trope in analysis, for it 'is the form that is typically foregrounded, rightly or wrongly, as emblematic of the aesthetic state of the medium [television] as a whole'.[32] This means that the majority of the work that argues for contemporary television to be understood as 'cinematic' is primarily focused on the drama series (and American drama series at that). This can, for example, be seen in Dunleavy's assertion that twenty-first century television has been in 'pursuit of a visual quality that has reduced the remaining aesthetic distinctions between television and cinema',[33] as evidenced by her analysis of *The*

[29] Caldwell, *Televisuality*, 5.
[30] Caldwell, *Televisuality*, 5.
[31] Frances Bonner, *Ordinary Television: Analyzing Popular TV* (London: Sage, 2003), 44.
[32] Jacobs, *The Intimate Screen*, 1.
[33] Trisha Dunleavy, *Television Drama: Form, Agency, Innovation* (Basingstoke: Palgrave Macmillan, 2009), 211.

Sopranos and *Lost* (ABC, 2004–10), whereby 'drama' comes to stand in for 'television'.

But is it possible to think of the cinematic for other genres? For example, both Su Holmes[34] and Glen Creeber[35] outline how *Who Wants to be a Millionaire?* (ITV, 1998–) might be thought of aesthetically, exploring in detail how the programme draws on the conventions of television quiz shows in its look and employs newer forms of technology that developed an influential style for the genre. For Holmes, key to the quiz show is the 'game space'[36] whereby the set construction, visual style, and shot and editing choices not only constitute a quiz show aesthetic but also function narratively and ideologically. But as the quiz show does not exist within cinema, is it possible to call such aesthetics 'cinematic', or is the distinction between the cinematic and the televisual predicated on readings of drama alone? In that sense, might the quiz show be a maligned genre, which can never 'aspire to cinematic visual style',[37] not because of anything to do with aesthetics but simply because some genres, it seems, are conventionally not thought of as cinematic? Similarly the British soap operas *EastEnders* (BBC, 1985–) and *Coronation Street* (ITV, 1960–) both switched to high definition broadcasting in 2010, rebuilding their sets to make better use of the increased quality of their imagery.[38] In that sense they took advantage of new technologies to foreground a 'density of visual texture', yet soap operas rarely, if ever, appear in debates about cinematic television.

Perhaps more important here, then, is the ongoing desire that seems to exist to argue that something might be seen as cinematic at all. Why might critics, viewers and academics be keen to highlight the supposed cinematic nature of (certain kinds of) television? It's clear that the term 'cinematic' is one associated with hierarchical ideas of quality, and is perceived to be a compliment when appropriated for television. Nelson's use of the word 'aspire' to describe what television does when it aims to be cinematic shows that there's an assumption here that not only is the cinematic something that television typically does not do, but also that it is felt that it is an ambition

---

[34] Su Holmes, *The Quiz Show* (Edinburgh: Edinburgh University Press, 2008), 67–70.
[35] Glen Creeber, '*Who Wants to be a Millionaire?*', in *Fifty Key Television Programmes*, ed. Glen Creeber (London: Arnold, 2004), 232–6.
[36] Holmes, *The Quiz Show*, 63.
[37] Nelson, *State of Play*, 11.
[38] Marc Chacksfield, '*EastEnders* Gets Ready for HD By Burning Down Queen Vic', *TechRadar*, 23 June 2010, http://www.techradar.com/news/home-cinema/high-definition/eastenders-gets-ready-for-hd-by-burning-down-queen-vic-698320 [accessed April 12 2012]; ITV, '*Coronation Street* Moves to High Definition', *ITV Online*, May 12, 2010, http://www.itv.com/presscentre/pressreleases/programmepressreleases/coronationstreetmovestohighdefinition/default.html [accessed 12 April 2012].

beyond the reach of 'normal' television. Indeed, there is a correlation between the use of the word 'cinematic' to describe television (drama) and the desire on the part of those who use the word to argue for television hierarchies that construct some television texts as better than others. In contemporary terms this is most apparent in writing about 'quality' television, where it's hard to find discussions where the words 'cinematic' and 'quality' don't appear in tandem. As Brunsdon notes, for such analyzes one of the key ways 'quality' is defined is via money; she refers to programmes that 'cost a lot, and, as importantly, looked as if they cost a lot'.[39] This equates with Nelson's analysis of such programming where he sees an exhibition of 'production values'[40] as vital to the categorisation of what he calls 'high-end' television drama. That a programme might *look* expensive (which may or may not correlate with whether it actually was expensive or not) is predicated on the ways in which imagery is used and, perhaps more importantly, how it is foregrounded as an element of a programme that audiences are invited to take pleasure in. That there's a correlation between the cost of television and its quality, and that such quality can be understood as 'cinematic', has been formalised in the UK Government's plans to give tax relief to '"cinematic television dramas" – those that cost at least £1m an hour to film'.[41] Here the relationship between cost and the cinematic is made clear, especially as this policy will align the tax system for these 'cinematic television dramas' with that already in place for British cinema.

But I would also want to ask what the consequences of an interest in something referred to as 'cinematic' has for television studies as a whole, and for debates about television style. That the 'cinematic' might be seen as a positive term when applied to (some) television can only be seen as a reassertion of a hierarchy that sees television as film's poor relation. This means that television style only seems to become of interest when it is seen to draw on the conventions of another medium which, in broad terms, has far more cultural legitimacy. For debates about television style, the examination of the cinematic might symbolise the lack of work on *other* ways in which the visual aspects of television can be thought about, showing we still need to work on the methods and terminology appropriate for the examination of how television 'does' style. The use of the term 'cinematic' not only simplifies cinema, its comingling with questions of quality and cultural hierarchies

[39] Charlotte Brunsdon, *Screen Tastes: Soap Opera to Satellite Dishes* (London and New York: Routledge, 1997), 142.
[40] Nelson, *State of Play*, 112.
[41] Nicholas Watt, '*Downton Abbey* Could Get Tax Break in TV Production Plan', *The Guardian Online*, March 16, 2012, http://www.guardian.co.uk/media/2012/mar/16/downton-abbey-tax-break-plan [accessed 12 April 2012].

demonstrates its use in television studies is never innocent. In that sense, it may be the fact that the term 'cinematic television' is used *at all* that tells us the most about television style; or, more accurately, the persistence of the term could be seen to represent an ongoing unease over the stylistic richness, diversity and specificities of the medium we say we study.

Bibliography

Bonner, Frances. *Ordinary Television: Analyzing Popular TV*. London: Sage, 2003.

Bordwell, David. *Poetics of Cinema*. New York and London: Routledge, 2008.

Brewster, Ben, and Lea Jacobs. *Theatre to Cinema: Stage Pictorialism and the Early Feature Film*. Oxford: Oxford University Press, 1997.

Brunsdon, Charlotte. *Screen Tastes: Soap Opera to Satellite Dishes*. London and New York: Routledge, 1997.

Caldwell, John Thornton. *Televisuality: Style, Crisis, and Authority in American Television*. New Brunswick, NJ: Rutgers University Press, 1995.

Chacksfield, Marc. '*EastEnders* gets Ready for HD by Burning Down Queen Vic.' *TechRadar*, June 23, 2010. http://www.techradar.com/news/home-cinema/high-definition/eastenders-gets-ready-for-hd-by-burning-down-queen-vic-698320 [accessed 12 April 2012].

Cohan, Steven. *CSI: Crime Scene Investigation*. London: BFI, 2007.

Corner, John. *Critical Ideas in Television Studies*. Oxford: Oxford University Press, 1999.

Creeber, Glen. '*Who Wants to be a Millionaire?*' In *Fifty Key Television Programmes*, edited by Glen Creeber, 232–6. London: Arnold, 2004.

Dunleavy, Trisha. *Television Drama: Form, Agency, Innovation*. Basingstoke: Palgrave Macmillan, 2009.

Feuer, Jane. 'The MTM Style.' In *MTM: 'Quality Television'*, edited by Jane Feuer, Paul Kerr, and Tise Vahimagi, 32–60. London: BFI, 1984.

Gould, Jack. 'Matter of Form: Television Must Develop Own Techniques If It is To Have Artistic Vitality.' In *Watching Television Come of Age: The New York Times Reviews by Jack Gould*, edited by Lewis L. Gould, 36–8. Austin: University of Texas Press, 2002 [1948].

Holmes, Su. *The Quiz Show*. Edinburgh: Edinburgh University Press, 2008.

ITV. '*Coronation Street* Moves to High Definition.' *ITV*, May 12, 2010. http://www.itv.com/presscentre/pressreleases/programmepressreleases/coronationstreetmovestohighdefinition/default.html [accessed 12 April 2012].

Jacobs, Jason. *The Intimate Screen: Early British Television Drama*. Oxford: Oxford University Press, 2000.

Jermyn, Deborah. 'Body Matters: Realism, Spectacle and the Corpse in *CSI*.' In *Reading CSI: Crime TV Under the Microscope*, edited by Michael Allen, 79–89. London and New York: I. B. Tauris, 2007.

Jones, Stuart Blake, Richard H. Kallenberger, and George D. Cvjetnicanin. *Film into Video: A Guide to Merging the Technologies*, second edn. Woburn: Focal Press, 2000.

Lavery, David. "Coming Heavy': The Significance of *The Sopranos*.' In *This Thing of Ours: Investigating the Sopranos*, edited by David Lavery, xi–xviii. New York: Columbia, 2002.

Lury, Karen. *Interpreting Television*. London: Hodder, 2005.

McCabe, Janet. 'Creating "Quality" Audiences for *ER* on Channel Four.' In *The Contemporary Television Series*, edited by Michael Hammond and Lucy Mazdon, 207–23. Edinburgh: Edinburgh University Press, 2005.

Mazdon, Lucy. 'Introduction: Histories.' In *The Contemporary Television Series*, edited by Michael Hammond and Lucy Mazdon, 3–10. Edinburgh: Edinburgh University Press, 2005.

Nelson, Robin. *State of Play: Contemporary 'High-End' TV Drama*. Manchester: Manchester University Press, 2007.

Pearson, Roberta E. and Máire Messenger-Davies. '"You're Not Going to See That on TV": *Star Trek: The Next Generation* in Film and Television.' In *Quality Popular Television*, edited by Mark Jancovich and James Lyons, 103–17. London: BFI, 2003.

Watt, Nicholas. '*Downton Abbey* Could get Tax Break in TV Production Plan', *The Guardian Online*, March 16, 2012. http://www.guardian.co.uk/media/2012/mar/16/downton-abbey-tax-break-plan [accessed 12 April 2012].

4

Rescuing television from 'the cinematic': The perils of dismissing television style

Deborah L. Jaramillo

'Cinematic' should be a contentious word in the field of television studies. It should raise the eyebrows of anyone who thinks and writes about television; instead, it has become commonplace for scholars and popular critics to use the term as shorthand when discussing the complex visual and aural style in scripted series such as *The Sopranos*, *Mad Men*, and *Breaking Bad*. 'Cinematic' connotes artistry mixed with a sense of grandeur. A cinematic movie is one that requires a theatrical viewing in order to extract every ounce of visual and aural depth from it. The term is reserved for films that reveal the exploitation of filmmaking technologies in the service of skill and creative vision. It is an inherently positive, even boastful word that many people rally around and ascribe to the best of the best on TV.

The use of the term 'cinematic' to describe sophistication and beauty on television demands a critical examination for at least three reasons. First, it perpetuates an audio-visual media hierarchy that is hopelessly antiquated. Second, it does not advance our understanding of where the look and sound of television are going in any meaningful way. Finally, it implicitly argues that film has a clearly understood essence that can compensate for television's lack thereof. This chapter seeks to highlight and interrogate the widespread use of a term that muddles a serious discussion of television aesthetics.

Better than TV

In the new conversation about good-looking series, television is positioned as its own limiter, and cinema can somehow liberate TV from itself. For example, Allen characterizes HBO's miniseries *From the Earth to the Moon* as 'a television production with aspirations toward the cinematic'.[1] Pearson describes how the critical praise heaped upon the pilot episode of ABC's *Lost* hinged on its alleged similarity to a film.[2] Nelson optimistically posits that the 'former denigration of television in the face of cinema has itself been revalued', but he follows that by equating the 'improved imagery' of television with the aesthetics of cinema and concludes by referring to TV's prestige series as 'high end, cinematic TV dramas'.[3] In sum, the look of cinema, mapped onto television, has elevated the smaller medium and wiped out the hierarchy.

In her work on TV liveness, Levine argues that this hierarchy was never levelled. She writes that the 'cultural denigration' of television reached a new stage when discourses about television sought to create 'an additional level of distinction, this time among types of television'.[4] But these discourses reinforced this level of distinction by invoking other media, particularly cinema. Levine refers specifically to the way in which certain US television series since the mid-1990s have been described as novelistic, as cinematic, and – most famously, thanks to HBO – as 'not TV'. Although Levine cites television's 'ongoing association' with domesticity and femininity as reasons for its 'low cultural status', we might also point to the way in which the discussion of television style has been side-lined historically.[5]

In Newcomb's decisive intervention on behalf of television, *TV: The Most Popular Art* (1974), he writes that the goal of focusing on aesthetics 'should be the description and definition of the devices that work to make television one of the most popular arts'.[6] Newcomb did not want to ignore what critics felt were television's shortcomings; rather, he wanted to celebrate the features

---

[1] Michael Allen, '*From the Earth to the Moon*', in *The Essential HBO Reader*, (eds) Gary R. Edgerton and Jeffrey P. Jones (Lexington: The University Press of Kentucky, 2008), 119.
[2] Roberta Pearson, '*Lost* in Transition: From Post-network to Post-television', in *Quality TV: Contemporary American Television and Beyond*, (eds) Janet McCabe and Kim Akass (London: I. B. Tauris, 2007), 245.
[3] Robin Nelson, 'Quality TV Drama: Estimations and Influences through Time and Space', in *Quality TV: Contemporary American Television and Beyond*, (eds) Janet McCabe and Kim Akass (London: I. B. Tauris, 2007), 43, 51.
[4] Elana Levine, 'Distinguishing Television: The Changing Meanings of Television Liveness', *Media, Culture & Society* 30:3 (2008): 393–4.
[5] Levine, 'Distinguishing Television', 393.
[6] Horace Newcomb, *TV: The Most Popular Art* (Garden City, NY: Anchor Books, 1974), 245.

of a medium able to attract an enormous audience at any given point in time. Indeed, one of the qualities that Newcomb pointed to was the small screen, which encouraged an intimate relationship with viewers through the display of 'faces, reactions, explorations of emotions'.[7] Intimacy was also achieved through the emphasis on interior spaces – the living rooms of TV families, for instance – and not the expanses exploited in the cinema through various widescreen technologies.[8] The 'expansiveness' of a Hollywood western was, for Newcomb, 'meaningless' on television.[9] The television aesthetic that Newcomb formulated drew also from the narrative complexity of serialised programmes and the negotiation of history within a medium that exists so firmly in the here-and-now. Most striking about his conceptualisation is his assertion that, in 1974, 'it should no longer be possible to discuss "violence on television" without recognizing the aesthetic structure within which that violence occurs'.[10] Furthermore, the 'values' that television espoused should not be disconnected from 'the artistic context of those values as presented on television'.[11] Newcomb challenged thinkers to insert art into the conversation about television, but that conversation did not happen easily.

In a 1978 article in the *Journal of the University Film Association* (a title that inherently underscores the marginalisation of television in the academy), Zettl lamented the dearth of scholarly writing about television aesthetics. Two reasons for such a lack, according to Zettl, were television's commercial imperative and its reputation as a 'distribution device for ready-made messages', which divorced content from the 'process of television'.[12] These two reasons remain relatively intact. HBO's ascent as a creator of original series in the late 1990s and 2000s may have quelled the anxieties of some who wanted to embrace the medium but were turned off by its commercialism. HBO's ad-free subscription model meant that scholars and critics could ignore the economic foundation of the rest of television and enjoy this new, 'cinematic' television available for an additional fee.

To Zettl's list I would add at least three other historical obstacles to the consideration of television aesthetics. The first was the embrace of television by the field of mass communication, which has no use for art. The second was the focus on television's capacity for liveness, which, though a novel and important opposition to cinema, actually constrained visual and aural flair. And

---

[7] Newcomb, *TV: The Most Popular Art*, 245–6.
[8] Newcomb, *TV: The Most Popular Art*, 248.
[9] Newcomb, *TV: The Most Popular Art*, 248.
[10] Newcomb, *TV: The Most Popular Art*, 263.
[11] Newcomb, *TV: The Most Popular Art*, 263.
[12] Herbert Zettl, 'The Rare Case of Television Aesthetics', *Journal of the University Film Association* 30:2 (1978): 3.

third was the shoddiness of the technology and quite frankly, the screen. Attention was drawn to narrative structures and genres, possibly the most interesting text-based aspects to write about in a medium with budgets much smaller than those of mainstream cinema. Newcomb's appreciation for small-screen aesthetics sought to rescue visual strategies from the limitations of the technology. Instead of criticising them for being so unlike cinema's strategies, he wanted to redeem them because they existed within a specific set of constraints. At this point in the development of television we need to ponder the aesthetic consequences of the loosening of those constraints.

Bad language

The early works of Newcomb and Zettl evince a struggle for television's aesthetic legitimacy, while more recent studies embrace terms that stunt our understanding of that aesthetic. In 1995 Caldwell elaborated on a drastic shift in how meaning was made on television in the 1980s. Part of that shift involved excess, 'performance' and 'stylization'.[13] The name Caldwell assigned to this shift was 'televisuality'. Consisting of 'several axes', televisuality manifested formally either as 'cinematic' programmes or 'videographic' programmes.[14] For Caldwell, 'spectacle, high-production values, and feature-style cinematography' were cinematic attributes that endowed an 'air of distinction' to programmes like *Moonlighting*.[15] Videographic programmes lacked such distinction; aided by new technology, these programmes revelled in active stylisation.[16] Caldwell places MTV and CNN firmly within the videographic realm.[17] Certainly, US cable news and other subgenres of reality television have only escalated their reliance upon graphics, quick editing and attention-grabbing music. And those who assign the 'cinematic air of distinction' to certain TV programmes would easily exclude reality TV from their canon. Although Caldwell expounds on the style of this era, he wishes to avoid ascribing to television a 'Kantian aesthetic essence'.[18] As he articulates it, televisuality is dynamic rather than static, and as a 'cultural operation with

---

[13] John Thornton Caldwell, *Televisuality: Style, Crisis, and Authority in American Television* (New Brunswick, NJ: Rutgers University Press, 1995).
[14] Caldwell, *Televisuality*, 12.
[15] Caldwell, *Televisuality*, 12.
[16] Caldwell, *Televisuality*, 12–13.
[17] Caldwell, *Televisuality*, 13.
[18] Caldwell, *Televisuality*, 352.

marked political consequences' it can encompass a multiplicity of 'looks'.[19] Despite his disclaimer, the idea of televisuality as excess lingers.

For a scholar like Deming (2010), 'televisuality' is too restrictive a term.[20] In her analysis of televisuality during the Golden Age of TV, Deming actively avoids the term's connection to excess and opts to construct a different paradigm. Whereas Deming attributes a different set of meanings to the term, Butler (2010) abides by Caldwell's original construction. In *Television Style*, Butler reviews the literature that has attempted to make aesthetic judgements about television series – *positive* aesthetic judgements. He remains unconvinced as to the success or even necessity of these writings, opting instead to wait for the development of a television-specific 'aesthetic system that goes beyond taste and dominant culture norms'.[21] He also seems uncertain that one is even possible. So he offers terms that serve his purposes, one of which is 'zero-degree style', the 'lack of style' that he associates with the visual signifiers of liveness.[22] He moves between lack and excess, both of which expose an easy acceptance of *negative* aesthetic judgement.

The issue that arises, then, is that the loaded terms 'excessive', 'cinematic' and 'videographic', defined explicitly in relation to televisuality, indelibly colour the larger concept. If we stand back and assess the situation, we can ascertain that television is a stylistic vacuum ('zero-degree'), excessive ('televisual'), or derivative ('cinematic'). Television is implicated in bombarding the viewer with hyperstylisation or no style at all while, in special spaces, it imitates another medium of higher esteem. We see this play out in the constant comparisons of television to other media across time. In the early 1950s critics applauded the similarities between the live anthology drama and the legitimate theatre. But the style of 1970s multiple-camera sitcoms – the zero-degree style that Caldwell and Butler write about – also maintained a strong link to the theatre, so 'theatrical' has conflicting connotations when applied to TV. Most recently HBO helped to usher in a period of television that critics and scholars alike commend for its 'cinematic' look and feel. But when television is 'televisual' it is excessive. I am not arguing against the presence of a multiplicity of styles on television. I am, however, arguing that we have become reliant on terms that characterize television as a stylistic dumping ground that must pray the cinema will rescue it from its excessive or sheer lack of style.

---

[19] Caldwell, *Televisuality*, 353.

[20] Caren Deming, 'Locating the Televisual in Golden Age Television', in *A Companion to Television*, ed. Janet Wasko (Malden, MA: Wiley-Blackwell, 2010), 127.

[21] Jeremy Butler, *Television Style* (New York and London: Routledge, 2010), 19.

[22] Butler, *Television Style*, 15.

Cinema has an essence?

Levine argues that liveness is still used as a marker of distinction, despite the ascent of other technologies that perform this function more often than TV does. The key aspect of this argument – and the reason why I invoke it – is the long-held assertion that television had an essence, and that essence owed in part to TV's capacity to broadcast images and sounds as they happened. Levine and others have worked to disconnect TV from liveness ultimately to combat the notion that TV has an essence. By invoking the term 'cinematic', other writers are not only embracing essentialism, they are also arguing that film has an omnipotent and entrenched essence.

In *Theorizing the Moving Image*, Carroll (1996) deconstructs 'medium-essentialism' in order to create a definition of cinema that avoids relying on such a principle.[23] Medium-essentialism embodies the notion that 'each art form has its own distinctive medium, a medium that distinguishes it from other forms'.[24] Carroll writes that it is a widely adopted 'doctrine' that appealed to film theorists who wanted to 'block accusations that film was merely a subspecies of theatre'.[25] Staiger (2000) likewise claims that arguing for television's specificity or essence 'repeats the process common to most new technologies in which their supporters try to mark them out as novel and revolutionary'.[26] We are left with a curious situation, then. Film theorists sought to emancipate their medium from another. Apparently unconcerned with freeing television from the hierarchy in which film is privileged – and even going so far as to import that privilege to legitimise the look of TV – television scholars employing the term 'cinematic' appeal to film's essence which, according to Carroll, is a dead end.

The situation becomes more complicated the more we focus on language. There is one television-specific phrase that scholars use to describe good-looking, well-written, well-produced, sophisticated television. That phrase is 'quality television'. That banal couple of words is the highest praise that can be heaped upon a programme without resorting to 'cinematic'. Who needs art when you have 'quality'? And even critics and scholars who argue for the use of the term 'quality television' tend to employ 'cinematic' to support the aesthetic legitimacy of their chosen programmes. Granted, basic formal elements and rules do stem from the craft of filmmaking, but 'cinematic'

---

[23] Noël Carroll, *Theorizing the Moving Image* (Cambridge: Cambridge University Press, 1996), 49.
[24] Carroll, *Theorizing the Moving Image*, 49.
[25] Carroll, *Theorizing the Moving Image*, 49.
[26] Janet Staiger, *Blockbuster TV: Must-See Sitcoms in the Network Era* (New York and London: New York University Press, 2000), 27.

implies something more than just a shared formal ancestry. 'Cinematic' removes the television text and its style from the medium we are studying and transplants it elsewhere.

In a striking denial of the capabilities of TV, one creator-producer evoked yet another unproductive term when communicating his vision for *Six Feet Under* to his director of photography. McCabe and Akass (2008) cite Alan Ball's use of the phrase 'anti-TV language' and assert that 'the search for a quality TV aesthetic plunders already established "high-end" media – theatre, European art cinema and painting – to determine and legitimize the new'.[27] But, really, Ball's choice of words lays bare the search for a lexicon rather than an aesthetic; there is no linguistic legacy to aid the discussion or labelling of a quality aesthetic. Besides, what is anti-TV language? Has there ever been one coherent language of television?

As we examine TV's history, we see that different sets of circumstances have engendered different visual and sonic choices. Live scripted drama of the 1950s used one language that live news did not. The switch to film in the mid-1950s interestingly did not represent a shift to the 'cinematic', because these productions were typically made very cheaply with limited sets. At that time the networks were afraid that Hollywood would stain the prestige of *theatrical* TV projects by imposing a cookie-cutter visual sensibility. The launch of quality TV in the 1970s reveals a pendulum swinging from *The Mary Tyler Moore Show*'s proscenium-style multiple-camera setup shot on film, to *All in the Family*'s proscenium-style multiple-camera setup shot on video, to the single-camera *M*A*S*H*, which was shot on film and disallowed a laugh track during certain scenes. The stylistic choices could not have been more different, yet all live under the umbrella of 'quality' – the early conceptualisation of which stressed the complexity of the narrative and characters, the independent production house, and the makeup of the audience.[28]

Moving to the present, we still do not have one coherent language, one coherent style. Multiple-camera sitcoms use a more static aesthetic, while single-camera comedies have come to use very quick editing as a means to communicate comedy. Hour-long dramas range from staid and subtle (*In Treatment*) to hyperstylised (*CSI: Miami*) to hallucinatory (*Breaking Bad*). *Louie* defies easy generic categorisation and manifests as vignettes and a mix of styles from one week's episode to the next. As television series continue to disrupt conventions tied to genre (and continue to disrupt simplistic generic

[27] Janet McCabe and Kim Akass, 'It's Not TV, It's HBO Original Programming: Producing Quality TV', in *It's Not TV: Watching HBO in the Post-television Era*, (eds) Marc Leverette, Brian L. Ott and Cara Louise Buckley (New York and London: Routledge, 2008), 88.

[28] Jane Feuer, Paul Kerr and Tise Vahimagi, (eds) *MTM 'Quality Television'* (London: BFI, 1984).

formulations), the job of identifying and naming these welcomed disruptions becomes incrementally harder.

Moving forward

Auteur Theory plays a role in keeping TV aesthetics off the table. Butler writes, 'I ... reject the definition of style as the mark of the individual genius on a text'.[29] I reject the notion that the next logical step after identifying beauty is to invoke the spectre of the auteur. We can successfully connect beauty to the talent involved in creating it as well as to the circumstances that enable and sometimes impede that talent. Gitlin achieves this in a compelling way in his work on *Hill Street Blues*.[30] Precisely what makes a television aesthetic so important is the web of relations behind it. We do not need to move backwards in order to make these connections. Too many binaries have clouded the discussion and have posited that aesthetic judgements imply a dismissal of the critical project. At the same time, very little attention is paid to the liberal use of a lexicon that privileges cinema. So I wonder how we, biased by a hypercritical attention to television style and a hypocritical attention to the dominance of cinema, can write about TV aesthetics as existing within the complicated relationships that make TV so interesting to study and also as something that can be positive and is deserving of its own name.

Bibliography

Allen, Michael. '*From the Earth to the Moon.*' In *The Essential HBO Reader*, edited by Gary R. Edgerton and Jeffrey P. Jones, 116–24. Lexington: The University Press of Kentucky, 2008.

Butler, Jeremy. *Television Style*. New York and London: Routledge, 2010.

Caldwell, John Thornton. *Televisuality: Style, Crisis, and Authority in American Television*. New Brunswick, NJ: Rutgers University Press, 1995.

Carroll, Noël. *Theorizing the Moving Image*. Cambridge: Cambridge University Press, 1996.

Deming, Caren. 'Locating the Televisual in Golden Age Television.' In *A Companion to Television*, ed. Janet Wasko, 126–41. Malden, MA: Wiley-Blackwell, 2010.

---

[29] Butler, *Television Style*, 15.
[30] Todd Gitlin, *Inside Prime Time* (Berkeley: University of California Press, 2000).

Feuer, Jane, Paul Kerr and Tise Vahimagi, (eds) *MTM 'Quality Television.'* London: BFI, 1984.

Gitlin, Todd. *Inside Prime Time.* Berkeley: University of California Press, 2000.

Levine, Elana. 'Distinguishing Television: The Changing Meanings of Television Liveness.' *Media, Culture & Society* 30:3 (2008): 393–409.

McCabe, Janet, and Kim Akass. 'It's not TV, it's HBO Original Programming: Producing Quality TV.' In *It's Not TV: Watching HBO in the Post-television Era*, edited by Marc Leverette, Brian L. Ott and Cara Louise Buckley, 83–94. New York and London: Routledge, 2008.

Nelson, Robin. 'Quality TV Drama: Estimations and Influences through Time and Space.' In *Quality TV: Contemporary American Television and Beyond*, edited by Janet McCabe and Kim Akass, 38–51. London: I. B. Tauris, 2007.

Newcomb, Horace. *TV: The Most Popular Art.* Garden City, NY: Anchor Books, 1974.

Pearson, Roberta. '*Lost* in Transition: From Post-network to Post-television.' In *Quality TV: Contemporary American Television and Beyond*, edited by Janet McCabe and Kim Akass, 239–56. London: I. B. Tauris, 2007.

Staiger, Janet. *Blockbuster TV: Must-See Sitcoms in the Network Era.* New York and London: New York University Press, 2000.

Zettl, Herbert. 'The Rare Case of Television Aesthetics.' *Journal of the University Film Association* 30:2 (1978): 3–8.

PART TWO

Aesthetics and style of television comedy

5

Why comedy is at home on television

Alex Clayton

This chapter will flesh out an intuition that television readily lends itself to comedy, and provide reasons for this special affinity. My explanation will appeal to the idea of television as a hybrid medium marked by the inheritance of a winning combination of conditions and tendencies that have individually allowed comedy to flourish in other media. This understanding emerges not from a set of general presuppositions about television, but through a piece of criticism on a single comic sketch, an attempt to account, primarily, for its particular pleasures and for its distinct achievement *as* a work of television. Here I follow Stanley Cavell's caution to the effect that we understand the conditions and possibilities of a medium not by thinking about its mechanics but only by appreciating the significance of its works – and we can only appreciate the significance of its works by considering their particular qualities, specifically through criticism.[1]

The 'Four Yorkshiremen' sketch was televised in the first series of *At Last the 1948 Show* (Associated Rediffusion, 1967), featuring Tim Brooke-Taylor, Graham Chapman, John Cleese and Marty Feldman. The programme's sketch show format and absurdist-satirical sense of humour makes it an important precursor to the more celebrated *Monty Python's Flying Circus* (BBC, 1969–74), with whom it shares Cleese and Chapman, and indeed the Yorkshiremen sketch is probably best remembered from its reprisal as part of a Monty Python stage show released as a concert film, *Live at the Hollywood*

---

[1] Stanley Cavell, *The World Viewed: Reflections on the Ontology of Film*, enlarged edition (Cambridge, MA: Harvard University Press, 1979), 31.

Bowl (1982). Many of the episodes of *At Last the 1948 Show* were thought wiped and only in recent years has a significant proportion of its output been recovered and restored. A compilation of highlights from the show, including 'Four Yorkshiremen', has happily now been released on DVD (Boulevard, 2007), and readers may wish to know that this original version of the sketch can (as at the time of publication) be watched online.[2]

It opens with a view of four men in bold white tuxedos, smoking cigars and drinking wine around what seems to be an outdoor café table (south of France maybe), accompanied by classical music (suggesting somewhere exclusive). The figures appear in a symmetrical composition, in their matching outfits, to form a cohesive cluster in a horseshoe around the table, an image of group balance about to be upset, four heads ready to talk. The semi-circle assembly may also faintly suggest the seating arrangement for a card or parlour game, an association which will be developed as the sketch proceeds The men gaze variously outwards, chuffing on their cigars, setting the mood for wistful reflection and pompous self-congratulation.

The script seems to have been composed collectively by the main performers. It is exceptionally well-crafted, and worth printing here in full:

FIRST YORKSHIREMAN (Marty Feldman):
(Referring to the wine) Aye, very passable, not bad at all.

SECOND YORKSHIREMAN (Graham Chapman):
Aye. Nothing like a good glass of Château de Chasselas, eh, Josiah?

THIRD YORKSHIREMAN (Tim Brooke-Taylor):
Aye, you're right there, Obadiah, dead right.

FOURTH YORKSHIREMAN (John Cleese):
Who'd have thought, forty years ago, we'd be sittin' here drinking Château de Chasselas.

FIRST YORKSHIREMAN:
Aye, we'd have been glad of the price of a cup o' tea, then.

SECOND YORKSHIREMAN:
A cup o' cold tea.

FOURTH YORKSHIREMAN:
Without milk or sugar.

---

[2] http://www.youtube.com/watch?v=DAtSw3daGoo [accessed 15 June 2012].

THIRD YORKSHIREMAN:
Or tea.

FIRST YORKSHIREMAN:
Out a cracked cup, at that.

FOURTH YORKSHIREMAN:
We never 'ad a cup. We used to drink out of a rolled up newspaper.

SECOND YORKSHIREMAN:
The best we could manage was to suck on a piece of damp cloth.

THIRD YORKSHIREMAN:
But you know, I often think we were 'appier then, although we were poor.

FIRST YORKSHIREMAN:
Because we were poor. My old Dad said to me, 'e said, 'Money won't bring you 'appiness, son'.

FOURTH YORKSHIREMAN:
'E was right. I was 'appier then and I had nothin'. We used to live in this tiny tumbledown old house with great 'oles in t' roof.

SECOND YORKSHIREMAN:
'Ouse?! You were lucky to live in a 'ouse! We used to live in one room, twenty-six of us, all there, no furniture, 'alf the floor was missing, and we were all 'uddled together in one corner for fear of falling.

THIRD YORKSHIREMAN:
Room?! You were lucky to 'ave a room! We used to 'ave to live in t' corridor!

FIRST YORKSHIREMAN:
Corridor?! Oh, I used to dream of livin' in a corridor, that would ha' been a palace to us. We used to live in a water tank on t' rubbish tip. Aye. Every morning we'd be woke up by having a load of rotting fish dumped all over us! House! Huh.

FOURTH YORKSHIREMAN:
Well, when I say 'ouse, it were only 'ole in the ground covered by a couple o' foot o' torn canvas, but it were 'ouse to us.

SECOND YORKSHIREMAN:
Oh well, we were evicted from our 'ole in the ground; we 'ad to go and live in the lake.

THIRD YORKSHIREMAN:
Eh, you were lucky to have a lake. There were over a hundred and fifty of us living in a small shoebox in t' middle o' road.

FIRST YORKSHIREMAN:
Cardboard box?

THIRD YORKSHIREMAN:
Aye.

FIRST YORKSHIREMAN:
Aye, you were lucky. We lived for three months in a rolled up newspaper in a septic tank. Aye. Every morning we'd 'ave to get up at six, clean out t' rolled up newspaper, eat a crust of stale bread, then we'd 'ave to work fourteen 'ours at t' mill, day in, day out, for sixpence a week! Aye, and when we'd come home, Dad would thrash us to sleep with his belt.

SECOND YORKSHIREMAN:
Luxury. We used to get up at three, clean the lake, eat a 'andful of 'ot gravel, then we'd work in t' mill for twenty hours for tuppence a month, then we'd come home, and Dad would beat us about the head and neck with a broken bottle. If we were lucky!

THIRD YORKSHIREMAN:
Paradise. We 'ad it tough. I used to 'ave to get out of shoebox at midnight, lick road clean, eat a couple of bits o' *cold* gravel, work twenty-three hours a day at mill for a penny every four years, and when we got home Dad used to slice us in half with a bread knife.

FOURTH YORKSHIREMAN:
Right. We used to get up in morning, at 'alf past ten at night, 'alf an 'our before we'd gone to bed, eat a lump of poison, work twenty-nine hours at mill for ha'penny a lifetime, come home and each night Dad would strangle us and dance about on our graves.

FIRST YORKSHIREMAN:
Aye. You try and tell that to the young people of today. Will they believe you?

ALL TOGETHER:
No!

As is customary in British comedy, class-cultural stereotypes are boldly invoked from the outset.[3] For a native English viewer, at least, the repeated (comically gratuitous) use of 'aye' in the first three lines identifies the stereotype of a Yorkshireman: plain-speaking, down-to-earth, sharing the values of his forebears (as befits a man with a Victorian name), and taking excessive pride in all of the above. The stereotype is meant immediately to jar with the dazzling tuxedo (one might have expected a tweed flat cap), and with the topic of discussion, the quality of fine wine (not ale) identified pretentiously by its French estate (not by its colour). 'Nothing like a good glass of Château de Chasselas', spoken bluntly and with an upward inflection at the end of the line as if it were a well-known adage, involves a clash between content and idiom, cosmopolitan (effeminate) discourse spoken as provincial (manly) common sense. Whilst the opening establishes a satire of social posturing, the tone is fond and the mockery playful. The ostentatious rich ham up their working-class credentials, but there's another layer of pretence in play here: the Northern accents are notably wobbly because the performers are all Southern and middle class. Rather than this necessarily being a flaw of the sketch, it's best thought of as part of its texture, lending an atmosphere of the amateur masquerade. Consider the relish with which the performers articulate their lines, for each other as much as for us. Why else would such an extraneous detail as the name of the wine be repeated other than to savour its glottal pleasures when pronounced in a Yorkshire accent? One's appreciation of the sketch will depend whether one is willing to accept this invitation to a community of convivial playacting.

The palpable camaraderie between performers sets an important tone, but also serves a key theme of the sketch: the relationship between competition and cooperation. Finding happy agreement on the quality of the wine, the Yorkshiremen begin to reflect on their humble lives forty years previously (although no effort has been made to disguise the fact that none of the men are conceivably over forty – another acknowledgement of playful pretence). They are of one mind in their recollection that in those days they would have been glad for the price of a cup of tea. 'A cup o' cold tea', notes Obadiah. 'Without milk or sugar', the Fourth Yorkshireman observes. 'Or tea', adds Josiah. The men are forging an account together, individually appending clauses to a statement with ostensive application to the whole group. The humour of 'Or tea' comes not just from the absurdity of self-contradiction (tea without tea), but from its demonstration that the rhythms of amiable

---

[3] Andy Medhurst's book, *A National Joke: Popular Comedy and English Cultural Identities* (London: Routledge, 2007), presents a valuable and involved account of how class and other forms of identity have figured in twentieth-century English comedy.

conversation can so easily railroad its members into unreasonable consensus. That consensus is expressed aurally by means of the rhythmic interjection of 'Aye' after each addition, and visually by holding the balanced four-shot for almost the entire first minute of the sketch. Yet even in these early stages the collective building amongst identically besuited Yorkshiremen is starting to contain notes of rivalry. In the space between 'we'd have been glad of the price of a cup o' tea' and 'we used to drink out of a rolled-up newspaper', the reference for the first-person plural has imperceptibly morphed from collective present company ('we Yorkshiremen') to individual and absent clans ('we: my family').

A slow zoom into John Cleese and Graham Chapman, the two Yorkshiremen at the middle of the four-shot composition, is the first shift in camera perspective, and inaugurates a new phase of more blatant one-upmanship. From now on, the Yorkshiremen will more systematically try to outdo one another with embellished reports of juvenile hardship. Ironically, the shift starts on a point of general agreement that 'money won't bring you happiness' ('"E was right: I was "appier then and I had nothin"'). Cleese leans in like he's about to deliver a homily on the topic, and the camera responds as if settling into position to receive his unifying wisdom. Yet the camera's inference proves unfounded. Cleese's utterance turns out not to be nothing more than the first in a series of competitive boasts – and not of happiness, but of deprivation. The camera has apparently been wrongfooted in its prediction of relevance, its attempt to 'cover' the conversation by anticipating where things will go next, as in a documentary. As the scene proceeds, the découpage seems (pretends) to learn, with us, the rules of the game, such as the unvarying rule that each participant will speak strictly in turn. This motivates, for instance, a cut to a shot favouring Marty Feldman a beat *before* his outcry of 'Corridor?!', where previously the selection of views had seemed to play catch-up. From this point forward, the editing becomes more anticipatory, synched with the regular rhythms of the dialogue. Cutting before and after each delivery itemises the contributions as individuated units, shown from a range of angles including tight close-ups and over-the-shoulder two-shots across the table, pitting Yorkshireman against Yorkshireman. The paradoxical result is to stress the breakdown of solidarity by strengthening the impression of an orderly, turn-based game, in which each player must respond punctually to the previous 'hand'.

The sketch invites us to chart its development almost as one might follow the course of a sports match. It would have been possible for each testimony to lay claim to an entirely new form of destitution and suffering, unrelated to those that precede it. More pleasurable by far is the recognition that each new avowal takes evident inspiration from previous claims, seeking to better those claims by building on them. Surveying the process of accretion and variation is a semi-abstract pleasure of this sketch: the accusations of having been lucky which develop into hyperbolic exclamations of envy ('That would 'a been a palace to us!' – 'Luxury!' – 'Paradise!'); the early recourse to fairy-tale imagery ('tiny tumbledown old house') which permits a move to fantastical miniaturisation ('over a hundred and fifty of us livin' in a small shoebox'); the idea that eating hot gravel is preferable to eating cold gravel, following the same logic that hot porridge is more desirable than cold porridge, and so on. Living space becomes more inhospitable, work more gruelling, pay more measly, food more inedible, domestic violence more extreme. The pattern of escalation culminates in the sight of Cleese's Yorkshireman, puckering his lips in close up: 'Right...' he exclaims, *almost* acknowledging the rules of the game, steeling himself to invent something unsurpassable. His hyperbolic, impossible report is held together only by the sheer force of assertion: he glowers around as he speaks, daring the others to call his bluff. They can't, of course, because to challenge one claim would be to open them all up to query. The investment is too heavy: their entire identities are staked on wild accounts of miraculous social climbing. They swiftly find a common adversary – the cosseted youth of today – and unite in agreement once more. The classical music of the opening moments has resumed and we close with the balanced four-shot with which the sketch began.

Immanuel Kant defined humour as that which arises 'from a strained expectation being suddenly reduced to nothing'.[4] Whilst this isn't a sufficient definition, it captures the structure of 'Four Yorkshiremen', with its abrupt collapse, after so much wrangling for top spot, to the self-same state of equilibrium with which the sketch began. This is a structure we may associate with television more widely. The quintessential example is the sitcom, which typically works to get the characters back into position for another round of events next week.[5] Yet even without the demands of the series format (we expect no return to these characters: *that* sketch show convention had not yet been founded), 'Four Yorkshiremen' ends where it began. The greater reason seems to be the aesthetic pleasure of a circular return, and the apprehension of *design* which is of critical importance for comedy.[6] The convention that a sketch will be a miniature work entire (set up its own premise, establish ground rules, settle its own little drama) encourages us to survey and

---

[4] Immanuel Kant, *Critique of Judgement* (Oxford: Oxford University Press, 2008), 161.
[5] This cyclical return to normalcy is generally seen to be one of the sitcom's most decisive structural features. See, for example, the entry on situation comedy in Brian Geoffrey Rose and Robert S. Alley, *TV Genres: A Handbook and Reference Guide* (London: Greenwood Press, 1985), 115.
[6] For elaboration on this matter, see Alex Clayton, 'Playacting: A Theory of Comic Performance', in *Theorizing Film Acting*, ed. Aaron Taylor (London: Routledge, 2012), 47–61.

savour its emerging shape (for instance, a pattern of escalation) with an eye towards its imminent completion. Contrast the more forward-looking mode of perception which would result if we took 'Four Yorkshiremen' to be the opening scene in a feature film, for example. The expectation that the sketch's resolution, as convention demands, will be laughably expedient, without further consequence, fosters a mode of perception less geared to 'what will happen next' and more attentive to comic patterns, repetitions and variations.

Somewhat against Raymond Williams' idea that the definitive character-istic of television is its 'flow', the blending of one part into another in a stream of broadcasting, John Ellis has stressed the way television output is blocked out as a series of discrete units.[7] For Ellis, the principal unit of television is not the programme or the series but the segment, 'a relatively self-contained scene [rarely exceeding five minutes in length] which conveys an incident, a mood or a particular meaning'.[8] Ellis's examples of formats which are built out of segments include the news bulletin, the commercial break and the soap opera, but he might well have added the sketch show, perhaps the most manifest instance of this compositional tendency. The sketch show epito-mises television's condition as a medium of discrete chunks, the individual success of which matters far more than the order of their conjoinment. Ever since the silent clowns moved to multi-reel movies, film comedy has always struggled with the problem of duration. How to sustain laughs for more than two reels, let alone the length of a feature presentation? Even if the material doesn't flag, the audience probably will. Tying bits of comic business together through story is the usual attempted solution, but it turns out to take a rare genius, in the medium of film at least, to combine humour and extended narrative without them diluting or diminishing one another (for one reason, because a punchline is ruined by the addition of 'and then...'). The shorter formats of television, constructed more brazenly out of segments, lend themselves more readily to solve this problem. Although film is often considered television's closest cousin, the most evident forerunner to this condition is variety theatre.

Along with segmental composition, television derives from variety theatre a number of other features. One such feature is its partiality for formal routines, capable of being reprised on a regular basis with minor variations, similar phraseology and recognisable personnel, and usually involving some degree of direct address. The post-match analysis, the weather report and

---

[7] Cf. Raymond Williams, *Television: Technology and Cultural Form* (London: Routledge, 2003), 77–120, and John Ellis, *Visible Fictions: Cinema, Television, Video* (London: Routledge, 2000), 116–26.

[8] Ellis, *Visible Fictions*, 148.

the game show provide instances of this tendency. Comic sketches may or may not involve returning characters or reprisals of previously-seen set ups, but invariably draw on the same handful of performers across sketches, playing all the roles. This is not just a cheap option; instantly recognizing members of a troupe through disguises of accent and costume is part of the sketch show's appeal. For a sketch like 'Four Yorkshiremen', the familiar appearance of performers immediately trumps the appearance of 'new' characters. Moreover, the flavour of a comic routine is established in part by the regularity and melodic qualities of delivery, each performer supplying his line in a manner which is more like contributing a line or verse to a communal sing-song than it is like weighing in to an exchange of views. Something like a refrain is established − 'You were lucky!' − worthy of a music hall ditty.

The proscenium arch arrangements of variety theatre may also be an influence on the tendency towards frontal composition in television, especially comedy. The three-wall space of many sitcoms, at least before recent experiments with the form, typifies this tendency.[9] The front-on, non-naturalistic horseshoe arrangement of figures in the opening shot of 'Four Yorkshiremen' is not merely the plainest method of providing a clear view of four faces. The resultant effect of symmetry does everything it can to present the characters as interchangeable types, and to suppress, for the moment, the considerable physiognomic differences between the four identically-dressed individuals. Squeezed into the 4:3 frame and thereby restricted in their capacity for physical movement, the stiff, linear appearance of these figures might recall marionettes in a puppet show. Indeed, whimsical as it may seem, puppet theatre − another form in which comedy has traditionally flourished − strikes me as an importantly close relative to a medium which also involves peeping into a box and is so commonly accused of presenting a collection of 'talking heads'. What television shares with puppet theatre above all is that sense of being open about its own mechanics. For instance, TV studios are not inordinately disguised for much non-fiction programming, appearing cavernous, shiny, candidly multi-purpose. Breakfast shows routinely refer to aspects of their own production process, especially when little things go wrong, and microphones are clipped to collars not for concealment but to dramatise the event of interview − like the visible strings and sticks which contribute to a puppet's poignancy and humour.

---

[9]Antonio Savorelli highlights the use of the proverbial fourth wall and tendency for the couch to define a frontal shot in what he calls 'classic sitcom'. He then shows how some recent TV comedies have departed from such conventions. *Beyond Sitcom: New Directions in American Television Comedy* (Jefferson, NC: McFarland, 2010), 23–6.

Television's habitual candour about contrivance works positively to comedy's advantage. Rather than making efforts to camouflage the signs of constructedness, comedy is so often disposed to declare its own artifice, relieving viewers from an absorption in fiction to follow the workings of comic operation as such. There is no attempt, in 'Four Yorkshiremen', to give the impression of eavesdropping on a conversation in progress. Indeed, the lengthy pause before dialogue begins (letting the audience settle) and lack of reference to any prior utterance seem to announce 'beginning of routine' rather than 'we join our protagonists as...'. There is no real sense of a world beyond the frame: nobody gestures or glances outside of the performance space, and contextual questions, such as whether these are industrialists at a break in a business conference, for example, or old schoolmates at a reunion, lack pertinence and do not arise. The premise has been stripped down to its bold essentials. As with the recounting of a joke, there is no attempt to embellish the scenario with layers of naturalistic detail (it is, after all, a 'sketch'). Such details would only cloud the line of comic development and produce a mood less conducive to a voyage into the absurd. The idea that those who can't afford tea might resort to sucking on a piece of damp cloth is possible to entertain only in a realm without serious claims to representation.

I wrote earlier of the sketch's invitation to join the performers in savouring the sounds of speech and the stylised rhythms of its dialogue. In this aspect the sketch draws on conditions and tendencies which television shares with radio. The relative prominence of sound against a small screen makes it a more naturally voice-led medium than film and fosters its compulsive interest in talk. 'Four Yorkshiremen' exploits this interest by emphasising the musical qualities of conversation, for instance, the rhythmic repetition of 'Although we were poor'/'*Because* we were poor'. Like musical phrases, grammatical structures find echoes and variations: 'We used to 'ave to live in t' corridor!'/'I used to *dream* of livin' in a corridor!' Establishing this internal convention means that a moderate shift in the pattern can yield a comic effect of surprise which is principally rhythmic, such as when the First Yorkshireman begs a further detail from the Third Yorkshireman ('*Cardboard* box?'), breaking the momentum before taking up the thread once again.

Television is also like radio in that, unlike cinema's easy resort to sensorial abundance, it manifests a proclivity to appeal to the imagination of deprived senses – hence the draw of TV cookery shows, serving the ostensible function of culinary instruction whilst really providing the opportunity to dwell on tastes untasted and smells unsmelt. 'Four Yorkshireman' arranges its frames quite simply, and minimizes the movement within them, as if to allow the stream of images roused by the dialogue to layer itself over the top. No amount of visual enhancement (for instance, cutting to an image to illustrate each fantasy of childhood poverty) would better the effect of keeping what is invoked absent from view. The humour so often lies with our *efforts* to envision what is lucidly described but effectively impossible to picture: say, a stream of urchins trailing from a shoebox at dead of night to lick the road clean. The imagery appeals to the mind's eye, but also, and most vividly, to the mind's mouth. To entertain the daft idea of drinking tea from a rolled-up newspaper, as the insistence of delivery compels us to do, is (for British viewers) perhaps to recall the comfort provided by fish-and-chips (traditionally consumed from a folded tabloid) and, against the background of that, the image of a gathered family, passing a rolled-up newspaper like an opium pipe as the disappearing tea darkens the white sheets, the dreamlike frustration of trying to slurp what has already been absorbed, the texture of soaked paper on parched lips.

Such features would work well on radio (and indeed a number of successful TV comedy series, at least in the UK, had former incarnations as radio series).[10] What the image track gives us is a photographic presentation of the contrasting physiognomic features of its performers. These four men may dress alike, speak alike, and think alike, but these interchangeable types are embodied by unique individuals. However many times one has seen Marty Feldman on screen, one cannot help but be struck by the wonderful peculiarity of his facial appearance, with its bulbous eyes and crooked nose. His Yorkshireman is a swivel-eyed nutcase who rants and taps the table as if blaming others for his condition. Graham Chapman's Yorkshireman is a straight-backed simpleton with the facial appearance of a startled ferret. Tim Brooke-Taylor's Yorkshireman is a mincing old sourpuss who conveys his superiority by turning away for theatrical emphasis and blowing cigar smoke through tight lips. John Cleese's Yorkshireman is an insecure Babbitt who follows the crowd and perpetually seeks affirmation from the others, peering out from under furry eyebrows, trying to assert himself. These are what Stanley Cavell, discussing film's use of types, calls 'individualities': 'particular ways of *inhabiting* a social role', in which the individuality of the human subject 'naturally takes precedence' over the role.[11] For Cavell, film's tendency to stress the specific embodiment of the type is a consequence of the photographic basis of moving pictures, which automatically attends to the physical qualities of the figure on-screen, making the particularity of the performer its primary subject (rather than the depicted character). This is a condition that television importantly shares with film. It is difficult to imagine

[10] For example, *Hancock's Half Hour* (BBC, 1956–60), *Whose Line Is It Anyway?* (Hat Trick Productions, 1988–98) and *Little Britain* (BBC, 2003–6) all started out as BBC radio series.
[11] Cavell, *The World Viewed*, 33, 34–5 (italics added).

a more defined and rigid type than that of 'The Yorkshireman' as established in this sketch. Yet even here the individual performers create unique variants on 'The Yorkshireman', each offering a different inflection on the type. These inflections manifest each Yorkshireman's unshakeable separateness, even in the midst of a like-minded group. Each man's boasting about his own past deprivation seeks to assure his place as an authentic member of the group, with an unquestionable right to that status. Yet each effort to secure this acceptance, to adhere to type more completely, drawing out as it does certain idiosyncrasies of appearance and temperament, ironically serves to distinguish and individualize that member. The relationship between eccentricity and conformity is a ripe subject for comedy, and one which is well-served by television's disposition to offer 'individualities'.

Alongside his writing on film, Cavell has endeavoured, in a provocative but neglected essay, 'The Fact of Television', to sketch some dimensions of television's distinctness as a medium. Reflecting on the enduring appeal of a range of formats – news broadcasts, sports coverage, commercials and quiz shows, for instance – Cavell finds crucial to an understanding of the medium the intuition that television is disposed to 'cover (as with a gun), to keep something on view'.[12] Accordingly, television calls upon a mode of perception Cavell characterizes as 'monitoring', continuous with the way a security guard might attend to a bank of CCTV monitors. We are thus placed, through television, to monitor 'the eventful', but equally, Cavell claims, to monitor its opposite, 'the *uneventful*, the repeated, the repetitive'.[13] This characterisation of the medium chimes with my sense that the core appeal of 'Four Yorkshiremen' has to do with monitoring the drift of an essentially uneventful conversation, tracing its rhythms and repetitions as such. This mode of attendance is rather different, for instance, from identifying with the plight and activity of comic protagonists, as we do with Chaplin and Keaton. Rather than encouraging immersion in a comic universe, what 'Four Yorkshiremen' offers is a surface of social behaviour made available for more or less amused inspection. The sketch presents nothing more grandiose than a trivial competition between acquaintances as something worth following, perhaps for instruction in how better to conceal our own efforts to secure the respect of others. The security-guard implication of the word 'monitoring' furthermore matches my sense that the humour of the sketch contains a shadow of anxiousness. Part of what we monitor is the prospect of one party's bluff being called out, to prepare ourselves for the regular rhythms of the uneventful to be disrupted. The displayed struggle for status is so determined and the manoeuvres so

---

[12] Stanley Cavell, 'The Fact of Television', *Daedalus* 111:4 (Fall 1982): 85.
[13] Cavell, 'The Fact of Television', 89.

transparent that we are placed to glimpse a distorted mirror of our own restless concerns for esteem management, along with the attendant threats of exposure.[14]

We also monitor the progress of the sketch as a comedic performance unfolding in a continuous slice of time. A viewer does not need to be in possession of the fact that the sketch was shot with several cameras in a single 'take', and edited live, to be able to appreciate the effect of uninterrupted continuity. That one or two lines are slightly bungled only adds to the impression of liveness and improvisation. Cavell's surprising suggestion for why television obsessively 'monitor[s] signs of life', as he puts it, is that the medium seeks to reassure the paranoid intuition of the 'growing uninhabitability of the world',[15] a desperate feeling that the world no longer 'can humanly be responded to'.[16] Foregrounding the capacity for improvisation, aliveness to one another (Cavell calls improvisation 'as apt a sign of human life as we have to go on'[17]), is one way in which the medium pacifies this terrible thought. The 'Four Yorkshiremen' depicts a realm where even mundane conversation is a skirmish filled by meagre lies and boasts of suffering – yet what I earlier referred to as a community of convivial playacting affords the hope of human company.

It may be that monitoring is properly thought of as merely the *default* mode of perception invited by television. Indeed, the *range* of ways in which we are invited and able to attend to television's material, switching modes of attention as we switch channels, may itself be a significant fact about the medium. Yet the attitude invoked by monitoring serves the appeal of comedy in its obsessive attention to the surface of social life, with its varied forms of more or less harmless pretence. In other ways I hope to have shown, if 'Four Yorkshireman' is as exemplary as I take it to be, that television lends itself to comedy – at least, to comedy astute enough to acknowledge the medium's possibilities, which means seeing its conditions as opportunities. The conditions I find most apt to support comedy reflect television's mixed inheritance from a range of other media: from variety theatre, its tendency towards segmentation and partiality for formal routines; from puppet theatre, its candour about contrivance and stripped-down composition; from radio, its privileging of the sound of the spoken voice and appeal to the imagination of deprived senses; and from film, its preference for 'individualities', the individual fleshing-out of social types. Together they allow for the creation of

---

[14] See Clayton, 'Playacting' 47–61 for more on this relation between comedy and Erving Goffman's vision of social life.

[15] Cavell, 'The Fact of Television', 95.

[16] Cavell, 'The Fact of Television', 88.

[17] Cavell, 'The Fact of Television', 88.

humorous forms without need to strain against the medium's own inclinations. And that's why comedy is at home on television.

Bibliography

Cavell, Stanley. *The World Viewed: Reflections on the Ontology of Film*, enlarged edn. Cambridge, MA: Harvard University Press, 1979.

—'The Fact of Television', *Daedalus* 111: 4 (Fall 1982): 75–96.

Clayton, Alex. 'Playacting: A Theory of Comic Performance.' In *Theorizing Film Acting*, edited by Aaron Taylor, 47–61. London: Routledge, 2012.

Ellis, John. *Visible Fictions: Cinema, Television, Video*. London: Routledge, 2000.

Kant, Immanuel. *Critique of Judgement*. Oxford: Oxford University Press, 2008.

Medhurst, Andy. *A National Joke: Popular Comedy and English Cultural Identities*. London: Routledge, 2007.

Rose, Brian Geoffrey, and Robert S. Alley. *TV Genres: A Handbook and Reference Guide*. London: Greenwood Press, 1985.

Savorelli, Antonio. *Beyond Sitcom: New Directions in American Television Comedy*. Jefferson, NC: McFarland, 2010.

Williams, Raymond. *Television: Technology and Cultural Form*. London: Routledge, 2003.

6

Situating comedy: Inhabitation and duration in classical American sitcoms

Sérgio Dias Branco

Consider a moment from an episode of *Will & Grace* (1998–2006), 'Something Borrowed, Someone's Due' (4.18), which is filmed employing a single 40-second shot. Best friends Will (Eric McCormack) and Grace (Debra Messing) have moved into a huge new apartment, and are alone in their bedrooms. Will is upstairs. Grace is downstairs. We cannot see them and they speak loudly to each other so that their voices traverse the rooms of the apartment. The shot is wide enough to include the stairs to Will's room, on the left, and the door to Grace's room, on the right. Here is their exchange of words:

> *Grace*: Will, I'm having a clothing crisis. Will you come down here?
>
> *Will*: No. You come up here.
>
> *Grace*: No. You come down here.
>
> *Will*: No. You come up here.
>
> *Grace*: No. You come down here.
>
> *Will*: No. You come up here.
>
> *Grace*: No. You come down here.
>
> [*pause*]

Will: No. You come up here.

Grace: Please?

Will: No, and stop bothering me.

[*the telephone rings*]

Will: Hello? Grace, I'm not coming down there!

Grace: Will, I miss our old apartment.

Will: Me, too. I wanna go home.

Grace: Me, too.

Will: Let's talk about this.

Grace: Yeah, let's. [*pause*] Will you come down here?

Right after this scene, they decide to return to their old apartment. Their off-screen, disembodied, voices convey the suggestion that they are communicating as if they were in different spaces instead of a shared space. Furthermore, their absence from the shot captured by a stationary camera expresses that this is already an uninhabited place, an empty location – not really a home.

Moments like these stress the significance of inhabitation (of living in a space and finding a place in it) and duration (of experiencing time and valuing it) in sitcoms like *Will & Grace*. This chapter focuses on these two topics to examine the style of classical American sitcoms. Such programmes are filmed scene by scene, instead of shot by shot, in a sound stage and relying on a virtual proscenium that the multiple cameras do not cross, in what may be described as aspects of traditional sitcom aesthetics.[1] The term 'classical' signals that this was the first structure used in the making of sitcoms. Yet, this unified employment and exploration of the means of studio television production, which creates a sense of place and time through the filming of continuous action, is not tied to an era. It is followed by some contemporary sitcoms that may therefore be aptly described as classical.

Jeremy Butler claims that these programmes follow an editing pattern that he perceptively terms *attenuated continuity*, the opposite of the *intensified continuity* identified by David Bordwell.[2] In the former, techniques of

---

[1] Brett Mills, *The Sitcom* (Edinburgh: Edinburgh University Press, 2009), 6.
[2] David Bordwell, *The Way Hollywood Tells It: Story and Style in Modern Movies* (Berkeley and Los Angeles: University of California Press, 2006), 121–89.

visual continuity such as the 180° rule for camera positions or the eyeline matches for shots and reverse-shots are 'reduced to the bare'.[3] In the latter, the same techniques are amplified to the point of redundancy. Butler's work has changed the perception that these television programmes have, as he describes, a 'zero-degree style', a styleless style. This is an impression that of course did not extend to single-camera sitcoms such as *Scrubs* (2001–10) because these series do not rely on a fixed system of several cameras and so stylistic choices become *more evident*. My contribution with this text follows from these considerations and ideas, but has a different purpose. This is a piece of television criticism that aims at illuminating the nuanced uses of these techniques calling attention to the way the 'stagy' feel of these series is connected with the closeness of the characters and with their delimited, intimate world. It makes claims about the handling of stage-like settings in classical American sitcoms, namely the bar in *Cheers* and the living room in *Frasier*, whose particular worlds are connected. It therefore scrutinises their exploration of concerns around inhabitation and duration, or dwelling and time, and the connections between the two.

The sitcom (situation comedy) is generally defined as a type of series in which an established set of characters are involved in recurring comic situations.[4] This generic definition is not, nor could it be, attentive to the stylistic properties of particular sitcoms. This is especially true of those sitcoms that follow the classical structure of the genre that, as we have seen, are thought to be even more undistinguished. Details of performance and framing, rhythm and flow, characterize how characters inhabit a place throughout time and demonstrate that classical sitcoms may be alternatively described as a form of *situating comedy*. That is, as a way of grounding and inscribing the comic idiosyncrasies and rapport of a small group of characters in a defined and regular spatial and temporal context. *Cheers* (1982–93) and its spin-off *Frasier* (1993–2004) provide examples from three different decades. They also show different modes of being an inhabitant and of experiencing time that will be studied by drawing on philosophers who have meditated on these matters. This may be unusual in television studies, but we shall see that philosophy provides meditations that allow us to understand aspects of human existence and interaction that are at the center of these series. Both the bar in *Cheers* and Frasier's apartment in *Frasier* become homes, even though the bar is a public space and the apartment is a private space. In fact, there is often a fusion between these two kinds of space in classical American sitcoms – the coffee shop in *Friends* (1994–2004) that becomes a third apartment, beyond

---

[3] Jeremy G. Butler, *Television Style* (London: Routledge, 2010), 83.
[4] See, e.g.: Brett Mills, *Television Sitcom* (London: BFI, 2005).

the two where the main characters live, is but an example. In *Cheers*, the bar is a place where the characters spend a lot of their time and where they feel content and at home. In *Frasier*, the apartment is Frasier's, but his family and friends occupy and reside in it, sporadically or continuously.

Martin Heidegger calls attention to how inhabitation is tied with being.[5] We *are* by inhabiting. Inhabitation in human terms is called *dwelling*, which is the building of *our* world, of a place where we feel at home, physically and spiritually comfortable. According to Heidegger, not all buildings are devised for dwelling, but the bar in *Cheers*, which bears the same festive and warm name as the series, certainly *allows* for dwelling. The cameras were set up for the series in front and across the counter where the costumers sit and drinks are served. This piece of furniture structures the *mise-en-scène* with its central position. It has the centripetal function of, not only aggregating the characters' actions, but also of establishing the camera's positions and angles. Long shots abound so that the presence of the counter remains visually dominant. Yet, because this is an establishment, it is open to the public. *Cheers* presents a limited sphere, but a porous one that let us see what lies behind its limits. It is subterranean, but the fact that it is out of sight for the passer-by does not mean that it is not welcoming. Cheers' inhabitants treasure the open door and take pleasure in greeting and taking a stranger in. The narrative of each episode frequently develops from someone, like the Englishman in 'The Spy Who Came in for a Cold One' (1.12), or something, like the fortune-telling machine in 'Fortune and Men's Weight' (2.17), crossing the threshold of the bar. Halfway through 'Let Me Count the Ways' (1.14), a fan of the baseball team Celtics walks in from the street. We see him walking from the street to the stairs that lead to the bar: the camera follows his movement, from a straight-on position to a high-angle position. He enters the bar in the next shot, with the camera already in its habitual place. Much like the regular costumers, the camera adopts positions that become usual. It is the first time that we see such a transition, which shows the journey of a character from outside to inside, revealing the outer world while at the same time emphasising the inner border of the bar. Yet there are many transitions between the bar and the adjacent, secluded spaces that lie beyond its delimited space: Sam's office and the poolroom. The office of the owner, Sam Malone (Ted Danson), is disconnected from the bar by a door, whereas a passageway separates it from the poolroom. To reinforce the centrality of the bar, both of them are repeatedly employed as off-screen spaces, that is, spaces that are linked with the one we see on screen, but that are simultaneously outside the

---

[5]Martin Heidegger, *Poetry, Language, Thought*, trans. Albert Hofstadter (New York: Harper Colophon Books, 1971), 145–61.

limits of the frame and of the room with the counter. In addition, the office door allows whoever uses that space to hide from the eyes of the people in the public area of the bar. They can only know what is going on in the office if they listen in through the door – as they do many times. In contrast, characters communicate between the bar and the billiard room, across the passageway. These differences between spaces and their use within *Cheers* explore the fusion and the degrees between the private and the communal.

In other words, the series establishes the topology of its fictional world, outlining the other spaces against the bar. This main space feels like a stage, a place where people enter and leave sideways (from or to the street, the office, or the billiard room) or upwards (from or to the restaurant above). This staginess is related to the clearly defined limits of the space as well as to its unity that the elements of the setting and the set camera positions enhance. How do the characters live in this unified space? How do they dwell in it? There are noticeable differences between Diane Chambers's (Shelley Long) pensive and elegant gestures and Carla Tortelli's (Rhea Perlman) careless, graceless actions. But what is more striking is their dynamic as a community, the communion of different people. 'Manager Coach' (2.08) opens with Carla singing a lullaby to her baby on the phone. Her colleagues and the bar's customary clients join in, little by little, and the shot widens to accommodate all the impromptu singers. The particular and intimate moments of a character usually have the magnetic power to summon the other characters, turning them into shared moments and moments of sharing. This is a place where 'everybody knows your name' and the 'troubles are all the same', as the lyrics of the theme song say. The bar's inhabitants are clustered around a character or an unfolding event forming a kind of family in which the worries, joys and interests of one of them occupy them jointly. There is a similar interconnection in 'The Heart Is a Lonely Snipe Hunter' (3.14), this time in the form of a chain instead of a gathering, when a costumer starts singing 'On the Sunny Side of the Street' and then one character after another picks up where the other one has left off. They see a possibility to connect to each other as if in a chain of fellowship. When such opportunities of becoming a fellow become plain, time is seen as that which opens up new possibilities of being.[6] Revealingly, the characters are in tune. They respond to each other, continuing in their own way what the other has started, forming a community which does not erase their individuality and which arises not only from the sharing of space, but also of time. The last one to participate, Coach (Nicholas Colasanto), seems to be at odds with the rest because he begins singing

---

[6]Heidegger, *Being and Time* [1927], trans. John Macquarrie and Edward Robinson (Oxford: Blackwell Publishers, 2005), 488.

the country song 'Jingle Jangle Jingle'. He does not do this intentionally to stand out. The other characters and the regular viewers know how forgetful (and self-effacing) he is. Then and there, he still lives this moment with them through his forgetfulness.

Besides these recurrent events, another aspect that conveys the characters' bond with and in the bar is the way workers and costumers have found a specific spot for them, which grounds them in this site and to which they repeatedly return. Norman Peterson's (George Wendt) presence is the most eloquent example of this. He seats at the right extremity of the counter and drinks beer after beer. The teaser for 'They Called Me Mayday' (2.09) shows him in pyjamas as Sam walks into Cheers to open it for business. Norman has been residing at the bar. By the end of the ninth season, in 'Uncle Sam Wants You' (9.26), the bartender Woody Boyd (Woody Harrelson) receives the mail and gives every envelope to Norman – not just the ones addressed to 'Mr. Peterson' or 'occupant', but also an item sent to 'Mr. Boyd'. Woody's automatic distribution demonstrates how usual it has become for all the post to be Norman's.

As in the initial example from *Will & Grace* that explores the characters' gradual uneasiness, this sense of belonging arises in *Cheers* from the fluent and continuous unravelling of situations. Shots are sequenced without individuation, framing an uninterrupted performance and weaved to preserve this continuity. This feature is highlighted in *Frasier*, through the titling of scenes. The scenes of classical sitcoms are unusually long when compared to sitcoms that follow the single-camera mode of production. The episode evocatively called 'Space Quest' (1.02) begins with a scene of more than five and a half minutes. Frasier Crane (Kelsey Grammer), is a psychiatrist and radio-show host first seen in *Cheers* as a customer. Recently returned to his hometown Seattle, he has just woken up and walks into the living room with an open robe as if he were alone. The scene is titled 'Dear God, it wasn't a dream'. His father Martin (John Mahoney) has moved into the apartment with his caretaker, Daphne (Jane Leeves), and his dog, a terrier named Eddie (Moose). There are other repeated spaces beyond the apartment, such as the coffee shop, where characters meet, or the radio studio, from where Frasier broadcasts his show. Yet *his* space is the apartment, particularly the living room, and the episode deals with the feeling that they have intruded into it. The series uses a smaller proscenium, but a more extensive set with even a small, salient part that includes the apartment door. The relation between camera and set is more diverse than in *Cheers*, because the compositions in the original series tend to be plain, with the camera in a perpendicular position in relation to the bar counter. In *Frasier*, the two windows of the living room make an edge and the sofa, table, steps, walls, and shelves have different orientations. The bar in *Cheers* is larger and more densely occupied, which creates the noted chances for interaction, participation, and transformation. As we have seen and will see, the apartment in *Frasier* provides opportunities for integration, reinvention and realisation on the part of the characters. Later, in 'Space Quest', he arrives at the apartment and (still with his coat on) calls for the three new occupants. He says 'Eddie' with a loose mouth, disparaging the dog, because up to this point the most uncomfortable moments had been those when Eddie followed or stared at him. Frasier's movements are slow and cautious at first, but when he is certain that no one is home, he grins and takes off the coat with ample and energetic gestures. He uses a back cushion of the sofa as pillow on top of which he places a book and then prepares a glass of wine, humming the Toreador song from Georges Bizet's opera *Carmen*: 'Toreador,/Don't spit on the floor,/Use the cuspidor-a/What do you think it's for-a?' The emphasis on the appended '-a' is a sign of his relaxed state, which is confirmed when he sits on the couch, drink in hand and eyes on the book. Frasier's now companion residents barge in right after he finally concentrates on the book. Andrew Klevan says of the relation between performer and place that they 'find each other, so that the discovery of location is inseparable from the investigation of psychology: the performers look to their environment to realize their characters'.[7] The performer Kelsey Grammer also looks to Frasier's apartment and its contents to realize the character. He reorganizes the sofa and improvises an operatic aria with spontaneity, but with a formal, almost ceremonial, attitude. He bubbles over with an enthusiasm that is restrained. Developing Klevan's idea, we may say that it is the ways in which a performer occupies a place and manages time that realize a character, moment by moment.

Afterward, the tension has not vanished and Frasier convinces his father to have a three-minute conversation. He uses an egg timer to count the time, which he carefully places in front of them on the dining table, where they are seated. Martin shouts about the stupidity of the situation after the first second – 'One second? That's our personal best?', asks Frasier. They argue and forget about the timer. Already up, they agree that it will take years not minutes to forge a bond – Martin believes it will go by before they know it, whereas Frasier hypothesizes 'it will seem like eternity'. Augustine writes about time as a distension of the soul. Time gains meaning subjectively and continually through our attention. In this sense, it may only be measured spiritually. He notes how the vanishing of the present is continuous, opening the way to what we expect and what we remember: 'So the future, which

---

[7] Andrew Klevan, *Film Performance: From Achievement to Appreciation* (London: Wallflower, 2005), 71.

does not exist, is not a long period of time. A long future is a long expectation of the future. And the past, which has no existence, is not a long period of time. A long past is a long memory of the past.'[8] This measuring is therefore qualitative and not quantitative. Behind this idea is a focus on time as experienced, related with the dynamic view of time of philosophers like Aristotle.[9] This is an understanding of time as heterogeneous, *felt*, which cannot be separated into static instants. The timer that Frasier uses, like a clock, is a device that quantifies and indicates time as homogenous. It may show that three minutes have lapsed, but that may be lived as a flash or an era. Experienced time, which is always the experience of the freedom of choice, is what Henri Bergson calls *duration* in which moments 'are not external to one another'.[10] Frasier and Martin's friction endures, but it is smoothed with understated moments of rapport that glide. In 'Look Before You Leap' (3.16), they split the newspaper in a casual manner. Frasier sits on the sofa and Martin lies back on his recliner. Frasier is now somewhat used to his dad, just like he had to adapt to Martin's old recliner that changed the arrangement of the room. The series does not stress the moment, cutting to Daphne when Martin picks up a part of the paper.

This last-mentioned particular editing choice does not stress the flow of action, but underlines the relaxed nature of a gesture. *Frasier* is, however, mainly interested in the notion of *timing*, in the control of action and the awareness of inhabitation that this notion includes. Frasier tries to act elegantly and to be sophisticated – and this is something that he has in common with his brother Niles (David Hyde Pierce). 'Fathers and Sons' (10.22) explores the similarities between Frasier and Leland Barton (David Ogden Stiers), his mother's former research assistant, which raises suspicions about Leland being Frasier's biological father. They are both psychiatrists. They both appreciate fine art and drink sherry. They also have many of the same mannerisms. At one point, they seat on opposite ends of the sofa, graciously holding a glass of the fortified wine with the top of their fingers, cross their legs, sip, and then sigh with pleasure, simultaneously. The suspicion comes from the way gesture and posture *incarnate* identity throughout the ten seasons of the show. Such a feeling is connected with the way Frasier had been seen elegantly occupying and using his apartment and savouring the passage of time in it in previous episodes.

[8] Augustine, *Confessions* [398], trans. Henry Chadwick (Oxford: Oxford University Press, 1998), 243.
[9] Aristotle, *Physics, Or Natural Hearing* [350 BC], trans. and ed. Glen Coughlin (South Bend, IN: St. Augustine's Press, 2005), book IV, chap. 11.
[10] Henri Bergson, *Time and Free Will: An Essay on the Immediate Data of Consciousness* [1889], trans. F. L. Pogson (New York: Dover Publications, 2001), 226.

The multiple-camera proscenium schema that these classical sitcoms follow underlines the flow of time as inscribed in space, situating the comedic action. This is why it is so fitting to use the word 'moment', which has the same origin as 'movement' (*movere*), instead of 'instant' or 'point', to discuss them. This chapter has held on to moments in particular classical sitcoms, attending to their details in order to understand the handling of time[11] and space in these programmes. Such details show particular uses of the unbroken action that the several cameras can track and of the theatrical feel that a studio production is able to create. The scene from *Will & Grace* dislocates the protagonists to a new environment that they do not know how to inhabit and presents the continuous unravelling of their sense of discomfort and disconnection. *Frasier* and *Cheers* locate comedy in specific places, an apartment and a bar, investigating communal and private inhabitation and duration, and opening up possibilities for the emergence of significant moments. Both series give similar importance to the finding of a place where the characters can settle in and enjoy their time, but they do it differently. Frasier desperately seeks a home from the first episode and ends up leaving the apartment to his family in the last episode, 'Goodnight Seattle' (11.23–4). His apartment vanishes from *Frasier* as he begins the search for a new home in a new city, Chicago. In contrast, *Cheers* ends with Sam realizing that the bar is the love of his life, as Norman suggests earlier in the closing scene of the series. He touches the counter with the palm of his hand and knocks on its wood and then tells a potential costumer, who stays outside, isolated by the closed door, that the bar is closed. Sam decides to be alone to better contemplate and appreciate Cheers before it is filled again with people – hence his contact with its objects, which asserts his personal attachment to them. He adjusts a picture frame on the wall, tidying up as a host does in preparation for a party, and then disappears into the darkness of the poolroom instead of leaving. This is where he lives.

Bibliography

Aristotle. *Physics, Or Natural Hearing* [350 BC], trans. and ed. Glen Coughlin. South Bend, IN: St. Augustine's Press, 2005.

Augustine. *Confessions* [398], trans. Henry Chadwick. Oxford: Oxford University Press, 1998.

Bergson, Henri. *Time and Free Will: An Essay on the Immediate Data of*

---

[11] Cf. Steven Peacock, 'Holding onto Moments in *The Age of Innocence*', *Film Studies: An International Review* 9 (2006), ed. Sarah Cardwell: 49.

Consciousness [1889], trans. F. L. Pogson. New York: Dover Publications, 2001.

Bordwell, David. *The Way Hollywood Tells It: Story and Style in Modern Movies*. Berkeley and Los Angeles: University of California Press, 2006.

Butler, Jeremy G. *Television Style*. London: Routledge, 2010.

Heidegger, Martin. *Being and Time* [1927], trans. John Macquarrie and Edward Robinson. Oxford: Blackwell Publishers, 2005.

—*Poetry, Language, Thought*, trans. Albert Hofstadter. New York: Harper Colophon Books, 1971.

Klevan, Andrew. *Film Performance: From Achievement to Appreciation*. London: Wallflower, 2005.

Mills, Brett. *Television Sitcom*. London: BFI, 2005.

—*The Sitcom*. Edinburgh: Edinburgh University Press, 2009.

Peacock, Steven. 'Holding onto Moments in *The Age of Innocence*'. *Film Studies: An International Review* 9 (2006), ed. Sarah Cardwell: 40–50.

7

Arrested developments: Towards an aesthetic of the contemporary US sitcom

Timotheus Vermeulen and James Whitfield

Television – as a piece of technology, as a medium, as an art form – has undergone dramatic changes over the past few years. There have been significant shifts in the ways in which programmes are produced, distributed and consumed. As scholars like Kim Akass and Janet McCabe, Robin Nelson and Jason Mittell have demonstrated, television also looks markedly different today.[1] Much has been written in recent years about contemporary US television drama with the phrase 'Quality Television' often used as a rather problematic descriptor.[2] In contrast, relatively little attention has been devoted to the concurrent changes that have taken place in contemporary US television comedy.[3] This chapter seeks to help redress this critical lacuna.

---

[1] Compare: Janet McCabe and Kim Akass, (eds) *Quality TV: Contemporary American Television and Beyond* (London and New York: I. B. Tauris, 2007); Jason Mittell, 'Narrative Complexity in American Contemporary Television', *The Velvet Light Trap* 58 (Fall 2006): 29–40.
[2] Compare: Sarah Cardwell, 'Is Quality Television Any Good? Generic Distinctions, Evaluations and the Troubling Matter of Critical Judgement', in *Quality TV: Contemporary American Television and Beyond*, (eds) Janet McCabe and Kim Akass (London and New York: I. B. Tauris, 2007); Charlotte Brunsdon, 'Problems with Quality', *Screen* 31:1 (Spring 1990): 67–90.
[3] Specific examples include Greg M. Smith, *Beautiful TV: The Art and Argument of* Ally McBeal (Austin: University of Texas Press, 2007) and David Lavery and Sara Lewis Dunne, (eds) *Seinfeld, Master of its Domain: Revisiting Television's Greatest Sitcom* (New York: Continuum, 2006).

Employing close textual analysis of one recent sitcom – *Arrested Development* (Fox, 2003–6, Netflix, 2013) – we suggest that specific industrial and technological changes have facilitated an alteration in the style and meaning of the US sitcom. Focusing on one particular aspect of this aesthetic shift, we will examine the ways in which the programme redevelops the classic 'pull back and reveal' gag structure, reconfiguring the interrelationships between narrative, style and fictional world. The viewer of this sitcom, much like the viewer of contemporaneous dramas such as *The Wire* (HBO, 2002–8) and *Mad Men* (AMC, 2007–), is thus encouraged to engage with the series in new and different ways.

I was sitting there, minding my own business, naked, smeared with salad dressing and lowing like an ox ... and then I got off the bus.

Stewart Lee[4]

In a 2006 newspaper article on the differences between British and German humour, British stand-up comedian Stewart Lee offers the above gag as an example of the 'pull back and reveal', a form of joke reliant on the withholding of a key piece of information until its very endpoint.[5] The actions described – the nudity, the food play, the oral mimicry of oxen – encourage us to imagine one type of situation before the punch line suddenly places us in a different one altogether, one in which such actions appear comically out of place. As Lee notes, the flexible sentence structures of the English language make gags of this type particularly easy to construct and it is thus no surprise that we find them repeated over and over again in English-language comedy, from prose to the stage, from radio to film, and from television to YouTube.[6]

Yet as the medium changes so, often, does the form of the joke. Television and radio comedy producer Gareth Edwards has described how he finds 'pull back and reveal' jokes much harder to pull off on television than on radio because radio, a purely aural medium, gives you much more 'control over how the information is released', whereas the television image necessarily 'give[s] people quite a lot of information at the start'.[7] For Edwards the visual dimension of television comedy appears to be a hindrance to this particular type of language-based gag. Yet, as the term 'pull back and reveal' itself suggests, calling to mind the image of a camera tracking back or zooming

[4] Stewart Lee, 'Lost in translation', *The Guardian*, May 23, 2006. http://www.guardian.co.uk/world/2006/may/23/germany.features11 [accessed 15 December 2011].
[5] Ibid.
[6] Ibid.
[7] 'BBC Writers Room – Sanjeev Kohli and Gareth Edwards: 7 on 7', http://www.bbc.co.uk/writersroom/insight/sanjeev_kohli_4.shtml [accessed 15 December 2011

out to reveal a wider view of a particular action, this form of joke is in no way restricted to purely verbal forms of humour. It has, indeed, become just as much a matter of visual and aural style as it is a form of wordplay. Nowhere is this more noticeable than in the contemporary American sitcom.

In recent years, scholars such as Brett Mills, Jeremy G. Butler and Antonio Savorelli have begun to discuss the differences and similarities between what one can tentatively call 'traditional' sitcom and the sitcoms of our contemporary moment.[8] In terms of style, Mills details how sitcoms are conventionally shot 'as if the performance was taking place in a proscenium theatre, with the audience positioned as the fourth wall'.[9] Other key stylistic elements of the 'traditional' sitcom include a three-camera set-up, a live studio audience (providing the conventional laugh track) and the resultantly inflexible standing sets.

This 'traditional' sitcom style has certainly not disappeared. As Mills noted in 2009, *Two and a Half Men* (CBS, 2003–) remains the highest rated American sitcom.[10] Yet the contemporary multichannel television landscape, with the opportunities for repeated and 'binge' viewings provided by DVD and the Internet, has introduced an increasing number of decidedly unconventional sitcoms – from *Arrested Development* and *Community* (NBC, 2009–) to *Curb Your Enthusiasm* (HBO, 2000–) and *Parks & Recreation* (NBC, 2009–). *Arrested Development*, for example, is a text that Mills has already discussed as one of a group of new sitcoms that stand out from 'traditional' sitcom by making 'an explicit display of [their] use of the image'.[11] It exhibits a playful approach to seriality, a concept traditionally foreign to a genre concerned with maintaining the diegetic status quo, employing frequent flashbacks, callbacks and foreshadowing. It eschews both live studio audience and laughter track, and employs single-camera shooting across a variety of sets and outdoor locations. Its mobile handheld cameras, forever reframing the action through rapid movements and sudden zooms, together with its rough editing style and voiceover narration give the sitcom a quasi-documentary feel not entirely dissimilar to that displayed in the mockumentary-sitcoms that Mills terms 'comedy verité'.[12] Finally, much as Jeremy G. Butler describes in relation to another recent sitcom, *Scrubs* (NBC/ABC, 2001–10), the freedom

[8] See Brett Mills, *Television Sitcom* (London: BFI, 2005); Brett Mills, *The Sitcom* (Edinburgh: Edinburgh University Press, 2009); Jeremy G. Butler, *Television Style* (New York and London: Routledge, 2010); and Antonio Savorelli, *Beyond Sitcom: New Directions in American Television Comedy* (Jefferson: McFarland, 2010).

[9] Mills, *Television Sitcom*, 31.

[10] Mills, *The Sitcom*, 127.

[11] Mills, *The Sitcom*, 129.

[12] Mills, *The Sitcom*, 128.

from proscenium-style staging increases the possibilities for staging in depth rather than simply across the x-axis, permits increased control over framing, and gives greater licence for the cameras to invade the stage-space.[13] As the following textual analysis demonstrates, a number of these 'unconventional' elements very much inform *Arrested Development*'s specific deployment of the 'pull back and reveal' gag and, in turn, the audience's understanding of the programme's fictional world.

Arrested Development tells the story of the Bluths, a wealthy Californian family who risk losing their entire fortune when the head of the family, George Bluth Sr. (Jeffrey Tambor), is imprisoned for his fraudulent running of the family business. The remaining, highly dysfunctional, members of the family prove entirely incapable of handling their own, now comparatively impoverished, lives, let alone the running of the Bluth Company, so it is left to the series' reluctant 'hero', second eldest son Michael (Jason Bateman), to take charge, running the family business and taking on a parental role for all his adult relatives as well as his own teenage son. A running joke that continues throughout the sitcom's lifespan concerns Michael's attempts at persuading his relatives to find gainful employment.

Early in the first season's second episode ('Top Banana'), Michael walks into the living room of the family home to find his sister Lindsay (Portia de Rossi) and her husband Tobias (David Cross) sprawled out on the couch. A long shot of what appears to be the entire room establishes the space of the scene and the three characters within it. Michael complains that the couple has not moved from the couch all day long and harangues them for not job-hunting. Lindsay's reply that her job is simply to support her husband compels Michael to retort, 'You certainly haven't been shopping. The only thing I found in the freezer was a dead dove in a bag.' At this point the voice of Gob (Will Arnett), Michael's older brother, is heard off screen exclaiming, 'You didn't eat that, did you? Cos I've only got a couple of days to return it', and, as Michael turns his head, we cut to an over-the-shoulder point-of-view shot depicting Gob slumped on a couch in the neighbouring room.

Gob is not even supposed to be living in the family home at this point. Yet, lying on his side, his head poking out over one of the couch's arms and his inelegantly splayed legs hanging over its other edges, he is even more flagrant in his idleness than his relatives. Thus, a 'pull back and reveal', achieved not through reframing but through the use of off-screen sound and editing, is employed to humorously exacerbate the sense of the Bluth family's apathetic immobility. The exact same gag is then repeated later in the scene. As Michael calls for his sister to think about the example she is setting to her daughter,

---

[13] Butler, *Television Style*, 173–218.

Maeby (Alia Shawkat), expressing his concern that she will end up just like her mother, a quick lateral camera movement reveals Maeby to be lying on the floor behind the very couch on which Lindsay has been lounging. 'Yeah, shoot me when that happens', responds Michael's previously unseen and unheard niece, yet her appearance – flat on her back, her eyes never leaving the screen of her handheld gaming device – suggests it may already be too late.

In both cases, the 'pull back and reveal' device is used not only to add an extra phase to a running joke. Humour is here also created through the repeated confounding of the audience's expectations regarding the scene they are viewing. Despite the use of establishing shots – devices conventionally used to provide coverage of the entire setting and the various actors within it – as well as a constantly mobile handheld camera, seeming able to rove into the many corners of the Bluth's open-plan abode, we are twice surprised to find that an additional character has been lying there unnoticed all along. Thus a tone is set, an instability created between the show's stylistic register and the diegesis it purportedly represents.

What interests us here is not simply that *Arrested Development* uses the 'pull back and reveal' gag, since that in itself is not new. We are interested in the particular ways in which the programme uses the gag to expressive effect. By using the 'pull back and reveal' gag in the way it does in the scene described above, the programme problematises the relationship between style and meaning. It tells the audience to expect one thing, only to then present it with something else. It says: 'This is what this scene, and by extension, this world is about, so pay attention to that', but then suggests something else is equally, if not more, important and could have been watched instead. It draws into doubt the nature of its story world by displacing and in some instances dissolving it into what one may call the not-yet-and-not-necessarily story world. For when Michael is talking to his sister and her husband and Gob interferes, the privileged, closed space of the plot is interrupted, and increasingly dispersed into, an even more complex world of familial relations. Our point here is not that the 'pull back and reveal' gag draws everything into the plot, but rather that the plot can be drawn into everything. It indicates that everything can potentially become significant, that what is foregrounded is not by definition more important than what is in the background, that what is large is not necessarily more important than what is small, that what is onscreen is not more important than what is off screen, and so on. The joke, after all, emerges precisely from the conflict between narrative progression and what Seymour Chatman would call a *temps mort*,[14] but what we may also

---

[14] Seymour Chatman, *Antonioni, or, The Surface of the World* (Berkeley: University of California Press, 1985), 125–31.

term, indeed, an *arrested development*: a moment in time which does not necessarily further the plot but reflects upon it and opens it up to plethora of other potential plot lines and meanings.

In the scene described above, the privileged situation of the plot is democratised, as it were, with the underprivileged situatedness from which it emerges. Each time the programme sets out to represent the world via the categories of the plot, action or agent, the world appears to impose itself upon it, speaking up through Gob unexpectedly, suddenly entering the conversation via Maeby.[15] The 'pull back and reveal' gag thus problematises the relationship between what conventions imply should be watched, and what may also be watched in order to understand another dimension of the text's humour, encouraging the audience to always be on the lookout for the most insignificant of details that may or may not come to be influential later on, or hold subtle appeals to significance. It is here then, also, that the correlation between new technologies and industrial practices, on the one hand, and style, meaning, and viewing practices, on the other, becomes apparent. At the level of production, the shift from proscenium staging to single-camera set up makes available a more elaborate form of visual comedy, with humour more easily derived from elements of visual style. The comic success of the scene described above – hiding elements in plain view before revealing them at the exact required moment – is dependent on the tight framing, mobile camerawork and staging in depth that this new mode of production allows. At the level of consumption, the new methods of watching television offered by the digital age – the repeat viewing opportunities offered by DVD box-sets, internet distribution and marathon broadcasts of specific shows on niche channels, together with larger, widescreen and high-definition televisions – positively encourages the inclusion of humorous aspect that can only be derived from close and repeated scrutiny.

Viewers are thus not just asked to watch the programme more closely, but to watch it differently, paying attention to the plot and its visual implications, but also to other details on display; in the foreground and background, centre and periphery. In the scene described above, for example, Maeby's hand is already visible on numerous instances before she is introduced as a character. Whilst the hand is never central in the frame, it is nonetheless always there, competing for our attention as a marker of further narrative

---

[15] Our argument is influenced here by Jacques Rancière's work on the nature of images in *The Politics of Aesthetics: the Distribution of the Sensible* (London and New York: Continuum, 2004) and *The Future of the Image* (London and New York: Verso, 2007). For a discussion of Rancièrre's work in relation to television aesthetics, see Timotheus Vermeulen and Gry Rustad, 'Watching Television with Jacques Rancière: (Quality) Television, Mad Men, and the Late Cut', *Screen* 54:3 (2013).

possibilities. Indeed, in the following episode ('Bringing Up Buster'), the 'pull back and reveal' is used so often that the viewer is almost primed to notice each instance of the device's use in advance. In this episode, Lucille (Jessica Walter), the family's matriarch, palms off her youngest son, Buster (Tony Hale), a socially underdeveloped man-child, on Michael. Michael is thus left to babysit Buster for the remainder of the episode. Yet, as in the previously discussed scene, selective framing and editing is used on a number of occasions to obscure Buster from a scene right up until the point that a 'pull back and reveal' divulges his continued presence. For example, in separate scenes Michael is depicted having conversations with each of his parents. On both occasions Buster's 'condition' is discussed in terms so frank ('he's not the sharpest knife in the drawer') that, when Buster's presence is eventually revealed the conversations suddenly appear humorously inappropriate. Crucially, by the time we get to the second of these discussions, we have now seen so many 'pull back and reveals' that we start to expect them. The series is thus able to play with this expectation, George Bluth Sr describing Buster in terms so ridiculously forthright ('he turned out a little soft ... a little doughy', 'the doctor said there were claw marks on the walls of her uterus') that we, as the audience, are positively encouraged to anticipate the 'reveal'. The humour is thus no longer simply a result of the outside fictional world suddenly impinging on the seemingly closed space of the plot. As Bluth Sr's descriptions of Buster become increasingly insensitive, the attentive viewer, now aware of the increasingly comedic implications of Buster being in the room, is able to enjoy the additional pleasures of predicting the 'reveal', of being 'in on the joke'. The audience, then, is left in a position of always already expecting such an intrusion, always aware that there is more to *Arrested Development* than its advancing plot.

As the episode nears its end, however, the trick receives another tweak. Lucille decides she wants Buster back and goes to the Bluth Company offices to get him. A somewhat emotional conversation ensues and, as mother and youngest son depart, Lucille leaves Michael with a word of advice about his relationship with his own son, George Michael (Michael Cera). Michael, seemingly left alone in the room, breathes out and closes his eyes in a contemplative moment as the camera pulls back from him and inspirational guitar chords build up on the non-diegetic soundtrack. This is a classic trope traditionally used at the end of a narrative: pulling back from our protagonist to place him or her within the outside world at the same point that we too, as the audience, leave the protagonist's story and return to our own lives. Here, though, the device is used differently. Totally undercutting this emotional moment, the camera movement instead reveals a full boardroom of Bluth Company staff. 'So, er, can we go now?', asks one employee before at least seventeen previously unseen characters slowly trickle out of the room. Pulling back to reveal that the intimate conversation between Michael and his mother was, in fact, shared by numerous board members, the programme momentarily arrests narrative progress in order to announce another kind of narrative. It shows that beyond the privileged space of the plot there are other, peripheral spaces that may contain elements running parallel to the main plot, or indeed, that may intersect with it. Rather than simply pulling out from the story space and into the wider outside world as a marker of the narrative's endpoint, this particular aesthetic choice accentuates the uncomfortable but perpetual relationship between these two realms. Viewers of *Arrested Development* are thus encouraged once again to watch the programme differently, just as alert to these peripheral spaces as they are to the central space of the narrative, and, furthermore, always already aware that what is now peripheral or unseen may well become a key constituent of the programme's future.

Unfortunately, we do not have the space here to compare *Arrested Development*'s use of the 'pull back and reveal' gag to the ways in which it is employed in other contemporary US sitcoms. *Community*, for example, includes a 'clip show' episode. Whereas 'clip shows' conventionally return to moments the cast has shared with its audience through the recycling of footage from previous episodes, thus affirming the viewers' integration in the story world, the *Community* 'clip show' pulls back to reveal memories, i.e. episodes, that the programme has never shared with the viewer. Similarly, *Curb Your Enthusiasm* consistently draws plotlines, meanings and comic potential from the most apparently insignificant and peripheral moments: a rude remark, an impolite gesture, personal hygiene. We realize that our discussion of *Arrested Development* is too brief to make a definitive statement about the nature of the programme, let alone about the nature of the contemporary US sitcom. However, we do feel that its use of the 'pull back and reveal' gag is not merely a matter of an arbitrarily placed and conventional stylistic flourish but reconceives firstly, the correlation between style and meaning; and secondly, the relationship between the programme and its viewers. In *Arrested Development*, the 'pull back and reveal' gag signifies a democratisation between the representative categories of plot, action and agent and pure presence, necessitating another mode of viewing that is possible only due to recent technological developments: appreciating the expressive relationship between plot and place.

Bibliography

BBC. 'BBC Writers Room – Sanjeev Kohli and Gareth Edwards: 7 on 7'. http://www.bbc.co.uk/writersroom/insight/sanjeev_kohli_4.shtml [accessed 15 December 2011].

Brunsdon, Charlotte. 'Problems with Quality'. *Screen* 31:1 (Spring 1990): 67–90.

Butler, Jeremy G. *Television Style*. New York and London: Routledge, 2010.

Cardwell, Sarah. 'Is Quality Television Any Good? Generic Distinctions, Evaluations and the Troubling Matter of Critical Judgement'. In *Quality TV: Contemporary American Television and Beyond*, edited by Janet McCabe and Kim Akass. London and New York: I. B. Tauris, 2007, 19–34.

Chatman, Seymour. *Antonioni, or, The Surface of the World*. Berkeley: University of California Press, 1985.

Lavery, David, and Sara Lewis Dunne, (eds) *Seinfeld, Master of its Domain: Revisiting Television's Greatest Sitcom*. New York: Continuum, 2006.

Lee, Stewart. 'Lost in translation'. *The Guardian*, May 23, 2006. http://www.guardian.co.uk/world/2006/may/23/germany.features11 [accessed 15 December 2011].

McCabe, Janet, and Kim Akass, (eds) *Quality TV: Contemporary American Television and Beyond*. London and New York: I. B. Tauris, 2007.

Mills, Brett. *Television Sitcom*. London: BFI, 2005.

—*The Sitcom*. Edinburgh: Edinburgh University Press, 2009.

Mittell, Jason. 'Narrative Complexity in American Contemporary Television', *The Velvet Light Trap* 58 (Fall 2006): 29–40.

Rancière, Jacques. *The Politics of Aesthetics: the Distribution of the Sensible*. London and New York: Continuum, 2004.

—*The Future of the Image*. London and New York: Verso, 2007.

Savorelli, Antonio. *Beyond Sitcom: New Directions in American Television Comedy*. Jefferson: McFarland, 2010.

Smith, Greg M. *Beautiful TV: The Art and Argument of Ally McBeal*. Austin: University of Texas Press, 2007.

Vermeulen, Timotheus, and Gry Rustad. 'Watching Television with Jacques Rancière: (Quality) Television, *Mad Men*, and the Late Cut'. *Screen* (forthcoming 2013).

8

Better or differently: Style and repetition in *The Trip*

James Walters

Television situation comedy (sitcom) has always exhibited a strong investment in the rhythms and patterns of everyday life.[1] Much of that close affinity is bound up in the genre's fundamental reliance upon and exploitation of repetition, evident in the regular return to an established set of characters and environments. Likewise, plot structures that hinge upon those characters interacting with scenarios allow familiar attitudes, beliefs and motivations to be visited and revisited. This pattern of repetition fuses the television sitcom to the everyday and, as a result, even relatively early examples such as *The Phil Silvers Show* (CBS, 1955–9) or *Hancock's Half Hour* (BBC, 1956–60) achieve their dramatic and comedic impacts precisely by placing (or even trapping) their characters in a series of circumstances that often vary only to a fractional degree. It would be fatuous, therefore, to claim in any strong sense that an attention to the everyday and its repetitions is a novel occurrence in television sitcom.

However, it is nevertheless useful to note that a number of more recent examples from the UK and the US have incorporated this investment in the everyday to a much greater extent in their aesthetic composition. One potential marker of this would be the widespread removal of the pre-recorded audience laughter track (formerly a standard feature of the sitcom) which took away the convention of the comedic punch line occurring as a pronounced, even unnaturally forced, (audio) event. Likewise, the migration away from the

---

[1] A key text that explores the complex relationship between television and the modern (or postmodern) world in theoretical terms is Richard Silverstone's *Television and Everyday Life* (London: Routledge, 1994).

studio in preference for filming on location breaks from comedy performance as a rehearsed and choreographed theatrical event. We might also recognize a greater emphasis upon uneventfulness in plot structures, an eagerness to linger upon the uneven, broken patterns of 'ordinary' speech, a more subdued tone of comedy performance, the frequent use of natural light, or the increased employment of a handheld or roving camera that recalls the 'fly on the wall' style of television documentary and, consequently, can be said to attempt a more pronounced sense of authenticity.[2] Such aesthetic changes define a new dedication to a more accurate – often starkly accurate – depiction of the everyday, and further represent an effort to construct a fictional comedy world that is hermetically contained to a far lesser degree than was previously the case in more traditional sitcoms, where attempts at verisimilitude were arguably less pronounced.

The successful comedy writer and performer Victoria Wood made reference to this new direction for sitcom in rather bleak terms during an acceptance speech for her outstanding achievement award at the British Comedy Awards in 2005. Wood suggested that:

> The sitcom is dead. I think it died after *Dinnerladies* when *The Royle Family* and *The Office* came on. Suddenly, the whole landscape changed and you couldn't go back to that studio audience sitcom because *The Office* was too good. So people don't know what else to do. Everything's naturalistic and semi-ironic now, whereas before it was contrived to make people laugh.[3]

Wood's assertions make reference to her own sitcom, *Dinnerladies* (BBC), which ran from 1998 to 2000 and followed the then established studio audience format. Her choice of terms suggests a striking shift in the tone and style of sitcom and, furthermore, her selection of Caroline Aherne and Craig Cash's *The Royle Family* (BBC, 1998–) and Ricky Gervais and Steven Merchant's *The Office* (BBC, 2001–3) as examples is pertinent, given that these programmes epitomise the new 'naturalism' she describes and, indeed, were undeniably instrumental in its rise.

---

[2] It may seem unsatisfactorily imprecise to talk of a 'sense of authenticity', but this lack of definition is guided by the complexity of the debates surrounding that central issue of authenticity in the documentary form. Stella Bruzzi's evocative claim that documentary might be seen as 'the perpetual negotiation between the real event and its representation' encapsulates a key tension in this respect. Acknowledging that a 'negotiation' is always taking place goes some way to understanding that reality and representation are in constant flux in documentary, as Bruzzi maintains: 'distinct but interactive'. Stella Bruzzi, *New Documentary: A Critical Introduction*, second edn (London: Routledge, 2001): 9.

[3] Cameron Robertson, 'Victoria Wood: The Sitcom is Dead', *Daily Mirror*, 16 December 2005.

We might find cause to moderate the severity of Wood's claims, however, given that innovative studio audience sitcoms like *Miranda* (BBC, 2009–) in the UK and *Two and Half Men* (CBS, 2003–) in the US have thrived despite any perceived shift away from this format. With these examples in mind, the notion of the traditional sitcom being 'dead' perhaps risks exaggerating the true extent of the evolution in aesthetic style. Nevertheless, Wood makes precise reference to a new wave of sitcoms inspired, perhaps, by *The Office* and *The Royal Family* in the UK and equally prevalent in US series such as *The Larry Sanders Show* (HBO, 1992–8) and *Curb Your Enthusiasm* (HBO, 2000–) that seek to depict an everyday employment reality behind the scenes of the Hollywood entertainment industry. The prevalence of shows being produced in the style of these frontrunners certainly gives plausible justification for the strength of Wood's claims. The use of the term 'reality' in describing the ambitions of these comedy programmes reminds us that this move towards a new authenticity in television sitcom coincided with the emergence of reality television as a discernible genre in global television during the 1990s and 2000s.[4] In the UK, for example, an achievement of *The Office* lies in its ability to confidently build upon and meticulously parody the style and tone of existing workplace-based reality television series such as *Airline* (ITV, 1998–2006) and *Driving School* (BBC, 1997). Indeed, Ricky Gervais recounts his frustration that, at the time of its first broadcast, many viewers mistook *The Office* for a genuine television documentary about life in a Slough-based paper company, with some apparently finding it less funny when they were made aware of its fictional status.[5] The close dovetailing of aesthetic styles within reality television and sitcom is suggestive of the kinds of exchanges that can occur between genres and formats, to the extent that one might be mistaken for the other. It also helps us to understand Victoria Wood's view of these sitcoms as 'semi-ironic', given that they are closely matching and often satirising a television documentary style that involves genuine, candid subjects: 'real people'.

Broadcast in 2010, *The Trip* (BBC) might be regarded as simply another addition to the already swelled mass of 'naturalistic' television comedies. Directed by filmmaker Michael Winterbottom and starring Rob Brydon and Steve Coogan as fictionalised exaggerations of themselves, the six-part series works on the premise that Coogan has been commissioned to write a series of reviews of Michelin-starred restaurants in the north of England

---

[4]See Su Holmes and Deborah Jermyn, (eds) *Understanding Reality Television* (London: Routledge, 2003); Dolan Cummings, ed. *Reality TV: How Real is Real?* (London: Hodder Arnold, 2002).
[5]Gerard Greaves, '"Me? A leading man? Are you having a laugh?" Ricky Gervais Takes on Hollywood', *Daily Mail*, 23 October 2008.

for *The Observer* newspaper. When his American girlfriend returns home in preference to the trip they had planned together in Coogan's native north, Brydon takes her place. The sparseness of this plot recalls the economy of programmes like *The Royle Family* or *The Office*, which both avoid eventful narratives, whilst the device of actors playing versions of themselves is familiar from shows including *Curb Your Enthusiasm* and *Extras* (BBC/HBO, 2005–7). Winterbottom, Brydon and Coogan had previously collaborated in this way on the film *A Cock and Bull Story* (Michael Winterbottom, 2006); Brydon and Coogan had also collaborated on the series *Marion and Geoff* (BBC, 2000–3), which, as Steven Peacock has noted, is also representative of the 'stripped down' style common among contemporary sitcoms.[6]

The familiarity of *The Trip*'s thematic structures and aesthetic style prompts questions of ambition and originality, especially given that comparable programmes had already received considerable critical praise. This risk is certainly courted and, indeed, a number of reviews took a negative view both of the programme's lack of narrative action *and* its reliance upon actors playing 'themselves'. Writing for *The New Statesman*, Rachel Cooke provides the following assessment of the entire first episode:

> Does it work? No. It's the strangest, most self-indulgent thing I have ever seen, though I will keep watching, mesmerised as I am by both its peculiarities and its brass neck. In the first programme, the two of them set off up the M6 to the Forest of Bowland in Lancashire. What happened next? Not a lot. On arrival, when it seemed they were going to have to share a bed, they made a few we're-not-homosexuals-don't-you-dare-touch-my-bottom jokes. Then they went to lunch in the hotel bar, where they had scallops (Brydon) and soup (Coogan), and Brydon annoyed Coogan by periodically lapsing into impressions. Coogan, of course, would secretly love to out-impression his upstart rival – that was how he began his career – but now he thinks of himself as a film star, he must affect a terrible boredom at the distinctive tones of Michael Caine and Jimmy Savile. After lunch, Coogan took a call from his agent, and there followed one of those clichéd agent-client conversations: the client wants a movie; the agent is offering a role as a baddie in *Doctor Who*. Finally, in the gloaming, Coogan lumbered up the nearest hill and rang his estranged girlfriend. She didn't sound too happy to hear from him.[7]

---

[6]Steven Peacock, 'In Between Marion and Geoff', *Journal of British Cinema and Television* 3:1 (2006): 115–21.
[7]Rachel Cooke, '*The Trip*: This comedy vehicle is too knowing for its own good', *The New Statesman*, 4 November 2010.

Cooke's charge of self-indulgence is curious, given the lengths that both Brydon and Coogan go to in making their screen personas less than flattering. Nonetheless, her somewhat acerbic evaluation of this episode outlines in concise terms the series' resistance to the eventful as it discards a conventional structure of increasing dramatic tension and comic relief. It is telling that, in attempting to provide a short account of *The Trip*'s sparse plot texture, Cooke is drawn to moments that might appear to possess the greatest potential for heightened drama – the prospect of two heterosexual men sharing a bed, the conversations with the agent and the girlfriend – even though these events are afforded only a fraction of attention within the episode and are certainly not exploited for dramatic or comedic impact. It is as though a frustrated search for discernible plot points has been conducted and, if Cooke did indeed persevere with the series, one can only assume her frustration deepened and intensified as the programme deviated very little from those patterns established in this first episode.

On this basis, we might concur with the words of another newspaper critic, John Preston, that *The Trip* is 'determinedly uneventful',[8] but it is also *repetitively* uneventful, placing its characters in recurring scenarios across an entire series whilst resisting conventional plot development. Indeed, a crucial tension is contained within the notion that, despite the physical progression inherent in their trip together, the characters do not apparently move forward as a result of their experiences. Coogan in fact makes dark humorous reference to this in episode three when Brydon asks him whether they just have the same conversation in every restaurant. Coogan concurs:

> We start out being a bit awkward with each other. Have a little bit of wine and exchange a few frivolities. Enjoy each other's company. Have a bit more wine, get cantankerous, pick fault with each other, and it descends into a kind of bitter, unhappy end to the meal.

Coming at the midpoint of the series, this statement serves to both highlight a pattern that has already formed and provide an indication of its perpetuity. This might well be perceived as a limitation, especially when viewed only in broad narrative terms, but there are also ways in which *The Trip*'s lack of dramatic emphasis can be seen as its defining strength. We may take guidance on this from Andrew Klevan's study of undramatic achievement in cinema.[9] In his book, Klevan reaches the succinct conclusion that 'The

---

[8] John Preston, '*The Trip*', *Daily Telegraph*, 5 November 2010.
[9] Andrew Klevan, *Disclosure of the Everyday: Undramatic Achievement in Narrative Film* (Trowbridge: Flicks Books, 2000).

achievement of the undramatic films is to reveal significance without the assertion of revelation.'[10] Klevan's understanding of undramatic films and their achievement is pertinent to an appreciation of *The Trip* as, due to the lack of dramatic stress within its plot events, slight details such as a glance, a shift in posture, a pause or a sigh take on weight and meaning: they become the evidence upon which we base an awareness of and even insights into these people performing a series of apparently minor routines like eating, driving, walking or brushing teeth. By refusing to communicate that information emphatically (through a brand of plotting devoted to the creation of conflict and revelation, for example) *The Trip* dedicates itself to processes of display rather than relay, trusting its audience to search for significant details within its aesthetic design rather than pronouncing or embellishing such information. Nevertheless, the programme is far more self-conscious about these processes than those examples contained within Klevan's study of undramatic film.[11] This self-awareness clearly emanates from the central conceit of Brydon and Coogan playing versions of 'themselves', meaning that *The Trip* is always alert to the effects of its unemphatic moments. At times, this extra layer of self-reference perhaps results in *our* heightened awareness of the programme's efforts to achieve certain effects even when this takes place through its aversion to revelatory dramatic climax.

We might suggest that *The Trip* asks us to draw upon a set of interpretative skills we employ every day in our interactions with others, but it is also true that as television viewers we have honed these processes of intimate analysis through our regular involvement with various genres. For example, Rachel Moseley reminds us that makeover programmes – not normally singled out for their aesthetic or thematic complexity – 'ask us as viewers to draw upon our repertoire of personal skills, our ability to search faces and discern reactions (facilitated by the close up) from the smallest details – the twitch of a muscle, an expression in the eye...'.[12] *The Trip* similarly invites its viewers to engage with the minutiae of human behaviour and discover the significance within the rhythms and repetitions of everyday life.

This discussion goes some way to discerning the general character of the programme but, given that it is unremarkable in 2010 for a sitcom to be built around the repetitions of everyday life, it is necessary to develop our

---

[10] Klevan, *Disclosure of the Everyday*, 207.

[11] Klevan's book contains four main case studies: *Diary of a Country Priest* (Robert Bresson, 1950), *Loves of a Blonde* (Milos Forman, 1965), *Late Spring* (Ozu Yasujiro, 1949) and *A Tale of Springtime* (Eric Rohmer, 1990).

[12] Rachel Moseley, 'Makeover takeover on British television', *Screen* 41:3 (2000): 314.

assertions in order to describe aspects of *The Trip*'s achievement: what it manages to express through this chosen mode. In addressing this concern, we might move to consider the manner in which the series develops its repetitive structure in order to create resonances within and across scenes. A clear example of this is presented in the repeated instances of Coogan and, particularly, Brydon, performing comedic impressions of famous actors to one another. In these exchanges, the actors allow their impressions to go beyond the point at which they could be appreciated for accuracy and skill so that they become incessant and almost redundant in terms of their quality. Brydon is especially alert to this as he takes virtuoso impersonations – of Alan Bennett or Roger Moore, for example – and overuses them in unremitting rearticulation, potentially obscuring any admiration we might hold for their craft and artistry. By allowing the impressions to become repetitive, the programme asks that we look beyond the immediate pleasure of performance and begin to consider what motivates these people to engage in – often competitive – shows of impersonations. Rachel Cooke's review made reference to insecurity in relation to this, pointing out that Brydon's career has relied far more upon 'variety' entertainment whereas Coogan has attempted to pursue a different, more artistically credible, path. This is certainly true – and the programme makes regular reference to the relationship between impressions and professional credibility – but, as the series progresses and the repeated impressions build into a pattern, it becomes evident that these performances are replacing opportunities for these individuals to interact meaningfully within one another or, rather, have become the means for these two performers to interact meaningfully. Inherent in this is a lack of emotional articulation shared by both men, an inability to converse without the protection of an act, but also a fundamental need to impress one another. Getting the impression right, and getting the better of one another through getting it right, might then represent a genuine dedication to the friendship and to one another. It is not enough for one of them to think their performance is skilful; it has to be debated between them. The relentless revision of the same impressions therefore suggests a lingering desire to continue that conversation, to prolong the engagement, without making explicit reference to the desire. In this way, Brydon and Coogan communicate with each other and even express their affection for one another through the repressed form of comedic impersonation. In doing so, these men display characteristics that are opposite to those Sarah Cardwell observes in the work of Stephen Poliakoff. On the subject of repetition in Poliakoff's work, Cardwell notes that: 'Rearticulation is a primary means by which the characters convey their thoughts and feelings to other, and think through their own dilemmas.'[13] The comparison is effective because we might say that, in *The Trip*, rearticulation is a primary means for characters to *avoid* conveying their thoughts and feelings to others but, as a result, we are compelled to consider the thoughts and feelings that they avoid precisely through persistent re-articulation.

In an attempt to tighten these suggestions about uneventful repetition into a closer appreciation of *The Trip* in terms of its aesthetic style, I would like to turn to a moment from Brydon and Coogan's final car journey back to London. Car journeys have become a recurring motif in the series; necessary due to the reviewing task the pair embark upon but developed into small, delicate portraits of two men amusing each other to pass time between destinations. We might suggest that the inclusion of these car journey sequences within the programme's narrative is representative of its dedication to the otherwise inconsequential facets of everyday life as travelling to a location is afforded sustained attention despite little occurring that could be classed as 'plot development'. The pleasure of these sequences, therefore, lies in Brydon and Coogan's efforts to fill these spaces of 'dead' time by amusing one another with imaginative and often comically surreal conversation. It is notable that the car journeys are characterized by an improvisatory freedom that the scenes in restaurants, for example, are not. The formality and ceremony of the restaurant table seems to give rise to the characters' competitive and more rigidly defined exchange of impressions. As in-between spaces, the car journeys are somehow less defined, perhaps less of an event, and so result in a different register of interaction between the pair.

The uneventfulness of the car journeys is reflected in their style and composition. The final journey sequence utilizes six camera setups: an extreme long shot of the vehicle on the motorway, two medium close-ups of Brydon and Coogan through the windscreen, a long shot from a position in front of their vehicle, and two close-ups of Brydon and Coogan from the backseat of their vehicle. There is nothing elaborate in the selection of these camera positions and their functionality is matched by a relatively rapid editing pattern that does not sustain or privilege a particular viewpoint but, rather, is motivated by the direction of speech within the vehicle. This unassertive visual style invites the viewer to interpret the significance of the scene without definite cues or, indeed, signifiers, which might otherwise focus our attention. The sequence's aesthetic composition avoids emphasis

---

[13] Sarah Cardwell, '"Television aesthetics" and close analysis: style, mood and engagement in *Perfect Strangers* (Stephen Poliakoff, 2001)', in *Style and Meaning: Studies in the Detailed Analysis of Film* (eds) John Gibbs and Douglas Pye (Manchester: Manchester University Press, 2006): 179–94.

and punctuation, curtailing the creation of clear dramatic points through visual accenting. Likewise, the conversation between Brydon and Coogan tends to veer away from dramatic tension or climax: the subject of Coogan's liaisons with various women on their trip is raised but left to dwindle and, similarly, the question of whether he will move to America in order to be with his girlfriend, Mischa (Margo Stilley), is only briefly debated. It is conceivable that these matters might be prolonged for their dramatic or even comedic potential but, instead, the exchanges move fluidly through different topics, never settling on a single theme and never confronting directly Brydon or Coogan's intimate thoughts or feelings.

When asked about his dilemma regarding Mischa and America (Brydon having posed the question in a comedy Irish accent) Coogan begins to express his love for her but then breaks off, saying that he doesn't want to talk about it. He is allowed to leave the subject unresolved as Brydon picks up his words and uses them to segue into the opening lines of ABBA's 'The Winner Takes it All', an opportunity that Coogan takes up as he joins in reciting the lyrics. Although prompted by Coogan's choice of words, Brydon's choice of song is not entirely random: the pair had debated its merits in a previous episode, going on to ironically perform 'The Winner Takes it All' in the style of the chef from *The Muppets*, Christoph Waltz's Nazi from *Inglourious Basterds* and Roger Moore. Thus, its rendition in this sequence occurs within the series' overarching patterns of repetition, taking its place alongside other aspects such as comic impressions and car journeys. The duo's performance of the song retains an ironic quality as they begin by speaking the lyrics, both men affect slight Swedish accents at certain points, Brydon provides a hi-hat accompaniment at the start of a new verse, and they both end on an exaggerated, high-octave crescendo.

The playfulness of the song's performance also gives way to unexpected moments of sincerity, however, as both Brydon and Coogan allow themselves to be drawn into the underlying tone of regret that this somewhat trite pop record manages to achieve (and which they briefly identified in the earlier episode). For a moment, their expressions relax to become passive and distant as they indulge in fleeting reflection, both staring out at the road ahead as though briefly lost in private contemplation. Coogan's earlier remark that a particular line sends a shiver down his arm now seems genuinely felt. But this subtle change in mood is not indulged as the camera resists lingering on their faces while each proceed to correct the other's lyrics and, as they begin their finale, Coogan looks across at Brydon and sweeps his hand across in a flamboyant gesture, as though marking a shift from private reflection to self-conscious performance once more. And yet, their closing flourish does not obliterate totally the thoughtfulness they each briefly engage in during

the song. Rather, it brings these men together again in an unspoken acknowledgement of the regrets they might both hold. Singing together in this way
becomes a mediated method of sharing the fact that the song has touched
them without defining, analysing or labouring that sentiment. It might be
that this is the only way they can properly communicate with one another –
through performance – in an effort to find perfection, to please each other,
but at the same time acknowledging that perfection is impossible (hence
the constant recapitulation of the same performances) and that pleasure is
always a passing sensation (hence the need to keep on attempting to please
each other). It is appropriate, therefore, that this moment of shared reflection
should dissolve into a contest to see who can sing the most octaves: who
can get closest to perfection? Whose performance can give the greatest
pleasure?

This portrait of male emotional inarticulateness makes a simple point that
it can be difficult to talk to even close friends about ourselves. It is especially
suitable that situations such as car journeys and restaurant meals should be
chosen as environments for this point to be made, given that they contain
certain social rules (not making a scene in a restaurant, not making a long
journey uncomfortable for a companion) that restrict the opportunities for
emotional expression. *The Trip's* aesthetic style responds to this subdued
emotional register, refusing to embellish moments of significance and
suppressing opportunities for heightened dramatic tension or release. The
awkward hug through a car window that Brydon and Coogan share when they
finally part in London seems especially representative of this: displaying their
inability to show emphatic affection for one another but simultaneously not
allowing this to become an exaggerated theme as the embrace is divided up
into four separate shots. We are denied an opportunity to become immediately intimate with their uncomfortable intimacy. The reprised performance of
'The Winner Takes it All' not only falls into this pattern of emotional inarticulateness but also forms part of *The Trip's* structure of repetition. The subtle
differences between the two performances of the songs create resonance,
making us aware of a slight change of register in the two men as they sing.

Although the programme takes its place within a new wave of 'naturalistic'
sitcoms that invest in the repetitions of the everyday, its achievement lies in
its ability to develop those repetitions into points of subdued significance and
meaning. In doing so, *The Trip* avoids the easy temptation of asserting those
meanings too heavily, making them facile. We might appreciate that Brydon
and Coogan experience regret when they sing 'The Winner Takes it All' for a
second time, but the programme allows that emotion to remain ambiguous,
obliging its audience to revisit preceding episodes in order to interpret the
moment. Ultimately, given the programme's subtle aesthetic composition,

we are encouraged to engage repetitively with these characters and their everyday, to watch and listen again and again, so that we might seek out those moments we find to be significant. As a belated addition to the canon of naturalistic sitcoms that exists within UK and US television, *The Trip* certainly risks accusations of unoriginality. Yet, in the ways I've attempted to outline in this discussion, I would contend that the programme works innovatively within those pre-established generic parameters, defining its dramatic tone through an engagement with the conventions of naturalistic sitcom. The fact that the programme shares characteristics with earlier programmes therefore does not negate claims for its originality. Indeed, as Rob Brydon notes at the beginning of the road trip, 'It's 2010; everything's been done before. All you can do is do something someone's done before but do it better or differently.'

Bibliography

Bruzzi, Stella. *New Documentary: A Critical Introduction*, second edn. London: Routledge, 2001.

Cardwell, Sarah. '"Television aesthetics" and close analysis: style, mood and engagement in *Perfect Strangers* (Stephen Poliakoff, 2001)'. In *Style and Meaning: Studies in the Detailed Analysis of Film* edited by John Gibbs and Douglas Pye, 179–94. Manchester: Manchester University Press, 2006.

Cooke, Rachel. '*The Trip*: This comedy vehicle is too knowing for its own good.' *The New Statesman*, November 4, 2010.

Cummings, Dolan, ed. *Reality TV: How Real is Real?* London: Hodder Arnold, 2002.

Greaves, Gerard. '"Me? A leading man? Are you having a laugh?" Ricky Gervais Takes on Hollywood.' *Daily Mail*, October 23, 2008.

Holmes, Su, and Deborah Jermyn, (eds) *Understanding Reality Television*. London: Routledge, 2003.

Klevan, Andrew. *Disclosure of the Everyday: Undramatic Achievement in Narrative Film*. Trowbridge: Flicks Books, 2000.

Moseley, Rachel. 'Makeover takeover on British television.' *Screen* 41:3 (2000): 314.

Peacock, Steven. 'In Between Marion and Geoff.' *Journal of British Cinema and Television* 3:1 (2006): 115–121.

Preston, John. '*The Trip.*' *Daily Telegraph*, November 5, 2010.

Robertson, Cameron. 'Victoria Wood: The Sitcom is Dead.' *Daily Mirror*, December 16, 2005.

Silverstone, Richard. *Television and Everyday Life*. London: Routledge, 1994.

9

The presentation of detail and the organisation of time in *The Royle Family*

James Zborowski

The Royle Family (BBC/ITV, 1998–2000), in addition to its popularity and critical acclaim, has been discussed academically in relation to various topics: the sitcom,[1] the programme's creation of a sense of place,[2] its eschewal of 'classical' conventions of storytelling and of spatial and temporal representation,[3] its representation of family, memory and television viewing[4] and its densely textured treatment of class.[5] In what follows I wish to supplement these illuminating overviews by taking a slightly different approach: my account will be structured around reflection upon a pair of short moments from a single episode, and around a pair of ways of looking suggested by two television scholars.

The first way of looking is provided by John Caughie, who in the course of a chapter titled 'Small Pleasures: Adaptations and the Past in the Classical Serial' expresses an interest in 'thinking about detail

---

[1] John Hartley, 'Situation Comedy, Part 1', in *The Television Genre Book*, second edn, ed. Glen Creeber (London: Palgrave Macmillan, 2008), 81; Brett Mills, *The Sitcom* (Edinburgh: Edinburgh University Press, 2009).

[2] Karen Lury, *Interpreting Television* (London: Hodder Education, 2005), 158–61.

[3] Kristin Thompson, *Storytelling in Film and Television* (London: Harvard University Press, 2003), 136–7.

[4] Amy Holdsworth, *Television, Memory and Nostalgia* (Basingstoke: Palgrave Macmillan, 2011), 16–19.

[5] Andy Medhurst, *A National Joke: Popular Comedy and English Cultural Identities* (London: Routledge, 2007), 144–58.

as part of a poetics which is specific to television'.[6] Helen Wheatley[7] and Iris Kleinecke-Bates[8] have engaged with Caughie's suggestion in relation to period drama. I am interested here to take it up as a way of approaching a programme perhaps less concerned with ostensive display, but at least equally concerned with detail. The second way of looking is provided by Paddy Scannell. Using Martin Heidegger's phenomenology, Scannell argues that 'dailiness' constitutes 'the unifying structure of all [broadcasting] activities';[9] it is the specific 'care structure' of broadcasting – the thing that explains both the institutional framework that generates broadcast content and the textual features of that content. By focusing on *The Royle Family*'s details and its particular 'care structure', my dual aim is to arrive at a fuller account of the programme's treatment of time, and of what the programme reveals (or reminds us of) regarding the relationship between two sets of concerns or modes of experience that '[a]t first glance [...] might seem slightly at odds',[10] but which television, and, perhaps, Television Studies, may be particularly well positioned to bring together: aesthetics and the everyday.

The first of my chosen moments comes from around halfway through the fifth episode of *The Royle Family*'s third and final series. Dave (Craig Cash) is called upon by his wife Denise (Caroline Aherne) to show Barbara (Sue Johnston), Denise's mother, 'what you can do with your finger – that trick'. Dave demonstrates, using his right forefinger to flick back and forth the top joint of the fourth finger of his left hand. The dialogue is as follows:

Barbara: How long have you been able to do that Dave?

Dave: Hmmm, think it was about last March or April. Summat like that. About last March or April wasn't it Denise?

Denise: Think it was about... yeah, last March or... April, summat like that.

Barbara: How did you find out you could do that Dave?

---

[6]John Caughie, *Television Drama: Realism, Modernism, and British Culture* (Oxford: Oxford University Press, 2000), 213.
[7]Helen Wheatley, 'Rooms within rooms: Upstairs Downstairs and the studio costume drama of the 1970s', *ITV Cultures: Independent Television Over Fifty Years*, (eds) Catherine Johnson and Rob Turnock (Maidenhead: Open University Press, 2005), 146.
[8]Iris Kleinecke, 'Representations of the Victorian age: interior spaces and the detail of domestic life in two adaptations of Galsworthy's *The Forsyte Saga*', *Screen* 47:2 (2006), 139–62.
[9]Paddy Scannell, *Radio, Television and Modern Life: A Phenomenological Approach* (Oxford: Blackwell, 1996), 149.
[10]Ben Highmore, *Everyday Life and Cultural Theory: An Introduction* (London: Routledge, 2002), 19.

Dave: Well I was in the doctor's surgery, and they had no magazines, you know, so I was just messing about going like that [he shifts to striking his finger from above only] and then suddenly it just went to that [he returns to his original motion].

Barbara: Oh! It's *great* that Dave. Isn't it great Denise?

Denise: Yeah!

Dave: [Still demonstrating] Just went to that.

Denise: He's always been great doing anything like that, Dave.

Dave does not have to be asked twice to perform his demonstration. There is no apparent worry that it might meet with an indifferent reception, and indeed, Barbara is sincerely delighted. (It is only Denise who exhibits pride though: Dave treats his ability with the mild wonder of a detached observer.) I believe that the transcription alone captures some of the humour of the moment. Dave is not only called upon to demonstrate his skill but to account for the moment of its discovery. Denise's final comment is balanced skilfully by the programme's writers (Aherne and Cash) between being misplaced in its object but commonplace in its phrasing.

The absurdity of this moment is kept 'unforced'[11] rather than explosive by the studiously unemphatic camera work and, more importantly, by the fact that the moment occurs at home. Jim (Ricky Tomlinson), the father of the family, points to the relevance of this consideration when he sarcastically exclaims at the end of Dave's display that he had 'better book the bloody Palladium'. A diversion which might reasonably, if briefly, command the attention of family members may well not be up to the task of securing the interest of the paying public. Similarly, when the sphere of interaction is the settee/sofa, H. P. Grice's conversational maxims of quality, quantity, relevance and manner – which become what we might call the general to-be-heardness of broadcasting[12] – can be relaxed. This friction between what we, the viewer/listener, often expect to be provided with by broadcasting (and art, and fiction) and what we understand to be appropriate to sociable encounters among close family is what makes the anecdote of Norma (Liz Smith) later in the episode humorous and plausible: 'I know they stopped at a hotel. Now I don't know what it was called or where it was, but I do know that every night they had a mint chocolate put on their pillow.'

---

[11] Medhurst, *A National Joke*, 150.
[12] See Paddy Scannell, 'Introduction: the relevance of talk', in *Broadcast Talk*, ed. Paddy Scannell (London: Sage, 1991), 5.

So the burden of what might legitimately claim one's attention is significantly lowered when one is among family and friends. But how does the programme justify its claim on *our* attention, given that it is being offered to the (licence fee paying and/or DVD purchasing) public as art and entertainment? As has been repeatedly observed, when we watch *The Royle Family* on television, we watch the Royle family watching television. Holdsworth seeks to account for the significance of this as follows:

> Arguably, it was in its audience's identification with the everydayness of the Royles and the role of television viewing that the programme found its biggest draw. *The Royle Family* managed to situate television not just as part of daily life but as part of a system of everyday memory-making; the family's squabbles, laughter, banalities, celebrations and tragedies all caught in the act of viewing.[13]

The Royle Family, we might say, does not only capture, or represent, the everyday, but becomes a programme *about* how the everyday is *structured*, a reflexive feat it achieves in part by being about the everyday activity that the viewer must participate in if they are to be a viewer. We might say, then, that *The Royle Family* invites reflection upon the artistry with which it excavates and represents its subject. If we are treating the programme aesthetically, then our engagement with its details will, in addition to having a reflexive dimension, probably seek to account for the place of those details within a larger whole. These two matters are related, and I shall return to them below.

Caughie's discussion of detail is prompted by Naomi Schor's treatment of the topic in her book *Reading in Detail: Aesthetics and the Feminine* (1987). Caughie quotes a passage in which Schor refers to the detail's 'participation in a larger semantic network, bounded on the one side by the *ornamental* [...] and on the other, by the *everyday*', before concluding that 'the detail is gendered and doubly gendered as feminine'.[14] 'The ornamental, the everyday, and the feminine: the resonances for television criticism are suggestive', Caughie notes.[15] However, in the interests of being reflexive rather than succumbing to a reflex, I think it is worth pausing rather than following through upon the idea of details as feminine in this particular instance. I have no desire to challenge Schor's overall thesis (even if I were in a position to do so), but to apply her connection between the detail and the feminine too swiftly to *The*

---

[13] Holdsworth, *Television*, 18.
[14] Naomi Schor, *Reading in Detail: Aesthetics and the Feminine* (London: Methuen, 1987), 4, quoted in Caughie, *Television Drama*, 213–14 (italics in Schor).
[15] Caughie, *Television Drama*, 214.

Royle Family runs the risk of falsifying it, as the programme does not allow its viewer to map details onto gender binaries straightforwardly. Jim, to be sure, is an unreconstructed male in, to take perhaps the two most pressing examples, his attitude to housework, and in his proprietorial attitude towards the television remote control. However, it is Jim rather than Barbara who seems tied to the domestic space that we see. We know that Barbara goes out to work, and that Jim does not. In the series as a whole, it is more common for Barbara to be out of the house – or out of her seat! – than Jim. We do occasionally see Barbara engaged in housework, or, in one episode, testifying to her oppressive existence, but for the most part, we see the whole family in moments of leisure. Indeed, on the basis of what we see directly, the primary domestic drudge is not Barbara, but Antony (Ralf Little), who is repeatedly, and to humorous effect, compelled to make cups of tea or bacon sandwiches, or dispatched to buy food or alcohol, or given Baby David to tend to. (This is not to suggest that we are not left with the impression that off-screen, as it were, it is Barbara who does the most domestic work. However, the fact that this work is largely left off-screen should not be ignored.) I am in overall agreement with Andy Medhurst that class, rather than gender or another element of identity, provides the programme's 'primary axis of orientation' and 'emotional lodestone'.[16] (That said, throughout this piece I am implicitly arguing against Medhurst's absolute tethering of the programme's representation of the everyday to its treatment of class. I believe that the two concerns can be *partially* separated. To (inadequately) summarize: many aspects of the specific *content* of the programme's representation of the everyday are class-specific, but underpinning this is a form – we might call it a poetics of the everyday – that is much less particular. The specific milieu depicted in *The Royle Family* is not that of my upbringing, but I most certainly recognize the conversational content and rhythms captured by the programme, and I know I am not alone in this.)

There is one more line of thought prompted by Caughie that I would like to briefly work through. In a striking moment within his chapter on 'the classic serial', Caughie speaks of 'quality' television as a category that 'seems to speak of pleasures without demands'.[17] The lowering of the demands that a work of art places upon us is usually taken to signal compromise and a lessening of value. However, as Caughie has also noted, a shift in the 'terms of engagement' between viewer and medium can lead to a range of aesthetic effects, all potentially legitimate. Jim is right to observe that Dave's finger is not worthy of the Palladium. I do not want to say *The Royle Family* is not

---

[16] Medhurst, *A National Joke*, 144.
[17] Caughie, *Television Drama*, 210.

worthy of the cinema, but would it *work* there, and in the same way? I am certain that the answer to both of these questions is no, but I am equally certain that this is not to be counted against the programme. (Just as my sense is that I would not want to see *The Royle Family* try to sustain itself across the twenty or so episodes per series usually demanded of US sitcom – and that again I do not take this to be a point against it.) My academic training prevents me from watching *The Royle Family* distractedly, but these words do seem a good fit with my appraisal of it:

> '[G]ood' television asks for our perceptual intelligence rather than our anxious love; and [...], in both its location in everyday space and in its formal rhetoric, it may offer an exteriority to be appraised rather than a [sic] interiority in which to lose ourselves.[18]

A few moments after Dave's finger trick, there is one of many moments in *The Royle Family* where we witness a pause, but not a silence. As well as the sound of potatoes being peeled by Antony, we hear a female voice coming from the (off-screen) television: 'Meanwhile, with just twenty minutes to go before fifty guests arrive, things in the kitchen are starting to hot up.' As Lury has observed, the television programmes that the Royles watch (with a spectrum of engagement that ranges from not watching at all right through to rapt attention) will often subtly relate to what is going in the living room.[19] The use of *Shopping City* (BBC, 1999/2000) here highlights the fact that it is not only fiction on contemporary television that tends to organize time dramatically. At the same time that we hear the above line, we also hear a mobile telephone ringing. Remarkable from a distance of only thirteen years is Barbara's warm reaction: she smiles and turns in the direction of the sound, evidently pleased by what remains a novel event, and (it seems to me) by the fact that someone is about to receive greetings from a friend. (Barbara's smile soon gives way to a confused frown, as Antony communicates with his friend in the medium of an impersonation of then-modish 'Ali G', one of the fictional personae of British television comedian Sacha Baron-Cohen.) During the course of the conversation, Antony confirms an existing arrangement ('What, about half eight, nine-ish, yeah?'). We may hypothesize that this meeting will be the beginning of Antony's trip down to London, which has already been the subject of much discussion (and mockery) in the episode. However, the conversation does not appear to supply Antony with any new information.

---

[18] John Caughie, 'Telephilia and Distraction: Terms of Engagement', *Journal of British Cinema and Television* 3:1 (2006): 15.
[19] Lury, *Interpreting Television*, 159–60.

Kristin Thompson has suggested that '[t]he most distinctive aspect of [*The Royle Family*] is its lack of continuing causal lines, which in an ordinary series would be the primary source of dramatic conflict'.[20] Thompson can help to draw our attention to a truly remarkable strand of abstemiousness in *The Royle Family*. Not only does the camera never leave the Royle household, and not only do episodes almost always unfold without temporal ellipses (and often within a single space – most often the living room), but the handling of the flow of time in the series is never dramatic, and is usually anti-dramatic. 'Before' and 'after', or 'cause' and 'effect', will give us no purchase on the programme's temporal flow.

This freedom from a causal matrix provides an alternative framework, better equipped to accommodate moments such as Dave's finger trick, the story of the chocolate on the pillow and Antony's phone call. The latter, which continues for a good while after the confirmation of the meeting, and descends into a phatic exchange of recycled catchphrases, is able to achieve a degree of sociability that is (all too) rarely achieved elsewhere in television fiction, if we understand a sociable exchange as one that 'lacks a content', and whose 'medium is conversation, talk for talk's sake'.[21]

In the concluding chapter of *Radio, Television and Modern Life: A Phenomenological Approach*, Paddy Scannell commences with a meditation upon Martin Heidegger's 'discovery of care as the specific mark of all possible and all actual ways of being human in the world':

That things matter for us (no matter what), the ways in which they matter and the extent to which they do so, mark out the boundaries of our concerns. Concern is all such things as noticing, remarking upon, attending to, observing, picking out, foregrounding and bringing to bear a focused attentiveness upon phenomena (upon each other and ourselves and circumstances) in such ways as to find and make the matter to hand significant and meaningful in some way or other. Concern is being caught up in. It is engagement *with*, involvement *in*.[22]

For Scannell, the care structure that is particular to broadcasting is 'dailiness':

[T]he effect of the temporal arrangements of radio and television is such as to pick out each day as *this* day, [...] caught up in its own immediacy, with its own involvements and concerns. [...B]roadcasting delivers a service

---

[20] Thompson, *Storytelling in Film and Television*, 136.
[21] Scannell, *Radio, Television and Modern Life*, 23.
[22] Scannell, *Radio, Television and Modern Life*, 145 (original italics).

whose most generalizable effect is to re-temporize time; to mark it out in particular ways, so that the time of day (at any time) is a particular time, a time differentiated from past time-in-the-day or time that is yet-to-come.[23]

This fascinating passage can alert us to the fact that *The Royle Family* does not replicate the overall care structure of broadcasting. When we further contrast the programme's treatment of time with the dramatic organisation of time that Thompson points to in television fiction, usually less marked by 'dailiness' than other types of broadcast output but often no less urgent in its itinerary of events, and even the dramatic treatment of time in non-fiction formats gestured to above in relation to *Shopping City*, we can see that *The Royle Family* is swimming against the tide. To continue with the metaphor a moment longer, its apparent stasis requires, and conceals, a great deal of work.

As theorists including Victor Shklovsky and Bertolt Brecht have taught us, aesthetics is in part a question of one's orientation towards an object, or an experience. Shklovsky, in one of my favourite passages, writes: 'Habitualization devours work, clothes, furniture, one's wife, and the fear of war. [...] And art exists that one may recover the sensation of life; it exists to make one feel things, to make the stone *stony*. [...] *Art is a way of experiencing the artfulness of an object: the object is not important.*'[24] What is important is the fact that, as beholders and critics, we 'bring to bear a focused attentiveness', and contemplate (in varying mixtures) both what we think the artwork wishes to make us notice and what we wish to attend to within it. Artistic creation and criticism are two halves of this same care structure.

If we think of aesthetics as being concerned with renewing perception and of studies of the everyday as being concerned with reclaiming experience, then it is not hard to see the connections between the two endeavours. Returning, finally, to *The Royle Family*, we can observe that its care structure is particular, and subtle. It does not contain – in fact, it eschews – the modes of organisation of most other television. Within the context of a culture that teaches us to treat time as a commodity, a programmes which lavishes attention so generously on a double-jointed finger, a chocolate on a hotel pillow, or a sociable encounter between two friends, is both defamiliarizing and, in a roundabout way, utopian. We might describe *The Royle Family's* care structure as one which, painstakingly, and via an aesthetics of strict and consistent abstention, excavates aspects of experiences from beneath the

---

[23] Scannell, *Radio, Television and Modern Life*, 149.
[24] Victor Shklovsky, 'Art as Technique', in *Literary Theory: An Anthology*, (eds) Julie Rivkin and Michael Ryan (Oxford: Blackwell, 1998), 18 (original italics).

structures and impulses that often bury them. The programme is fascinatingly and strangely poised between enacting and counteracting other televisual experiences of time and the everyday.

Bibliography

Caughie, John. *Television Drama: Realism, Modernism, and British Culture.* Oxford: Oxford University Press, 2000.

—'Telephilia and Distraction: Terms of Engagement.' *Journal of British Cinema and Television* 3:1 (2006): 5–18.

Hartley, John. 'Situation Comedy, Part 1.' In *The Television Genre Book*, second edn, edited by Glen Creeber, 78–81. London: Palgrave Macmillan, 2008.

Highmore, Ben. *Everyday Life and Cultural Theory: An Introduction.* London: Routledge, 2002.

Holdsworth, Amy. *Television, Memory and Nostalgia.* Basingstoke: Palgrave Macmillan, 2011.

Kleinecke, Iris. 'Representations of the Victorian age: interior spaces and the detail of domestic life in two adaptations of Galsworthy's *The Forsyte Saga.*' *Screen* 47:2 (2006): 139–62.

Lury, Karen. *Interpreting Television.* London: Hodder Education, 2005.

Medhurst, Andy. *A National Joke: Popular Comedy and English Cultural Identities.* London: Routledge, 2007.

Mills, Brett. *The Sitcom.* Edinburgh: Edinburgh University Press, 2009.

Scannell, Paddy. 'Introduction: the relevance of talk.' In *Broadcast Talk*, edited by Paddy Scannell, 1–13. London: Sage, 1991.

—*Radio, Television and Modern Life: A Phenomenological Approach.* Oxford: Blackwell, 1996.

Schor, Naomi. *Reading in Detail: Aesthetics and the Feminine.* London: Methuen, 1987.

Shklovsky, Victor. 'Art as Technique.' In *Literary Theory: An Anthology*, edited by Julie Rivkin and Michael Ryan, 17–23. Oxford: Blackwell, 1996.

Thompson, Kristin. *Storytelling in Film and Television.* London: Harvard University Press, 2003.

Wheatley, Helen. 'Rooms within rooms: *Upstairs Downstairs* and the studio costume drama of the 1970s.' In *ITV Cultures: Independent Television Over Fifty Years*, edited by Catherine Johnson and Rob Turnock, 143–58. Maidenhead: Open University Press, 2005.

10

The man from ISIS: *Archer* and the animated aesthetics of adult cartoons

Holly Randell-Moon and Arthur J. Randell

'**S**terling Archer, code name: "Duchess"'. A heavily accented voice intones these words over a close up of a pair of blue eyes scanning left and right. As the camera pans back, we are shown a darkened room where the blue-eyed man (Agent Archer) is manacled and, apparently, on the verge of being tortured. That is, until he begins criticising the interrogator's implement of torture, a golf cart battery, and 'inauthentic' accent. At this point, the lights in the room are turned on and a middle-aged woman, Malory Archer, watching the scene unfold through a plate glass window, implores Archer to treat this 'training simulation' seriously. 'How can I?' he retorts and begins to list a further series of shortcomings regarding his interrogator such that he eventually receives an electric shock. Falling down and crying out in pain, Archer complains, 'Mother did you see that?' An over-the-shoulder shot reveals Malory's reflection in the glass as she watches Archer surrender to further shocks in the room beyond. A smile forms on her face. The opening credits roll and we are introduced in this first episode to the world of espionage in *Archer* (2010–), an animated programme airing on North American cable television.

In this chapter, we will examine how *Archer* exemplifies a particular genre of animated comedy that appeals to an adult demographic by offering coarse satirical content alongside a limited animated format traditionally associated with children's cartoons. The emergence of niche cartoon programming on cable television in the 1990s facilitated a mode of production that favoured an inexpensive and minimalist animation aesthetic. Programmes such as *Archer* utilize this aesthetic to address material that live action television cannot due to the exigencies of performance and censorship that broadcast content is subject to. *Archer* makes creative use of the limited animation format to achieve a greater economy of visual humour and style with a focus on complex dialogue and characterisation, complemented by an idiosyncratic intertextuality.

Despite the high level of technical and aesthetic proficiency involved in the creation of animated television, and perhaps due in part to the medium's beginnings and concentration in children's programming,[1] it is generally perceived to be less 'serious' than its live action counterpart. Carol A. Stabile and Mark Harrison write for example, that animated television is 'doubly devalued' because of its association with both cartoons and the comedy genre.[2] With the increasing number of adult oriented cartoons, critical interest in and public perception of animated television has shifted over the last two decades. *The Simpsons* (1989–) has been enormously influential in demonstrating that the format, style and aesthetics of animated television are broad enough to allow a range of thematic concerns for both younger and older audiences. In line with the 'processes of imitation and distinction/ innovation' in television production,[3] later shows such as *South Park* (1997–) and *Family Guy* (1999–) followed the programming and marketing model of *The Simpsons* whilst pushing the boundaries of acceptable prime-time content in terms of 'politically incorrect' subject matter. In 2001, the cable television channel Cartoon Network created an influential animation programming block called Adult Swim. Adult Swim was an attempt to consolidate the growing niche market for cartoons with more mature subject matter and was successful in capturing a significant share of the 18–24 year-old male demographic leaving broadcast television.[4]

Adult Swim's brand of animation programming is characterized by irreverent and profane comedy with trappings of the absurd. Some of its original programmes included *Aqua Teen Hunger Force* (2000–), featuring

---

[1] See Jason Mittell, 'The great Saturday morning exile: scheduling cartoons on television's periphery in the 1960s', in *Prime Time Animation: Television Animation and American Culture*, (eds) Carol A. Stabile and Mark Harrison (New York: Routledge, 2003), 33–54.
[2] Carol A. Stabile and Mark Harrison, 'Prime time animation – an overview', in *Prime Time Animation: Television Animation and American Culture*, (eds) Carol A. Stabile and Mark Harrison (New York: Routledge, 2003), 2.
[3] Stabile and Harrison, 'Prime time animation', 8.
[4] Justin Peters, 'Toon In', *The Washington Monthly*, June 2004, 27–31.

a super-trio comprised of a milkshake (Master Shake), fries (Frylock) and a meatball (Meatwad), and *Harvey Birdman, Attorney at Law* (2000–7), where the titular character defends stock Hanna-Barbera characters in the court of law: be it charges of drug possession for Scooby-Doo and Shaggy or Yogi Bear's alleged terrorist links. Some of the original Adult Swim programmes re-edit and reuse stock Hanna-Barbera animations cells as a result of the Cartoon Network's acquisition of the Hanna-Barbera back catalogue and as an inexpensive method of programme production. *Sealab 2021* (2000–5) consists entirely of revoiced and re-edited footage from the short-lived environmentally themed programme, *Sealab 2020* (1972). The programme juxtaposes the seemingly innocuous animation with lewd dialogue. These and other Adult Swim programmes 'are united by a shared postmodern ethos that plays upon the metaphors and tropes of bad TV'.[5] The programmes do not attempt to displace or disguise their limited production values and basic animation. Many of the programmes rely on genre as a traditional televisual framing device whilst also explicitly resisting narrative techniques of character consistency and plot resolution. Characters may be dispatched at random and plot development discarded in favour of extended non-sequiturs.

Although appearing on the cable channel FX, *Archer* shares similarities with the animation style, production and subject matter of Adult Swim cartoons. Its creator Adam Reed was responsible for *Sealab 2021* (with Matt Thompson). With its Saul-Bass inspired opening credits, *Archer* is ostensibly a parody of the spy genre in the vein of *Get Smart* (1965–70), *I Spy* (1965–8) and *The Man From U.N.C.L.E* (1964–8). *Archer* shares with these programmes a tendency to 'put style and process ahead of political harangues' and favours 'comic distancing and irreverent parody'[6] in its portrayal of covert intelligence. The show's eponymous hero is secret agent Sterling Archer who works for the organisation ISIS (the International Secret Intelligence Service), run by his mother Malory. The programme features storylines typical of the spy genre, such as kidnappings, bomb threats and espionage. As the opening scenes of the show indicate, these crises are only ever half-heartedly pursued due to the characters' general self-absorption. Archer is cast in the mould of both James Bond and Maxwell Smart in that he has considerable skill as a spy but often lacks self-awareness, humility or tact. For example in the fourth episode of the first season 'Killing Utne' (1.4), Archer's proficiency with firearms is revealed in a flashback where we are shown a room full of dead men in

[5] Peters, 'Toon In', 30.
[6] Rick Worland, 'The Cold War Mannerists: The Man From U.N.C.L.E and TV Espionage in the 1960s', *Journal of Popular Film and Television* 21:4 (1994): 152.

blindfolds with Archer holding a gun and exclaiming, 'Oh my God. I can't believe they fell for that!'

The programme combines the characters' comically inflated self-absorption with a wilfully vague setting that appears to draw on a number of generic allusions to real and fictitious political and military operations. As with *The Man From U.N.C.L.E*, *Archer* has a 'deliberately playful confusion between reality and artifice'.[7] For instance, one of the main antagonists in the show is the Russian intelligence and national security agency KGB. Coupled with fashion and décor styles from the 1960s and 1970s – mini-skirts, formal suits for men, basic computer technology such as punch cards – this would suggest a Cold War setting. However, the characters use contemporary technology such as mobile phones and the Internet and frequently reference recent historical events and popular culture items. In one episode alone ('Killing Utne'), we found references to *The Simpsons*' Truckasaurus, an allusion to the Styx song 'Mister Roboto', *Star Wars* (1977), an REM song, baseball player Johnny Bench, *Sesame Street* (1969–), film director John Woo, an eastern European indie band called the Fantastiques, and a little known form of self-defence, Krav Maga, among others.

As with other animated programmes such as *The Simpsons*, these intertextual references function as a commentary on the show's narrative and genre as well an elaborate form of intratextual comedy for its own sake. For instance, the Johnny Bench reference becomes a recurring insult to describe characters with large hands, Kenny Loggins' 'Danger Zone' song from the film *Top Gun* (1986) appears periodically as an Archer catchphrase alongside quotes from the Burt Reynolds oeuvre. The programme also makes allusions to its generic forebears. In one episode ('Dial M for Mother', 1.10), Malory retrieves a gun hidden under the book *Greenmantle* (1916) by John Buchan, part of a series of novels featuring a secret agent in the early part of the twentieth century. The show builds these occasionally obscure references into an increasingly intricate and self-referential diegetic world. Another running joke throughout the series, for example, involves Archer claiming responsibility for the use of a black turtleneck sweater in covert operations. 'I was the first to recognize its potential as a tactical garment', he complains in 'The Rock' (1.8). Both *Archer* and Archer balance this self-awareness of how a 'spy' must look and perform with the competent execution of the generic staples of televisual and filmic espionage.

Writing on *The Simpsons*, Simone Knox suggests that there is 'inherent spectacle' in animation because it ostensibly 'strives toward the impression of verisimilitude' but due to 'its lack of a referent, [it] is at the same time

---

[7]Worland, 'The Cold War', 155.

freed from the constraints of liveaction representation'.[8] Within the diegesis of an animated text, there is relatively little narrative constraint in terms of historical setting, character action and plot resolution. Paul Wells suggests that animation has a 'particular form of anarchy' because it 'operates as a potentially non-regulatory or subversive space by virtue of its very artifice, and the assumed innocence that goes with it'.[9] The inherent artifice and spectacle of animation allows animated programmes to foreground and draw attention to their 'own textuality'.[10] *The Simpsons* is famous for exploiting its animated format to embed intertextual and intratextual visual references into each of its animated scenes so that repeated viewing and consumption of the text is necessary in order to recognize these references.[11]

In contrast to the complexity of *The Simpsons*' animation style, *Archer*, like its Adult Swim predecessors, is removed from 'the burden of spectacle'[12] due to the employment of a limited or reduced animation aesthetic. Wells defines limited animation as 'essentially the reduction of animation to its most essentialist form' resulting in 'little animation, no complex choreography, repeated cycles of movement, a small repertoire of expressions and gestures, stress on dialogue, basic design, and simple graphic forms'.[13] Characters in *Archer* are drawn in thick black outlines and are based on photographs of models and actors.[14] This gives the characters relatively realistic colouring and facial features but they have limited movement and are placed against delicately coloured, static backgrounds. The style is reminiscent of the limited animation of Hanna-Barbera cartoons.

Wells notes that this style was employed by Hanna-Barbera animators to reduce costs and speed up production.[15] Likewise, the production methods utilized by *Archer*'s creators emerged out of their previous experience with the Cartoon Network's restricted animation budget. Far from constraining the potential for textual complexity however, a limited animation style can lead to greater ingenuity in the animation available and the subject matter

[8] Simone Knox, 'Reading the ungraspable double-codedness of *The Simpsons*', *Journal of Popular Film and Television* 34:2 (2006): 80.

[9] Paul Wells, '"Smarter than the average art form": Animation in the television era', in *Prime Time Animation: Television Animation and American Culture*, (eds) Carol A. Stabile and Mark Harrison (New York: Routledge, 2003), 16.

[10] Wells, '"Smarter than"', 16.

[11] Knox, 'Reading the ungraspable', 74.

[12] Peter Moyes, 'Behind the Flash Exterior: Scratching the Surface of Online Animated Narratives', *Animation Studies: Online Journal for Animation History and Theory* (Animated Dialogues) (2009): 85–6.

[13] Wells, '"Smarter than"', 17.

[14] Bill Desowitz, 'Spy Spoofing in *Archer*', *Awn*, January 14, 2010, http://www.awn.com/articles/2d/spy-spoofing-archer/page/1 [accessed 5 April 2012].

[15] Wells, '"Smarter than"', 15.

that accompanies it. This is because narrative action and humour can be achieved with remarkable economy. For example, returning to the 'Killing Utne' episode, a pair of German assassins have killed the guest of honour at Malory's dinner party and fled the scene. In order to convey this we are shown a shot of Malory and Archer at the entrance of her kitchen with two grappling hooks and rope extending from the bench to the open window. Accompanying this static image, a single line of dialogue by Malory is used to illustrate what has occurred – 'Oh, for shit's sake'.

Archer's animation style allows for fast-paced humour and complex comedic sequences which are not typically achievable in live action situational comedies. Where live action production centres on the physical *mise-en-scène* and the performative aspects of working with actors, animation is able to exploit editing and timing for greater comedic effect such that physical or prop comedy and line delivery can be executed in quick succession. Take, for example, the following scene between Archer and Malory which occurs at the beginning of 'Killing Utne':

Mallory: … And as you may or… (Archer is rattling ice cubes in his glass with his finger) … probably don't know, for six years running, the contract has gone to Odin.

Archer: Ugh. The Organization of Douche-bags in … in … wait, I had something for this.

Mallory: Douche-baggery notwithstanding

Archer: Nowheres-ville.

…

Mallory: … this party is different and very important, so absolutely nothing can go wrong.

Archer: Well, then we better keep Dr Bellows away from Jeannie.

Mallory: No! No dates!

Archer: From 'I Dream of Jeannie'.

Mallory: No one is bringing a date, so don't you bring a date.

The dialogue for Archer and Malory overlaps and weaves in and out of an individual strand of conversation. Archer continues and finishes his joke about the location of Odin and *I Dream of Jeannie* (1965–70) independently of the exposition from Malory about the party and plot of the episode. Scenes such as this, where characters can discuss and muse on several different topics at once, would require significant direction, rehearsal and blocking, all of which are unnecessary for an animated programme like *Archer*. The complexity of *Archer*'s dialogue is achieved despite the scheduling requirements of recording the voice actors' dialogue individually.[16] This means that the long scenes of dialogue in the programme are the result of seamless editing which reconstructs separately recorded lines of dialogue into a flowing conversation between several different characters.

A preference for extended scenes of dialogue can be explained by the limited mobility of the characters in terms of their interaction with sets and props. The sets for the show are rendered in three-dimensional models and then painted for texture using Photoshop.[17] Some of the props and texturing are quite specific and as with the characters' illustration are based on photographs of already existing rooms, furniture and architecture. Different types of wood panelling or metal work are visible in the delicate paintwork. Because the sets are expensive and time consuming to build, action in *Archer* is typically contained within one or two locations. As a result, dialogue often focuses on squabbling between the characters. This petty bickering can lengthen the delivery of a simple set of instructions or expository material, as in the scene from 'Killing Utne' with Malory and Archer, and flesh out the intricacies and personal histories of character relationships. These relationships are often presented with a mixture of pathos and mocking humour.

In another first season episode, 'Job Offer' (1.9), Archer casually mentions that his mother sent him to boarding school for thirteen years and then quickly follows this up with a defensive explanation of how much he enjoyed school and his 'many friends'. This is followed by a cutaway to a forlorn looking young Archer, sitting alone in a park. Leaves swirl around him and plaintive piano music is briefly heard on the soundtrack. The awkward humour of the scene reveals a knowing insight into the fractured gender and sexual politics that inform a significant portion of Archer and his mother's relationship; one that is hinted at in the opening scenes of the show. The time spent within the show developing the psychological and sexual backgrounds of the characters diverges with the Adult Swim model of cartoon production. These programmes pair the limited animation format with limited characterization, resulting in surreal and absurd narratives. *Archer* moves this format in a different direction by attempting to supply motivation for its characters and

---

[16] Vlada Gelman, 'Interview: Adam Reed', *The A.V. Club*, February 24, 2011, http://www.avclub.com/articles/adam-reed,52336/ [accessed 5 April 2012].

[17] Desowitz, 'Spy Spoofing'; admin, 'Go Behind the Scenes with Aisha Tyler', *Archer.com*, December 7, 2009, http://archer.blogs.fxnetworks.com/2009/12/07/go-behind-the-scenes-with-aisha-tyler/ [accessed 5 April 2012].

their relationships within a fully realized diegetic world – albeit with its own eccentric and at times, peculiar logic.

Adding resonance to these interpersonal relationships are the cinematic flourishes used to underscore particular shots and scenes. Freed from the exigencies of live production, animation allows for a more adventurous framing and shooting style than traditional television formats. As we explained in the beginning of the chapter, the first episode 'Mole Hunt' contains a very precise sequence of shots in the introduction of Archer and Malory to both establish and then subvert the spy genre. We first see Malory through a shot above Archer (observing the training room through an overlooking window), with his head and outstretched arms framing the bottom of the screen. We then see a reverse shot over Malory's shoulder looking through the glass window with her reflection overlaying the manacled Archer in the room beyond. Although Archer is introduced as the central character of the show, this sequence of shots establishes his dependency on Malory's caprices and suggests that her reflection shadows his actions and personality. The turning on of the lights and the revelation of the training simulation also foregrounds *Archer*'s self-referential awareness of the generic construction of espionage. Archer clues the audience in on his 'interrogator's' fake Russian-sounding accent, the buzzing electricity of an ostensible weapon of torture is actually a golf cart battery and the torture room is revealed in full light (and in a running gag throughout the series) to be the office snack room.

Because action and humour in limited animation is reliant on the economical use of a static space, Peter Moyes argues that the visual reading required of this type of television is similar to that of comic strips. Audiences must 'join the dots, complete the illusion, and make the narratives their own'.[18] For Moyes, limited animation draws attention 'to the constituents and mechanics of the text; audiences are asked to invest life in overtly inanimate forms, and to collaborate with the text (and author) in creating narrative coherence'.[19] A scene towards the end of 'Killing Utne' has a long continuous shot of a partially opened apartment door and we hear rather than see the characters discussing the macabre details of how to dispose of the dead bodies of Malory's assassinated party guests. The audience is required to visualize and complete the narrative based on the dialogue, sound effects and vocal perfor- mances. The comedy is heightened precisely because we imagine rather than see the characters' reactions to this grizzly task. At other times, limited spatial movement is used for humorous effect. In an episode set in a space station ('Space Race: Part 1', 3.9), Archer is leaning against a wall tossing a ball with

---

[18] Moyes, 'Behind the Flash', 85.
[19] Moyes, 'Behind the Flash', 86.

a catcher's mitt. Expressing one of his typically expletive filled soliloquies over the incompetence of the other characters, he pauses as the ball he pitches slowly returns to his outstretched hand. After watching the returning ball for a considerable silence, he sighs, 'Fuck you space.'

Scenes like this demonstrate how *Archer* is able to extract humour from the limited animation style and exploit the potential for visual economy and framing, punctuated by succinct dialogue, usually with an invective turn of phrase. Employing a mode of production borne out of the rise of niche cartoon programming on cable television, *Archer* is able to rework televisual animated aesthetics to create a slyly parodic, occasionally crass but stylish take on both the spy and cartoon genres.

Bibliography

admin. 'Go Behind the Scenes with Aisha Tyler.' *Archer.com*, December 7, 2009. http://archer.blogs.fxnetworks.com/2009/12/07/go-behind-the-scenes-with-aisha-tyler/ [accessed 5 April 2012].

Desowitz, Bill. 'Spy Spoofing in *Archer.*' *Awn*, January 14, 2010. http://www.awn.com/articles/2d/spy-spoofing-archer/ [accessed 5 April 2012].

Gelman, Vlada. 'Interview: Adam Reed.' *The A.V. Club*, February 24, 2011. http://www.avclub.com/articles/adam-reed,52336/ [accessed 5 April 2012].

Knox, Simone. 'Reading the ungraspable double-codedness of *The Simpsons.' Journal of Popular Film and Television* 34:2 (2006): 73–81.

Mittell, Jason. 'The great Saturday morning exile: scheduling cartoons on television's periphery in the 1960s.' In *Prime Time Animation: Television Animation and American Culture*, edited by Carol A. Stabile and Mark Harrison, 33–54. New York: Routledge, 2003.

Moyes, Peter. 'Behind the Flash Exterior: Scratching the Surface of Online Animated Narratives.' *Animation Studies: Online Journal for Animation History and Theory* (Animated Dialogues) (2009): 84–90.

Peters, Justin. 'Toon In.' *The Washington Monthly*, June 2004.

Stabile, Carol A., and Mark Harrison. 'Prime time animation – an overview.' In *Prime Time Animation: Television Animation and American Culture*, edited by Carol A. Stabile and Mark Harrison, 1–11. New York: Routledge, 2003.

Wells, Paul. '"Smarter than the average art form": Animation in the television era.' In *Prime Time Animation: Television Animation and American Culture*, edited by Carol A. Stabile and Mark Harrison, 15–32. New York: Routledge, 2003.

Worland, Rick. 'The Cold War Mannerists: The Man From U.N.C.L.E and TV Espionage in the 1960s.' *Journal of Popular Film and Television* 21:4 (1994): 150–61.

PART THREE

Critical analyzes of television drama

11

Don Draper and the promises of life

George Toles

'We distinguish two forms of rhetoric which, if not always debased, are certainly suspect: propaganda and advertising. They are suspect because their approach is ironic: an advertiser attaches very little real commitment to what he says, nor does he expect a committed response from the public.' Northrop Frye, *Words With Power*.

Don Draper's defining moment in the pilot episode of *Mad Men*, 'Smoke Gets in Your Eyes', occurs during a meeting with Lucky Strike executives. Don makes a strangely affecting speech which solves an advertising dilemma created by the growing public awareness of research linking cigarette smoking to cancer. What I mean by defining moment is a point of dramatic confluence when the components of an ambiguous character's public and private identity harmonise in an arresting fashion. Our emotional investment in Draper's means of presenting, withholding, and beholding himself suddenly deepens. We are supplied the right aperture for glimpsing, powerfully, the 'something more' in him that may link up with the unsolved mystery of ourselves. One might call such a connection 'identification', but that term is lazy and imprecise, and has grown ever more vaporous from overuse. In any event, what we may *identify* in Draper's defining moment, and feel compelled to acknowledge as a shared attribute, is an intricate helplessness. Helplessness is a behavioural response that immediately provokes discomfort unless it is somehow reckoned with, and triumphantly subdued. Don is as prone to evading and denying helplessness, when it arises, as anyone, but he also has an intriguing way of managing it – in fact, turning it to good account. Don's desperate skirmishes with helplessness, which introduce fracture lines in his commanding image of male strength, are what fully ignite our interest in him. It is the nature of his contention with this split between solidity and weak dispersal that makes him not only a representative of his time (1960), for satiric purposes, but also someone who casts a long shadow forward. The problems attending Don's inner workings extend to the present, and the darkness we discern there mingles, in an alternately enticing and troubling fashion, with our own.

We understand Don in the key Lucky Strike scene in terms of what resists being 'put together', though he is clearly a master of image assembly. Within a half hour of first encountering Draper and taking his measure, we are required to revise substantially our first strong impression of the sort of man he is likely to be. This necessary revision of judgement will be an ongoing feature of our relationship with the character. But it's not merely a matter of being deprived of certain puzzle pieces from Draper's past that might answer the questions: 'Who is he, really? What is he hiding?' It is more the case of seeing how a man who gives every indication of being unsettled, fearful, a tense jumble is so often able to bring proportion out of disproportion, to build a *saving* set of appearances for himself that somehow holds together emotionally as well. Our image of Don Draper, and our way of thinking about him, will consistently return to his 'man in a gray flannel suit' fitness for inspection. The composed outward form is an endlessly renewable source of beguilement. But it is his struggle to keep helplessness in check and the resources he summons for that task that makes him a 'large' figure, one we are disposed to imagine and inquire about on a grand scale. What we learn about his navigation through infirmity prevents Don from dwindling into a David Mamet-like power broker, whose conflicts fall into a reliable pattern in which the external testing of competence and the unleashing of ruthlessness predominate.

The haunting graphics that accompany the *Mad Men* credits at the beginning of each episode present Don's immaculately tailored silhouette in desperate, though graceful, slow motion freefall. All the lavish trappings of his office domain fail to solidify and contain him. They gently scramble, dissolve and sink beneath his feet before he begins his plummet. We catch up with him in mid-air as he drops past skyscrapers and billboards covered with images of pleasure and security – the sort he devises and dispatches to the anonymous consumer world 'out there'. More sturdy than he, the images stand impervious and continue to broadcast their promises as he tumbles earthward. But, crucially, the silhouette somehow draws strength from this array of remote images – the lustrous backdrop to panic – and Don magically averts what seemed to be certain disaster. Don's silhouette re-organizes itself; he takes his final form with his back to us, resting on an office couch

– arm outstretched on the rear cushion to perform relaxation for whoever encounters him. He is the embodiment of focused composure: alert, ready to do business, ready to confront and prevail over muddle. The music that flows alongside Don's voyage through helplessness (an RJD2 instrumental) is tinged with anxiety and melancholy, but the tones of distress are muted. They feel only half-asserted. Even during the worst moments of Don's plunge through emptiness, the musical pulse is subdued, almost soothing, as though a nightmare were threading a needle, and sedating its dread with a lullaby. As Don regains his equilibrium, restored by a kind of mesmerism to a shielded repose, the music offers a tinkling cascade to allay the disquiet of the lingering bass line. The tinkle converts the shuddering descent into the plink of cubes in a whiskey glass. The revival of spirit emerges, musically, through a liquid haze.

I will have more to say later in the essay about Don Draper's character in its full-scale development, and will address in some detail its central paradox: ever-expanding dimensions within what continues to impress the viewer as a tight, restrictive outline. But let us engage with him first during the Lucky Strike meeting, and discover what aspects of Draper are highlighted there. The struggle that most concerns me is between his overt, surprisingly complete surrender to helplessness and his recovery, through improvisation, of a forceful, if tantalisingly elusive, belief.

Like many great scenes in film, the Lucky Strike meeting misleadingly prompts us to think, at the outset, that we know exactly what is at issue and that we are equipped with exactly the right sort of understanding to make quick work of it. In this instance, we come in with the flattering sense of possessing an appropriately ironic awareness, pitched well above the heads of the characters, an awareness which permits our evaluation of their dilemma – as beleaguered tobacco executives and ad men – to be automatically superior to theirs. We are further flattered by the implication that our higher cultural understanding is derived in part from our commandingly unnaive life in the demanding present, which has left behind so many of the crude assumptions about tobacco advertising to which the characters in the scene (stranded in 1960) are still prey. In fact, the knowledge that we think we have will swiftly be taken away from us, or at least be set joltingly at odds with our emotional participation in the scene. Our 'knowledge' becomes an intriguing, indeed baffling, obstacle to our evolving realisation of the outcome of the meeting that we desire. We are instantly certain, for example, that we should be suspicious, to the point of scorn, of Lucky Strike representatives seeking to find fresh slogans and ploys to bamboozle cigarette buyers. (We likely find an opportunity to congratulate ourselves for not sharing the pervasive gullibility of our consumer forebears. As always, we note and savour

our separation from the woeful ignorance to which the past, recent as well as distant, is incurably susceptible.) The spectator is additionally encouraged to regard whatever solution to the advertising problem that Draper and his Sterling-Cooper associates may come up with as pointedly absurd – and perhaps troubling to dwell on were it not so comfortingly ridiculous. And yet, by scene's end, we will be fiercely committed to finding an honourable solution to the puzzle.

How well we know our way around high level conference rooms, in movies and television shows, especially those whose decision-making involves malign scheming against the collective well-being of ordinary folk. Our voyeuristic interest, as we enter such gatherings, has to do with being let in on trade secrets and watching at close range as the levers of power are manipulated. At the same time we can easily appoint ourselves the unseen advocate and conscience of those unfortunates whose rights are being abused. It is as though the simple act of witnessing a damaging board room policy being ratified is tantamount to exposing wrongdoing to the light. Our awareness that objectionable plans are being made right before our eyes, which will then be hurried to execution, carries us forward, imaginatively, to the remedy for such a repellent design, which we have sensibly figured out. Our being privy to the schemers' intent sounds an alarm, of sorts. We become, in effect, secret holders of confidential information. We would promptly deliver it to the right parties, were that possible, before the feared result transpired. The moral answer to the crisis lies with us, and mentally we have done our part to avert it.

As the Lucky Strike meeting commences, we are handed an easy joke that confirms our privileged position at the conference table. The joke is there to assure us that we are historically and ethically situated *above* the proceedings. Several of the company representatives who are nonchalantly smoking in the Sterling-Cooper meeting room begin coughing in unison after Lee Garner, Sr, their boss, refers to 'government interference' infringing on tobacco industry freedoms. Garner harshly declares that with such a policy in place they might as well be 'in Russia.' These opening remarks by Garner in a smoke-congested room, backed by a chorus of hackers, succinctly confirms the viewer's superior grasp of Cold War shibboleths, the wisdom of government monitoring of mendacious tobacco interests and the business-men's wilful blindness to the dangers of their own product. Chiefly we are alerted to the fact that Garner is an elderly conservative patriarch concerned solely with profits, and that we should summarily reject whatever values he espouses. He is coarsely concerned about the possibility of Lucky Strike being sued, as one of his competitors, represented by a rival ad company, has been, over misleading claims about health threats. We attend closely to Don

Draper's visible attitude from the outset, since we have been given ample hints that he is not adequately prepared to make a presentation. However, at this stage in the pilot episode, our attachment to him is still tenuous enough that we have no reason to feel anxious on his behalf. We have watched him fret and grow frustrated over his lack of inspiration, but his performance of a successful pitch is of only abstract concern to the viewer. We are thus far disengaged from his brooding self-absorption. It does not matter to us whether he distinguishes himself in this primitive world of PR jousting for position and preferment. We would be hard pressed to say how his creation of a successful sales pitch for a tobacco giant would count as meaningful. Perhaps Don's best chance of impressing us, we calculate, would be for him to take a principled stand (that is, *our* stand) against Sterling-Cooper's disagreeably complacent, rapacious clients. That option, however, is unlikely. In an earlier meeting with Rachel Menken, the manager of a department store, Don has behaved intemperately and with a boorish resentment of his client's judgement and air of assured independence.

Also on display in the earlier meeting was Don's reflex discomfort with Rachel's Jewishness (a response perfectly in accord with that of the other representatives of the agency taking part in the interview). Don's casual indignation over his client's moxie and strong opinions climaxes with a fit of pique. He abruptly walks out of the meeting, in part because he dislikes having his authority challenged by a female know-it-all, and in part (as he confides to his 'underling', Pete Campbell) out of worry over the pending Lucky Strike presentation. He directly acknowledges that he is stymied, that his efforts to devise an effective campaign have come to nothing, and we do not doubt him. Up to this point in the episode, Don's smoothness and aura of self-command have nearly been overshadowed by an impression of his coarse typicality. He seems very much, and regrettably, a man of his time, someone who swims with the current of all the prevailing attitudes about masculine prerogatives, and who profits from them without giving them a moment's thought. He appears clever but not introspective, and perfectly embodies the business 'values' of his agency rather than covertly chafing against them.

After the preliminary review of Lucky Strike's predicament is finished, Roger Sterling, Draper's boss, confidently directs the group's attention to him, noting with smiling professional aplomb that the conversation has arrived at Don's 'cue' to enter, and (implicitly) be dazzling. What follows is a strikingly prolonged, humiliatingly conspicuous exhibition of Draper's ineptitude. It is like a slow motion nightmare of a public fiasco, with all eyes in the no exit chamber fixed upon him. Don fumbles through the papers in his leather briefcase, in bewildered search of notes that do not exist, and strenuously avoids eye contact with both his Sterling-Cooper colleagues and the

triad of tobacco clients seated across from him. As he stumbles unconvinc-
ingly through some 'stalling for time' prefatory remarks, the viewer's verdict
on Draper's dismal performance is sharply reinforced by a cut to the impatient
executives, who are at one in their immobility and frozen-faced displeasure.
Don's immaculate grooming, topped off with a scalpel-clean part in his hair,
works against him here. For the first time, he has the look of a pretender
in his image-proclaiming garb, not so dissimilar from the nameless Jewish
employee who was whisked from the mail room and rigged up in a suit for
a mute demonstration of ethnic 'fellowship' at the Rachel Menken meeting.
Though we have not yet, in all likelihood, formed a resilient attachment to Don
(which might oblige us to share his anxiety and shame over this derailment of
expertise), I think there is an immediate viewer concern, more visceral than
reflective, that the situation be saved.

We adopt, for hard to explain reasons, a sudden loyalty to Sterling-Cooper's
interests at this juncture, and keenly hope that one of its team members
can find rhetoric potent enough to appease the disgruntled tobacco baron.
I shall return shortly to the crucial, protracted rendering of Don's descent to
a childlike 'uselessness'. Let me merely note for now that Don's unnerving
vulnerability – amounting to all-out, splashing panic – is not, by itself, the
element that brings us into emotional alignment with him. It is helplessness in
combination with Draper's resources for rapid image rebuilding and decisive,
clean-edged emotional recovery that grant him his formidable, labyrinthine
mystique. It is important, for purposes of crystallisation, that we discern his
helplessness first in a pure, isolated state, and that we have ample time to
feel its abject writhing, with no recourse to a conceivable remedy. The delay
that Matt Weiner makes part of the scene structure, prior to Don's retrieving
his voice and proficient bearing, is essential to make us participate fully in the
culminating grand moment of self-determination – when prostrate weakness
and mastery coalesce. The mastery will be that of a supreme escape artist, a
Houdini of the inner life.

As Don's initial presentation crumbles, his rival in the agency, Pete
Campbell, sees an opening and literally *rises* to the occasion: a tidy young
man in a blazing blue suit who must stand up to become captain and seize the
helm of the foundering vessel. Although we have even less reason to admire
Pete's qualities than Draper's, we have cast in our lot with the ad men and
require someone to cover for Don's ruinous lack of focus, before it is too late,
and complete his task successfully. There are few dramatic circumstances
more propitious for enhancing spectator involvement than a daunting, unfin-
ished task. Campbell's readiness to intervene is soon strengthened by our
surprised realisation that he is more poised, shrewd, eloquent and intellec-
tually nimble than we had supposed. He offers an appealing, adroitly phrased

variation of the existential approach to cigarette smoking which a laughably 'Viennese' female psychology consultant had earlier outlined for Don in his office. Campbell's pitch feels bold and ingenious and it is seductively presented to the viewer as the kind of cunning, glitteringly roguish solution we might imagine coming up with ourselves in a pinch. For several artfully calibrated beats, Pete seems to have hit upon an idea that cuts the Gordian knot and meets our wised-up consumer selves precisely where we presently live. Pete's slogan, in other words, leaps past the restriction of 1960 tobacco industry wisdom and acquires an aura of prescience. His logic speaks directly to our only half-acknowledged, perverse appetite for self-wreckage. 'Cars are dangerous', Pete begins, with his best 'let's be grown-ups' smile. 'There's nothing you can do about it. You still have to get where you're going.' The 'You still have to get where you're going' assertion implies that without cigarettes as part of your danger tool-kit, you'll probably lack the requisite toughness to bear down and push all the obstacles to your goals – including the timorous brand of human being – out of the way. The sentence also manages to weave a strand of romantic Hemingway fatalism in with the cocky, trampling brute will.

Our provisional positive assessment of the first portion of Pete Campbell's pitch effectively dismantles the satiric framework that was our tonal guide at the opening of the meeting. Without being fully conscious of the sea change, we have been drawn into the advertising mind set: Campbell's unexpected association of cigarettes and men of the road and his tingly phrasemaking are a fetching lure. From now on we are playing the game on the same terms that the others in the room are; we have taken a seat of our own at the table, rather than maintaining our former droll detachment. Lee Garner Jr speaks admiringly of Pete's angle, but we sense as he does so that he is merely a 'yes' man, who will capitulate immediately to his father's position, whatever that might be. We are meant to be taken aback by Garner Sr's swift, uncomprehending, contemptuous dismissal of Pete's idea. By this point it had become *our* idea as well. Our surprised delight at Campbell's skill in unfurling it and his grace under pressure have made us collaborators in excellence, a familiar viewer response in movie scenes where creativity is on exhibit. We credit ourselves – in a fantasy of validation – with being co-authors. Yet as soon as Pete proceeds to clarify his thinking and begins ill-advisedly to meander about a collective death wish, we effortlessly abandon him and side instead with the indignant Garner Sr. It does not take more than a few moments of backpedalling adjustment to revise our earlier impulse to approve. We *must* have known from the outset that Campbell's proposal was flawed, and inadequately thought through. Don is returned to prominence at the table with a close-up view of him drawing back sceptically from Campbell's increasingly murky logic. Draper seems to have recovered enough presence of mind to be inwardly amused at Campbell's flailing effort to soldier on with an already lost argument. Prior to Don's re-entry into the discussion we are prodded to affiliate ourselves with him: he is once more the person with the most capacious sense of what's going on.

As the meeting verges on irretrievable collapse, Don seems fully prepared to let the Lucky Strike account go, along with any lingering embarrassment over his own spectacular maladroitness. He is somehow unfazed by the atmosphere of quiet doom emanating from Roger, his beleaguered boss. Somewhere in the brief interval in which we have been deprived of visual contact with Don, his self-possession has been reactivated, by a cryptic feat of prestidigitation. This return to form, it must be noted, is not the result of Don having (yet) the slightest inkling of a rescue plan. He merely manifests a capacity to take a tranquil step back from the pervasive turmoil (his own included) and survey the scene with dispassionate alertness. He appears, paradoxically, remote from the crisis while being tuned in to all the particulars. I should also mention the curious transformation of the viewer's attitude to Garner Sr. As we watch this elderly man wield his power with careless authority and speak his mind plainly, without pretence or undue oafishness, he loses the ready-to-wear blackguard label that he possessed in the scene's introductory segment. He strikes us now as a raffish, two-fisted patriarch of the old school, who unmistakably *loves* the product he sells. (A certain nostalgia for the demands of tobacco cultivation and curing – over the genera-tions – creeps into the smoke-filled air of the board room.) We are enticed into forming a makeshift new alliance with the colourful tycoon, replacing our still garden-fresh connection with Pete Campbell, who suddenly takes on (by contrast) the objectionable, oily smoothness of a wet-behind-the-ears upstart. Lee Garner Sr's bewilderment at Campbell's *outlandish* slogan, which in his mind boils down to 'You're going to die anyway. Die with us', persuades us (in our fickleness) to re-join the traditionalist ranks, applauding common sense while scoffing at fancy theories that, a minute ago, may well have excited our admiration. A knee-jerk resistance to 'cheap' Freudianism ties the bow on our repudiation of Campbell.

Noting that his father's patience with the stalled proceedings is exhausted, Garner Jr adopts the pose of self-directed assertiveness, giving imperious voice to his father's transparent mood. ('Come on, dad. Let's get out of here.') Then, at almost the same stroke that he confirms our sense of him as a feckless 'Yes' man, he makes a throwaway comment that holds a veiled solution to the advertising impasse. I should stress that the spectator, however adroit he may imagine himself in slicing through the wiles and chicanery of cigarette promotion, misses the cue, the clue, and the inferences to be drawn from Garner Jr's 'unthinking' words. ('The bright spot is, at least we know that if we have this problem, everyone has it.') Garner Jr appears to be belabouring the obvious, and merely restating what has already been said. The emphasis here is on common difficulties, those that belong to 'everyone' (equally and disagreeably) rather than the sort of bright, singular, creative notion a clever individual might come up with. Such a notion as that would not be the property of everyone, but a secret held in isolation by Lucky Strike. Don Draper sees and seizes his opening here, wresting it – by virtue of what he himself is – from the shadow of *everyone's* problems. Draper's character embodies a familiar type of American split between being 'no one in particular' (the product of a shameful, 'under the heel' past that needs to be lost, forgotten, forcefully displaced and surmounted) and a highly inviting individual presence (strong enough to block all efforts to read and understand him). The conviction of being, at bottom, a nothing, a fraud who cannot withstand close scrutiny, somehow drives Don to be a compulsive borrower from 'everyone', or rather from every intriguing individual he runs up against. He furtively appropriates the coveted bits and pieces of the temporary behaviour model he appraises, and from them adds additional material to the imposing drapery of his personage. He has some of the mixed freedom that Walter Kerr attributed to Chaplin's tramp in his study, *The Silent Clowns*. Because the tramp is fundamentally no one, he can effortlessly impersonate, and temporarily be filled up by, any aspect of any stranger he encounters.[1] An attribute once taken on and taken in affords fleeting refuge, a gratifying hiding place. It will serve to stave off instability and core confusion for the time being, but Don, like Chaplin's tramp, knows that every improvised identity gesture is likely to fail him, and he'll be 'out in the cold' once again.

This quasi-pathological freedom to be elusive and indeterminate connects with advertising's equal adeptness at playing upon social anxieties while contriving, almost in the same breath, images of reassurance. Robert Warshow, in his 1952 essay 'The Movie Camera and the American' (which is mostly concerned with Arthur Miller's *Death of a Salesman*) speaks of

a broad concept of American society which in fact we all assent to. The American stands outside any fixed social framework, and so he must create his own place, indeed he must create himself, out of the resources of his personality. If he believes still that the world lies open to him, he believes also, and with greater clarity, that if he fails to measure up to his opportunity he will find himself an outcast.

---

[1] Walter Kerr, *The Silent Clowns* (New York: Alfred Knopf, 1975), 84–5.

The fate of a contemporary American male (and, by implication, female), tied to some large bureaucracy, 'depends primarily on pleasing his superiors, or if not his superiors, then simply "pleasing", in the most general sense ... failure is a kind of insidious disease, like cancer; you may find out at any moment that you had it all along'.[2] Warshow concludes by saying that this picture of how things work is undeniable. Parents naturally fear that their children may 'miss that exact balance of the physical, intellectual, and social graces without which these gifts will go to waste ... On some level of our minds we go in expectation of the word of rejection that will leave us jobless, loveless, without a place'.[3]

Don Draper is an American 'nobody', like Jay Gatsby, who has somehow managed to generate a 'Platonic conception of himself' out of his vague, shifty, hardscrabble temperament and the good fortune of possessing the right look and voice.[4] This conception, which is not merely fraudulent since everything that America *is* backs it up, springs full-blown from his assumed name and invented history. He has an impressive talent for externally vindicating the Platonic ideal, which is powerfully ratified by the strength of his projected image, without needing, or being able to, live inside it. He is *of* it, but not *in* it; however, he has an abiding faith that this gap can eventually be closed. In a sense it is the fantasy of being *everyone*, in their collective aspiration, as opposed to the 'nobody' of his shameful, buried beginning, that gives Don's creative work its special edge, and keeps him afloat, professionally. Don feels he can intuit what 'everyone' wants because he is constantly seeking reinforcing ballast for the Everyman dimension of himself. What holds an ad idea together as a potent fantasy of betterment and self-consolidation for the striving souls comprising the multitude, is equally a means for Don to adjust his own inner fragments so they too show signs of coalescing. The imminent prospect of his many competing roles merging in one grand story steadies him. His ability to conjure up a unified vision of possibility that the public could embrace is always (though he does not know it) a simultaneous effort to reassemble the puzzle pieces of himself into a new, more durable and readable picture.

The camera tracks in on Don as soon as Garner Jr announces that it's time to leave. Father and son are already en route to the door. Don's arm is half-upraised and motionless, as though it had plucked a thought from mid-air and held it, aflutter, while it gains definition. His face is transfixed by

---

[2] Robert Warshow, *The Immediate Experience*, enlarged edn (Cambridge, MA: Harvard University Press, 2002), 148–9.
[3] Warshow, *Immediate Experience*, 149.
[4] F. Scott Fitzgerald, *The Great Gatsby* (New York: Charles Scribner's Sons, 1953), 99.

something that seems to bridge phrases employed in swift succession by the two Garners. 'We're selling America', Lee Sr had noted, without a trace of irony or cynicism. His son then mentioned 'everyone' being stuck with the same problem of the cigarette–cancer linkage. A solitary blink on Don's otherwise immobile, unreadable face attests to the sudden crystallisation of an intuition. 'Gentlemen, before you go, could I just say something?' Don expresses courtly deference with his caressing use of the word 'gentlemen', and appears to concede that the executives have made up their minds, appropriately, and that what he has to add, by way of a parting thought, will not detain them for long. His phrasing accomplishes something more, though. It acknowledges that his earlier fumbling remarks have demoted him to 'on the sidelines', underling status. He will only win the right to speak if he asks permission first. At the same time, the statement subtly revises the narrative of his previous muddled state of mind. The reconstituted figure addressing the group is not a man scrambling to make amends for prior blunders. Rather, he conveys the impression of one who has been sagely observing the group's deliberations from the outset, and who waited patiently for the two Lees fully to articulate their concerns before weighing in with his own considered response. Don does not defensively recoil from whatever demonstrable foolishness happened before. Because he has dropped all signs of being tied to his previous lavish display of weakness, it does not limit his present stance in any way.

Roger's dryly ironic rejoinder to Don's request ('Could I say something?') is 'I don't know, Don. Can you?' This deflating joke neatly resolves the awkward business of acquiescing to Don's casual petition for a second chance. By needling Don (half-privately but still audibly) Roger takes the onus off the tobacco executives, who are not obliged to say if they intend to delay their departure. Roger deftly answers on their behalf, without appearing to do so. The fact that he can jest at Draper's expense relieves spectator worry that Roger is still dismayed by the fiasco of the botched presentation. Roger's mockery operates slyly to re-establish solidarity between the two men, and a slight resurgence of team spirit. Roger's feigned poise enhances our impression of Don's *restored* poise, which seems the genuine article, and gives Don room to manoeuvre. Whatever qualms Roger may have about Don's fitness to carry on, the offer of a congenial, sharp-edged challenge signals to the viewer that Roger, who in all likelihood is a reliable assessor of Don's past performances, is prepared to believe in him once again, and to be favourably surprised.

Don rises from his chair for the first time in the scene. He makes this decisive move not in the manner of one who girds himself with power-broker confidence but instead as someone awakening to an understanding. We see him entering into a more intimate relation with his own freshly seized thoughts, and with himself into the bargain. His improvised presentation is divided into two parts. The first smoothly establishes the argument that because all the major tobacco companies are in the same boat, none can make a health claim against the others. (The second will involve a feat of self-discovery.) The *sameness* of the product and the shared predicament of those selling it is framed as a rich source of opportunity to be inventive, without constraint by facts. The companies are free to say whatever they want about their own product's magical, inimitable attributes, without fear of another company resorting to scare tactics or a discrediting of, say, Lucky Strike's proclaimed virtues. There is no direct appeal to spectator feeling in the first portion of Don's pitch. However, we are meant to identify with his relaxed determination to persuade and prevail. He is now placed in the time-honoured movie hero position of having to bring a near-impossible task to completion, as I noted earlier, and to do it expeditiously. Instead of remaining unable-to- be-duped consumer advocates (our role at the beginning of the scene), we have grown comfortable with the exhilarating, unanticipated role of the even more wised-up designer of irresistible falsehoods. It is quite easy for us to become cozy with perfidy and the sweet logic of those planning to wreak havoc at arm's length. We prefer, at least temporarily, the scintillating callousness of the insider's view to the traditional hand-wringing over adver-tising foul play. Perhaps we remind ourselves, censoriously, of the gullibility and doltishness of those, unlike ourselves, who are so pathetically taken in by glib phrases and exaggerated ad images. These abstract cancer victims of the past, though they, of course, warrant our sympathy, bear some responsibility for their plight. They should have been more savvy interrogators of ad rhetoric. If we take the bait in the scene's multi-level manipulation of us, we may well succumb to 'serves 'em right' tough-mindedness as we figure out how Don proposes to work the angles. To be *against* Don as he pulls himself together and weaves his beguiling tale may strike us as a tediously inflexible position. Let us by all means disavow any vestiges of a prim, Puritan uptightness. Don's use of a 1950s schoolroom chalkboard to make notes on group suggestions introduces a reassuring note of near-innocence and technological quaintness in the undertaking.

Don's transition line, as he launches a search for the right slogan, is 'We can say anything we want.' He accompanies this revelation with a genial shrug. Don is hardly in a position – in this meeting or in any other area of his life – where he can authentically avail himself of such freedom. The spectator no doubt is in a similar quandary, so she is unlikely to stave off the appeal enshrined in the 'presto' dispensation from the need to 'watch what one says'. We skate from a situation where the word cancer can barely be mentioned to the grumpy tobacco men without triggering embarrassment and upset, to a declared spree, where dangerous language of every sort seems, for the nonce, powerless and permissible. After printing the words 'Lucky Strike' on the blackboard, Draper requests a primer lesson in how cigarettes are made. Junior acknowledges that he has no idea, which prompts a swift rebuke from Lee Sr: 'Shame on you.' What transpires in this split second sounding of a minor father–son rift is that the scene dynamic subtly yet decisively shifts once again. Lee Sr instantly becomes one of the disappointed, successful self-made fathers (in 1950s film melodrama and beyond) who is in search of an appropriate surrogate son. This replacement will make up for the deficient 'my own flesh-and-blood' version that an 'unlucky' strike has forced upon him. Draper, we feel, is auditioning for paternal acceptance, as well as trying to please a client, and we grow increasingly hopeful that Don will win the elusive prize of paternal validation. Lee Sr answers Don's question about the story of tobacco with a fond listing of steps: seeding, planting in the 'North Carolina sunshine', cutting, curing and then (as a savoury capper) 'toasting'. Lee Sr lays particular prideful stress on his wise employment of 'insect repellant' seed. 'Insect repellant' jousts a bit in our ear with the not quite silenced (or banished) spectre of cancer. Don recognizes, perhaps a couple of beats ahead of the spectator, that the word 'toast' is redolent of breakfast togetherness and the inviting warmth of a day commenced with fresh resolve. It is a word that simultaneously connotes fragrance, heat that browns (moderately) without burning, daybreak and venerableness (grandpa's dear tobacco pipe). It also salutes the benign comforts supplied by modern kitchen appliances. (Who can be sceptical hearing the cheerful pop of a shiny, reliable toaster?)

Adopting the tone of a pleasantly surprised, quietly encouraging teacher, Don rewards Lee Sr with the gracious admission that the old man has held the solution to the insoluble tobacco ad puzzle all along. 'There you go', he announces twice, printing the unassuming phrase 'It's toasted' on the blackboard. Implicit in Don's inspired culling of the word from Lee's dry list is the smiling sense that 'You, Lee, have been holding out on us.' In a sense, Lee's exciting 'suggestion' makes Don and the executive crafty co-conspirators who have *jointly* refrained from showing their hand till the exact propitious moment. The simplicity of the phrase, even before we assent to its rightness, combined with the elementary school blackboard lettering offhandedly, and a trifle crudely, produced by Don, intimate that we are in a time earlier and more Edenic than that when smoking gave pause to the anxious choice maker. We're looking at tobacco still in the *garden*, basking in the North Carolina sunlight, needing only a bit of 'toasting' refinement to achieve the perfected natural goodness that smoker and non-smoker alike yearn for. In this garden, the child's garden of tobacco, it's all as simple as 'one-two-three'.

Lee Sr, turning literal-minded briefly and still not quite able to bring his apparent cleverness into proper focus, remonstrates that 'everybody else's tobacco is toasted'. Don, who until now in his speech has been the ebullient champion and spokesman for 'everybody' in the basic pursuit of ordinary satisfactions, abruptly transforms into a sly backer of the elect and its warranted privileges. The men and women who select Lucky Strike are those who deserve to rise above the crowd, even if their elevation is the result of a somewhat underhanded bit of sales malarkey. Ruses are forgivable when the outcome is appropriate, and works to the benefit of all concerned. 'No', Don says, gently correcting Lee Sr, his most talented, mature pupil. (The son is about to open his father's eyes.) 'Everybody else's tobacco is poisonous. Lucky Strike's is toasted.' The main pitch is now concluded, but the even more important character-defining work to be accomplished in the second part of the presentation is still – unanticipated – ahead of us. As Don is obliged to clarify his thinking further, he establishes a perspective on advertising that becomes beautifully and movingly indistinguishable from who he thinks he is. In this metaphysical elucidation stage, the pleasure of watching a demoralised salesman regain his moxie and control of the audience with a headily intriguing idea gives way to something deeper. What is avowed, by way of conclusion, is unfeignedly emotional.

Roger Sterling re-enters the discussion at this point, sensing – as boss – an unmistakable shift in the atmosphere of the room. Trying to shore up the favourable mood by vocally lending Don his support, he speaks before he has had time to absorb fully the nuances of the pitch. (I suspect most viewers share his cloudiness about where precisely things have arrived.) 'Well, gentlemen, I don't think I have to tell you what you just witnessed here.' What, indeed, *have* we witnessed? I think we await something that is not flummery to be added to the mix, before we can take the measure of Draper, as protagonist of *Mad Men*. Behind Roger, Pete Campbell, abashed and perhaps imploding, looks down at the table. We have time to recall the premature elation that flourished fleetingly in the wake of his own speech. The two-shot of Roger's and Pete's contrasting reactions to Don and the effusive 'faking it' of Roger's comradely intervention highlight the fact that a split and some unresolved discord remain in the meeting room. Garner Junior is confident enough in assessing his father's lingering perplexity to respond quickly to Roger's misty claim with an obdurate 'I think you do.'

Don immediately continues, ignoring Roger's bid for recognition of their linked and like-minded position. Clearly he doesn't need or even wish for Roger's endorsement. He has absorbed all of the leadership capacity available on his side of the table into himself. He is coming fully into his own now as someone who is not merely 'making business sense' but stumbling onto a pivotal private realisation in the process. His recognition has to do with uncovering a viable foundation not simply for a smoker's happiness, but his own. Don seizes upon the ever-present link between every piece of effective advertising and happiness, and then dares to raise the question 'Do you know what happiness is?' without having the answer securely in hand. Don gives the irresistible impression of chancing upon the secret wellspring of happiness in a forest glade, making it real for himself as the words to evoke it come to him, unbidden. Happiness is 'the smell of a new car', he begins, referencing a childhood of plenty, of middle-class 'having', and convivial family occasions that had nothing to do with his actual cold, shabby upbringing. Nonetheless, the Proustian madeleine sense recollection of that bygone (in fact, fantasy) car's revivifying smell penetrates Don as he speaks it. The world as he might have known it and belonged to it is alive to him as breathes in the car's fragrance. Don follows up the 'new car smell' with an abstraction: 'It's freedom from fear.' The camera view has shifted to Lee Sr. The speech is transformed into a subterranean colloquy between this would-be father, who can dispense acceptance (a kind of anointing) and, by extension, all good things, and Don, who is embarked on replacing every trace of his genuine parent – fearsome, remote – with the newfound 'maker' who sits before him, silently appraising. Don liquidates his own fear of paternal rejection and brutality by connecting happiness to a *freedom* from fear that he possesses just by speaking the phrase, with understated conviction. Don supplies a third example before gathering his meaning to himself one last time, and bringing it home. 'It's a billboard that you see by the side of the road that *screams* with reassurance ....'. Don gives emphasis to the word 'screams'. The camera is by now settled on him alone, in close-up. From this enclosed private frame he appears to be at one with what he perceives, a bridge perhaps leading from his own isolation chamber to a place of imagined fellowship. The 'scream' (without the reassurance) belongs to his own desolate apartness, his loneliness, for which he has no available explanation, and maybe very little insight. The looming billboard offers a loud promise, loud enough to vanquish the past. The past is everything that must be overcome or subdued if Don is to arrive safely at his emotional destination. Maybe it can ALL be left behind. He envisions the traveller on a long journey stopping by the side of a strange road for a short rest, then seeking refreshment from an image that someone has planted there, whose immensity and promise are so much greater and more commanding than himself. 'Screams with reassurance that whatever you're doing (pause) it's okay (a lengthier pause). You ... are okay.'

Cigarettes seem to have fallen out of the picture for Don as he arrives at his cherished point of equilibrium. He has summoned it through high-wire imaginative intuition, and given it substance through the grace of untrammelled, uncalculated utterance. Don hasn't so much *willed* his finding of restored security, from which his small audience might draw sustenance. Rather, he has ventured, with calm audacity, in the direction of a condition, a station, a niche he could not quite bring into focus. He doesn't preordain his arrival vocally, and inwardly, at 'okay' – a word which marks the successful staving off of helplessness, for now. He takes mental hold of the 'okay' barely one step in advance of landing there. He manifests an almost blind faith that he can secure, in a state of psychic emergency, what he needs, and somehow call 'himself' into existence in the process (whatever 'himself' might mean, here and now). 'I am present and accounted for', Don's face undeceptively proclaims, 'as I pronounce the benediction of "Okay".' The faith element, which Don hardly recognizes as such, allows selfhood to be retrieved *as* a state of being okay. And the fact that he has found this life-giving reassurance – synonymous with happiness – after running the risk of another massive defeat (he speaks with no safety net) is exactly what makes the 'You're okay' place of arrival visible, and meaningful, to his listeners.

When Don comes to a halt, Pete Campbell is shown looking up at him, before we are granted Lee Sr's definitive judgement. Pete is swayed: he has the demeanour of someone who accepts his punishment as his due. He has been beaten back down after his earlier misguided attempt to usurp Don's authority. Pete may also be struck, as the viewer is, by Don's apparently genuine release from his established office manner: sovereign aloofness. Don has embodied his pitch rather than acted it out. It carried the listeners beyond the reach of language, however artful. Pete's involuntarily admiring gaze is followed by a close-up of Lee Sr, who is smiling beatifically. The hard to satisfy 'parent' has been completely won over and bowled over by Don's delicate, quietly impassioned finish. The moment has a force comparable to John Wayne's dispensing of a smile of unconditional paternal affirmation to his adopted son, Montgomery Clift, at the conclusion of *Red River*. The grin overflows the banks of its dramatic context. Instead of a business meeting we are now part of some sort of homecoming. 'It's toasted. I *get* it', Lee announces. What precisely has he, in company with us, gotten? Lucky Strike has been made part of a plausible place that ratifies one's desire to belong, to be taken care of, to be at one's ease. It is a place where one does not live by making false impressions (or needing to). It somehow permits one to leave behind the strain of anxious pretending. The place Don sees – which carries us through the billboard, beyond the blandishments of 'mere' advertising – is one that solidly welcomes him, and makes him feel whole. Lee Sr *gets* the force of Don's connection with whatever it is he has sighted. In the lengthy close-up of Don becoming 'Okay' in spite of 'whatever he has done', we understand anew what Noel Burch means when talking of the close-up's 'erotic vocation'.[5] Don looks down, half-smiling, and humbly receives the peace that has been granted to him. The viewer's emotional pact with Don Draper as the unquestionable, worthy protagonist of *Mad Men* is fully formed and settled in the course of this reaction. Draper (as Jon Hamm powerfully incarnates him) is not making himself vulnerable to others here – not even to the father surrogate whose approval he has gained. He is rather made vulnerable to himself, locating (again?) a vital lost key that enables him to emerge from a deep, familiar darkness and a sham existence. He passes into a light that bewilders, consolidates and frees him all at once. He has awakened, cleansed. The rest, as Hamlet knew, is silence.

The next scene, set in Don's office, is set in motion by a sound cue of ice cubes being dropped into a whiskey glass. The visualized drink, which Roger is pouring for Don, immediately follows. Replacing Don's tender, surprised, saved-from-darkness-and-drowning expression at the close of the tobacco meeting, the ice cubes, viewed at close range in their tantalising, translucent hardness, shift our perspective on Don once again. He has already retreated into hardness himself; his genially opaque, imperial mask has been reinstated. The contact he just secured with a happiness neither willed nor comprehended has already been severed. Although in a relaxed mood, with his feet propped up on his desk, and jubilantly smoking a cigar, he is not accessible to Roger's probing – except as a cheerful impersonator of 'Don' – nor to ours. One should not underestimate, however, the relief that comes from controlled male pullaways from vulnerability. The restored detachment is presented with a dash of irony, blended with a recognition that a prolongation of Draper's thawed openness would diminish its impact. We admire Don for mastering his former precarious uncoveredness. We have identified a mysterious clearing in Don, alive with emotional need, as well as a possible means of that need's fulfilment, but such a clearing signifies more to us when quickly obscured by the dense, enfolding wilderness. No sooner does one find such a clearing, ancient myths tell us, than one is likely to lose touch with it, and one endows such a clearing – where a knight's soul is glimpsed taking form – with even more value in the losing. Our relationship with Don, in this respect, comes to resemble our hide-and-seek relationship with ourselves.

Roger confesses that Don had had him 'worried'. With a very limited conception of how to explain what took place, Roger facilely asks whether Don, in fact, had been drunk or not drunk. He can imagine no other options. The word 'drunk' is Roger's way of conceding that he had lost his customary mode of 'winking, stylish bullshitter' connection with Don. He had noted Don's confusion in the meeting, and the odd process by which he had turned

---

[5] Quoted in David Trotter, *Cinema and Modernism* (Oxford: Blackwell Publishing, 2007), 40.

it, by some feat of legerdemain, to good account. He congratulates Don for having been 'inspired'. Don's reply to Roger's query indicates that he is equally mystified by what happened in the meeting, and by what he had managed to salvage in his trance-like trawl of his psyche, and in the ensuing silence. 'For the record, I pulled it out of thin air. Thank you [casting his eyes heavenward] up there.' Don cobbles together a version of his performance that appeals to contingency, dumb luck, and flying by the seat of one's pants. He does not credit imaginative faith, or indeed belief of any kind. In the afterglow he is fully prepared to own up that nothing he created on the spot 'out of thin air' was drawn meaningfully from his own experience, or from his baffled, thwarted, dolorously questing hope for a more capacious vision of life. He is pleased to regard himself as a mere confidence man (though highly resourceful), one who knows full well that the rhetorical ploys involved in his sloganeering cannot be tested for a foundation. Don has forgotten his silence at the end of his happiness speech – a real silence, out of the reach of speech, in which he found himself, unencumbered, and at peace with himself, in another place. He does not take counsel from the silence, and once he has returned from it, appears entirely willing to dismiss its effect on him. What difference, after all, could such a brief lapse of presence and control be expected to make? Perhaps he was simply appeased by the knowledge that his presentation had had its desired *theatrical* effect.

A few scenes later, when Don meets Rachel Menken in a restaurant, in an attempt to repair the damage of his business meeting walkout earlier in the day, he opens up to her, to a degree, offering a fully worked out speech about his pervasive distrust of 'deeper values'. He is led to this disclosure by Rachel's admission that she has never been in love, with the 'rider clause' implication that if she had been, it would naturally have mattered a great deal to her. Don is genuinely perturbed that someone who professes independence and strength of mind would hold on to the fantasy of a transforming depth of attachment within a male–female relationship. Going into seducer mode, he presents her with what he takes to be a saleable version of himself as an admirably disenchanted man of the world. He is someone making do with his bereft of illusions condition. He realizes, in a sad grown-up way, that love was a 'gimmick invented by guys like me' as a means 'to sell nylons'. He then endeavours to impress her with his alluringly perilous commitment to a streamlined, shrink-wrapped form of existentialism, seasoned with the exotic spice of nihilism. 'You're born alone and you die alone and this world just drops a bunch of rules on top of you in order to make you forget those facts, but I – never forget. I'm living life like there's no tomorrow, because there – isn't one.' Don is striking what he regards as a tough-minded, manly stance of 'mature pessimism'. This resonant phrase was employed by Robert

Warshow to describe the all-but-inevitable post-Holocaust Jewish world view. But Don is, in fact, trafficking here in the shoals of an immature pessimism – a cynicism acquired cheaply, defensively and without close examination. Although he believes the sentiments he espouses belong to him, and require a certain audacity to utter, he is actually re-indoctrinating himself in the ethos of his power player, business mystique: Don as solitary buccaneer, the man above conventional laws, who lives hard and fast because he must, but exhibits Hemingway's difficult grace under pressure.

The spectator does not necessarily hear this speech (at least not immediately) as re-indoctrination. It might sound as though Don is articulating a code that is meant to set him apart from his peers rather than placing him comfortably in their midst. His manner of presenting his case indicates that he is someone resigned to live fatalistically, with the dark face of things steadily before him. He *never* forgets the most alarming facts about human isolation, and that social rules in toto are just a game. He proposes that tomorrow is but a senseless reiteration of the muddle confronting us today. Groping for meaningful change isn't likely to change anything, except cosmetically. Don and the viewer are equally taken aback, I suspect, by Rachel's rejoinder to Don's absurdist mission statement. She tells him that she realizes, possibly for the first time, that a man's lot is pitiable, chiefly because it shares many of the weaknesses of her own position. Don had neither sought nor anticipated pity: he felt that his avowal of a world-weary futility and his stoic persistence in a struggle without meaning would excite a fearful admiration. But it is Rachel, impressively, who is able to pinpoint exactly where Don is. She looks past his worked-up language and returns us to the supplementary language of body and face, the teeming expressive silence that his speech was intended to obscure. She directs us back to the silence of Don at the tobacco meeting, and to his prior display of helplessness. After Don nervously fends off her acknowledgement of pity for him with a stammered 'Excuse me?' Rachel fixes him with her gaze and supplies an unflinching appraisal of his existential camouflage and his true (however embarrassed) preoccupation with the pressing matter of belief. 'Mr. Draper, I don't know what it is you really believe in but I *do* know what it feels like to be out of place, to be disconnected, to see the whole world laid out in front of you, the way other people live it.'

One of Don's paramount strengths is his capacity to listen attentively to unwelcome words in tough and irksome situations. In this instance, Don seems to release his pugnacious air of death-defying bravado in a flash, and reverts to the forsaken state of inner scrambling (oh, for some, any sort of purchase on myself!) that we witnessed in his abject failure to 'come through' at the start of the tobacco meeting. It is clear that Rachel's penetrating description of Don has both surprised and unmasked him. He regards her feat of detection with a measure of distress, but at the same time he is trying on her picture of him for size, and gauging to what extent it might indeed make sense of him. He does not argue further for any portion of his previous credo. Inwardly he attends, I think, with special concentration to her idea of disconnection and distance. Yes, the world does appear to be 'laid out' plainly and in a more accessible form to others, but for him there is a persistent gulf between himself and almost anything he struggles to experience. It is the world in its baffling farawayness that is the *billboard* for him, one tableau after another awaiting an infusion of authentic life. Instead of screaming reassurance, the billboard's noise is a keening, blurred lament. To be made real enough for Don to believe in (as something of intimate proximity and concern rather than a semblance, a dumb show, a place of feigning, guarded poses), either Don or the world must give way and move closer. Belief is the strong counter-urge to Don's need for control (and thus a saving distance) at all costs.

The power of love is always linked for Draper to the rekindling of belief; it is his best means (apart from his creative bursts in his advertising sessions) of interrupting his daily struggle with inner estrangement, and of being *found* – by a discerning other – on different, ameliorating terms. His too easily activated desire is, at its best, a desire to attend, temporarily, to the possibility of another's reality: a readiness, in Gillian Rose's phrase, to 'be unsure' in someone else's presence. He craves relief from what is so much of the time a mechanized 'sureness of self'.[6] Don is, in certain respects, a male Blanche DuBois in his pattern of promiscuous courtship, seeking 'not realism, but magic'[7] from his partners, an opening for something resembling freedom, on both sides, and also, as Blanche eloquently puts it, 'a cleft in the rock of the world that I could hide in'.[8] The hiding for Don bespeaks the possibility of shortcuts to love, which might spare him love's work of knowing, and letting himself be known. Gillian Rose speaks of the comic condition, so basic to human life, of *euporia*: 'the always missing, but prodigiously imaginable, easy way'.[9] Don, of course, is almost never 'sure of himself'. He is '"sure" only of this untiring exercise', the aim of putting something over successfully. [10] It is odd and disquieting, and also amusing, that Don should exchange so readily the peace and grace found in his performance triumph earlier in the day for

---

[6] Gillian Rose, *Love's Work* (New York: NYRB, 2011), 125.
[7] Tennessee Williams, *A Streetcar Named Desire* (New York: New Directions, 1980), 145.
[8] Williams, *Streetcar Named Desire*, 147.
[9] Rose, *Love's Work*, 125.
[10] Rose, *Love's Work*, 134.

a nocturnal proclamation that nothing holds, nothing matters, and that things can only improve in the quest for meaning if one is delusional.

Don asserts to Rachel that there is no 'tomorrow', but this may be because yesterday has such an inexorable pull for him. The past is Don's exclusive, though sporadic reality focus, the place where reality makes itself felt. He is ceaselessly involved in fleeing from it, keeping it at bay, as though the past were always ready to pounce, wolf-like and ravenous. It is comic watching Don devise a quick route to seduction through an appeal to the glamour of nihilism, and then being caught in the lie, being exposed as both a *believer* and a self-deceiver. The 'mismatch between [his] aim and achievement' [11] reminds us of how tentative Don's grasp of his own 'good fortune' always is. Whenever he is touched by grace, and a vision of possible plenitude, an attendant guilt swiftly intervenes to curtail it, and casts him backwards into the dark. If his burden lightens for more than a short while and he feels raised above his own contradictions and bitterness, the most intransigent, small-time version of his 'I' awakens to protest. An earlier, truer time strikes home, the everlasting childhood hour where nothing can be pardoned, where the only law is shivering need and displacement. To cite Gillian Rose again, Don is placed 'at the mercy of his own mercilessness', [12] as is the case with so many proudly self-reliant men. Don's stammered response – and it is a *full* as well as an evasive response – to Rachel Menken's description of his 'Jewish exile' from the 'laid-out world' that belongs to privileged (mostly male) insiders is 'I don't know if that's true. (beat) Do you want another drink?'

Still later that same night, after Don has finally made his way to his literal current home, he is greeted in his bedroom by his still awake wife, Betty. This greeting is our introduction to her, and she comes as a total surprise. The improbable house, warmly lit from within, and its improbable welcoming occupant lead us to share, briefly, Don's difficulty *imagining* Betty or this secure environment as truly connected to his existence. The closing shot of the pilot episode presents us with a long shot view of Don standing between the beds of his two sleeping children, stretching out his arms to each of them simultaneously, with the accompanying sensation that they are both a bit beyond his reach. Nevertheless, his effort to make contact with them inside this space – this dream dwelling of his – is undeniably heartfelt, and achingly poignant. Betty stands at a distance watching him, a silhouette in a lighted doorway. Her literal distance as observer mirrors the distance within Don that he strains to overcome. At moments like this, he would give anything to be able to make himself something more than a mere observer of the

---

[11] Rose, *Love's Work*, 135.
[12] Rose, *Love's Work*, 136.

serene domestic picture lying spread out before him, awaiting his return. This unexpectedly piercing image of his sleeping children wants to receive him, to include him totally, yet he can't quite find his way into it. His arms, extended outward, confirm both a readiness to open himself and a desire to be a protector, to remove a disconcerting gap, to make everyone in his care safe at once. He would accomplish all this by a single, spontaneous, lived gesture (the wide reach), a gesture that ideally might gather the things that are near to his heart to himself. But the children impose the distance of their sleeping. They cannot see or feel what he is offering to them, or nearly offering. His wife, who can see, in her fashion, is too far away, and unfortunately his back is to her. The yearned-for embrace is unattainable. Don wants it to extend to everything in his life so as to make it all fit together, as though nothing within him need remain concealed or dissociated any longer. The missing parts could at last be accounted for. He would be large enough to protect this fully exposed being, this overgrown child that is Don, to shelter *him* from harm. I am reminded again of Scott Fitzgerald's Gatsby looking around wildly after declaring that 'of course you can' fix the past, 'as if the past were lurking here in the shadow of his house, just out of reach of his hand'.[13] Caught in the gap between two children settled in their own dream space, he tries to turn his arms into a bridge, for him and them to cross. He does not have enough material at his disposal to complete the span. There is not enough *of* him to make a good bridge, or to launch a rescue.

Don Draper fits into a long tradition in American literature and film of Gatsby-like figures who embark on a grand design after concocting a new identity (on the scale of a lofty childhood fantasy) and erasing their ties to a shameful past. James Gatz, like Don Draper, was the son of 'shiftless and unsuccessful farm people', who eventually found a way to re-fashion himself and to climb atop an almost entirely invented personal history. To a greater extent than Gatsby, Don manages to sell his version of the Draper persona to nearly all the people who matter in the ruthless 'new frontier' of Madison Avenue. He is not only feared but respected, and his air of unknowability enhances that respect, endowing him, as we have seen, with a potent mystique. (As Don puts it to Betty in the last episode of season one, 'The Wheel': 'No one knows why people do what they do.' Such a claim proposes that the enigma of Don, instead of being an aberration, is more or less the common lot.) As spectators we are meant, to a larger extent than we perhaps acknowledge, not only to partake of the mystique but eagerly to shore it up – as though it were as much in our own interests as Don's to preserve 'appearances'. Maybe holding on to the commanding image is a far more

---

[13] Fitzgerald, *The Great Gatsby*, 117.

palatable key to a workable identity than the messy pains of self-awareness. What is most unusual about the Draper persona is that it emerges from the shell of so many ruinous failures in male roles: he fails as a soldier in Korea, receives a Purple Heart under false pretences, fails to secure the affection of his impoverished parents and step-parent, and lays to waste the love that he does receive from his younger brother, whom he coldly repudiates in a crisis and inadvertently drives to suicide. Draper never finishes high school (leaves, in fact, less than halfway through) and is borderline illiterate. Finally, he obtains his major job break through flimflamming and wheedling, and is utterly unable (the reverse of Gatsby) to live up for long to any romantic commitment. His 'romantic readiness' is persistently undone by a fear of closeness, the unhinging terrors of dependency.

Like many isolated American heroes – Natty Bumppo, Captain Ahab, Huck Finn, the Thoreau of *Walden*, Thomas Sutpen in *Absalom, Absalom!* –he lives in fear of belonging too fully to a constricting social order, yet all of his work in advertising depends on his inspired fantasies of belonging. As I hope to have demonstrated in my reading of the Lucky Strike scene, which is the template for so many later instances of 'breakthrough', the solutions that seem to matter most in *Mad Men*'s fretwork of tawdry, emotionally deficient dreams and aspirations are advertising solutions. Or rather, the puzzle is always how to give an advertising image a temporary foundation of perilous conviction. On the one hand, *Mad Men* seems bent on confirming our long-held notion that selling products is venal and superficial, an enterprise steeped in deception. But secretly, advertising in *Mad Men* is enshrined as the most compelling locus of the creative imagination in full swing. Don's haunted negotiation with his emotional impasses and the 'vacant lot' of his selfhood achieves its provisional gains in the meetings where gossamer ad fancies find substance and take wing. Don gives voice repeatedly to his own deepest longings through ad inspiration, and his longings overlap, more often than not, with the part of us that shares Don's sense of exile. The ad visions are Don's most valuable means of linking himself closely to others, in an ironically reduced version of the struggle for democracy. Don's unconscious spawns gleaming reveries that will hold for the multitude, vividly articulated poems of fulfilment in which Don's person is somehow released from its habitual captivity and, like a figure reborn, scrubbed clean.

The most often cited segment of the entire series – Don's unveiling of the Kodak Carousel in the final episode of season one – is in some sense a replay of the Lucky Strike scene. It manages to unite Don's crucial discovery of a place to stand (where one is restored to self-acceptance and cohesiveness) with a mature, near-tragic recognition of loss. Loss is presented, indissolubly, as a thing of beauty, as well as a vehicle of imagined return. Don tells the

Kodak representatives that nostalgia provides a 'deeper bond' with a product than the more superficial excitement over newness. Nostalgia induces 'a twinge in the heart' that connects one more delicately and potently to objects than memory can on its own. He supplies a literal ancient Greek definition of nostalgia as the grounding for his pitch: 'the pain from an old wound'. This wound lends a counterpoint of blight to the pageant of wistfully reassuring slide images of Draper's own wife and children performing the rituals of family life in his company. In a previous scene, Don has talked about the caves of Lescaux with Harry, a member of his staff who is for the time being obliged to live in his office at Sterling-Cooper after his wife (whom he loves and keenly misses) threw him out of their home. Harry wonders about the handprints that the primitive cave dweller artists placed alongside other pictures of their life experiences on the walls. Harry felt, during his visit to the caves, the presence for an instant of 'someone reaching through the stone', right to him. It was as though 'I was him'. In the Kodak meeting, as Draper clicks his way through an assortment of his own visual handprints, arranged as a story of America in the demonstration carousel, he views his own photographed image repeatedly and persuasively in physical contact with loved ones. In one slide a child is resting on him, in another a child is being lifted up, in each instance Don smiles under a pleasing and effortless weight. He recognizes himself as *literally* taking part, being right in their midst, so in that sense he was *Don*, that unmistakable figure resurrected by the mechanically whirring time machine, *being there*. And yet, as many of us feel revisiting photos commemorating days of imagined felicity, there can be a wall as thick as stone separating us from our face and the role we assumed for the camera, to meet expectations. The aloneness, the apartness are faintly inscribed in the frozen visual record of that outing or ordinary bit of daily doing, like the 'pain from an old wound'.

My point then is that Don is looking at (and contending with) more than slide snapshots documenting happier times. It is not simply the case of photographs transmitting the ache of distance from experiences that had once been undeniably possessed and *felt*. Rather, I think, Don confronts his absence and exclusion *then*, in the time of pleasure, as though the images supplied a piercing burden of proof. Don witnesses a sleepwalker onscreen, going through the motions in a dreamland of life possibilities. (In one slide he is actually asleep on a sofa, with his daughter lying on his chest, asleep as well, as if in imitation. His son peers out, from a standing position beside the couch, self-consciously striking an awkward pose of collectedness for the camera-wielding spy to snap.) Sensing his failure to find the key of belonging then (and giving it a turn as one might to open a familiar, welcoming door), Don discovers, from his remote viewing distance that he might have the capacity to do so now. He sees – or imagines he sees – a way to make himself known and available to these expectant, forgiving others lit up in the images, to make his presence felt by them more strongly. All it would take is a modest inner adjustment, an emotional adding-in to the not quite fixed and final slide glimpses he beholds in the Carousel. The key, as it were, lies in his hand: the remote control button. He can touch it, like the alien hand that is his own pressing toward him through the stone of 'lost time', reviving the past and in so doing curing it. *Now* Don is awake; he has shaken off the sleepwalking stupor. He can feel his way in, past the strained stances and shadowy hurt and suppression. He can pour in the fatherly/husbandly balm that will mend the wounds in these quietly forsaken tableaux, and restore them to life (however belated his arrival).

Don has learned a short while ago that his younger brother, Adam, whose connection to him he refused to acknowledge and take up again, has committed suicide – anonymously – in a squalid hotel room. *That* wound, that severed tie, that lost, squandered remnant of Don's family history, are without remedy. Adam's rejected appeal to him, in its utter irreversibility, is surely in Don's mind as he runs his slide show for the Kodak executives. Don tells his audience in the darkened room that the carousel 'lets us travel the way a child travels … round and round and back home again, to a place where we know we are loved'. For a child, time can always move in more than one direction. It is never impossible for a bad situation to be undone, taken care of, by some wonder-working enchantment. A deus-ex-machina could always come clanking to the rescue, even if the odds are against it. Even death doesn't quite feel irrevocable. And home, that fluid entity, can be any door which, when opened, reveals someone behind it who is able to love us: as much as we deserve, or better.

Earlier in this season finale episode, Don's wife, Betty, desperate for someone to talk to, begs a young boy from her neighborhood who once requested a lock of her hair when she babysat him to listen to her for a few moments. Spotting him in a parking lot as he sits waiting for his own mother in the front seat of a car, she appeals to him for support through the 'screen' of a half closed car window, hovering helplessly next to the vehicle as the apprehensive child remains at a loss for what to say. 'Adults don't know anything', she tells him. At the end of her rope, Betty, an arrested child in so many ways herself, can think of no one other than this boy whom she might confide in during her crisis. After all, he had previously let her know that he *liked* her. Maybe he could elaborate on what he understood about her, and begin to explain who she is. The best he can offer is his mittened hand, which he is quick to withdraw after she takes it in hers. 'The Wheel' episode concludes with Don returning by commuter train to his house in the suburbs. His Kodak Carousel pitch (where the merry-go-round image seems to explain everything) has been rapturously received, and the resolutions he has made while performing the pitch are still alive for him. The viewer might begin to understand, after being moved by the Carousel talk himself, Jeanne Randolph's startling claim that somewhere around 1950, advertising surreptitiously but triumphantly took over the work of philosophy.[14] Don imagines, while homeward bound on the speeding train, that he might with luck arrive in time to accompany his family on a Thanksgiving weekend trip to the home of Betty's parents. (We recall that he had previously told a morosely reticent Betty that there would be no chance of his being able to get away from work.) We are shown two versions of his homecoming. The first, which does not feel like a fantasy as it unfolds, but proves to be after it draws to an inconclusive close, presents Betty reacting to his arrival in her customary stiff, emotionally wary state. Don's imagination has not found a plausible means of appreciably lightening her mood. She appears somewhat surprised at his change of plans, and mildly pleased, if confused, by his notable increase in responsiveness and availability. Don's daughter and son are considerably more elated by the prospect of their father joining them on the trip, but even in their case one has the sense of Don pushing for immediate results, willing his children into an ebullient, festive spirit that is hardly natural for them.

In the second homecoming, the *real* version, Draper enters an empty house. He has once again, staying true to his blurred role in the slide show, 'missed the moment', domestically. The family has departed without him, lacking any awareness of his projected, conciliatory gesture. In the fantasy, conceived in the afterglow of the Kodak presentation, Don was able to keep faith with the child's 'round and round' impression of reversible time, and like an emotional miracle worker, make good on his replenished chances for atonement. Don acquires (in his daydream of homecoming) Gatsby's knack of smiling his way past all resistance and seeming to face the whole external world for an instant, as though embracing and subduing its propensity for otherness. With the world on a string, he concentrates on the 'you-ness' of the heretofore isolated members of his family, displaying an 'irresistible prejudice' in favour of each of them in turn. His smile, like Gatsby's, 'understood you just as far as you wanted to be understood, believed in you as you would like to believe in yourself … Precisely at that instant [the smile] vanished.' [15] But the real homecoming is to a sad echo chamber. Adrift in his now doubly empty house, Don is restored to a chastened awareness of

---

[14] Jeanne Randolph, *Ethics of Luxury: Materialism and Imagination* (Winnipeg: YYZ Books, 2007), 35.
[15] Fitzgerald, *The Great Gatsby*, 48.

how things presently stand when his calling out is met with a pale, smoky, dispiriting silence. Don sits down, not in a chair, but on one of the lower steps of a stairway leading upwards behind him. He tries to take stock of his circumstances. He is subdued, perhaps despondent, no doubt freshly mindful of the difficulty of rekindling authentic connection, but not, I think, defeated. He has not abandoned his resolve to retrieve, somehow, more of the invigorating, demanding promises of life. The camera is moving in the downstairs area, for a short while managing to keep Don in sight, then, almost imperceptibly, losing him. He vanishes before having the impulse to turn around and look upwards. The ascending stairs loom, ambiguously, above him. He might accept their invitation to lift his gaze to a higher imaginative plane. The Dylan song, 'Don't Think Twice', plays over the end credits, its title reminding us of Don's double-ply effort to get home, and his failure to do so even when he is actually there. And yet Don Draper's drive to find placement, belief, a sure center above his helplessness that would allow him to give himself back whole to those he might finally learn to love, is still intact. He knows there are further moves to make, moves that will count for something, in due time. 'So don't think twice, it's all right.'

Bibliography

Fitzgerald, F. Scott. *The Great Gatsby*. New York: Charles Scribner's Sons, 1953.

Kerr, Walter. *The Silent Clowns*. New York: Alfred Knopf, 1975.

Randolph, Jeanne. *Ethics of Luxury: Materialism and Imagination*. Winnipeg: YYZ Books, 2007.

Rose, Gillian. *Love's Work*. New York: NYRB, 2011.

Trotter, David. *Cinema and Modernism*. Oxford: Blackwell Publishing, 2007.

Warshow, Robert. *The Immediate Experience*, enlarged edn. Cambridge, MA: Harvard University Press, 2002.

Williams, Tennessee. *A Streetcar Named Desire*. New York: New Directions, 1980.

12

Justifying *Justified*

William Rothman

Graham Yost has described his goal in creating *Justified* as bringing to life the world of Leonard's crime fiction, a world whose denizens, good talkers all, speak in the distinctive patterns that have garnered the author universal praise for his dialogue. The series is based on 'Fire in the Hole', a 2002 Elmore Leonard short story.[1] Timothy Olyphant, who proved in *Deadwood* how cool he looks in a cowboy hat, plays the story's protagonist, Deputy US Marshal Raylan Givens. The pilot, written by Yost himself, follows Leonard's story with remarkable fidelity, borrowing from it almost everything the characters do and say. Nonetheless, I argue in what follows, the pilot takes on a life of its own. And in doing so, it exceeds the story on which it is based. 'Fire in the Hole' is a very good story. But *Justified* is great television. Is it the equal of *Deadwood*? Perhaps not. *Deadwood* is staggering in the magnitude of its ambition and achievement. *Justified*'s achievement is more humble. It would be a mistake, though, to underestimate its deceptively modest virtues.

In a *New York Times* review of the story collection that included 'Fire in the Hole', Janet Maslin observed that Leonard's great gift is to be able to 'invent coolheaded characters who leap off the page, equip them with pricelessly terse dialogue and dream up the kinds of plots that might have worked for O. Henry if O. Henry had had a serious interest in lowlife, double-crossing, and crime'.[2] The reviewer for the *San Jose Mercury News* added the complementary insight that the voice in which Leonard's stories are told conveys

---

[1] Elmore Leonard, 'Fire in the Hole', in *When the Women Come Out to Dance: Stories* (New York: HarperCollins, 2002), 57–112.
[2] Janet Maslin, 'Nine Tales From the Underside, Where the Talk Is Terse: review of *When the Woman Come Out to Dance* by Elmore Leonard', *The New York Times*, December 16, 2002.

'a hint of what lordly amusement would sound like if God had worked at a Detroit ad agency'.[3] This lordly, amused narrator is the irreplaceable one of those 'coolheaded characters who leap off the page' that it is Leonard's gift to be able to invent.

Never standing on grammatical ceremony, the narrator's voice melds seamlessly with the voices of the characters whose stories he is telling, helping to give Leonard's prose its propulsive forward movement. In 'Fire in the Hole', the narrator continually segues – within single paragraphs, even single sentences – between quoting characters, paraphrasing them, asserting what they're feeling, thinking, imagining or remembering, and expressing his own thoughts. Typical is the exchange between Raylan and his boss Art Mullen (played in *Justified* by the great Nick Searcy), which sets up Raylan's fateful visit to the home of Ava Crowder (Joelle Carter in the series), who they hope will help them smoke out Boyd Crowder (Walton Goggins), her dead husband's brother, whom they suspect of blowing up a black church. (In the pilot, we see him do it.)

> Not a bad idea, Art saying yeah, that could bring him out. Saying then, 'There's another situation could do it. You know Bowman, Boyd's brother?' Raylan saw him in a football uniform. 'Sorta. He was a star running back in high school – this was after I got out. Boyd was always talking about him, how Bowman had the goods and would go on to play college ball and become a pro. I was never that sure.' Art said, 'You remember the girl he married, Ava?' Raylan's tone came alive as he said, 'Ava, yeah, she lived down the street from us.' He remembered her eyes. 'She's married to Bowman?' 'Was,' Art said. 'She ended the union the other day with a thirty-ought-six, plugged him through the heart.'[4]

Does the narrator identify with these characters whose thoughts are transparent to him and whose voices he mimics so deftly? His 'lordly amusement' conveys the impression, rather, that he takes himself to be a bit superior to them. Then again, the characters in the story – especially the men – are wont to look down on each other. The 'hint of lordly amusement' with which the narrator tells this story about characters who are (he wants us to know) open books to him reveals – despite himself, I want to say – his affinity with them. No less than the Sydney Greenstreet character in in *The Maltese Falcon*, Elmore Leonard likes a man who likes to talk, whether he be a criminal

---

[3]David L. Beck, 'No Mystery About It: Leonard's a Master Storyteller: review of *When the Woman Come Out to Dance* by Elmore Leonard', *San Jose Mercury News*, 5 January 2003.
[4]Elmore Leonard, 'Fire in the Hole', 73.

mastermind like Boyd, the colourful but clueless lowlife types who follow him, or a hero like Raylan, who struggles to reconcile the code of law vested in his badge with his own morality, symbolised by his cowboy hat.

Boyd is Raylan's nemesis. He's also a kind of soul mate. That he's Raylan's match as a sardonic wordsmith is evident from their charged exchange just before the climactic shootout in which – in the story, but not in the pilot – he mortally wounds Boyd:

> 'Your forty-five's on the table but I have to pull,' Raylan said. 'Is that how we do it?' 'Well, shit yeah, it's my call. What're you packing?' 'You'll pay to find that out,' Raylan said. 'Ice water in your veins, huh? You want a shot of Jim Beam to go with it?'[5]

The narrator is too amused by these characters, too intent on impressing on the reader that he, too, has ice water in his veins, to plumb their depths – or his own. Is this a failure of Leonard's writing? Rather, it's a condition of the story's way of achieving closure, of being complete unto itself. *Justified*'s pilot must *not* be complete unto itself. Viewers must perceive that beneath the ground it stakes out are rich veins to be mimed in episodes to come. But how is this even possible, given that its characters' actions and words are substantially unchanged from a story that is self-contained, complete in itself? How is it possible for the pilot to reveal in these characters depths unsuspected by Leonard's narrator – as it must if it is to fulfil its mandate *as* a pilot?

Part of the answer resides in the alterations the pilot does make to the original story. More crucial, however, is the fact that a television drama, like a movie, *shows* rather than *tells*. And the people the pilot shows are not the story's characters, although they fit their descriptions, have the same M.O.'s, and mostly speak the same words. The people on the television screen are flesh-and-blood human beings, subjects of a camera that really filmed them. Viewers don't have to imagine Raylan, but they also lack the freedom to do so. Compensating for this loss of freedom is the fact that the story cannot enable readers to imagine *this* Raylan. The Raylan Timothy Olyphant incarnates on screen is a particular human being. And because human faces and bodies and voices possess 'remarkable expressiveness', as Emerson puts it in his late essay 'Behavior', the pilot grants us access to a kind of beauty, a kind of poetry, out of reach of the story on which it is based.

Justified is realized so masterfully that it almost unfailingly achieves what Stanley Cavell calls the 'poetry of the ordinary', the perception that 'every motion and station, in particular every human posture and gesture, however

---

[5] Elmore Leonard, 'Fire in the Hole', 109.

glancing, has its poetry, or ... its lucidity'.[6] Leonard's readers cannot see in their mind's eye what viewers see with their own eyes when just these human beings, in just these settings, in just these situations, framed in just these ways, perform just these gestures. Nor can readers imagine the moods they express, and cast, when they break their silence to speak just these words in just these voices. The character Elmore Leonard invented can no more be the pilot's Raylan than George Kaplan, the character the Professor invented, can be Roger Thornhill, the human being Cary Grant incarnates as well as the character he plays in *North by Northwest* – a man 'with the holiday in his eye, who is fit to stand the gaze of millions' as Cavell (quoting Emerson's essay 'Manners') describes Grant, on screen, in *His Girl Friday*.[7]

In the pilot, Timothy Olyphant's Raylan – like Walton Goggins' Boyd, Nick Searcy's Art, Joelle Carter's Ava and Natalie Zea's Winona (and, in the second season, Margo Martindale's monstrous yet all too human matriarch Mags; with Mags, the series hits the mother lode) – incarnates, in the way every real human being does, the mystery of human identity: the fact that we are mysteries to each other and to ourselves; that our identities aren't fixed, that we are in the process of becoming. In the pilot, Raylan possesses an unfathomable depth, a dimension of unknownness, that cannot simply be the invention of a writer. Graham Yost didn't have to be the George Hearst of *Deadwood* to recognize that, to paraphrase the John Barrymore character in *Twentieth Century*, the gold is there – it is there in the camera's subjects, in the world recreated in its own image on the screen. Leonard's story provides Yost and his creative team with an instrument for mining it.

The ending of 'Fire in the Hole' is the exception that proves the rule that the story's Raylan lacks the depth Timothy Olyphant's Raylan brings to the screen:

> Art Mullen arrived wanting to know how the rear end of the Town Car got fragged, but saved asking when he saw Boyd on the floor. Raylan stood by, relating the scene step by step as Art rolled Boyd over to look at the exit wound.... 'He have any last words?' 'He said I'd killed him.' Raylan paused. 'I told him I was sorry, but he had called it.' Art was frowning now. 'You're sorry you killed him?' 'I thought I explained it to you,' Raylan said in his quiet voice. 'Boyd and I dug coal together.'[8]

---

[6] Stanley Cavell, 'The Thought of Movies', in *Cavell on Film*, ed. William Rothman (Albany: State University of New York Press, 2005), 96.

[7] Stanley Cavell, *Pursuits of Happiness: The Hollywood Comedy of Remarriage* (Cambridge, MA: Harvard University Press, 1981), 235.

[8] Elmore Leonard, 'Fire in the Hole', 109.

The phrase 'in his quiet voice' (rather than 'in a quiet voice') conveys that Raylan speaks the last line in a voice typical for him, not in an emotional voice. Nor does the narrator's voice betray emotion, whether Raylan's or his own. That Raylan is moved is conveyed only by the author's device – its effect can't be typical; no story can use it more than once – of letting Raylan have the story's last word – as if Raylan's quiet voice silences the narrator, who doesn't know what to say. There's nothing the narrator *can* say in *his* typical voice. And for the narrator to drop his mask of 'lordly amusement' would be like Raylan venturing hatless into the world. Ain't gonna happen. (The *Justified* episode titled 'Hatless' revolves around an exception that proves *this* rule.)

Walton Goggins is so charismatic that if in the pilot Raylan *had* aimed for Boyd's heart, the series would have taken the bullet. Because Boyd survives the shooting, the pilot has to alter the story's last scene. It is not to Art but to Ava, who isn't sorry – nor are we – that she had killed her abusive husband, that Raylan explains that he was sorry he had to shoot Boyd because they had 'dug coal together'. There is no narrator whose attitude filters our access to the characters. Whatever is revealed *to* the camera is revealed *by* the camera. From Joelle Carter's reaction to Raylan's words, we know that Raylan's explanation resonates with Ava. In the pilot, Ava, too, is deeper than her counterpart in the story. As a daughter of Harlan County, she knows the immutable bond forged between men who stared down the angel of death when they were miners together. And she has had a crush on Raylan, and he has wanted to kiss her, since they were minors together. Now that she and Raylan, too, have stared down the angel of death together, Ava has reason to hope that an immutable bond has now been forged between them.

In both story and pilot, sparks fly when Raylan and Ava first find themselves face to face after so many years. 'Ava was forty now,' Leonard's masterful passage begins, 'but he knew those eyes staring at him and she knew him, saying, "Oh my God – Raylan," in kind of a prayerful tone.'[9] Making Ava's words be 'Oh my God – Raylan' slyly intimates that he *is* her God. The slyness is Leonard's, not Ava's nor even the narrator's. But the narrator's gratuitous 'kind of' adds his typical 'hint of lordly amusement' to the implication that Raylan's arrival at her door is, for Ava, a prayer answered, a miracle.

The passage goes on:

'You remember me, huh?' Ava pushed the door closed. She said, 'I never forgot you,' and went into his arms as he offered them, a girl he used to like now a woman who'd shot and killed her husband and wanted to be held. He could tell, he could feel her hands holding on to him. She raised

---

[9]Elmore Leonard, 'Fire in the Hole', 77.

her face to say, 'I can't believe you're here.' He kissed her on the cheek. She kept staring at him with those eyes and he kissed her on the mouth … He saw her eyes close, her hands slipping around his neck, and this time it became a serious kiss … Now he didn't know what to say. He didn't know why he kissed her other than he wanted to. He could remember wanting to even when she was a teen.[10]

When this woman who has never forgotten Raylan is incarnated by Joelle Carter, and when the actress plays this scene the way she does, we no more look down on Ava than on Raylan, who has never stopped wanting to kiss the girl with 'those eyes'. In the pilot, 'those eyes' belong to an actress who is sexy in this scene not because Raylan – or the camera – 'objectifies' her, but because Ava's passionate desire, her longing for love, her *subjectivity*, shines so radiantly in Joelle Carter's eyes.

Raylan can tell that Ava wants to be held, the narrator says, but without saying whether Raylan can tell that what she wants is to be held by *him*. After their kiss becomes 'serious', we are told that Raylan – like the narrator himself at story's end – doesn't know what to say. Raylan would know what to say if he knew he had a reason for kissing Ava other than that he wanted to. Whether he has such a reason is something the story's Raylan doesn't know about himself. Nor is he troubled by this. Or, if it does trouble Raylan that he doesn't know himself, that is something the narrator doesn't know about him, or doesn't find worthy of mention.

At the end of 'Fire in the Hole', Art frowns when Raylan tells him what he said to Boyd after shooting him. At the end of the pilot, what troubles Art is that Raylan had *failed* to aim for Boyd's heart. In the story, there's no suggestion that Raylan finds it troubling that Art is troubled by him. In the pilot, Raylan *is* troubled by this. More generally, he is troubled by what he knows, and what he doesn't know, about himself. 'When is killing justified?' is a question the pilot raises, as does every episode in the series. And this question is inseparable from the questions, 'What kind of person is Raylan? What kind of person does he wish to be?'

That these questions haunt Raylan is explicit in the little scene that ends the pilot, a scene that has no equivalent in the story. Beer bottle in hand, Raylan shows up in the middle of the night at Winona's home, sneaking in through the garden door and almost giving a heart attack to current husband Gary (William Ragsdale).

In *Justified*, Raylan and Winona have no children, but in Leonard's story they have two sons who live in Georgia with their mother and step-father.

---

[10] Elmore Leonard, 'Fire in the Hole', 78.

Given *Justified*'s emphasis on father–son relationships, especially in its first season, these sons would have been another rich vein to mine. They would have been an encumbrance, though, to the renewal of Raylan's romantic relationship with his ex-wife, which proves an even richer vein that the series mines, at least in the first two seasons, in ways that link it intricately with the great Hollywood movies of the 1930s and 1940s that Stanley Cavell calls 'comedies of remarriage' in *Pursuits of Happiness*, his seminal study of the genre that includes such classic romantic comedies as *It Happened One Night*, *The Awful Truth*, *Bringing Up Baby*, *His Girl Friday*, *The Philadelphia Story*, *The Lady Eve* and *Adam's Rib*. The series comes by this inheritance naturally, insofar as Benjamin Cavell is one of *Justified*'s regular writers. *Justified* has done Ben's father proud. Father–son relationships, indeed!

Raylan's ex-wife is the only person to whom Raylan feels he can, and must, confess at least part of what is troubling him. In the pilot's opening scene, we see Raylan kill a man in Miami under circumstances so questionable he is transferred to the Lexington, Kentucky office, uncomfortably close to Harlan, where he was born and raised and where Arlo (Raymond Barry), his wily criminal father, still lives. The fear Raylan confesses to Winona is that he would have killed that man, in his eyes a murderer who deserved to die, even if he hadn't drawn his gun first; the fear that he had no reason to kill him other than that he wanted to; the fear that he, too, is a killer by nature. 'I've never thought of myself as an angry man', Raylan says thoughtfully. Winona replies, firmly but gently, as if to a child, but with a hint of amusement less 'lordly' than seductive, 'You're good at hiding it and most people may not see it, but you're the angriest person I have ever known.'

Raylan's silence acknowledges that Winona knows him better than he knows himself. How can he not wish for his relationship with this woman to have a future as well as a past? He can't have this kind of conversation with Ava. And yet, Ava, too, knows something about her hero that he doesn't know about himself – the fact that he *is* a hero. Ava is the part of what is troubling Raylan that he finds himself unwilling to confess to Winona. His desire for Ava, and hers for him, has reawakened his desire for his ex-wife. We sense that Raylan will eventually have to choose between them. But he doesn't yet know which woman he really wants.

Real estate agent Gary strikes Raylan – as he strikes us – as unworthy of Winona. Later episodes will bear this out, but not before we – and Raylan – learn that Gary possesses a trait that Winona isn't foolish for valuing so highly. Unlike Raylan, Gary knows what he wants. And to get and keep what he wants, he will move heaven and earth – and hell as well, as it turns out. To win her, Raylan will have to claim her, as the Cary Grant character must do to win back his ex-wife in *The Awful Truth*, *His Girl Friday* and *The Philadelphia Story*, three definitive remarriage comedies. To do so, he will have to overcome the passive, fatalistic streak in his nature that resonates with the Oscar Wilde line Hitchcock never tired of quoting, 'Each man kills the thing he loves.' The series teaches us to think of this darkness as the Harlan in Raylan's nature. No one has expressed it more hauntingly than Brad Paisley, in the song that accompanies the credits at the end of the second season finale:

> In the deep dark hills of eastern Kentucky
> That's the place where I trace my bloodline
> And it's there I read on a hillside gravestone
> 'You will never leave Harlan alive.'[11]

Harlan is a real place not far from modern Lexington, which might as well be – and in the series *is* – Los Angeles. But in *Justified*, Harlan is also a mythical place, as it was in Barbara Kopple's 1976 Oscar-winning documentary *Harlan County, USA*. Harlan pulls the series closer to the world Flannery O'Connor, or even *Medea*, than to the world of Elmore Leonard's crime fiction. As the series progresses, Raylan finds himself less engaged in the everyday work of a US Marshal and increasingly committed to the mission – at once a moral obligation and a spiritual quest – of saving this Chinatown of family feuds, corruption, corporate greed and drugs from being engulfed by chaos and violence. Between Ava and Winona, Raylan will choose Winona. But how can he possibly choose between this mission, which is his and his alone, and his dream of walking together with Winona, every day and every night, in the direction of what Emerson in 'History' calls the 'unattained yet attainable self'?

Raylan's dilemma is akin to that of Jeff, the Robert Mitchum character in *Out of the Past*, Jacques Tourneur's great film noir. But Jeff differs from Raylan in that he comes to know what he wants and struggles valiantly, if ultimately unsuccessfully, to extricate himself from his past so he can be free to marry the woman who loves him for who he is. Then again, Jeff doesn't trace his bloodline to the deep dark hills of eastern Kentucky.

---

[11] Brad Paisley, 'You'll Never Leave Harlan Alive.' As performed on his CD 'Part II' (Nashville, Arista Records, 2001).

Bibliography

Beck, David L. 'No Mystery About It: Leonard's a Master Storyteller: review of *When the Woman Come Out to Dance* by Elmore Leonard.' *San Jose Mercury News*, 5 January 2003.

Cavell, Stanley. *Pursuits of Happiness: The Hollywood Comedy of Remarriage*. Cambridge, MA: Harvard University Press, 1981.

—'The Thought of Movies.' In *Cavell on Film*, edited by William Rothman. Albany: State University of New York Press, 2005.

Leonard, Elmore. 'Fire in the Hole.' In *When the Women Come Out to Dance: Stories*. New York: HarperCollins, 2002.

Maslin, Janet. 'Nine Tales From the Underside, Where the Talk Is Terse: review of *When the Woman Come Out to Dance* by Elmore Leonard.' *The New York Times*, December 16, 2002.

13

HBO aesthetics, quality television and *Boardwalk Empire*

Janet McCabe

HBO's original series *Boardwalk Empire* (2010–) set in Atlantic City in 1920, on the eve of Prohibition, opens with an iris-in on a close up of a ticking period-perfect pocket watch. A fog envelops the smugglers' whiskey-boat adrift at night; beyond the jurisdiction of US border control. At once visually poetic, ethereal textures created by hues of midnight blue conjure ghostly echoes of films like *L'Atalante* (Jean Vigo, 1934), while offering an atmospheric tableau of beguiling menace. Next the scene shifts to a night-time heist in the New Jersey backwoods and then jumps back three days to a Women's Temperance League meeting held in Atlantic City. Both events deftly sketch the broader historic canvas defined by mobsters and moralists, profiteers and prohibitionists. The sepia-toned colour palette, chiaroscuro lighting and bravura tracking shots determine the distinctive look of this period piece told in a televisual present tense. Every detail from a cameo brooch to the silk threads of the temperance society's embroidered banners and a poster linking alcoholism with delinquency speak eloquently of a 1920s-specific vernacular. In delving into the past through these various acts of retrieval – of historical objects, formal techniques and iconography, US myths and generic memories – the aesthetics and visual style of the Pilot announce ambition. It visualizes an entangled, layered 'after-life' of images and historic objects, re-imagined into original television drama. This project involves a discursive dialogue involving aesthetic choices and film style *producing* historical verisimilitude, of understanding the past alive in the present; but the Pilot also propagates knowledge of HBO as a patron of TV creativity and its role within American cultural life. No wonder the lavish 80-minute Pilot filmed on Super 35 film, and using the latest VFX technologies, is allegedly the most expensive ever made in television history – reportedly costing around $18m (£11.5m)[1] – and won its director Martin Scorsese the 2011 Emmy for Directing of a Drama Series.

So far, so impeccably crafted. So staged to aesthetic perfection, in fact, that some critics sensed that 'the show was trying just that bit too hard to tick all the boxes … [and] there was something rather lifeless about it'.[2] Still, the creative intent of the *Boardwalk Empire* Pilot is exactly the type of original television we have come to expect from HBO, the premiere US subscription cable channel that has given us *The Sopranos* (1999–2007), *Deadwood* (2004–6), *The Wire* (2002–8) and the critically acclaimed miniseries, *John Adams* (2008). Since relying ever more on prestigious, big budget original programming to entice subscribers to pay the extra monthly fee, HBO has been occupied in a purposeful rebranding strategy to create a sense of itself as a purveyor of contemporary television art. Ex-HBO chairman and CEO Chris Albrecht even went as far as to claim, 'HBO is more than a place; it's an idea … In certain cases; it's like the Medicis, like we're patrons of the arts.'[3] Referencing directly the Renaissance mercantile family who sponsored a revolution in art is telling; it speaks directly to how HBO has taken meticulous care to institutionally position itself – while never letting us forget to think about the company – as *the* benefactor of an extraordinary wave of accomplishment in television drama that tell important stories for a nation. Such rhetoric also makes visible how HBO has imposed itself as a model for producing the highest quality television possible in the post-1996, post-network era.[4] The channel enforces specific notions of TV creativity by placing a high premium on selling its distinctive brand as something worth paying for each and every month, something that subscribers cannot get elsewhere.[5] The company has actively created an exclusive dominion, branding itself as producing television for anyone with discriminating cultural taste; or, as Amanda Lotz put it, 'HBO thrives by defying programme standards that appeal to the mass audience, and succeeds by exploiting limited access as the means of acceptance as

---

[1]Cynthia Littleton, 'HBO Lays Big-Bucks Bet on *Boardwalk*', *Variety*, 7 August 2010, http://www. variety.com/article/VR1118022673?refCatId=14 [accessed 29 November 2011].
[2]John Crace, 'TV Review: *Boardwalk Empire*', *The Guardian*, 2 February 2011, http://www.guardian. co.uk/tv-and-radio/2011/feb/02/tv-review-boardwalk-empire [accessed 19 April 2012].
[3]Bill Carter, 'He Lit Up HBO. Now He Must Run It', *The New York Times*, 20 July 2002, C11.
[4]Melissa Grego, 'Feared Yet Respected', *Variety* (Special on HBO at 30), 4 November 2002, A1–A2, A5.
[5]Deborah Jaramillo, 'The Family Racket: AOL-Time Warner, HBO, *The Sopranos* and the Construction of a Quality Brand', *Journal of Communication Inquiry* 26:1 (2002): 59–75.

high (or at least higher) elite art.'[6] The channel implants notions of exclusive access and an elevated sense of cultural and commercial worth into its original programming philosophy, which, in turn, translates elite values into aesthetic sensibilities and TV style. HBO has thus come to define and *make visible* the contemporary era of television art, and how the channel institutionalised that discourse of cultural prestige, power and influence into signature shows like *Boardwalk Empire* is the subject of my work here.

This chapter dissects the aesthetic sensibilities of the *Boardwalk Empire* Pilot. It explores how images and formal techniques are excavated, and established reputations appropriated, to announce and authenticate the importance of this creative endeavour from HBO. The layering of these borrowed iconographies and formal strategies helps create historical verisimilitude for a period rarely depicted on screen. The Pilot thus puts into discourse the unique response of the series to history, deliberately echoing past visual forms, techniques and genres *in* and *through* how its cinematography, aesthetics choices and VFX technologies conserves but reinterprets, to create prestigious television, a HBO original. Written by Terence Winter, the Emmy award-winning writer of *The Sopranos*, directed by Scorsese, and starring Steve Buscemi as politician-cum-criminal kingpin Enoch 'Nucky' Thompson, the first episode of the period drama set in 1920 Atlantic City, as the Volstead Act passed into law, had pedigree. It did seem, at first glance at least, that the show was as close as it got to a sure thing for HBO. With what Alessandra Stanley called, 'an artful reworking of the gangster myth',[7] *Boardwalk Empire* represented a bid by the channel to 'reclaim their crown as the masters of art-TV'[8] after losing its momentum in the mid-2000s and conceding creative ground to commercial rivals, Showtime (*Queer as Folk*, *The L Word*, *Dexter* and *Nurse Jackie*), FX (*The Shield*, *Nip/Tuck*, *Rescue Me* and *Damages*) and AMC (*Mad Men*, *Breaking Bad*). But the artistic and financial risk taken with *Boardwalk Empire* as somehow unique, something innovative, found HBO careful to manage what made its expensive new gangster epic stand out as a beacon of originality in the competitive television market.

Boardwalk Empire features powerful mobsters and ambitious musclemen and tells of greed, ambition and criminal corruption fuelled by bootleg liquor.

---

[6] Amanda Lotz quoted in Avi Santos, 'Para-Television and Discourses of Distinction', in *It's Not TV: Watching HBO in the Post-Television Era*, (eds) Marc Leverette *et al.* (New York: Routledge, 2008), 33.

[7] Alessandra Stanley, 'Jersey Shore, the Early Years', *The New York Times*, 16 September 2010, http://tv.nytimes.com/2010/09/17/arts/television/17boardwalk.html?pagewanted=all [accessed 23 November 2011].

[8] Benji Wilson, '*Boardwalk Empire*, HBO, Review', *The Telegraph*, 20 September 2010, , http://www.telegraph.co.uk/culture/tvandradio/8013543/Boardwalk-Empire-HBO-review.html [accessed 23 November 2011].

Nothing especially new, except for how that story, set in an era rarely depicted on film, let alone television, is told *in* and *through* its stylistically ornate and expensive-looking *mise en scène*. John Thornton Caldwell[9] charts the increased emphasis of excessive style on US television during the 1980s and the HBO originals are products of that encroachment. Nevertheless the channel has transformed that tradition into a 'rebirth' of television style, in parallel with the rise of new technologies, as well as institutional developments and business practices which occurred after 1996. If, as Jason Jacobs[10] claims, we can only determine the value of a television text by looking at it, then HBO has institutionalised that idea with programmes that command our undivided cultural attention. HBO want its texts to matter – and none matter more than the Pilots.

Pilots often prove the exception rather than the series norm. These initial episodes announce the new and introduce us to narrative worlds where characters are rudimentarily sketched and plot threads established. The Pilot for HBO, however, often acts as a showcase, where style and visual techniques (often never seen again in the series) announce the aspirations for new dramas and make visible why the company's originals matter most. These are the episodes international buyers will watch when deciding what to buy, but more importantly used to entice subscribers, both old and new. The HBO Pilot is thus conceived of as a modern masterpiece – and the first episode of *Boardwalk Empire* is no exception. Just as the series creates a protean world of mobsters, a mythology in the making in fact, the Pilot establishes its own artistic worth as a distinct and highly original piece of TV art. It does so by creating a hyper-reality, with an authentic-looking and ornately beautiful period style, achieved in and through its use of high-end image-making techniques and state-of-the-art VFX technologies. Such concepts of TV art includes a refining and elevating element, of making visible, as Matthew Arnold put it in 1865, the best that has been known and thought within a particular society. *Boardwalk Empire*'s bid for reputation as not just good but somehow the very best of what is possible in television drama absorbs the values of these debates about creative and commercial worth and a 'restricted' field of cultural production.[11] A belief in the exalted value of *Boardwalk Empire*'s artistic achievement is further generated and sustained by a consecrating consensus (a network involving critics, media experts and scholars) that helps us to think that way about the HBO series.

---

[9] John Thornton Caldwell, *Televisuality: Style, Crisis and Authority in American Television* (New Brunswick, NJ: Rutgers University Press, 1995).
[10] Jason Jacobs, 'Issues of Judgement and Value in Television Studies', *International Journal of Cultural Studies* 4:4 (2001): 427–47.
[11] Pierre Bourdieu, *Distinction*, trans. Richard Nice (London: Routledge and Kegan Paul, 1984).

When *Boardwalk Empire* first aired one could hardly pick up a newspaper or magazine without reading about the extraordinary look and 'feel' of the series. Credit for the artistry went, more often than not, to Oscar-winning director and acclaimed American *auteur* Martin Scorsese. He directed the Pilot as well as took an executive producer credit and reportedly continued as a hands-on consultant for the remaining 11 episodes. Reliance on someone with an uncompromising creative vision driving a project finds HBO placing a premium on the kind of authorship long associated with other privileged cultural forms such as theatre, international art cinema and literature. Scorsese, himself, even compared the creative latitude granted by HBO to the artistic freedoms enjoyed by filmmakers in the 1960s.[12] Artistic endeavour is not, however, something one simply judges; creative distinctiveness rationalises production, justifies inflated budgets and helps HBO distinguish its series from regular television.

HBO has longed been famed for its writer-producers (David Chase, Alan Ball and David Simon), but the channel is also known for its association with notable film *auteurs*, often closely linked with American independent cinema, including Susan Seidelman (*Sex and the City* Pilot), Walter Hill (*Deadwood* Pilot), Todd Haynes (five-hour miniseries, *Mildred Pierce*), Michael Mann (executive producer and director of the pilot of *Luck*, starring Dustin Hoffman) – and one of the most significant additions to that list is Scorsese. Drawing directly on the talents of *auteur* celebrities like Scorsese[13] known for bringing something unique to a particular genre enables HBO to sell its signature shows as exceptional, happening only once and never repeated. This is television designed to stand out from the competition and elevate the status of the medium as a consequence. It is a strategy that has paid dividend in terms of syndication and selling to international markets, with HBO agreeing a deal with BSkyB, reportedly worth around £150 million, for the sole rights to the entire back catalogue as well as current (and future) productions including *Boardwalk Empire*.[14] Venturing huge amounts of capital to purchase hit shows is about buying the exclusive HBO label to brand the identity of a particular channel (both

---

[12] Nikki Finke, 'TCA: Why Marty Scorsese Is Now Doing TV', *Deadline Hollywood*, 7 August 2010, http://www.deadline.com/2010/08/tca-why-marty-scorsese-decided-to-do-tv/ [accessed 26 November 2011]; Christina Radish, 'Martin Scorsese and Terence Winter Interview *Boardwalk Empire*', *Collider.com*, 14 September 2010, http://collider.com/boardwalk-empire-interview-martin-scorsese-terence-winter/47446/ [accessed 15 December 2011]

[13] Timothy Corrigan, 'Auteurs and the New Hollywood', in *The New American Cinema*, ed. Jon Lewis (Durham, NC: Duke University Press, 1998), 38–63.

[14] James Robinson, 'BSkyB Buys Complete HBO TV Catalogue', *The Guardian*, 29 July 2010, http://www.guardian.co.uk/media/2010/jul/29/bskyb-buys-hbo-tv-catalogue [accessed 27 November 2011].

at home and aboard). While, at the same time, drawing on the reputation of the *auteur* helps HBO sustain and even amplify a belief in the distinctive creative contribution of what the company believes it's making to contemporary TV culture based on more established hierarchies of restricted taste and aesthetic appreciation.[15]

HBO original series, especially the most critically acclaimed like *Boardwalk Empire*, rely heavily on the reassuringly familiar formula of the classic US genre system, even as these shows subvert the codes, revise conventions for television and build into the genre memory. Appropriating particular generic forms, and ones that enjoy such a privileged place within the American cultural canon, helps the HBO original determine its own value for the new. Little wonder, then, that having Scorsese attached to the project enabled the company to elevate *Boardwalk Empire*'s aesthetic disposition based on a hierarchy of generic and aesthetic value already in circulation. Scorsese has long had a reputation for understanding only too well America's fascination with the gangster as tragic hero, as well as the genre's privileged position within American cultural life, as he, at the same time, gives renewed representation to that love affair. In movies like *Mean Streets* (1973), *Goodfellas* (1990), *Casino* (1995) and *Gangs of New York* (2002), the director explores the tension between documenting the real (e.g. Method acting with its focus on the psychological realism of a character, the detailed sketching of specific times and places) with the artifice of cinema. Scorsese is recognized for his stylised techniques such as direct overhead shots, disjointed jump cuts (indicating the passage of time) and freeze frames. The way in which he has created, repeated and refined representational elements of the genre functions in relation to what has gone before, and through interplay of comparisons, the Scorsese look has established a privileged place within that order. This is not to suggest that the *auteur* guarantees great television, but that the *auteur* as discourse carries important creative meaning and cultural capital that help establish a reputation for a new series – particularly for HBO where series are sold as originals.

Scorsese delivers a visual template for *Boardwalk Empire*. He brings this series into being with a *mise en scène* full of authorial flourishes including the freeze frame on the half-lit face of a masked man armed with a shotgun overlaid with a woman's voice yelling, 'Coward! Monster! Vicious brute.' Other techniques include starting with a narrative segment from the end (when the timeline catches back up to that initial heist and [re]told with maximum tension by cross-cutting swiftly between distinct staging areas);

---

[15] Bourdieu, *Distinction*.

elaborate tracking shots (Hans Schroeder [Joseph Sikora] leaving his home and striding down the street, or Thompson strolling the length of a bustling gambling room); the discordant soundtrack (with source music, or the vaude-villian stand-up heard performing his routine over the cutting between an FBI raid on the illegal liquor factory and the violent roadside hold-up); and the jump cuts through the pages of *Vogue*, conveying the nervous unease of Margaret Schroeder (Kelly MacDonald) distractedly flicking through the magazine while waiting to see Nucky. And let's not forget the climatic *Godfather*-esque set piece, as we witness the demise of the old order and birth of the new with the assassination of Chicago boss, Big Jim Colosimo (Frank Crudele) and the more tawdry dispatch of Margaret's abusive husband, Hans. At some level, the viewer is constantly made aware that they are watching art (re) assembled, piece by piece, from familiar fragments of older cultural myths and Hollywood storytelling. These exquisitely filmed images function as an act of retrieval, reminding us of how the filmic image has profoundly tamed the gangster mythology into an ordained narrative sequence. Such moments of pure artifice are mnemonic of the celebrity *auteur* lending artistic legit-imacy and cultural kudos to the series (and, of course, the HBO brand). Someone who is already known for taking the visual and folkloric iconog-raphy established by Warner Bros. and RKO gangster movies during classical Hollywood era, and reworking those forms and styles filtered through his own revisionist contribution to the genre (involving identity politics, modern crime and violence).

The iconic filmic opening moment of *The Untouchables* (Brian De Palma 1987) with its direct overhead shot of people bustling around Al Capone (Robert De Niro) lying in a barber's chair is re-imagined with etched clarity for television with Thompson being shaved by his manservant, Eddie Kessler (Anthony Laciura). Of course Scorsese is also known for the direct overhead shot that make characters appear as pieces on a chess board; and in the interplay of associations this momentary fragment plays its part within the broarder narrative segment involving the assassination of Colosimo. But this detail is part of that story of power and the struggle for status nonetheless. With the Pilot shot in Super 35 film the more intimate portrait of this private, almost incidental moment (as opposed to the public, cinematic spectacle of Capone chatting convivially with the press while being shaved) is packed with visual information. From the Art Nouveau chandelier with its etched glass shades to the delicate lace net curtains and the pattern on the carpet, our eyes are in constant motion. Cinematographer, Kramer Morgenthau explains the decision to shoot on film:

We use the extreme ends of the gray scale. No zone is not visited. In my mind, the universe of the 1920s interior life depended on natural light. I push windows and other sources very hard, knowing that they will hold on film. You just can't do that with any other capture media.[16]

This visual clarity of the image allows us to see what is at the very edge of our peripheral vision, to somehow look again with fresh eyes at the gangster genre and the role of its iconography in the formation of history, myth and cultural identity.

TV critic Tom Shone[17] sees HBO has having taken up the task of producing the type of epics at which Hollywood used to excel – *The Godfather* (Francis Ford Coppola, 1972) and *Once Upon a Time in America* (Sergio Leone, 1984). But *Boardwalk Empire* is not simply a product of nostalgia for this kind of ambitious Hollywood filmmaking that *produced* and circulated cultural myths of America. Instead nostalgia for these past forms is implanted deep into the series' *mise en scène* as it conserves techniques and practises them anew. Certain stylistic touches used in the Pilot pay homage to the past contribution of Scorsese to the gangster genre (shocking violence, corporeal matter splattered over the lens), but also to the American cinema of the early twentieth century, including the archaic iris-in and iris out transitions bookending the episode. Its use is an obvious salute to early cinema and pioneering film techniques; but the iris-in/out shot also becomes embedded into the series DNA to tell and authenticate its story set in 1920. Furthermore, from the gramophone with its scratchy reproduced sound to the Fatty Arbuckle comedy about the dawn of Prohibition, which Jimmy Darmody (Michael Pitt) takes his family to see, the episode also fetishes older popular media culture and its 'new' technologies. Scorsese visualizes this entangled, layered 'after-life' of images and techniques, through his use of jump cuts, dissolves, the archaic iris-in/out transition, parallel editing, as well as a hybridised soundtrack full of music and songs from the period (commenting on the TV narrative). Given Scorsese's own passionate commitment to film conservation,[18] there is a sense that the foregrounding of techniques is another way of preserving and holding on to that movie legacy. In dialoguing with the border relation between past and present, both visually and aurally, these material techniques offer a

---

[16] David Heuring, 'Shooting *Boardwalk Empire* on Super 35', *Studio Daily*, 20 September 2012, http://www.studiodaily.com/2010/09/shooting-boardwalk-empire-on-super-35/ [accessed 26 April 2012]

[17] Tom Shone, '*Boardwalk Empire*, the "New *Sopranos*" from HBO', *The Telegraph*, 7 January 2011, http://www.telegraph.co.uk/culture/tvandradio/8244306/Boardwalk-Empire-the-new-Sopranos-from-HBO.html [accessed 26 November 2011]

[18] Christy Grosz, 'Scorsese Talks Preservation', *Variety*, 1 January 2012, http://www.variety.com/article/VR1118048017/ [accessed 28 May 2012].

depth of reference that Scorsese builds into the series memory for viewers to draw upon when comprehending *Boardwalk Empire*'s rich and complex engagement with modern American history. But, and more importantly, in keeping those methods in circulation, proficiently practising them while preserving, Scorsese is careful to place them in the context of our shared cultural history. It is thus a process that recognizes that film technologies and formal styles also have a rich background and past life.

Similarly, deliberately incorporated into the Pilot are various aesthetic motifs associated with the formidable visual history of the gangster genre already in circulation, but re-imagined and translated anew for television. One example includes when Thompson and his ambitious young protégé recently returned from the trenches of the First World War, Darmody, visit an illegal liquor factory hidden behind the walls of a legitimate funeral business. Mickey Doyle (Paul Sparks), the ever-so slightly unhinged racketeer who runs the illicit outfit, slides back a panel to reveal his operation. The camera glides in behind the protagonists and tracks into a familiar generic territory, accompanied by a ragtime melody coming from an unseen phonograph. Light streams through the slats in the wooden panelling, creating a low-key lighting scheme strongly associated with classic film noir and its stark light/ dark contrasts and expressionistic shadow patterning. Attached shadows cling to faces and cast ones loom large on the walls. Overhead shots and dynamic low-angle push-ins, close-ups of bottles and the alchemy of making bootlegged whiskey: the Scorsese touches are mixed with the aesthetic DNA of classic film noir. Foregrounding the artifice in this way allows for an exploration of the palimpsest nature of formal techniques and visual style to carry the DNA of a genre – how it constructs a story, how it constitutes cultural myths and remembers history.

With the Scorsese Pilot perpetually engaged in an entangled dialogue with the 'after-life' of images and formal techniques, the memory-journey of *Boardwalk Empire* directs the audience into a wider reconsideration of the role of the gangster mythology within American cultural life at the moment of its HBO renewal. Right down to dust specks floating through the air – spectacular in full HD – attention is trained onto the most inconsequential detail, as if only *now* the form can deliver something new, something not possible before: namely, a visceral engagement with the historic past. The long tracking shots inside Babette's Supper Club as the clientele celebrate the arrival of Prohibition, for example; or the carnival barker flanked by scantily clad chorus girls inviting us to a burlesque show, shot from a dynamic low angle with such compositional precision that nothing goes unseen: the wisps of chiffon fringe on the ill-fitting, handmade-looking dressing gowns and pink ribbons tied around the showgirls' face. There is also a naked female cadaver laid out on the embalming table: *Six Feet Under* meets *The Public Enemy* (William A. Wellman, 1931), a HBO original fused with gangster mythology. Breakfast at the Darmody household is another example, where a conventional shot-reverse-shot pattern with Jimmy and his wife, Angela (Aleksa Palladino), talking about the future is swiftly intercut with intimate close-up shots of their young son stirring his porridge (and his father laughing), to create the distracted rhythm of ordinary family life. The peripheral, the personal (which television has long taken seriously), those moments just before or after scenes of exposition, are represented by disorientating visual techniques, and draw us into the many layers of this story with its contested histories and counter narratives.

Shot on Super 35 film the cinematography references the above Hollywood films; and the lighting, generally dark in tone, capturing the harshness of the everyday, is heavily influenced by the Ashcan School (1908–13),[19] a painterly style of realism that documented prosaic urban subject matter around 1900 – a transitional time in US history and culture. Just as this important American art movement sought to capture spontaneous quotidian moments in its style of painting, the cinematography of *Boardwalk Empire* harnesses the authority of that rebellious project to authenticate its depiction of 1920 and absorbs past painterly techniques into its palimpsest creative mission. Using a similar dark, subdued palette, the series does the same with its kinetic portrayal of incidental sequences. For example, the hallway scene when Elias Thompson (Shea Whigham) goes looking for Darmody, only to find his wife at home. The high, distorted angle speaks to the uneasy but unspoken realisation of what Darmody has done (his maverick involvement in redirecting illegal whiskey), but the composition and lighting of the image draw attention to the artifice. While the Ashcan group was quite conservative in style, this defiant urban art was revolutionary in capturing a feel for a place where the struggling poor lived, which the Pilot, in turn, aims to retrieve and resuscitate. Similarly, with the Schroeder household (the knife cutting into soda bread, children sitting at the table) or the dark atmosphere of the dwarf-wrestling match (reimagining George Wesley Bellow's bold depictions of amateur boxing matches), these television images of the enfranchised are given representation and authenticated *in* and *through* referencing older but pivotal artistic strategies to give us the impression that *Boardwalk Empire*, as Matt Zoller Seitz put it, 'isn't interested in presenting life as it should have been, but life as it probably was'.[20]

The 1920s are a surprisingly underrepresented period in American history

[19] Heuring, 'Shooting *Boardwalk Empire* on Super 35'.
[20] Matt Zoller Seitz, '*Boardwalk Empire*: Episode One', *The New Republic*, 20 September 2010, , http://www.tnr.com/article/77765/boardwalk-empire-episode-one [accessed 25 April 2012].

(exceptions include *The Cotton Club* [Francis Ford Coppola, 1984]), but like other HBO histories (*John Adams, Deadwood*), *Boardwalk Empire* is set in a period on the cusp of seismic historic change: in this case, the end of the war, the beginning of Prohibition and women gaining the right to vote. No moment in history accidentally survives in our collective memory, but it remains, as Michel Foucault[21] demonstrates, in existence by virtue of discourses that support it, including material techniques and institutions of knowledge. *Boardwalk Empire* intervenes into founding myths of nationhood at the point where folklore is in the process of being written. Alessandra Stanley writes that 'imagined history can sometimes be more persuasive that fact'.[22] But is it not in how the *mise en scène* retrieves visual lexicons, material objects and formal techniques to *produce* its historical vicissitude that compels us to think that way? The VFX technology proves crucial.[23] The digital technologies reclaim the past and revitalise it into a HD televisual present tense. VFX re-imagines entire streets (Sewell Avenue with its 1920s beach bungalows, for example) and resurrects the historic boardwalk (using authentic, archival photographs). The digital technologies take fragments and create cultural remembrances; it further generates a visceral experience in its choice of matte paintings, with certain colours and textures reminiscent of the period.

Employing the latest software packages (compositing tools like NUKEX), the VFX team at Brainstorm Digital blur those borders between where the real ends and the verisimilitude begins; or, as the official HBO website tells us, how the specially constructed 300-foot (91m) pier abruptly ends at the foot of a giant blue screen, in which postproduction digitally insert footage, to bring the boardwalk back to its former glory. But how the pier is meticulously reconstructed from authentic period photographs speaks further about the capacity of images to carry a memory of how a particular historical time was once imagined. Taking relics of the past and transforming them into state-of-the-art TV style, the technology collapses any easy distinction between past and present, bringing new life and realism to its subject.

Just as the Pilot gives representation to a modern America on the cusp of momentous change, a shift of political power and economic influence, HBO originals continue to erase straightforward distinctions defining the medium. Of course television cinematography is evolving as is the entire home viewing experience. HBO anticipates higher audience expectations even as it contributes to changing our assumptions about that very experience through

---

[21] Michel Foucault, *The Archaeology of Knowledge*, trans. A. M. Sheridan Smith (New York: Pantheon, 1972).
[22] Stanley, 'Jersey Shore, the Early Years'.
[23] Vincent Frei, '*Boardwalk Empire*: Justin Ball – VFX Supervisor – Brainstorm Digital', *The Art of VFX*, 2011, http://www.artofvfx.com/?p=725 [accessed 26 April 2012].

its discrete distribution spaces and exclusive viewing domain. But in its aesthetic and formal acts of retrieval, in which the recovered iconography and styles are not only material objects with a past but also shape the palimpsest nature of the series, *Boardwalk Empire* is a work of *bricolage*, a stratagem of textual pleasures. The Pilot plays with visible trace on its surface (its originality, the HBO original) to invisible ones inside the image and film technique as it is used and practised (its cultural importance, established artistic worth). Responding to the almost 'messianic' talk surrounding the launch, TV critic Benji Wilson reported that, '*Boardwalk Empire* might be the most important thing to happen to television since John Logie Baird first turned the thing on.'[24] High praise indeed, but the sentiment nonetheless speaks to the continuing ambition of HBO to create original TV art while regulating that enterprise within established ideas circulating in American cultural life. In *Boardwalk Empire's* new history, knowing about the past is thus vital to the creative way forward.

Bibliography

Bourdieu, Pierre. *Distinction.* Translated by Richard Nice. London: Routledge and Kegan Paul, 1984.

Caldwell, John Thornton. *Televisuality: Style, Crisis and Authority in American Television.* New Brunswick, NJ: Rutgers University Press, 1995.

Carter, Bill. 'He Lit Up HBO. Now He Must Run It.' *The New York Times*, July 20, 2002.

Corrigan, Timothy. 'Auteurs and the New Hollywood.' In *The New American Cinema*, edited by Jon Lewis, 38–63. Durham, NC: Duke University Press, 1998.

Crace, John. 'TV Review: *Boardwalk Empire.' The Guardian*, 2 February 2011. http://www.guardian.co.uk/tv-and-radio/2011/feb/02/tv-review-boardwalk-empire [accessed 19 April 2012].

Finke, Nikki. 'TCA: Why Marty Scorsese Is Now Doing TV.' *Deadline Hollywood*, 7 August 2010. http://www.deadline.com/2010/08/tca-why-marty-scorsese-decided-to-do-tv/ [accessed 26 November 2011].

Foucault, Michel. *The Archaeology of Knowledge.* Translated by A. M. Sheridan Smith. New York: Pantheon, 1972.

Frei, Vincent. '*Boardwalk Empire*: Justin Ball – VFX Supervisor – Brainstorm Digital.' *The Art of VFX*, 2011. http://www.artofvfx.com/?p=725 [accessed 26 April 2012].

Grego, Melissa. 'Feared Yet Respected.' *Variety* (Special on HBO at 30), 4 November 2002.

---

[24]Wilson, '*Boardwalk Empire*, HBO, Review'.

Grosz, Christy. 'Scorsese Talks Preservation.' *Variety*, 1 January 2012. http://www.variety.com/article/VR1118048017/ [accessed 28 May 2012].

Heuring, David. 'Shooting *Boardwalk Empire* on Super 35.' *Studio Daily*, September 20, 2012. http://www.studiodaily.com/2010/09/shooting-boardwalk-empire-on-super-35/ [accessed 26 April 2012].

Jacobs, Jason. 'Issues of Judgement and Value in Television Studies.' *International Journal of Cultural Studies* 4:4 (2001): 427–47.

Jaramillo, Deborah. 'The Family Racket: AOL-Time Warner, HBO, *The Sopranos* and the Construction of a Quality Brand.' *Journal of Communication Inquiry* 26:1 (2002): 59–75.

Littleton, Cynthia. 'HBO Lays Big-Bucks Bet on *Boardwalk*.' *Variety*, 7 August 2010. http://www.variety.com/article/VR1118022673?refCatId=14 [accessed 29 November 2011].

Radish, Christina. 'Martin Scorsese and Terence Winter Interview *Boardwalk Empire*.' *Collider.com*, 14 September 2010. http://collider.com/boardwalk-empire-interview-martin-scorsese-terrence-winter/47446/ [accessed 15 December 2011].

Robinson, James. 'BSkyB Buys Complete HBO TV Catalogue.' *The Guardian*, 29 July 2010. http://www.guardian.co.uk/media/2010/jul/29/bskyb-buys-hbo-tv-catalogue [accessed 27 November 2011].

Santos, Avi. 'Para-Television and Discourses of Distinction.' In *It's Not TV: Watching HBO in the Post-Television Era*, edited by Marc Leverette, Brian L. Ott, and Clara Louise Buckley, 19–45. New York: Routledge, 2008.

Shone, Tom. '*Boardwalk Empire*, the "New *Sopranos*" from HBO.' *The Telegraph*, 7 January 2011. http://www.telegraph.co.uk/culture/tvandradio/8244306/Boardwalk-Empire-the-new-Sopranos-from-HBO.html [accessed 26 November 2011].

Stanley, Alessandra. 'Jersey Shore, the Early Years.' *The New York Times*, 16 September 2010. http://tv.nytimes.com/2010/09/17/arts/television/17boardwalk.html?pagewanted=all [accessed 23 November 2011].

Wilson, Benji. '*Boardwalk Empire*, HBO, Review.' *The Telegraph*, 20 September 2010. http://www.telegraph.co.uk/culture/tvandradio/8013543/Boardwalk-Empire-HBO-review.html [accessed 23 November 2011]

Zoller Seitz, Matt. '*Boardwalk Empire*: Episode One.' *The New Republic*, 20 September 2010. http://www.tnr.com/article/77765/boardwalk-empire-episode-one [accessed 25 April 2012].

14

Storytelling in song: Television music, narrative and allusion in *The O.C.*

Faye Woods

Karen Lury points out that 'music, like the human voice, is everywhere on television. It is ubiquitous',[1] yet television music is often neglected in studies of television aesthetics, where visual style has dominated.[2] Recent years have seen a rise in the presence of popular music in television soundscapes, with television's long-form storytelling having the potential to allow the rippling of music across episodes and seasons in interesting ways. Yet relatively little academic work has been produced on the role of music in storytelling and televisual expression,[3] with work on popular music in television tending to focus on performance and industrial exploitation,[4] whilst close analysis has largely been confined to score-based studies.[5]

---

[1] Karen Lury, *Interpreting Television* (London: Hodder Arnold, 2005), 71.

[2] See, for example, Jeremy Butler, *Television Style* (Abingdon: Routledge, 2010).

[3] Julie Brown, '*Ally McBeal's* Postmodern Soundtrack', *Journal of the Royal Musical Association* 126: 2 (2001): 275–303. Charles Fairchild, 'Flow amid Flux: The Evolving Uses of Music in Evening Television Drama', *Television and New Media* 12:6 (2011): 491–512.

[4] Simon Frith, 'Look! Hear! The Uneasy Relationship of Music and Television', *Popular Music,* 21:3 (2002): 277–90. K. J. Donnelly, 'Tracking British Television: Pop Music as Stock Soundtrack to the Small Screen', *Popular Music* 21:3 (2002): 331–43. Kay Dickinson, '"My Generation": Popular Music, Age and Influence in Teen Drama of the 1990s', in *Teen TV: Genre, Consumption and Identity*, ed. Glyn Davis and Kay Dickinson (London: BFI, 2004), 99–111.

[5] Ron Rodman, *Tuning In: American Narrative Television Music* (New York: Oxford University Press, 2009); James Deaville, ed., *Music in Television: Channels of Listening* (Abingdon: Routledge, 2011).

In order to explore the role of popular music in television storytelling, I will focus on *The O.C.*[6] a Teen TV programme that expressively utilizes popular music as both marker of character identity and storytelling tool. An ensemble drama set in the privileged Californian utopia of Newport, Orange County, the programme chronicles the after-effects of lawyer Sandy Cohen (Peter Gallagher) bringing misunderstood 'juvenile delinquent' Ryan Atwood (Ben McKenzie) into his family after Ryan is abandoned by his own. Sandy's sarcastic geeky son Seth (Adam Brody) embraces Ryan as his surrogate brother, whilst the Cohens' beautiful yet troubled neighbour Marissa (Mischa Barton) falls in love with the new arrival. *The O.C.* has often been discussed in terms of the industrial influence of its music supervisor Alexandra Patsavas and the programme's ability sell music and 'break' bands.[7] However, close analysis can help unpick the programme's offer of an at times complex interaction between popular music, narrative expression and serialised story-telling, which draws on music's allusive and referential qualities to particularly televisual ends.

The O.C. employs musical moments in a range of ways, with much of its use of popular music working to interweave narrative and soundscape, foregrounding yet simultaneously integrating popular music's presence. This is often found in contemplative moments, such as the episode-closing montages which draw together the strands of its ensemble storytelling.[8] However, I wish to focus here on the use of popular music as leitmotif, instances where tracks are repeated in episodes or across seasons. This is a form that can be playful or emotionally resonant and which engages with the serialised, interweaving narrative of ensemble drama.

Popular music also plays a key role in *The O.C.*'s shifting tonal address, which strikes a delicate balance between a playful reflexivity and a melodrama-informed emotional realism.[9] The programme draws on elements of *Dynasty*'s[10] prime-time soap camp and excess in its depiction of Newport society, yet works to contrasts this world with its protagonists. Presented as 'authentic' outsiders, Seth and Ryan view this society through a self-aware, slightly mocking distance. However, the emotive portions of *The O.C.*'s soundscape – plaintive indie-rock, new folk or singer-songwriter – allow music

---

[6] Dir. various (2003–7).

[7] Dorian Lynskey, 'How *The O.C.* Saved Music', *The Guardian*. 1 December 2004, http://arts.guardian.co.uk/features/story/0,,1363852,00.html [accessed 30 March 2006]. Emily Zemler, 'The O.C. Effect', *Popmatters*. 14 January 2005, http://www.popmatters.com/music/features/050114-indiesoundtracks.shtml [accessed 30 March 2006]

[8] Brown, '*Ally McBeal's Postmodern Soundtrack*', 285.

[9] Ien Ang, *Watching Dallas: Television and the Melodramatic Imagination* (London: Routledge, 1985).

[10] Dir. various (1981–9).

to provide the emotional connectivity that its playfully ironic pose could potentially deny. As a result, the programme allows a dual level of engagement for its audience, who could revel in the 'knowing' soap opera plotting and the boys' witty banter, yet at the same time be drawn to the emotional realism of its musical moments.

The O.C. often makes particular use of what Ian Garwood describes as the ability of 'a non-diegetic song to exceed the emotional range displayed by diegetic characters'.[11] Allowing a song to 'speak' for characters or to their feelings, contributing to melodrama's emotional affect by allowing us privileged access to character psyches. This is particularly true in moments when characters like sensitive, yet angry Ryan – or Seth in his tendency towards detached irony – withhold or struggle with their emotions. This can include literal lyrical interpretation, yet is more often a mood expressed through a musical quality or the abstract emotion of a lyrical phrase. One such example is 'The Links',[12] where Puddle of Mud's 'Away From Me' repeatedly breaks into the narrative to figure as Ryan's suppressed rage, which he struggles to contain as his girlfriend Marissa is manipulated by his rival, Oliver (Taylor Handley).

Drawing on a thrashing metal tone, 'Away From Me' is distinct from The O.C.'s dominant musical aesthetic of indie rock and singer-songwriter output, highlighting the track's disruptive presence. It first appears as the group of friends set off for a trip to Palm Springs where it signals Ryan's irritation at Oliver's presence, operating as a short stinger (a sudden musical phrase – often a dissonant scored chord – used to provide dramatic emphasis[13]). What begins as an echoing angular guitar element develops into a driving drumbeat, thrashing guitar and vocal wail as the scene closes on a close-up of Ryan grimly smiling through his frustration. The track appears here as merely a short fragment, its use as a stinger and disparity within the programme's soundscape signalling Ryan's jealousy as comedic. However, it later reappears in more fully developed form on a trip to a golf course, as Marissa remains oblivious to Oliver's needling of Ryan. The track's return signals an escalation in the boys' rivalry; as it builds to its thrashing crescendo during a duelling golf cart race, the singer's tale of anguish over being left for another man is given full range as it flows over the action as Ryan's jealousy breaks out. The track's return creates a musical leitmotif, signalling Ryan's developing anger to the viewer, to which Marissa seems oblivious.

---

[11] Ian Garwood, 'The Pop Song in Film', in Close-Up: 01, ed. John Gibbs and Doug Pye (London: Wallflower Press, 2006), 115.

[12] 1.16 Michael Lange 2004.

[13] Claudia Gorbman, Unheard Melodies: Narrative Film Music (London: BFI, 1987), 88.

The track's final appearance is at the episode's close as Marissa chooses to stay with Oliver after a suicide attempt that Ryan believes he has faked. After Marissa has angrily asked Ryan to leave, the track emerges in an echoing cross-fade from the score on his close-up reaction shot. Compared to its earlier appearances where it figured as comic with an underlying threat, this echoing cross-fade creates a more menacing tone as Ryan realizes that he has been bested. As with the earlier occurrences, the privileging of the audience – rather than Marissa – in this musical expression of Ryan's emotions heightens the melodrama of his inability to convince her of his misgivings. The episode ends with Ryan left alone outside the door of Oliver's penthouse, the connotations of danger in the track's metal guitar riff intensifying our access to Ryan's fear over Oliver's actions, together with our own concern over Ryan's potential for an angry reprisal. In the final shot the camera tracks away from him down the corridor, emphasising his isolation, yet also seemingly thrust by the power of the song's wailing refrain. The music figures as the release of the anger Ryan's coiled body language struggles to suppress.

The way 'Away From Me' repeats or echoes through this episode can be seen to function in a similar manner to the leitmotif within Classical Hollywood Cinema scoring, where 'repetition, interaction and variation' in a score's motifs acts as an emotive yet structural device.[14] However, whilst Claudia Gorbman describes these filmic themes as acting subconsciously, as 'Away From Me' demonstrates, *The O.C.*'s leitmotifs often utilize popular song's sonically disruptive nature. Jeff Smith problematically argues that the pop song's use as score is limited due to its structure being based on tonality and repetition, suggesting this renders it more obvious than a score's subconscious leitmotif.[15] In *The O.C.* these popular song leitmotifs often directly break into the soundscape, creating a playfully reflexive relationship between narrative, soundscape and audience, particularly when functioning as a stinger for comic effect. Yet whilst Smith suggests that the pop song's structure makes it unable to be segmented in the manner of a score's theme, *The O.C.*'s use of popular music leitmotif (which occurs in seven episodes across the four seasons), together with other music moments presents a more complex relationship than Smith allows. These moments often utilize both the 'obvious' nature of popular song for comic effect, successfully segment particular tracks, and at times build meaning *through* repetition, like the classical Hollywood score's leitmotif.

---

[14] Gorbman, *Unheard Melodies*, 91.
[15] Jeff Smith, *The Sounds of Commerce: Marketing Popular Film Music* (New York: Columbia University Press, 1998), 155.

Whilst the return of 'Away From Me' developed the track's meaning across the episode, other leitmotifs can be briefer and relatively simplistic. In 'The Rainy Day Women'[16] the same short burst of Louis XIV's 'God Killed the Queen' breaks into the soundscape each time Marissa and her new girlfriend Alex (Olivia Wilde) energetically kiss. The repetition of the song fragment signals the action as fun and exciting – a rebellious sexual experiment for Marissa – and whilst it never develops into the full track, the theme does pay off in a comic moment at the episode's close. The track's tapping drum and sharp rock guitar first briefly break into the soundscape to punctuate the girls sneaking a kiss at breakfast behind Marissa's mother's back. The 'awgh' cry of the vocal acts as a comic stinger to the music's abrupt cut (almost a needle scratch) as they part when she turns round. The sharp, raucous rock track acts as cheeky, reflexive commentary, coding the lesbian action as upbeat and sexy; not a meaningful exploration, but a short term, ratings-grabbing stunt.

The track later breaks into a scene at Alex's apartment when the girls make out, with the vocal cry and music cut signalling the end of the scene as they start to disrobe. It then recurs in a slightly longer fragment when Seth later encounters Marissa emerging half-dressed from Alex's room, the tapping drum arriving as Seth sees her, the angular guitar riff's appearance emphasising his drawn-out 'Oh. My. God'. As Alex throws Seth out the 'awgh' vocalises his play of comedic dismay at being excluded, with the cry and music cut acting as a comedic stinger, timed to the close of the door. Finally, a small section of the track – by now playing on its accumulated meaning – appears when Seth tells Ryan about the incident. Playing as they both sit quietly, the track implies the boys are contemplating the activity the theme is now associated with, the track again comically and abruptly cutting as Seth's mother Kirsten (Kelly Rowan) interrupts them. Whilst other romantic or melancholic moments in the girls' brief relationship are accompanied by more emotional, single-use tracks, the brief break-ins of 'God Killed the Queen' throughout the episode highlight the fun of the lesbian action, using the loud guitar style, vocal cry and sudden music cut to imply an amused and titillated audience reaction. In such a way, *The O.C*'s music use plays into the programme's combination of irony and emotional realism, its textual awareness allowing a playful relationship between its soundscape and narrative.

In these instances, popular song's referential and allusive dimension – which makes it such a rich signifier of time, place and identity – is constructed *within* the episode, intra-textually, rather than extra-textually. Its accumulated meaning can be called on through the employment of a small section of

---

[16] 2.14 Michael Fresco 2005.

the track, in essence, a leitmotif. Claudia Gorbman suggests that a theme or leitmotif can be fixed and static in its meanings or evolve and develop, contributing to narrative flow.[17] Whilst I have noted leitmotif return *within* episodes, the narrative space of a multi-season television text allows for the construction of a televisually-specific form of popular music leitmotif, one which can develop and echo across seasons, drawing on popular song's emotional resonance alongside series memory. In this way *The O.C.*'s use of Jeff Buckley's 1994 cover of Leonard Cohen's 'Hallelujah' can be viewed as a series leitmotif, having reappeared three times throughout the programme's run. Its use draws on the track's cultural connotations of melancholic indie credibility, yet also accumulates resonance within the narrative, developing musical meaning beyond individual moments and episodes to span the programme as a narrative whole. Amy Holdsworth has described the television viewing experience as one of 'accumulation, where viewing experiences and references are built up over time'.[18] The return of 'Hallelujah' explicitly draws on the ways 'the memory of 'afterimages' and 'moments' are accumulated over a life lived across television'.[19]

The track first appears in 'The Model Home',[20] diegetically motivated as a track playing from a mix CD Marissa has made for Ryan after he has run away from the Cohen's home. In the candlelit setting of a vacant house, the track accompanies a tentative, emotional conversation between the pair over her desire to stay the night with him. Marissa tells Ryan the song reminds her of him, and Buckley's tortuously melancholic vocals resonate with – yet do not directly express – Ryan's conflicted feelings for her. The rolling rhythmic pluck of the solo guitar that opens the track is compounded by the tracking camera that encircles the pair as they talk, giving the scene a swooning quality, with Buckley's softly fractured voice entering almost as answer to Marissa's request to stay, filling the space left by Ryan's silence as he struggles to articulate himself. As Buckley reaches his refrain, the repeated 'Hallelujah's build to emphasize Ryan's plaintive, 'We're from different worlds' and his demand that Marissa 'Go … Please… Go'. The track then shifts to the non-diegetic soundscape and we cut to the house exterior as Buckley moves back to the verse, singing of a woman's beauty in the moonlight and hinting at masochism as a weeping Marissa leaves and drives off into the night. The delicacy and passion of the track, alongside its underlying darkness contribute to *The O.C.*'s construction of the teenage couple's blossoming cross-class

[17] Gorbman, *Unheard Melodies*, 3.
[18] Amy Holdsworth, *Television, Memory and Nostalgia* (Basingstoke: Palgrave Macmillan, 2011), 34.
[19] Holdsworth, *Television*, 34.
[20] 1.2 Doug Limon 2003.

romance as a tragic 'great love'. The narrative appropriates the music's emotional complexity and existing cultural resonance to provide a depth that the relationship itself does not yet contain.

The song reappears at the close of the season one finale 'The Ties That Bind',[21] when Ryan has decided to leave Newport to return to his home town with pregnant ex-girlfriend Theresa (Navi Rawat), leaving a devastated Cohen family in his wake. The return of the track brings the connotations of its earlier involvement in a melancholically romantic moment of Ryan and Marissa's relationship and also provides a bookend to the season. It plays over and pulls together a montage of moments illustrating the effect of Ryan's decision on his friends and 'family': shots of Ryan and Theresa anxious and unsure in her car; Marissa isolated and drinking alone on the balcony of her stepfather's mansion home; Kirsten Cohen (Ryan's adopted mother) crying whilst clearing his room and Seth running away from home, sailing into the sunset in his boat. Buckley's rising refrain of 'I lived alone till I met you', which earlier related merely to Ryan and Marissa, expands here to refer to all the central characters and their relationship with Ryan. This sequence draws on the ability of the pop song montage to cohere the multiple moments of a televisual ensemble drama to construct narrative closure, creating a finality to a segment (a single episode and season) of an ongoing narrative whole.[22] Sequences such as this foreground the segmentation and flow of the television aesthetic as narrative fragments are woven together through the unifying flow of the track into an expressive whole.

The final appearance of 'Hallelujah' comes at the close of the season three finale 'The Graduates'[23] after Ryan and Marissa have suffered a car crash. Here an echoing and spare cover by Imogen Heap plays as Ryan carries a fatally injured Marissa away from the wreckage. This moment uses the allusive meaning of the song, drawing again on audience memory (potentially also figuring as Ryan's own) to recall previous narrative moments. This is compounded by the image of Ryan carrying an unconscious Marissa, a repeated visual motif within the programme, with past instances overlaid on the shot. This moment demonstrates long-term serialised narratives' ability to fold back upon themselves, 'the layering of traces, the return and retreat that enacts a rhythm of ebb and flow'.[24] 'Hallelujah's function as an emotive series

---

[21] 1.27 Patrick Norris 2004.
[22] This device is not confined to this show; Julie Brown, '*Ally McBeal's* Postmodern Soundtrack', 285, discusses its 'dramatic recapitulatory function' in *Ally McBeal* (dir. various 1997–2002), and it is now a prevalent televisual narrative and structural device, particularly in other music-centred melodramas such as *One Tree Hill* (dir. various 2003–12) and *Grey's Anatomy* (dir. various 2005–).
[23] 3.25 Ian Toynton 2006.
[24] Holdsworth, *Television*, 64.

leitmotif is compounded by the use of Heap, whose esoteric electro-pop had appeared multiple times across *The O.C*, including her 'Hide and Seek' closing the season two finale 'Dearly Beloved'.[25] This 'Hallelujah' brings traces of previous season finales and presents Marissa's death as a moment of anguish, but also as an inevitable conclusion to previous events. However, the use of Heap rather than the familiar Buckley version – her drawn out pacing and breathy, ghostly vocal echoed in Marisa's last breaths and Ryan's gasped entreaties – creates a sonic and memory disjunction which compounds Marisa's death as a moment of emotional and narrative fracture.

Jeff Smith suggests that popular song's filmic meaning is achieved through association and allusion,[26] its narrative affect often dependent on social and cultural resonance.[27] Marissa's death uses the intra-textual meaning of 'Hallelujah' to recall memories of previous emotionally resonant moments in the narrative. It draws on on the layering and return enabled by television's serialised narrative, where 'development and repetition feels more like the uncanny unfolding of fate, and is posed in direct recognition that we have, indeed, been there before'.[28] However, by the time this third use occurred, we had been there too many times before, as the song had perhaps been overburdened with *extra*-textual meanings. By the end of *The O.C.*'s third season in 2006, Buckley's 'Hallelujah' had become overused in popular culture, appearing in more than eight US series – including *The West Wing*[29] and *House*[30] – at moments of heightened drama and narrative climax.[31] Whilst *The O.C.*'s reuse of the song built on its original meaning within the narrative, drawing on audience memory, its cultural ubiquity ultimately polluted this climactic moment with many other televisual memories. The recognition factor and the crowd of allusions from other uses creates distance and reduces the emotional impact of this suturing of music and narrative.

Whilst *The O.C.*'s employment of pop song leitmotif is relatively rare in television, in exploring some of the ways in which the programme integrates popular music and storytelling I have sought to demonstrate the scope for analysis of television music. In particular, the chapter has explored how television's structure allows a song to evolve and contribute to narrative flow, accumulating meaning through repetition. In addition, musical moments can

[25] 2.24 Ian Toynton 2005.

[26] Smith, *Sounds*, 22.

[27] Smith, *Sounds*, 155.

[28] Jason Jacobs, 'Issues of Judgement and Value in Television Studies', *International Journal of Cultural Studies* 4:4 (2001): 434.

[29] Dir. Various (1999–2006).

[30] Dir. Various (2005–12).

[31] Jeff Tyrangiel, 'Keeping Up the Ghost', *Time*, 12 December, 2004, http://www.time.com/time/magazine/article/0,9171,1006590,00.html [accessed 1 July 2007].

sometimes contribute to *The O.C.*'s playful self-reflexive tone, yet at others provide the emotional resonance that the programme's ironic edge otherwise denies. Close analysis of textual and narrative uses of popular music across a serialised narrative can thus illustrate the depth of meaning and particular televisual quality of these moments of narrative popular music.

Bibliography

Ang, Ien. *Watching Dallas: Television and the Melodramatic Imagination.* London: Routledge, 1985.

Butler, Jeremy. *Television Style.* Abingdon: Routledge, 2010.

Brown, Julie. '*Ally McBeal's* Postmodern Soundtrack', *Journal of the Royal Musical Association* 126:2 (2001): 275–303.

Deaville, James, ed. *Music in Television: Channels of Listening.* Abingdon: Routledge, 2011.

Dickinson, Kay. '"My Generation": Popular Music, Age and Influence in Teen Drama of the 1990s.' In *Teen TV: Genre, Consumption and Identity*, edited by Glyn Davis and Kay Dickinson, 99–111. London: BFI, 2004.

Donnelly, K. J. 'Tracking British Television: Pop Music as Stock Soundtrack to the Small Screen', *Popular Music* 21:3 (2002): 331–43.

Fairchild, Charles. 'Flow amid Flux: The Evolving Uses of Music in Evening Television Drama', *Television and New Media* 12:6 (2011): 491–512.

Frith, Simon. 'Look! Hear! The Uneasy Relationship of Music and Television', *Popular Music* 21:3 (2002): 277–90.

Garwood, Ian. 'The Pop Song in Film.' In *Close-Up: 01*, edited by John Gibbs and Douglas Pye, 89–166. London: Wallflower Press, 2006.

Gorbman, Claudia. *Unheard Melodies: Narrative Film Music.* London: BFI, 1987.

Holdsworth, Amy. *Television, Memory and Nostalgia.* Basingstoke: Palgrave Macmillan, 2011.

Jacobs, Jason. 'Issues of Judgement and Value in Television Studies', *International Journal of Cultural Studies* 4:4 (2001): 427– 47.

Lury, Karen. *Interpreting Television.* London: Hodder Arnold, 2005.

Lynskey, Dorian. 'How *The O.C.* Saved Music.' *The Guardian.* 1 December, 2004. http://arts.guardian.co.uk/features/story/0,,1363852,00.html [accessed 30 March 2006].

Rodman, Ron. *Tuning In: American Narrative Television Music.* New York: Oxford University Press, 2009.

Smith, Jeff. *The Sounds of Commerce: Marketing Popular Film Music.* New York. Columbia University Press, 1998.

Tyrangiel, Jeff. 'Keeping Up the Ghost.' *Time.* 12 December, 2004. http://www.time.com/time/magazine/article/0,9171,1006590,00.html [accessed 1 July 2007].

Zemler, Emily. 'The O.C. Effect.' *Popmatters.* 14 January 2005. http://www.popmatters.com/music/features/050114-indiesoundtracks.shtml [accessed 30 March 2006].

15

Camera and performer: Energetic engagement with *The Shield*

Lucy Fife Donaldson

In a directors' roundtable discussion[1] on *The Shield* (FX, 2002–8), Peter Horton,[2] suggests that fully embracing a documentary aesthetic fights against closeness to characters' emotional states, and as a result the show potentially suffers from a loss of intimacy. On the contrary, close attention to the series' visual style, reveals impulses of intimacy and involvement with bodies. Strategies concerning camera placement and movement complicate the relationships between bodies and space, embedding patterns of tension between the willed direction of the camera and that of the performer in order to immerse the viewer in the unpredictability and risk of police work.

The Shield deals with a police department in the fictional LA district of Farmington, comprising uniformed officers, detectives, a gang task-force (the 'Strike Team'), senior staff and also city officials and other departments, as well as the gangs, criminals, citizens and family members they interact with.[3] The show routinely focuses on situations concerning brutal crimes and endangerment, underlining the physical risk involved in police work.

---

[1] Peter Horton, DVD 'Directors' Roundtable', season 2.
[2] Director of 3 episodes: 'Carte Blanche' season 2, episode 4; 'Co-Pilot' season 2, episode 9; 'Safe' season 3, episode 7.
[3] While there are various additions (and subtractions) over the 7 seasons, the core characters – Officer Danny Sofer, Officer Julian Lowe, Detective Holland 'Dutch' Wagenbach, Detective Claudette Wyms, Detective Vic Mackey, Detective Shane Vendrell and Captain/City Councillor David Aceveda – remain throughout.

The tensions of familial and working relationships result in physical assaults, sexual dysfunction, betrayal, murder and suicide. Violence and physical action are a main concern of the Police Series genre, which leads to an emphasis on the body, both as an object of violence and as the vehicle for expression of action and effort, as indicated by Jonathan Bignell: 'moments of character revelation by bodily means and not verbal ones characterize [*Hill Street Blues*, *Miami Vice*, *NYPD Blue* and *CSI*]'.[4] As he suggests, the impact of crime on the body, of both victim and cop, is important to programmes of various tones and registers.[5] Generic action is concerned with the physical labour of policing: crime scene detection, undercover work, chases and arrests. In *The Shield* the physical tension, energy and anxiety of this work are embedded in decisions about camera, bodies and space, so that the mechanics of our access to and knowledge of the fictional world are designed to immerse us in the exertion of policing.

The visual style of *The Shield* follows patterns established by US precinct dramas *Hill Street Blues* (NBC, 1981–7), *Homicide: Life on the Street* (NBC, 1993–9) and *NYPD Blue* (ABC, 1993–2005).[6] For these series, decisions concerning spatial arrangements of camera and performer attempt a documentary-like realism, suggesting that filming is reacting to events as they unfold, rather than as rehearsed, thereby framing action as the 'reality' of modern police work.[7] As Bignell has argued, the immediacy and intimacy of this stylistic approach are important to the genre, while

---

[4] Jonathan Bignell, 'The Police Series', in *Close-up 03: The Police Series, Weimar Cinema and Men's Cinema*, (eds) John Gibbs and Douglas Pye (London: Wallflower Press, 2009), 6.
[5] Examples include (but aren't limited to): *Cracker* (ITV, 1993–5, 1996 and 2006), *Homicide: Life on the Streets* (NBC, 1993–9), *Silent Witness* (BBC, 1996–), *CSI: Crime Scene Investigation* (CBS, 2000–), *Dexter* (Showtime, 2006–), *Southland* (NBC, 2009; TNT, 2009–), *Luther* (BBC, 2010–).
[6] Several key members of the crew, and returning directors worked variously as directors/actors/ writers/producers on these influential series, including: Scott Brazil (director, 11 episodes/ Executive Producer 2002–7) worked on *Hill Street Blues* as Associate Producer (1981–2), producer (1982–3), supervising producer (1983–6) and director (1984–6); Clark Johnson (director, 7 episodes) portrayed a central character on *Homicide: Life on the Streets* (in all 122 episodes) and directed 5 episodes (1996–8); Nick Gomez (director, 3 episodes) directed 6 episodes of *Homicide: Life on the Streets* (1993–8); Paris Barclay (director, 3 episodes) worked on *NYPD Blue* as producer/super-vising producer and directed 12 episodes (1997–9); Félix Enríquez Alcalá (director, 2 episodes) previously directed an episode of *NYPD Blue* (1994); Charles H. Eglee (writer, 15 episodes) writer of 3 episodes of *NYPD Blue* (1994–5); Kevin Arkadie (writer, 3 episodes) writer on *NYPD Blue and Homicide* (1 episode each).
[7] Although the issue of realism is beyond the scope of this chapter, it has been important to the Police Series in the UK and US since the 1960s, supporting concerns with presenting details of modern policing and framing violence as part of the routine of police work which made both *Z-Cars* (BBC, 1962–78) and *Hill Street Blues* such ground-breaking examples of the genre. See Lez Cooke, 'The Police Series/Hill Street Blues', in *The Television Genre Book*, ed. Glen Creeber (London: BFI, 2001), 19–23.

also being tendencies taken as specific characteristics of television.[8] *The Shield's* strategy of shooting with two cameras rather than one, usually a combination of handheld and steadicam, develops greater emphasis on action being in the process of unfolding, and therefore frames our epistemic position as responsive to and reliant upon the immediacy of performance and visual style.

Multiple-camera production is more typically associated with sitcoms, soap operas, game shows, sports programmes and newscasts, than drama. As noted by Jeremy Butler, there are key differences concerning treatment of performance and space: firstly, 'actors always perform the scenes straight through' and secondly, 'action may be missed by the camera and wind up occurring out of sight, off-frame, because the camera cannot control the action to the degree that it does in single-camera shooting'.[9] *The Shield* capitalizes on these impulses of continuous performance and incomplete coverage, contributing to an 'illusion of "liveness" and an apparent lack of control,[10] which support its interest in the risks of policing a violent and impoverished neighbourhood, while investment in the cameras' (and by extension our) lack of mastery over performance dramatises the nature of our access to the fictional world as partial and unpredictable.

The quality of access afforded to the body also informs how we engage with it, so by placing risk and incompleteness as central principles *The Shield* sets up the relationship between the body onscreen and our own as troubling the usual security of their reciprocity. Charles Affron discusses the joining of camera movement, sight and emotion, analogising the relationship between moving camera and character to a dance duet – a partnership which 'admits sharing and separateness, unity and individuality'.[11] In considering the role of spatial relationships in our emotional connection to cinema, Affron highlights the responsive dynamic of camera and performer, and how quality of movement can be affective. *The Shield's* dual camera approach complicates and inflects this dynamic to foster kinetic and emotional tension.

A chase involving members of the Strike Team dominates the pre-title sequences of 'Playing Tight'.[12] This opening, which starts with uniformed officers dealing with a domestic disturbance and then moves between the Strike Team and detectives Dutch (Jay Karnes) and Claudette (CCH Pounder) investigating a crime scene, is a strong example of the ways in which the

---

[8] Bignell, 'Police Series', 65.
[9] Jeremy G. Butler, *Television: Critical Methods and Applications*, second edn (Mahwah, NJ: Lawrence Erlbaum Associates, 2002), 166, 169.
[10] Butler, *Television*, 169.
[11] Charles Affron, *Cinema and Sentiment* (Chicago: University of Chicago Press, 1982), 100.
[12] Season 3, episode 1.

show habitually places the viewer in the midst of action already in progress.[13] After the attempted arrest of a drug dealer and subsequent car chase, Vic (Michael Chiklis) and Shane (Walton Goggins) follow the fleeing suspect on foot, via a number of alleyways, backyards and finally into the house of a Latino couple.

As Vic and Shane give chase, camera placement shifts rapidly, through editing and handheld camera movements, to combine continuity of physical exertion with visual complexity and incompleteness. As the suspect jumps over a gate in the background of a shot, Vic and Shane can be seen further behind him. The rest of the frame is filled with the contents of a washing line, the proximity of which overwhelms the space and impinges on the clarity of our view, so that action is intensified within a smaller pocket of space. Momentarily, the bodies onscreen are disconcertingly dwarfed by the washing, which then moves as each rushes past, the framing mindful of physical impact in this tactile space. Once the suspect gets nearer, the camera zooms out to show more of the yard into which they're running, and then remains in position as he runs past, followed by Shane and then Vic. In this brief shot, the compression of space, whereby action moves from foreground to background, rather than along the horizontal axis of the frame or through intercutting, forces attention to the complexity of performances within it. The rapid movement of three bodies within this cluttered space restricts capacity for sustained attention to details of expression. As we are acutely aware simultaneously of the proximity of police to suspect, his panic at being caught and their focused resolve to catch him, the shot emphasizes the spatial and physical dimensions of expressivity. The zoom out briefly prolongs this interaction between elements, while also adjusting the weight of attention to Vic and Shane's progress and allowing observation of the control in their compact actions in comparison to the suspect's looser panicked movements.

At the chase's climax, the movement from pursuit to capture, from exterior to interior, is elliptical in its rapidity. One handheld camera follows Vic and then Shane, before a sharp cut offers a momentary glimpse of Shane as he darts left to follow the suspect. A second rapid cut jumps us forwards to a medium long shot of the suspect outside a house as he changes direction to go into the doorway, at which point Vic appears from the left to grab him going up the steps. They fall into the room and there is a cut to a medium long shot of a couple sitting on their couch as Vic and the suspect plunge past, followed a beat later by a shot of both

---

[13] In some ways this opening also repeats the pilot's introduction of the series, which featured an extended chase, by way of introduction to police work and a central group of characters.

from outside the house, their bodies half hidden behind a wall, the camera zooming in fractionally as Vic receives a blow to the face. Here, changing perspectives omit increasingly substantial pieces of action. Rapid cuts to Shane and the suspect before Vic catches him seem to be ahead of the action's beat, and as the cameras catch up to the point of collision it almost happens without them. The precise spatial and temporal trajectories of the action are disrupted as camera placement and editing patterns reject the continuity or steady crescendo offered by match-on-action or direction of movement.

Experience of space is confusing and discordant, both in its partiality and in the handheld quality of movement. As with other instances of hand-held filming in TV drama, such as *24* (Fox, 2001–10) and *Battlestar Galactica* (Sci-Fi, 2003–9) the shaky movement and its rhythmic intensity encourages the feeling of being 'in' the action. Yet, while the cameras place us in the midst of things, the physical involvement this sequence invites more precisely encourages us to be concerned for Vic and Shane as their purposeful bodies direct our attention. Neither demonstrates outward anxiety or concern for risk as their gait and postures remain focused on their target – the assurance of Vic's leap through the doorway doesn't account for concerns of bodily harm. The cameras' reactive relationship to physicality, to movement and change, appeals directly to a sensory viewing experience by leaving an impression of effort and strain, even though we don't have the opportunity to observe this on the performers' bodies for any prolonged period. This process, whereby we are required to more fully imagine exertion, needing to 'flesh [action] out' through our bodies, is described by Vivian Sobchack as one in which the body 'fills in the gap in its sensual grasp of the figural world onscreen by turning back on itself'.[14] Without more sustained or perhaps choreographed access we flesh out the labour intimated by glimpses of bodies straining to increase their rhythms and capacity, in between the moments highlighting exertion, like Shane's abrupt change of direction.

This brief chase is instructive of how *The Shield* shapes our encounters with bodies in space, and the particular ways space is negotiated, compressed, shifted and interrupted, which foreground the exertion and propulsion of movement. Furthermore, the cameras' struggles to keep up are indicative of the way our relative epistemic, and often physical, proximity during the unfolding of events entails an experience of police work that is partial for us and for these characters. Our relationship to Shane and Vic doesn't centralise the act of detection in a way that is revelatory of investigative knowledge/

---

[14] Vivian Sobchack, *Carnal Thoughts: Embodiment and Moving Image Culture* (Berkeley: University of California Press, 2004), 82.

intuition, as the camera movements around Sarah Lund (Sofie Gråbøl) do in *Forbrydelsen/The Killing* (Danmarks Radio, 2007–).

The complication of bodies and space is not lessened in interiors. Like many Police Series, *The Shield*'s interrogation sequences frequently feature interplay between two spaces: interrogation rooms and an observation room. In 'Blood & Water'[15] attention is split between Dutch questioning a suspect in a gang killing, and his partner Claudette, accompanied by Shane and Vic in the observation room watching the live feed of the interrogation on a TV. Here the multiplicity of perspectives place Dutch's approach in tension with the motivations and methods of his observers, established through varying degrees of access to details of performance: a close-up Shane's of fidgety movements corresponds with his lack of sympathy and outward criticism of Dutch's subtle methods; repeated shots of Claudette's rigid posture and expressive constraint obscure her judgement; in a wider shot, Vic's initial relaxed lean into the sofa supports his position of confidence in comparison to the others who are sat forwards.

Dutch enters the interrogation room on the premise of obtaining a witness statement from Esteban (Jeremy Ray Valdez). Here, the shot reverse-shot pattern that might typically shape an interrogation to sustain the clarity of questioning/confession is renegotiated with the use of handheld and moving cameras. The sequence shifts between views of Dutch from roughly the same spatial position on his left side of Esteban (from over Dutch's shoulder), and the more infrequent insertion of something approximating a two-shot, including both of them in the frame. As such, the handling of space echoes patterns of capturing conversation familiar to television,[16] but modifies these using vertical and horizontal axes of perspective: our views of Esteban start level with the table, rather than his head, and continue at a lower angle even when he stands, whereas shots of Dutch, and Claudette in the observation room, are frequently from a higher angle. These adjustments to the dynamics of spatial perspective seep into the relationship between withholding and revelation at the heart of interrogation scenes more generally. The crescendo or rhythmic build potentially offered by the shot reverse-shot pattern is set off-kilter by the range of views and refusal to return to the exact same framing. Judgements of veracity, so important for comprehension of the interrogation for police and viewer, are thus problematised by inconsistencies in the interactions of camera, body and space so that the scene is opened

---

[15] Season 3, episode 2.
[16] As Jeremy Butler points out: 'In conversation scenes – the foundation of narrative television – directors rely on close-ups in shot-counter shot to develop the main narrative action of a scene.' Butler, *Television*, 168.

to the possibility of Dutch's failure to extract the information in time. The tensions between the differing experiences of the interview are dramatised by the way the cameras slide and hover around and past performers, as the sense of always being on the verge of movement and thus figuratively suspended intimates felt anxieties around Dutch's ability to perform.

As well as embedding a material anxiety into a scene where performers are moving little or not at all, decisions concerning framing display a desire to obscure perspectives. As the sequence progresses, views of Esteban are consistently framed by parts of Dutch's body, his face, shoulders or elbow, and in one instance through the gap between his torso and upper arm. This physical impingement results in a lack of clarity in our view, which in some ways matches that of Claudette, Shane and Vic, whose access to events are hampered by quality and scale of their view. It also draws out awareness of these bodies in relation to one another and in the context of this dramatically charged room: Esteban's awkwardness and then agitation is heightened by comparison to portions of Dutch's body framing him which remains still and angular. The cameras' proximity to performers entails closeness that draws attention to them as bodies, inviting us to view the body as a way to engage more fully with the expressivity of their physicality. Although anchored in a sitting position, Dutch's interrogations require certain postures – a relaxed gait and open arm movements as he first enters the space, which gives way to increasing fixity and control – and we see his questions in relation to these.

In their dynamics of revelation and withholding and the often tightly patterned methods of presentation, interrogation scenes can offer highly performative spaces, supporting the possible roles of 'good cop' 'bad cop', for instance. Just as the cameras are not settled, Dutch's role is not as defined, but attention to the body our access to him and the others affords, indicates the degree to which he is both playing a role and directing Esteban's behaviour. At first he presents a relaxed approach, engaging Esteban with a light tone of voice, gesturing flexibly with his hand, and looking down at the paper in front of him to make notes. As he starts to ask about details of what Esteban saw, Dutch's gaze becomes more attentive, his voice likewise more direct, with less inflection and stress only on certain keywords. The important role the body plays in detection is then confirmed when Dutch shifts the direction of the interrogation, leaning back in his chair as he says 'You know why you're in this room' and then again when he moves forwards to accuse Esteban of being involved. The expression of energy and release through the body communicates what is involved in police work, making the tension a material quality of performance and visual style. Our views of the observation room are mindful of the connection between bodies onscreen and off, as performers' postures dramatise the rise and release of anxiety: Vic leans forwards in his seat as Dutch builds the interview up, and then after Dutch reveals his knowledge of the killing, Shane leans back in his chair. The way Dutch uses his body reveals the importance of physical effort to police work, but in a way that communicates the differences between Dutch and the Strike Team; particularly in the way the ability to control the suspect and change pace dramatises the former's superior epistemic position.

Both chase and interrogation sequences indicate the sense that the cameras could go anywhere in their attempts to keep up with and cover action.[17] The decision to use two cameras utilizes the reactive and partial coverage afforded by this set-up, shapes involvement in the action as sponta-neous – presenting the action as everyone experiencing events for the first time.[18] Affron's sense of camera and performer being akin to dancing partners is modified here in the seeming absence of a choreographed unity, opening up a pattern of tensions between the degrees of control over events for camera and performer undermining unity between the onscreen body and camera to further reciprocation between camera and the offscreen body.[19] In doing so, the series internalises an acknowledgement of a lack of mastery of action and bodies that feeds through to our perspective on and experience of the fictional world. Although there is plenty more to say about the visceral nature of this programme, the unsteady and often anxious relationships between body and camera highlight the potential for highly physicalised change, communicating energetic engagement with the characters' ways of doing police work through exertion and propulsion be it active or not.

---

[17] This is confirmed by director of photography, Rohn Schmidt: 'Even if the shot starts over-the-shoulder, the operators have permission to follow what is more interesting. They'll tilt down and focus in on something or someone else. The actors have discovered that they can be on camera any time in any shot.' Anonymous, 'The Shield: How Rohn Schmidt breaks all the rules shooting in Super 16', *In Camera* (October 2003): 32.

[18] Director Paris Barclay describes his commitment to preserving this spontaneity while shooting, by secretly changing the blocking and not letting camera operators get used to doing a scene a certain way. Paris Barclay, DVD 'Directors' Roundtable, Season 2.

[19] There are a few notable exceptions to this throughout the series, where a sustained sequence of action is placed in conjunction with non-diegetic music (examples of this tendency occur during the closing of the pilot episode and 'Grave' season 4, episode 2), which stick out as overtly stylised and constructed, and less successfully engaging.

Bibliography

Affron, Charles. *Cinema and Sentiment*. Chicago: The University of Chicago
   Press, 1982.
Anonymous. 'The Shield: How Rohn Schmidt breaks all the rules shooting in
   Super 16.' *In Camera* (October 2003): 32–3.
Bignell, Jonathan. 'The Police Series.' In *Close-up 03: The Police Series, Weimar
   Cinema and Men's Cinema*, edited by John Gibbs and Douglas Pye, 3–66.
   London: Wallflower Press, 2009.
Butler, Jeremy G. *Television: Critical Methods and Applications*, second edn.
   Mahwah, NJ: Lawrence Erlbaum Associates, 2002.
Cooke, Lez. 'The Police Series/Hill Street Blues.' In *The Television Genre Book*,
   edited by Glen Creeber, 19–23. London: BFI, 2001.
Sobchack, Vivian. *Carnal Thoughts: Embodiment and Moving Image Culture*.
   Berkeley: University of California Press, 2004.

16

Flashforwards in *Breaking Bad*: Openness, closure and possibility

Elliott Logan

This chapter examines the interpretation and evaluation of the supposed puzzle nature of non-linear narrative designs in *Breaking Bad*. Against these claims I offer a close reading of the flashforward narrative of the penultimate episode of *Breaking Bad*'s first season.[1] My reading shows how the vocabulary appropriate to appreciating the achievements of a puzzle – one that implies fixed, inevitable solutions to a work – is inappropriate to the artistic achievements of the most profound works of contemporary television and inadequate to the concerns these achievements raise: concerns that do not lend themselves to solution.

Breaking Bad tells the story of Walter White (Bryan Cranston), who lives a life of quiet desperation: despite his once promising career as a research scientist, he is now a disrespected public high school chemistry teacher, working as a car wash cashier to make ends barely meet. In the pilot episode he is diagnosed with inoperable, terminal lung cancer, treatment of which would delay rather than prevent his death, giving urgency of purpose to what remains of his life.[2] Facing this apparently predetermined death, whose financial consequences would threaten the future possibilities of his family,

---

[1] Vince Gilligan and George Mastras, 'Crazy Handful of Nothin'. *Breaking Bad*, season 1, episode 6. Directed by Bronwen Hughes. Aired October 2 2008. Burbank, CA: Sony Pictures Television, 2008. DVD.

[2] Vince Gilligan, 'Breaking Bad', *Breaking Bad*, season 1, episode 1. Directed by Vince Gilligan. Aired August 28 2008. Burbank, CA: Sony Pictures Television, 2008. DVD.

Walt chooses to cook and sell methamphetamine with a former student, Jesse Pinkman (Aaron Paul), in order to financially secure his family's future. Through explosive moments of choice and the gradual accumulation of experience over the course of five seasons, Walt transforms himself, shaping a new life and identity as a ruthless criminal.

Many episodes of the series are distinguished by their use of enigmatic teaser sequences, or 'cold opens', that flashforward to elliptically suggest future catastrophes. Scattering strands of stories at the beginning, inviting anticipation of how they will be reconnected at the end, these initially confounding designs may present as puzzles in want of solution. For example, four interrelated flashforwards prefigure the devastating catastrophe of the second season's climax, in which, as an indirect result of Walt's terrible act of omission that allows a young woman's death, two passenger aircraft collide over the skies of Albuquerque. Lisa Coulthard claims these flashforwards function as 'retroactive clues' that may be used to unravel the season's 'mind game'.[3] Coulthard implies the design may be solved by properly understanding the clues, a solution that would constitute mastery in this 'mind game'. It is undeniable the initial puzzlement evoked by these designs is one of their intended effects. However, treating them as a puzzle in this way seems inappropriate when their relationship to story is considered. The flashforward designs in question withhold from the audience the nature of, and responsibility for, a gradually unfolding disaster of increasingly incomprehensible scale. This seems significant in relation to the fact that the principally involved characters are also unable to apprehend the nature of the catastrophe, or their responsibility for it. This design's significance does not ask for, nor is it amenable to, the solutions demanded of a puzzle. 'Solutions' may only be found when the design is evacuated of content. Reducing the narration of the second season's climax to a 'mind game' elides the tragically catastrophic blindness at its heart.

The grounds for this divorce between form and content are laid in Jason Mittell's interpretation and evaluation of what he calls moments of 'narrative special effect' in contemporary, narratively complex serial television.[4] Mittell interprets these moments as displaying an 'operational aesthetic', 'calling attention to the constructed nature of the narration and asking us to marvel at how the writers pulled it off; … we watch the process of narration as a machine rather than engaging in its diegesis'.[5] Viewers are invited 'to

---

[3] Lisa Coulthard, 'The Hotness of Cold Opens: Breaking Bad and the Serial Narrative as Puzzle,' *Flow* 13:3 (2010), http://flowtv.org/2010/11/the-hotness-of-cold-opens [accessed 10 December 2012]
[4] Jason Mittell, 'Narrative Complexity in Contemporary American Television', *The Velvet Light Trap* 56 (Fall 2006): 35.
[5] Mittell, 'Narrative Complexity', 35.

engage at the level of formal analyst, dissecting the techniques used to convey spectacular displays of storytelling craft; ... a level of awareness that transcends the traditional focus on diegetic action typical of most viewers'.[6] Mittell provides a pertinent example of such appreciation when arguing for the complexity of the narrative designs of *Lost* (ABC 2004–10), the third season of which concludes with the revelation that rather than an anticipated flashback, the expected narrative dislocation is a flashforward. Mittell writes of this choice:

> For once, the key question isn't 'What will happen?' (as we learn that at least Kate (Evangeline Lilley) and Jack will be rescued), but 'How will they tell us what happens?' To appreciate this moment requires viewers to think about the show's narrative mechanics, embracing the operational aesthetic to enjoy the storytelling spectacle provided by this narrational cliffhanger.[7]

Choices of narrative design are here valued for their capacity to draw attention away from fictional concerns, and to invite admiration of the creative intelligence that has shaped their presentation. The perverse consequence of this admiration is an underestimation of that intelligence and of those designs. Mittell suggests a principle by which narrative design, as well as representational content, should be valued for achieving decorative, rather than meaningful, effects.

We might imagine that the flashforward opening of 'Crazy Handful of Nothin'' functions similarly, to evoke anticipation, or the admiration of a creative intelligence. In it, Walt outlines to Jesse the future division of labour and ethical limits of their enterprise. The scene is punctuated by narrative dislocations that provide momentary, fragmented glimpses of an unidentifiable man striding away from the wake of what seems to have been an explosion in a rundown part of the city. The sequence climaxes with the revelation that the man is in fact Walt, enigmatically transformed, his nose bloodied, his head shaved, walking away from the violent scene clutching a bloodstained canvas sack.

By the episode's close the steps that led to this point have been retraced. Seeking to accelerate their earnings, Walt and Jesse looked to gain a supply contract with a notoriously violent mid-level distributor, Tuco (Raymond

---

[6] Mittell, 'Narrative Complexity', 36.
[7] Jason Mittell, 'Lost in a Great Story: Evaluation in Narrative Television (and Television Studies)', *Reading Lost: Perspectives on a Hit Television Show*, ed. Roberta Pearson (London: I. B. Tauris, 2009), 131.

Cruz). Tuco demanded that Jesse surrender thirty-five thousand dollars' worth of product on consignment. Jesse's refusal was met with a vicious beating. With Jesse in hospital, Walt met Tuco, and, by threatening him with explosives ingeniously disguised as meth, extracted an ongoing, favourable business arrangement. As the credits roll the pieces of the narrative puzzle have been restored to their correct order. Our anticipation has been pleasurably rewarded with clever surprise.

How can this solution adequately account for why it is that the episode unfolds the way it does? What else might the choice of the episode's opening suggest that cannot be accounted for by the solution of a puzzle, or the admiration of a creative intelligence revealed by the unexpected intricacies of a design?

'Crazy Handful' opens immediately after the previous episode, 'Gray Matter', closes. At that episode's end, having chosen to pursue chemotherapy, Walt returns to Jesse to restart their enterprise, having closed it down in the wake of the murderous violence it had unleashed. Jesse, having failed to produce on his own the high standard of product set by Walt, is packing away their equipment.[8] Thus 'Crazy Handful' opens with Walt leading Jesse back inside the RV that they use as a mobile meth lab, boxes of illegal lab equipment in hand.

The inside of the RV is a mess. The floor and benches are covered with broken glass, scattered equipment and supplies, and remnants of activities that have no place in Walt's treasured workspace: an empty malt liquor bottle and a particularly crass pornographic magazine. Testifying to Jesse's disastrous attempt to oversee his own 'cook' in Walt's absence, the RV's condition represents a crisis of position and authority within their partnership. The terms of this crisis are initially quietly expressed through the establishing shot of Walt and Jesse. Jesse skulks near the doorway, in the background of the lower left corner of the frame, out of focus, the right-hand third of the frame dominated by Walt as he takes in the chaos of the workspace. Although the tilt of Jesse's head seeks to avert Walt's judgemental gaze, his eyes look up to him, expectantly. I take this shot to be placing Jesse in relation to Walt as a student, or child, waiting to be disciplined or lectured to by a teacher, or parent. And indeed, a moment later, a lecture begins as Walt speaks the episode's first line. It is the clipped, declarative, authoritative opening of a teacher correcting a consistently recalcitrant student: 'Let's get something straight.' What follows sets out the terms of how this crisis of position and

---

[8]Vince Gilligan and Patty Lin, 'Gray Matter'. *Breaking Bad*, season 1, episode 5. Directed by Tricia Brock. Aired September 25 2008. Burbank, CA: Sony Pictures Television, 2008. DVD.

authority – what will emerge as a matter of identity – is to be settled, now and into the future.

The first sign of identity emerging as the subject of Walt's lecture to Jesse comes through two interlinked hand gestures that accompany the delivery of his next line: 'This – the chemistry – is my realm.' With 'this' Walt raises his left hand above the workspace, and, fingers outstretched, makes a number of tight circular movements, as if his hand were to encompass all that lies beneath it, in this space: 'the chemistry'. Walt then forcefully draws his hand, fingers still outstretched, back towards but not quite into his chest, as his emphatic pronunciation gives equal force to '*my* realm'. The second gesture's rhyme with the first crafts a link that makes the claim of Walt's domain over the chemistry consonant with his domain over himself. These two interlinked gestures that pass before us in the space of one line that is spoken in less than a full breath express that Walt considers himself to *be* what he *does*.

The authority of Walt's claims regarding his present identity and position is placed under pressure as he delivers his first line regarding Jesse and, implicitly, the future: 'Out there, on the street: you deal with that.' As Walt distances himself from the places and activities that he claims will, in future, constitute Jesse's position and identity within their enterprise, there is a cut to a scene that is something like this place, 'the street', which suggests a sense of what it will mean to 'deal with that'. We see two quick shots, slow-motion glimpses of a street in a rundown area, scattered with the debris of an explosion; onlookers move as if dazed, as the sharp peals of a ringing burglar alarm aggravate our temporal and spatial dislocation. These dislocating glimpses of crisis puncture Walt's claims with a tension that unsettles them.

Tension and unsettlement grow as the development and expansion of Walt's claims on the future attract longer, more detailed, and more intense glimpses of this crisis of indeterminate place and time, but occurring in suggestive relation to Walt and Jesse's futures. Walt next states that: 'As far as our customers go, I don't want to know anything about them. I don't want to see them; I don't want to hear from them. I want no interaction with them whatsoever.' This more detailed and emphatic claim, of superiority and distance, is answered by a lengthier, less fragmentary segment of the earlier street scene that places us more firmly, more intimately *within* its chaos. The shots are this time less glimpses than glares. Seemingly point-of-view, they confidently part the crowd of bystanders, who in dress and manner evoke motorcycle gang members, suggesting the very customers from whom Walt proclaims his separation. Moving through their midst we hear their idling engines and snatches of voices. A sense of proximity undermines the ideal of separation. The segment's final shot draws us in closer: it glides along the glass-strewn asphalt, following in close-up a man's calm footsteps as he walks from the unseen disaster, a man who walks with confidence through this crowd of 'customers'.

Developing duration, detail and proximity of involvement in relation to the expansiveness and emphasis of Walt's claims on the future, the two narrative dislocations heighten the ambiguous discord between the two simultaneous strands of narration. We experience neither one as 'past' or 'future', but each as unfolding in the *present*, a conflation of tense whose treatment does not obscure the strands' clear – and vital – before and after relation. The effect of the discord prefigured between them is to ratchet up a sense of the doom – ambiguously foreshadowed – of Walt's claims on the future constitution of his identity, and on the nature of his position in the criminal world in which he and Jesse are seeking to increasingly involve themselves.

This ambiguous sense of opposition between the imagination of the future and its realisation is made clear and emphatic in the final flashforward segment of the sequence.

We are prepared for the segment's heightened intensity and significance by the treatment of Walt's final claim. Walt moves in close to Jesse, face-to-face, less than an arm's length away, having gained Jesse's begrudging, indifferent consent to his position as the 'silent partner' in their two-man operation. The camera responds in kind, framing Walt in a tight close-up, canted slightly to the left, as if the disruptions of the previous narrative dislocations are felt even here, heightening the sense of crisis. In the intimacy of their standing to each other we may feel the weight of Walt's grave words: 'No matter what happens,' Walt says, his voice low and head shaking, as if to ward off the possibility of his words' violation, 'no more bloodshed.'

His words are violated, though, and with violence. The final segment, which confirms the sequence's status as a flashforward, is an image suggestive of violence, presented violently. Having made his vow of 'no more bloodshed', Walt pauses, to allow its weight to settle. The pause is seized from him, however, and its claim to peace shattered, by a cut back to the enigmatic feet striding along the glass-strewn asphalt. The cut's visual disruption is intensified as it arrives with a deep boom of percussion in concert with the backfire of a motorcycle exhaust. A steady, crashing beat now dominates the soundtrack as the feet march seemingly inexorably along; it nearly drowns Walt's voiceover delivery of 'No violence' that caps his proclamations. The volume and tempo build towards a climax as details of the mysterious figure are revealed, from the bloodstain on the canvas sack, to a glimpse of his shaved head and eyeglasses. The climax comes with an eruption of inhuman wailing on the soundtrack and a cut to a medium shot that reveals Walt – head shaved, nose bloodied, cheeks and eye sockets cavernous – nearly staring down the lens as he walks in slow motion away from the two-storey building behind, smoke and sparks issuing from its smashed windows. It is a disturbing image of previously unrealized self-possession and strength, evocative of violence, a violence that has already taken place in the past, behind us, but the sense of which is to be carried forward into the open future before us as the shot widens by retreating from Walt as he continues his march forwards and the opening titles begin.

This figure of Walt is an image of explosive self-transformation. The pilot episode's similar structure provides a basis to expect that this prefigured transformation will be the episode's predetermined narrative end. I take this predetermination of the end, and thus of everything in between that end and its beginning, to be a narrative model of the loss of possibility, in particular of the loss of the possibility of determining the future without bloodshed as imagined by Walt. It is the loss of a possibility of identity. It is also, necessarily, a gain. Dashing the hope of a more peaceful future, of the retrieval of Walt's better self, we are shown a picture of previously unrealized potency that, although violent, is also thrilling, exciting – unknown, primed with possibilities.

The articulation of this flashforward opening is telling us that we are to be concerned in what follows with the transformation of the self over time as an experience that registers the irretrievable loss of possibility but also its rejuvenating renewal.

It is therefore fitting that the episode moves through sequences that trace Walt's gradual existential decline as a result of his choice to extend the possibilities of his life by undergoing chemotherapy. These sequences register the passing of time, and with it the loss of possibility, in manifestations of financial and physical decline. Weekly payments to the private oncology practice erode what remains of Walt's cheque account, as his piles of ill-gotten cash increasingly dwindle, bringing him and his family closer and closer to ruin. Under this lengthening shadow, Walt's days are presented as moving between long stretches of immobile and impotent waiting as chemotherapy is administered, and violent episodes of sickness in which nausea and vomiting keep him from teaching and working. These sequences realize the feared possibility that Walt imagines during 'Gray Matter'. 'What good is it to just survive,' he asks Skyler, 'if I'm too sick to work? To enjoy a meal? To make love … ?' The loss of these capacities, whose exercise is constitutive of who Walt is, is a death in itself. He would become and be remembered as 'some dead man … some, artificially alive … just – marking time?' Walt claims to want above all else a choice. Throughout 'Crazy Handful of Nothin'' the realisation of that choice results in decay and decline: the loss of life's possibilities.

The episode's close provides a contrast. Moving beyond the terminal point prefigured by the flashforward, it gives us access to a private moment of Walt's emotional release, a moment of exhilaration and rejuvenation. It presents Walt's enactment of choice as opening up his personal possibilities, while opening out the series into new dramatic ones. If the flashforward structure provides a narrative model of doomed possibility that mirror's Walt's impending death, the episode's closure allows for the series' and Walt's mutual rebirth.

To simultaneously realize, lose, and renew possibility is a condition of serial television.[9] It is also a condition of the way we live and die. Through these conditions of the medium and of human life, 'Crazy Handful of Nothin'' and *Breaking Bad* articulate thinking about beginning and ending, life and death, and how we find vitality and significance in the possibilities between. The issues raised by this thinking go beyond the vocabulary of narrative designs as puzzles. Needed instead is a vocabulary adequate to the conditions of the medium, and to the conditions of life its best works seek to profoundly represent.

Bibliography

Coulthard, Lisa. 'The Hotness of Cold Opens: *Breaking Bad* and the Serial Narrative as Puzzle.' *Flow* 13:3 (2010), http://flowtv.org/2010/11/the-hotness-of-cold-opens [accessed 12 October 2012].

Gilligan, Vince. 'Breaking Bad.' *Breaking Bad*, season 1, episode 1. Directed by Vince Gilligan. Aired August 28 2008. Burbank, CA: Sony Pictures Television, 2008. DVD.

Gilligan, Vince, and Patty Lin. 'Gray Matter.' *Breaking Bad*, season 1, episode 5. Directed by Tricia Brock. Aired September 25 2008. Burbank, CA: Sony Pictures Television, 2008. DVD.

Gilligan, Vince, and George Mastras. 'Crazy Handful of Nothin'.' *Breaking Bad*, season 1, episode 6. Directed by Bronwen Hughes. Aired October 2 2008. Burbank, CA: Sony Pictures Television, 2008. DVD.

Mittell, Jason. 'Narrative Complexity in Contemporary American Television.' *The Velvet Light Trap* 56 (Fall 2006): 29–40. doi: 10.1353/vlt.2006.0032.

—'*Lost* in a Great Story: Evaluation in Narrative Television (and Television Studies).' In *Reading Lost: Perspectives on a Hit Television Show*, edited by Roberta Pearson, 119–38. London: I. B. Tauris, 2009.

O'Sullivan, Sean. 'Reconnoitering the Rim: Thoughts on *Deadwood* and Third Seasons.' *Third Person: Authoring and Exploring Vast Narratives*, edited by Pat Harrigan and Noah Wardrip-Fruin, 323–32. Cambridge, MA: MIT Press, 2009.

---

[9]Sean O'Sullivan, 'Reconnoitering the Rim: Thoughts on *Deadwood* and Third Seasons', in *Third Person: Authoring and Exploring Vast Narratives*, ed. Pat Harrigan and Noah Wardrip-Fruin (Cambridge, MA: MIT Press, 2009), 323.

17

The fantastic style of *Shameless*

Beth Johnson

Situated in a 'sink' estate on the outskirts of modern-day Manchester, UK, and known for its dramatic engagements with poverty, alcoholism and child abandonment, the contemporary 'cult' British drama series *Shameless*[1] has been contextualised by academics such as James Walters[2], Lez Cooke[3] and Glen Creeber[4] as a series that engages with the social realist tradition. Simultaneously however, as Creeber notes, *Shameless* also challenges the 'very notion of an objective and impartial 'reality' so integral to representing the 'original moral structures that defined British social realism in the past''.[5] Such an acknowledgement of the dynamic nature of social realism and, in the case of *Shameless*, the undermining of realist representations of the objective past, is also to be the jumping off point for this chapter. In particular, it explores how the series employs aspects of 'the fantastic' in its stylistic arrangements to complicate its apparent ties to the social realist tradition of British television drama.

As Marion Jordan notes, the demands of social realism in terms of British television drama can be understood thus:

---

[1] *Shameless* (television series) Channel 4, 2004–.

[2] James Walters, 'Saving Face: Inflections of Character Role-Play in *Shameless*', *Journal of British Cinema and Television* 3:1 (2006): 95–106.

[3] Lez Cooke, 'The new social realism of Clocking Off' in *Popular Television Drama: Critical Perspectives*, ed. Jonathan Bignell *et al.* (Manchester and New York: Manchester University Press, 2004), 183–97.

[4] Glen Creeber, 'The truth is out there! Not!: *Shameless* and the moral structures of contemporary social realism', *New Review of Film and Television Studies* 7:4 (2009): 421–39.

[5] Creeber, 'The truth is out there! Not!', 421.

Social Realism demands that life should be presented in the form of a narrative of personal events [...]; that though these events are ostensibly about *social* problems they should have as one of their central concerns the settling of people in life; that the resolutions of these events should always be in terms of the effect of social interventions; that characters should be either working-class or of the classes immediately visible to the working classes [...] and should be credibly accounted for in terms of the 'ordinariness' of their homes, families, friends; that the locale should be urban and provincial (preferably in the industrial north); that the settings should be recognisable (the pub, the street, the factory, the home and more particularly the kitchen); that the time should be 'the present'; that the style should be such as to suggest an unmediated, unprejudiced and complete view of reality.[6]

Jordan's definition is certainly apt for describing many elements of *Shameless*. Indeed, with a frequent focus upon the domestic, the ordinary, the everyday, the family, the Northern urban locale, the present and the working class/ underclass population of the Chatsworth estate, the series can be understood to adhere to and align itself with social realist demands. Yet, the latter aspects of Jordan's definition – the suggestion of an 'unmediated, unprejudiced and complete view of reality' – is certainly more problematic. In contradistinction to older British television dramas such as *Boys From the Blackstuff*,[7] *Shameless* often demonstrates a hyper-aware and hyper-mediated view of reality. As Creeber notes of the opening monologue spoken by drunken and inept father of five, Frank Gallagher (David Threlfall) in season one, *Shameless*'s narrative perspective is, from the outset: 'both unstable and unreliable, articulated through a narrator who is so much part of the community of which he speaks that he is clearly unable to be objective about it'.[8] Indeed, going on to discuss the unrealistic elements of exposition evident in the show further, Creeber notes that the hyper-mediated perspectives often presented to the audience are articulated as 'stylistic flourishes, [...]freeze frames, whip pans, surreal flashbacks, still images, and fantasy sequences that draw an audience's attention to the artificial construction of the narrative on offer'.[9] While all of these elements are of academic interest, this chapter is to focus in particular on a discussion of the style and aesthetics

---

[6] Marion Jordan, 'Realism and Convention', in *Coronation Street*, ed. Richard Dyer *et al.* (London: BFI, 1981), 28.
[7] *Boys From the Blackstuff* (television series) BBC, 1982.
[8] Creeber, 'The truth is out there! Not!', 432.
[9] Creeber, 'The truth is out there! Not!', 434.

of fantasy sequences in *Shameless*, and their implications for and in the undermining of traditionally British televisual social realism.

Formal contradictions to social realism associated with 'the fantastic' establish themselves at clear intervals within *Shameless*. As Rosemary Jackson notes, the 'escapist qualities' of fantasy, the fact that in many ways fantasy resists definition, can be understood as part of its textual attraction.[10] Arguing that fantasies often involve a refusal to 'observe unities of time, space and character, doing away with rigid distinctions between animate and inanimate objects, self and other, life and death',[11] Jackson goes on to note that fantasy is 'produced within, and determined by, its social context'.[12] Though writing dominantly of literary rather than televisual texts, Jackson's ideas themselves seem unlimited by the constraints of time or genre. Discussing, for example, the writings of Dostoevsky, Jackson cites him: 'What other people call fantastic, I hold to be the inmost essence of truth.'[13] This expression of understanding regarding the crossovers between the fantastic and the truthful or real, underpin the ways in which reality and fantasy interact in *Shameless*. In addition, as argued by Catherine Johnson: 'the representation of the fantastic enable[s] the metaphorical treatment of social anxieties'.[14]

Via fashioning, foregrounding and incorporating fantastic elements, *Shameless* simultaneously subverts and underscores the importance of the social realist aesthetic. The fantasy elements function to ask important socio-political questions and address underclass domestic concerns. For example, in series five, episode one, Frank meets his childhood self after drunkenly urinating on an electricity generator and being told (wrongly) at a subsequent medical check-up that he has a serious and terminal heart-condition. Asking Frank (aged 12) why he is haunting him, adult Frank is forced to recall the death of his mother, its traumatic impact upon him, his difficult relationship with his father and the question of what his own legacy will be. In series six, episode one, Frank's new-born daughter, aptly named after the larger brand Stella, fantastically and miraculously speaks asking of the Chatsworth residents:

Who are these people? How did they survive the evolution of the series? Breeding like rabbits. Kids having kids. Dwellers of the underbelly.

---

[10] Rosemary Jackson, *Fantasy: The Literature of Subversion* (London and New York: Routledge, 1998), 1.

[11] Jackson, *Fantasy*, 1–2.

[12] Jackson, *Fantasy*, 3.

[13] Dostoevsky cited by Jackson, *Fantasy*, 135.

[14] Catherine Johnson, *Telefantasy* (London: BFI, 2005), 29.

Scavengers on the edge of society. Maybe the tabloids are right. Point and laugh. Ridicule 'em. Lock 'em up and throw away the key. Why would anyone choose to live here?

In series eight, episode one, the drug addled patriarch of the Gallagher family is again subject to a fantastic invasion of space when, amidst worrying about his upcoming wedding and the end of his relationship with his first wife, Monica (Annabelle Apsion), he sees his spiritual home, the grotty Jockey (pub), turned into a flying alien spacecraft. Later in the series in episode seven, Kelly Maguire (Sally Carman), driven to despair by the loss of her baby, overdoses on ketamine and, akin to Mark Renton's (Ewan McGregor) heroin overdose in *Trainspotting*,[15] sinks surreally into the carpeted floor.

Seen through rapid camera movements, lurching tilts and visual distortions, this type of fantasy vignette is employed in the series, I argue, to signal a new model of the real in which the fantastic, surreal and otherworldly fragments of life (the drunken illusions, anxiety inspired dreams, grief stricken episodes of insanity or inertia, unexpected moments of revelation) can be understood as important and underrepresented aspects of real human experience. Moreover, the habituality of these types of experiences is conveyed through the transformation of everyday spaces – the kitchen, the pub, the street, neighbour's lounge, the hospital. Indeed, it is these recognisable spaces, these fragments of normality that become all the more powerfully transformed when suddenly rendered strange and alien. The invasion of the everyday by the fantastic is, in the words of John Hill: 'consistently harnessed to a narrative purpose', indicating in *Shameless*, the multiple narrative complexities of the series as well as the divided loyalties and the extensive psychological depth of the characters.[16] Drawing attention to the present tense of twenty-first century television, the visual fantasy elements within the series (often represented via special effects akin to the spectacle of cinema) coupled with the socially and politically aware dialogue of the characters (the talk of television), highlight a strange and at times, strained relationship. Focusing on the stylistic distortions of *Shameless*, the analysis below affords a critical reflection on what Jason Jacobs refers to as 'moments' or 'cherished fragments' of the televisual.[17] As such, close analyzes of the striking visual style of fantastic interludes in episodes 8:1 and 8:2 are to be the unashamed focus of this chapter.

---

[15] *Trainspotting* (Dir. Danny Boyle, 1996).

[16] John Hill, *Sex, Class and Realism: British Cinema 1956–1963* (London: BFI, 1997), 140.

[17] Jason Jacobs, 'Television aesthetics: an infantile disorder', *Journal of British Cinema and Television* 3:1 (2006): 20.

Cogito ergo sum: Fantasising close encounters of the third kind

Concentrating largely on three *Shameless* characters, namely the unemployed, alcoholic father of nine children, Frank Gallagher, his manipulative ex-wife (and mother of seven of his children) Monica Gallagher and his new fiancé Libby Crocker (Pauline McLynn), series eight, episode one opens by detailing Frank's anxiety regarding his forthcoming marriage. Relayed as an off-beat, self-consciously philosophical and fantastical sequence, Frank's first words are spoken not in English but in Latin: *Cogito ergo sum* (I think, therefore I am). Questioning his reality and nominating his fears about his existence and his future, Frank laments that he may only exist as a figment of others' imaginations. Pictured in a manic state building a model out of beer cans, boxes of matches, torn- up newspaper and pots of glue on the kitchen table of his home, the episode soon sees Frank's domestic space penetrated by fantastic and seemingly alien powers. Though Frank's alien encounter is interesting on many levels, for example, the encounter could be read as a penetration of his masculinity or as an example of Frank's childlike imagination, it is the telegraphing of borders – borders that, on breaking down or being breached, reveal a blurring between the real and the fantastical – that are most dominantly problematised and probed in this episode.

Visually echoing the third alien encounter from Steven Spielberg's 1977 film *Close Encounters of the Third Kind* (an encounter involving a young child, Barry Guiler [Cary Guffey] whose toys come to life, as well as the model making of character Roy Neary [Richard Dreyfuss] who becomes plagued by mental images of a mountain shape after an alien encounter), episode 8:1 visually commences with an out-of-focus, blue-tinted, dream-like close-up shot of Frank's lank brown hair and sweaty anxious face, side-on. Focusing on and simultaneously fragmenting the image of Frank building a model, the camera moves rapidly and jerkily, consciously makes the audience aware of its presence in this sequence – an alien interloper straddling diegetic and non-diegetic worlds. Followed by the penetration of a brilliant yellow light shining through the glazed glass of the kitchen door (a light that functions to frame Frank as some sort of otherworldly, sickly looking figure), the character's body is cast as alien and hollowed out – given a yellow tinge and fragmented into strange and disparate parts – a disembodied arm, a freakish hand, a staring pair of eyes.

On completing his model building, Frank lights a cigarette before turning in response to a noise behind him. Looking downward, a medium shot reveals a child's remote controlled car inexplicably driving toward him. Frank's eyes are then caught by a strange vision to his right. A shot reverse shot shows two toy tin robots (a couple – one male and one female) marching mechanically in his direction. Set against a net curtain and overshadowed on the left hand side of the screen by a toddler's plastic drinking cup as well as being framed by piles of untidy paper spilling into the borders of the frame, Frank is then distracted again by an additional toy tin rabbit mechanically playing the drums behind him. This invasion of Frank's alone time and, in particular, his usual pub worship by children's toys, arguably signifies the threat of repetition; of another domestic cycle with Libby – marriage, children, more noise, less freedom. The coming to life of the toys can be seen to index Frank's anxieties, literally making visible the haunting alienation, unmanageable multiple demands and domestic tensions that made up Frank's previous experiences of marriage and fatherhood.

As the sequence continues, a kitchen lamp adorned in pink love hearts (a prop perhaps literally highlighting the unruly mixing of love and domesticity) suddenly begins to flicker on and off. The kitchen microwave lights up and turns on. The taps of the sink then flow with water, the taps turning as if by an alien force. Lastly, the radio/CD player in the kitchen springs to life blaring out David Bowie's cosmically inspired music track *Starman*. This direct diegetic reference to an alien encounter by Bowie is followed by the nets of the kitchen windows suddenly blowing and the kitchen door bursting open. As the music and lights shut off, Frank stares at the model he has created. Grabbing his parker coat, Frank then turns and runs out of the house leaving the door gaping behind him. The camera then returns in clear focus to a close-up shot of Frank's model, the fragments now joined together to reveal a mock-up of the character's spiritual home, the Jockey pub.

The combination of the self-reflexive refusal of naturalism, character driven plot-line, playful intertextual references and expositional framework allow here for a revelation of the ways in which the show simultaneously subverts and underscores the importance of the social realist aesthetic. Indeed, the very introduction of fantasy elements such as the coming to life of inanimate objects plays on the tension between the supposed 'other worldliness' of fantasy and the recognisability and familiarity of the everyday. *Shameless* engages with fantasy via purposefully domesticating it, by making the ordinary extraordinary.

The next televisual fragment shows an impressive, computer-generated superimposition as the model pub is replaced by the 'real' Jockey pub situated on the Chatsworth estate. The advanced aesthetics of the scene could be read as a conscious reference here to the increasing quality of computer-generated images in contemporary quality television. As Stacey Abbott notes: 'Gone are the days where we assume that all effects on TV will be the low budget Styrofoam sets or paper maché backdrops of *Star Trek* or *Doctor Who*. Instead series […] have redefined expectations of TV SF with stunning computer generated visuals.'[18] Accompanied by strange non-diegetic music, the shot of the pub is then penetrated by a thick white mist before transitioning to reveal Frank in a medium shot running toward the building. Standing outside of the pub, Frank stares directly at it as if it were not familiar to him while watching strange multi-coloured lights filling the space of the windows and penetrating the borders of the building. Accompanied by a five tone musical score, the fantastic style, colours and sound here clearly replicate the alien encounters and communication strategies of Spielberg. In response to seeing the lights and listening to five tone phrases, Frank deliberately closes and then reopens his eyes as if trying to see 'straight'.

The notion that Frank silently contemplates here – the fact that his vision is deceiving him – is important in that, I suggest, it provides a context through which we can analyze the show's precise, filmic treatment of tele-fantasy. Frank's vision (and, by proxy, our own) is clearly one not associated with 'this' televisual world and as such, the vision accords the strangeness of the space of television as one that is invaded by the spectacle and convincing quality of the cinematic. The sequential fragments of the scenes described above are significant in that they point to the intertextuality of the series (its shameless references and parodies of famous filmic fantasy texts), as well as literally demonstrating the invasion of tele-vision by physically plausible filmic images. Considering the special effects and CGI employed on the show, it is pertinent to note here that *Shameless* invokes an aesthetic style, a 'look' that is recognisably dense, convincing and of high resolution. Employing a 16:9 aspect ratio (an aspect ratio most commonly associated with widescreen cinema), *Shameless* clearly situates itself as larger than life, fantastical and spectacular.

Doctoring whose reality?

In 8:2, the emphasis on the spectacular is envisioned differently. While the theme of invasion remains at the forefront of the episode, the entry point to it is intertextually televisual rather than cinematic. Specifically, 8:2 injects a sense of televisual otherness in the form of a direct spoof of the UK television series *Doctor Who*, with Frank styled as the fourth doctor (played by Tom Baker) and his ex-wife Monica styled as the Doctor's sexy companion, Leela

---

[18]Stacey Abbott, 'CFP: Special F/X and Television', *Critical Studies in Television Online*, 20 April 2011, http://cstonline.tv/cfp-special-fx-television [accessed 12 June 2011].

– a character who (much like Monica) refused to be civilised. Originally aired in 1977/78, the temporal similarity between this reference and Spielberg's *Close Encounters* reference in 8:1 is notable. 8:2, however, sees Frank missing from his home. While his fiancé Libby frantically searches for him, the audience are given narrative privilege as to his whereabouts. Appearing on-screen in a sudden close up shot, the colour of Frank's skin is notably desaturated, rendered pale and ghostly. The notion of Frank as an 'Other', a ghost perhaps, is thus writ large from the outset of the episode. Frank is simultaneously on the screen and missing from it, present and absent. The alterity of Frank here – his 'Otherness', can be connected directly to his questioning of existence in 8:1. Indeed, as Tamise Van Pelt (2000) argues: 'As half of a signifying binary, the "Other" is a term with a rich and lengthy philosophical history dating at least from Plato's Sophist, in which the Stranger participates in a dialogue on the ontological problems of being and non-being, of the One and the Other.'[19] The overexposed lighting of the background reveals only white blank surfaces and the fact that the motion of the camera is purposefully out of sync with Frank's small movements creates a sense of surreal alienation, a decentred visual discourse experienced both by Frank and the viewer. As Frank stands before a mirror, his voice echoes as he laments over his appearance and age. Studying his face he avers: 'Lines. Veins. Older. Older. Older. Older.' Frank's recognition of the significance of time, and more specifically, the passing or travelling of time and space, is rendered visually present in the next shot. Inexplicably styled as *Doctor Who* in his new alien world, Frank addresses the blank space: 'What the fuck am I doing here? And where is here? I need to get back. Back where?' As the echo of Frank's self-questioning reverberates in the white empty space, a screeching, disembodied voice shouting 'Doctor! Doctor!' invades the frame.

Probing the limits of his alien world, Frank is then shown to inexplicably and immediately travel to a new, dark, dank and smoky alternate space. In it stands Monica, his ex-wife dressed as Leela. Prompting Frank/the Doctor's action, Monica/Leela demands that he do something: 'Quick Doctor! The Cidermen are coming.' The urgent grain of her voice serves to both spoof the expressed fear of alien invasion on screen, as well as to build the anticipation of the shot. Accompanied by a new non-diegetic pounding beat, a sudden close-up shot reveals a silver boot marching mechanically into the frame from the left hand side. As the camera tilts upwards, the visual revelation is temporarily obscured by a lens blur. Shortly however, the figure is revealed as Libby, Frank's fiancé. Dressed head to toe in an amateur styled silver costume

---

[19] Tamise Van Pelt, 'Otherness', *Journal of Postmodern Culture* 10:2 (2000), http://muse.jhu.edu/login?auth=0&type=summary&url=/journals/pmc/v010/10.2vanpelt.html [accessed 28 May 2012].

with the word 'CIDERMAN' printed on it on large capital letters, Libby's mechanical actions and outstretched arms visually render her as the enemy, an enemy who will attempt to invade Frank's freedom and domestic space.

This obvious play on visuals and words – the exchange of the term 'cybermen' for 'cidermen' – speaks to the ways in which the show both spoofs and shamelessly adapts the world of *Doctor Who* to draw attention to its own visual gags and constructed reality. This parodic reference also demonstrates the overlap between spaces, places and genres that have perhaps traditionally seemed strange, disparate and out of sync. The clear social and, to Frank, very real anxieties regarding his forthcoming marriage to Libby and his feelings for his ex-wife are divulged then in the fantastic style of the series. An additional stylistic element of importance is the science-fiction soundscape that serves as an important backdrop to the visuals on screen. From the first instance of the fantastic *Doctor Who* fragment, what Sean Redmond nominates as the 'sound of science fiction' can be heard.[20] The generic sound of science fiction, both diegetic and non-diegetic, can be heard in amplified screeches, strange static sonics and the eerie reverberation of percussion echoes. At once familiar and yet unsettling to the viewer, the synthesised sounds project a 'vocalisation of invasion' lending an alien energy and further layer of fantastic style to the show.[21] In addition, more explicit musical references to the multi-layered intertextuality of *Shameless* are invoked via the inclusion of the KLF/Timelords track *Doctorin' The Tardis* – a track which is itself an alien mixture of the *Doctor Who* theme music, Gary Glitter's *Rock and Roll (Part Two)*, *Block Buster!* by Sweet and *Let's Get Together Tonite* by Steve Walsh.

Conclusion

The depth and multiple layers of 'alien' style in series eight of *Shameless* arguably expose and reveal to Frank (and the audience) not the ultimate strangeness of the 'Other' – other worlds, peoples, races, spaces, ideologies, values and social circumstances – but the fantastic extraordinariness of the everyday. If the everyday is rendered as fantastic and extraordinary in and by *Shameless* however, apt questions to ask here include: what is the series attempting to achieve or highlight via these fantasy vignettes? What does the series express of, say, Frank's standing in and attitude toward the world?

---

[20] Sean Redmond, 'Sounding alien, touching the future: beyond the sonorous limit in science fiction film', *New Review of Film and Television Studies* 9:1 (2011): 43.
[21] Redmond, 'Sounding alien', 52.

The stylistic strategy employed here points, I suggest, to the complex relationship between *Shameless* and its viewers. As *The Guardian* journalist James Donaghy noted recently, speaking of the eighth series: '*Shameless* has always been a show that split opinion. Critics say it has descended too easily into a chav cartoon, but such thinking fundamentally misunderstands the show.'[22] What Donaghy draws attention to here in his reference to the show as a 'chav cartoon' is, firstly, the centrality and importance of social class within *Shameless* and secondly, the social expectations and class categorisation of the shows' audience. Indeed, while various critics and viewers have branded the series shameful in its representation of the under-class and accused it of promoting 'class tourism' (in essence, functioning as a show that allows middle-class viewers to watch underclass behaviour repre-sented from a safe distance), I contend that this is not the case. In line with Sally Munt who argues that showrunner Paul Abbott's acknowledgement that *Shameless* is a recreation of his childhood allows for an: 'aura of authen-ticity that is crucial to framing the series' critical reception', I argue that the rendering of the everyday as extra-ordinary and fantastic works similarly.[23] That is to say, the fantastic extraordinariness of the everyday pushed front and centre in the visual style of the series, works to complicate and critique the notion that some middle-class viewers may regard the working or under-class environs of the Chatsworth as 'alien' and exotic. Indeed, the fantastic and shameless alien interludes point to specific truths about alterity – truths bound up in the series' concerns – in a way that social realist strategies would not. The visual vocabulary of *Shameless* works then to draw attention to the ways in which we, the audience, view, see and classify the 'Other' rather than looking at the alterity within ourselves.

The underclass positioning of Frank, slurring and swearing larger than life on our screens, in our homes, will undoubtedly continue to be seen by some as a domestic assault, an alien invasion of middle England's 'green and pleasant lands' by underclass values. Yet, such a reading entirely misses the socio-political point of the show. As Frank's comedic direct address monologue tells us at the beginning of each episode in series 8: 'Anybody who thinks that we know fuck all about fuck all better watch their backs.' Opening us up to that outside of dominant value systems, Frank's fantastic experiences convey the message that the real and the fantastic are intrinsically linked. As Jackson argues: 'The fantastic cannot exist independently of the "real" world which

---

[22] James Donaghy, 'Shameless: Why Frank Gallagher must die', *The Guardian*, 10 January 2011, http://www.guardian.co.uk/tv-and-radio/tvandradioblog/2011/jan/10/shameless-frank-gallagher-must-die [accessed 10 June 2011].
[23] Sally R. Munt, *Queer Attachments: The Politics of Cultural Shame* (Farnham and Burlington, VA: Ashgate, 2008), 133.

it seems to find so frustratingly finite.'[24] Thus, while the injection of the real with the fantastic may be viewed by some as an uneasy assimilation, it is in fact a merger that should serve to remind audiences that nothing is stable, and the fantastic elements of our everyday reality must be considered anew, both in life and on television.

Bibliography

Abbott, Stacey. CFP: Special F/X and Television, *Critical Studies in Television Online*, 20 April 2011. http://cstonline.tv/cfp-special-fx-television [accessed 12 June 2011].

Cooke, Lez. 'The new social realism of *Clocking Off.'* In *Popular Television Drama: Critical Perspectives*, edited by Jonathan Bignell and Steven Lacey, 183–97. Manchester and New York: Manchester University Press, 2004.

Creeber, Glen. 'The truth is out there! Not!: *Shameless* and the moral structures of contemporary social realism.' *New Review of Film and Television Studies* 7:4 (2009): 421–39.

Donaghy, James. 'Shameless: Why Frank Gallagher must die.' *The Guardian*, 10 January 2011. http://www.guardian.co.uk/tv-and-radio/tvandradioblog/2011/jan/10/shameless-frank-gallagher-must-die [accessed 10 June 2011].

Hill, John. *Sex, Class and Realism: British Cinema 1956–1963*. London: BFI, 1997.

Jackson, Rosemary. *Fantasy: The Literature of Subversion*. London and New York: Routledge, 1998.

Jacobs, Jason. 'Television aesthetics: an infantile disorder.' *Journal of British Cinema and Television* 3:1 (2006): 19–33.

Johnson, Catherine. *Telefantasy*. London: BFI, 2005.

Jordan, Marion. 'Realism and Convention.' In *Coronation Street*, edited by Richard Dyer, Christine Geraghty, Marion Jordan, Terry Lovell, Richard Paterson, and John Stewart, 27–39. London: BFI, 1981.

Munt, Sally. R. *Queer Attachments: The Politics of Cultural Shame*. Farnham and Burlington, VA: Ashgate, 2008.

Redmond, Sean. 'Sounding alien, touching the future: beyond the sonorous limit in science fiction film.' *New Review of Film and Television Studies* 9:1 (2011): 42–56.

Van Pelt, Tamise. 'Otherness.' *Postmodern Culture* 10:2 (2000). http://muse.jhu.edu/login?auth=0&type=summary&url=/journals/pmc/v010/10.2vanpelt.html [accessed 28 May 2012].

Walters, James. 'Saving Face: Inflections of Character Role-Play in *Shameless.'* *Journal of British Cinema and Television*.3:1 (2006): 95–106.

---

[24] Jackson, *Fantasy*, 20.

PART FOUR

Non-fiction and history

18

'Let's just watch it for a few minutes': *This is Your Life* in 1958

Charles Barr

On Friday 3 February 2012, the main morning story on the Sky News channel in the UK concerned a government minister, Chris Huhne. It had just been announced that he and his ex-wife were to face a police charge, to do with the alleged falsification of evidence after a speeding offence. The question at once arose, would he resign his post? The news media gathered outside the conference building where his party was holding a closed session, waiting for him to emerge and face questions.[1]

The viewpoint of the Sky camera, transmitting (as announced at the top right of the screen) live from Eastbourne, merely showed a set of office doors, untroubled by human movement. Apart from a few cutaways to other locations, this image was on screen for at least half an hour. This particular shot was held without interruption for more than five minutes: static camera, nothing happening, the only movement coming from the 'Breaking News' strapline, endlessly repeating itself, in parallel with the repetitive commentary speculation: when would Huhne appear and what would he say?[2]

The fact of coming 'Live from Eastbourne', at this date and this precise moment, is – or, rather, was – the entire point of it. As a recording, the footage of the broadcast has no use-value; the value resides in the record of the

---

[1] A year later Huhne pleaded guilty to the charge of perverting the course of justice and resigned as an MP.

[2] I rather regret the policy to eliminate illustrations from the book, and thus from this article – in particular the striking initial image taken from Sky News.

man's eventual emergence, with his statement of resignation. The past tense of a film newsreel would have shown just this, without the 'dead' period of waiting – as duly happened in later summaries on Sky News itself. But if there is such a thing as pure television, as distinct from however we define pure cinema, it resides above all, I would argue, in passages of live duration like this one that are inconceivable in cinema. However much cinema may at times envy, and mimic, this effect of real time – a point to return to later – it cannot by definition do present tense.

It is striking, and indeed reassuring, that broadcast TV can still in 2012 offer passages like this, at a time when the main channels, in Britain anyway, so frequently demonstrate a terror of letting shots, or scenes, or final credit sequences, run on, in case this might tempt casual viewers to switch channels. In the Huhne episode, in contrast, Sky News sustains the shot in order, precisely, to keep viewers hooked, waiting and waiting for the anticipated event to take place. There is a strong continuity here with the more common experience of viewers in the formative years of the medium, the years where live transmission dominated. One reason I found the Sky News moment so compulsive was the way it echoed a classic one from half a century earlier.

Dissolve back through time, then, to an image from near the start of a BBC programme, *This is Your Life*, broadcast at peak viewing time, 7 p.m., on 31 March 1958: a drab long shot, looking out from inside a theatre towards a dark street. The modern Sky News image has colour and fancy graphics, but the shots are otherwise similar. We look towards a door, waiting for something to happen, for a man to emerge.

The 1958 shot runs without a cut for a minute and a half. The programme's compere speaks over the first 25 seconds and the last 15, but for the 50 seconds in between there is virtually nothing: no voice-over, no camera movement, no noise apart from some very indistinct sounds coming from the group whom we glimpse beyond the door. And 50 seconds is a very long time for a stretch of silent nothing, when the context is peak-time popular television rather than the avant-garde cinema of an Andy Warhol or a Michael Snow. Even if the producer is embarrassed by this 'dead time' and itches to cut it out, he cannot do so, since the programme is going out live; but no embarrassment is called for, since the long pause is perfectly in tune with the aesthetic that gave *This is Your Life* its phenomenal long-term popularity.

Note the present tense in the title. *This is Your Life* (hereafter TIYL) was developed in, and for, live television, and prospered as a live programme for many years both in America and in Britain. When, for a variety of reasons, live broadcasting found itself progressively phased out, TIYL preserved, in a recognisable residual form, some of the qualities of live TV, continuing to invoke an element of here-and-now spontaneity and unpredictability. For weeks on end, for years on end, into the 1980s, it regularly attracted more viewers in Britain than any other programme, even including the then twice-weekly *Coronation Street*, holding down a peak-time slot of, or adjacent to, 7 p.m. It continued, intermittently and less successfully, into the new millennium, before finishing in 2003, though the idea of further revivals is not inconceivable.

Since the programme no longer runs, and since there are, at least for the British version, no DVD packages, a summary may be useful.[3] Each week an individual, generally a celebrity in some sphere, is taken by surprise, and is sat down to meet a pre-assembled succession of people who have played a part of some kind in her or his life. The half-hour programme has a classical structure: beginning, middle and end. The beginning is the springing of the surprise on the unsuspecting (we hope) subject, or 'victim'. The middle is an accumulation of small surprises and pleasurable (we hope) reunions and reminiscences. The end is the bringing on of a particularly dramatic and gratifying guest, followed – though this was not yet standard in 1958 – by a sentimental music-backed assembly, in tableau formation, facing the camera, of all those who have been involved, the victim at the centre.

This particular episode of the programme, whose subject is the singer and comedian, Harry Secombe, is of special interest because it comes exactly at the culmination of the *pre-videotape* era of television. Just two weeks after its transmission, on 14 April, the still single-channel BBC demonstrated, within its weekly *Panorama* programme, the new technology of recording the electronic image on to tape, as opposed to film: at that stage it was known by the acronym VERA (Vision Electronic Recording Apparatus). Although the machinery was at first bulky, clumsy and inflexible, like the initial sync-sound technology in cinema, it soon, likewise, became less so, and was succeeded by ever more sophisticated means of electronic recording and editing, thus progressively narrowing – though never closing – the gap between the aesthetics of the two media.[4]

The Secombe programme, like the *Panorama* demonstration two weeks later, is a remarkable 'time capsule'. It encompasses and exploits every aspect of the medium's pre-videotape technology, and does so in a disarmingly, and revealingly, self-conscious way.

---

[3]A three-disc DVD package, 'This is Your Life: the Ultimate Collection' is available in the US. It brings together eighteen of the American shows, most of them featuring film or TV stars. A certain amount of British material can now be found on YouTube.

[4]I trace and discuss this process in more detail in '"They Think it's All Over": The Dramatic Legacy of Live Television', in *Big Picture, Small Screen: The Relations between Film and Television*, edited by John Hill and Martin McLoone (Luton: John Libby Press, 1996), 47–75. For more details of VERA, and a link to the original Panorama footage, see http://www.vtoldboys.com/vera.htm#btm [accessed August 2011].

At the start, behind the title, theatrical curtains part, and the regular compere, the all-purpose Irish broadcaster Eamonn Andrews, comes forward to address the audience: that is, the TV audience watching at home, and also the studio audience whose applause we will hear throughout without, except at the very start, ever seeing them – they function as our surrogate. He gives us some hints about the identity of tonight's subject, and then sets the scene:

> Tomorrow he leaves for Central Africa. Tonight he's on his way, or in fact outside this theatre, completely oblivious of our plans. He's here to do a filmed interview with Peter Haigh about this trip of his. Now outside our theatre are cameras and lights and microphones to film his arrival, but hidden among the mass of gear is a live television camera, and this is what that hidden camera is seeing right now.

Immediately, then, there has been a foregrounding of the technology, centred on the sharp distinction, with which the audience is assumed to be familiar, between film and television. The cameras that are outside waiting to *film* the guest's arrival are simply a diversionary tactic, they will not feed images into the programme – how could they, when the film would first have to be taken off for processing and editing? As for the TV camera, it is not the flexible lightweight recording device with which we are familiar today, but a cumbersome, cable-bound image-relaying machine which has to be hidden in case a sighting of it immediately gives the game away, Having cued the shot, Andrews is entirely dependent on the action developing as planned, and is understandably nervous:

> I don't know if you can recognize any faces there, but they're out on the street, they're preparing for the trip, having jokes about it, we've got to watch carefully because the camera's so well hidden that we can't see all we might, like, want to see. [*He pauses to see if things are moving yet, but they aren't*]. Let's just watch it for a few minutes.

What a great line! The period of silent watching certainly feels more like several minutes than the 50 seconds that actually elapse. The deadlock is broken by Andrews calling out to Secombe's escort, almost in desperation: 'Just a moment, Peter Haigh, hold everything.' He then tells Secombe, at a distance, that 'Tonight, This is Your Life', and we can see in long shot the victim's authentically startled reaction. Haigh brings him in, the camera finally pans right from doorway to studio set, and proceedings begin, without, obviously, any break during which Secombe could compose himself: he is swept up in the real-time momentum of what has been planned for him.

This turns out to consist of fourteen segments.[5] Mostly, friends or relatives speak from behind the curtains, then come on for their intense two minutes of hugs and reminiscence; the multiple live studio cameras transmit all this in a straightforward way. But three of the segments take us outside the comfort of the studio.

(1) The initial guest is the classical singer Adèle Leigh, whose collaborations with Secombe had become an important validation of his own credentials as a serious singer, as well as a comedian famous for his membership of The Goons. She can't be there in person, as she explains: '...There was just one hitch and that was that I was going to be in America, three thousand miles away. But they have a wonderful thing called telerecording, so here I am after all.' 'Here' is on a big screen on the studio wall, now a very familiar device, but not so familiar then, and Andrews has to give Secombe a prompt both physically with his hands and verbally: 'Now if you look up on the wall here, Harry...'. These days, the words of someone in America would either be relayed live via a satellite link, or painlessly recorded from there in advance and simply played in to the programme at the appropriate time. But in 1958 there was no live transatlantic connection, and (pending the development of VERA) no way of recording the TV camera's image other than, somewhat crudely, on film – this is 'the wonderful thing called telerecording'.[6] Since there is no attempt to suggest an American background in the shot of Leigh talking, we can assume that she simply spoke into a TV camera in England before she left, the footage being recorded onto film as she spoke – much simpler than flying a can of film back from America. It is interesting, too, that her input was not simply shot with a *film* camera: the likely reason is that the telerecorded image of a talking head, when inserted into the live programme, created a more consistent visual texture than was then easy to achieve with an image actually generated on film. In any case, they do here use telerecording, and Leigh makes an explicit point of it.

(2) Soon after the half-way point, Secombe's wife is brought on, and we learn that their two children are being looked after at home. But they too come up quickly on the screen within the screen. Andrews gives another prompt: 'There they are, watching you.' As was not possible with Leigh, there is

---

[5] In fact the distinction between segments is not always clear-cut. Two successive guests may be connected, and could be counted together (as I have done) or separately. The figure of fourteen gives a neat average of two minutes within the half-hour programme.

[6] It is, of course, the same process that we are indebted to for preserving the episode itself in full: unlike so many TV programmes of that time, it was telerecorded and stored on film, enabling it to be rebroadcast on BBC2 in a 1980s retrospective series, recorded off-air on to VHS by me as no doubt by many others, and later transferred to DVD, and thence to a computer file, from which I have worked in writing this article ... complexities undreamed-of by the pre-VERA pioneers.

genuine interaction, and parents and children exchange excited greetings. We see in the foreground the TV set on which they are watching the programme, and Secombe asks Andrews the incredulous question, 'Is there a camera in the house?', which doesn't need answering, because clearly there must be one, moved in there in his absence by an Outside Broadcast team.

(3) Near the end, we get more images of children, in a hospital where Secombe is a regular visitor and benefactor. But these images are different, a shot of the ward and then a short montage of faces, photographed and edited on film; if it were live, it would have had to involve a separate camera for each face, and the same would apply in the case of a telerecording. Once again, the technicalities are spelled out, to the participants and to us: the hospital nurse makes her entrance on to the set, and Andrews tells her 'We were just looking at the *film* of your patients.' Back in the ward, the children wave goodbye, but this can only be a pretend interaction, in contrast to the one involving the Secombe home with its live camera.

The programme has, then, exploited the full range of technologies then available, pre-videotape. What is particularly striking is the way it has so carefully drawn attention to each. At the start, we are told to concentrate on the viewpoint of the hidden TV camera in the studio. Adèle Leigh acknowledges 'the wonderful thing called telerecording'. Secombe marvels at the placing of a live OB camera in his own home, and the images from the hospital are identified as film ones.

So what does all this demonstrate? It takes us back to a time when a TV show was not a taken-for-granted commodity but still rather miraculous, reaching us despite multiple obstacles and risks of which the audience was well aware. 'Do not adjust your set' is an obsolete formula now, but was in regular use then to warn us of a technical breakdown beyond the viewer's control. In live TV drama, cameras could break down on air, actors could dry or collapse or even, in one notorious case, drop dead during a transmission, and the show would have to go on somehow. TIYL was vulnerable to all such risks, and to special ones in the opening stages of each episode: the victim might not get to the right place at the right time – hence the nervousness at the start of the Secombe show – and the victim might refuse to take part, as famously happened on more than one occasion.[7] And however closely pre-planned the format of the show itself might be, hitches could always occur. In this one, there is no disaster, but (a) one guest jumps the gun with his off-screen verbal entry, before Andrews has finished cueing him,

---

[7] Two who refused were Richard Gordon, author of the novel *Doctor in the House* and its successors, and the footballer Danny Blanchflower, who captained Tottenham Hotspur and Northern Ireland. Tele-recorded back-up items had to be hastily substituted.

(b) another guest dries up and has to be prompted, (c) the comedian Eric Sykes is supposed to come on in the final segment, along with Spike Milligan and others, but Andrews calls for him repeatedly in vain, and (d) one of the final credit titles is not quite in place when the time comes to show it, so we see it having to be straightened.

These items, like the 50 seconds of nothing at the start, are flaws that modern producers would want to smooth out by retakes or editing; in its later years, the norm was, predictably, for TIYL to be safely pre-recorded and tidied up, even while its makers took care to preserve, particularly in the opening pick-up of the unsuspecting victim, the crucial residue of as-if-live excitement.[8]

The transformation in TV technology in which VERA was such a portentous landmark created many gains, but also losses, like the adoption of synchronised sound by the cinema three decades earlier. In this same year of 1958, the film director Jean Renoir cited the aesthetics of live TV as a fresh inspiration for his work in cinema, embracing exactly the kind of rough edges that we have observed in TIYL; Roberto Rossellini, alongside him, spoke in the same spirit. Discussing plans for his next production, Renoir told their interviewer:

I would like to make this film ... in the spirit of *live* television. I'd like to make the film as though it were a live broadcast, shooting each scene only once, with the actors imagining that the public are directly receiving their words and gestures. Both the actors and the technicians should know that there will be no retakes: that, whether they succeed or not, they can't begin again.[9]

The interviewer was André Bazin. No film critic could have been more in sympathy with Renoir's words. It was he who had memorably pinned down the special qualities of the 1950 film of Thor Heyerdahl's *Kon-Tiki* expedition: its very gaps and rough edges became positive virtues, vivid testimony to the authenticity of the record of a sea voyage whose dangers meant that severe

---

[8] Pre-recording of this opening segment was a positive advantage, in that it made it easier to contrive a genuine surprise; the victim could be caught anywhere, at any time. In the live days, this had to happen at a specific time of the week, close to the studio itself, and the production team had to take care not to arouse suspicion when an appointment was fixed up for that time-slot – as with Secombe and the elaborate decoy of the pre-Africa film crew. As against this, something was lost when, between the pick-up and entering the theatre, the victim made a journey, changed clothes, and was able to prepare mentally, in contrast to Secombe's palpably tenser real-time experience.

[9] 'Cinema and Television: Jean Renoir and Roberto Rossellini interviewed by André Bazin', *Sight and Sound* 28:1 (Winter 1958): 26–30: translated from original publication in *France Observateur*.

limits were placed on the camera's use. And it was he who had famously used the scene of seal-hunting, in Flaherty's *Nanook of the North*, to praise a mode of filming opposed to the classic montage style:

> Editing could have suggested the passage of time; Flaherty is content to *show* the waiting, and the duration of the hunt becomes the very substance and object of the image. In the film this episode consists of a single shot. Can anyone deny that it is in this way much more moving than 'editing by attraction' would have been?[10]

I feel he would have relished the opening of the Secombe TIYL, and the Sky News handling of the Breaking News about Chris Huhne.

But Bazin died in 1958, the interview being one of his last publications. He had written extensively about television as well as cinema, an element of his work that is only now starting to be rediscovered. All kinds of irony attach to the fact that he died at precisely the time when developments in electronic recording were starting to transform not only television, but also – in the longer term – cinema itself and our means of access to it; and that Renoir was exploring, with him, the potential of live TV aesthetics just at the moment when the process of phasing out live performance was beginning.

1958 was indeed an extraordinary year. The year of VERA, as yet a cloud no bigger than a man's hand. The year of the Nigel Kneale drama serial *Quatermass and the Pit*, as impressive as TIYL in its deployment of a wide range of the formal strategies available to pre-videotape TV.[11] The year of the publication of the first volume of Bazin's collected essays, of his death, and of the launch of the Nouvelle Vague which owed so much to him, to Renoir, to Rossellini, and to the ideas about TV-like spontaneity that their great interview of that same year discussed; François Truffaut, Bazin's protégé, began shooting his first film *Les 400 Coups* on the very day of his death, and would dedicate the film to him in a prefatory title. It is also the year of *Vertigo*, which functions as Alfred Hitchcock's valedictory summation of, and reflection on, the sumptuous visual pleasures of classical cinema; contrast *Psycho* in 1960, a very calculated response to the rise of television and its effects on cinema, shot not by his regular film collaborators but by the crew

---

[10] André Bazin, 'The Evolution of Film Language' in *The New Wave*, translated and edited by Peter Graham (London: Secker and Warburg, 1968), 29. Original French publication in *Que est-ce que le cinema?*, volume 1 of 4 (Paris: Editions du Cerf, 1958), which also contains his account of *Kon-Tiki*, in the essay on 'Cinema and Exploration'. Both these essays are included in *What is Cinema?* (volume 1 of 2), translated by Hugh Gray (Berkeley: University of California Press, 1967).

[11] *Quatermass and the Pit*, written by Nigel Kneale, directed by Rudolph Cartier: broadcast in six episodes on BBC TV between 22 December 1958 and 26 January 1959.

of his TV show. And 1960 is also the year of Michael Powell's *Peeping Tom*. If the Secombe TIYL lays out all the formal parameters of the TV of its time, *Peeping Tom* does the same for cinema, showing us celluloid *film* being shot, processed and projected, in all of its different gauges and contexts: home movie, documentary, feature.

For some years after that, anyone wanting to teach about TV had to send to the BFI for 16mm *films* of programmes or extracts, obtained via telerecording; video remained the preserve of professionals. Now, of course, the reverse obtains: instead of accessing TV via film, we access not only TV but cinema almost exclusively by electronic means. *Peeping Tom* becomes an essential aid for teaching about the lost film mechanisms of the past; TIYL can serve the same function for the evolution of the technologies of television. But they are both, like Bazin's writings, much more than museum pieces. *Peeping Tom* remains a profound film, TIYL taps into strategies and pleasures of live television that still have a meaning today, as the Sky News item of 2012 happens to confirm.

Another article – many articles – could be written, from this starting point, on developments since 1958 in cinema and in television and in the relations between the two, but I will leave it there, with the suggestion that those key transitional years 1958–60 deserve as close attention, in terms of technical change and responses to it, as the years 1928–30 habitually receive in terms of the technology of cinema.

Bibliography

Barr, Charles. '"They Think it's All Over": The Dramatic Legacy of Live Television.' In *Big Picture, Small Screen: The Relations between Film and Television*, edited by John Hill and Martin McLoone, 47–75. Luton: John Libby Press, 1996.

Bazin, André. 'Cinema and Television: Jean Renoir and Roberto Rossellini interviewed by André Bazin.' *Sight and Sound* 28:1 (Winter 1958): 26–30: translated from original publication in *France Observateur*.

—*What is Cinema?* (volume 1 of 2), translated by Hugh Gray. Berkeley: University of California Press, 1967.

—'The Evolution of Film Language.' In *The New Wave*, translated and edited by Peter Graham. London: Secker and Warburg, 1968.

19

Gaudy nights: Dance and reality television's display of talent

Frances Bonner

This chapter will explore spectacle, gender and class as aesthetic elements in the appeal of high rating reality talent show formats based on dancing. It will look briefly at the *So You Think You Can Dance* (GB/US. 19 Entertainment/ Dick Clark Productions) format, but its main examples will be *Strictly Come Dancing* (UK, BBC, 2004–) and *Dancing with the Stars* (Australia, Seven Network, 2004–), with some reference to the latter show's US version. That format, which is owned by the BBC and internationally traded as *Dancing with the Stars*, is presented as an exemplar of the sub-category 'reality talent show' and as the site where several precursors converge. The format's aesthetic, which is remarkably consistent across its versions, will be analyzed both in terms of its apparently conservative gendering and as an instance of 'cheerful vulgarity'. The discussion of this latter term refers both to the spectacle offered within the programme and aspects of the performance and address, including traces of vaudeville or music hall and other class-based referents in the way ballroom dancing is displayed on television. Despite aesthetic consistencies, varying screening practices lead to a different quality of national engagement between the programme and the viewers of the British and Australian versions of the format.

Internationally franchised programmes provide a valuable opportunity to examine aesthetic aspects of global television as they retain and vary elements in the process of localising the format. The extent to which they are able to do this varies according to how tightly the format licence is enforced.

There may be little variation allowed in the set (*Who Wants to be a Millionaire* (*WWtbaM*) is an example here) but all formats become localised through the people involved on-screen and the way that, if successful, they interact with their audiences. The Indian version of *WWtbaM* accrued immediate prestige through its employment of the venerated Bollywood actor Amitabh Bachchan as host. Lately, it has been building on this by targeting poor areas and under-privileged people as the pool from which to draw contestants and promote its key message of success through the acquisition of knowledge.

Despite the productivity of considerations of formatted quiz shows like *WWtbaM*, as shown by work by Albert Moran and Anthony Fung among others,[1] this chapter will as indicated investigate reality talent shows, where individuals or small groups compete on the basis of exhibitions of performing skills, primarily singing and dancing, but more occasionally other activities which once would have been seen as part of a variety bill, like ventriloquism or acrobatics. The way in which these programmes differ from the older talent quest shows and thus deserve to be included in the broad reality television grouping, is that together with the display of talent and its evaluation by a panel of judges, the process of moulding performances between programmes forms part of the show. In addition, viewer voting usually contributes to the eventual decision on the winner. This latter element increases the salience of audience reception of the programmes and their interaction with their paratexts, such as websites and spin-off programmes formally related to the core 'mothership', as well as mediated discussion on-line and in newspapers and magazines not formally so linked. I believe it is easily possible to include the display of talents not conventionally seen as performance ones, like cooking, fashion design, modelling and home renovation, in the grouping (the *Masterchef* franchise clearly operates similarly in many regards) but will not be doing so here, mainly because these variants do not engage viewers through voting and a surrogate studio audience, but also because the spectacle provided is more muted. As shall be demonstrated below, spectacle is a key part of the performance element of the core grouping of reality talent shows.

Reality talent shows are important components of broadcast television's attempt to retain an audience. The near live quality and viewer engagement through voting mean that there is a premium on watching at the time of broadcast, or within that short period that Misha Kavka calls the 'zone of

---

[1] See Anthony Fung, 'Coping, Cloning and Copying: Hong Kong in the Global Television Business', in *Television across Asia: Television Industries, Programme Formats and Globalization*, ed. Albert Moran and Michael Keane (London: Routledge, 2011); Albert Moran, *New Flows in Global TV* (Bristol: Intellect, 2009).

liveness' where an audience can think of itself as 'belonging to an imagined community of viewers *at the moment of watching*'.[2] Delaying for more than a few hours means missing out on national conversations about the progress of the contestants, the mini-scandals of the moment and tabloid 'outrages' about bad judgements. Timeliness is especially important for those formats which have mass appeal, like the *Idol*, *X Factor* or *Got Talent* franchises, though it is also significant for those of more niche appeal, such as *Next Top Model* or *Project Runway*, which may be screened on pay, rather than broadcast, channels where there may be a slightly lengthier 'zone of liveness'. More usually such channels screen foreign versions of successful formats or ones which have not been locally franchised, attracting smaller audiences and without the national engagement of localised programmes. This is not to deny that such programmes can have their own appeal to audience members who may enjoy the diverse deployments of the format, find one particular version more pleasurable or more adept, or just have different tastes from those judged popular by format buyers.

Although both singing and dancing reality talent shows stress music and movement, the priorities differ and the concern here with visual components in the performance spectacle means dancing talent shows are the focus. Those sections of the programmes not immediately concerned with the spectacle, which include the preparation, discussion with presenters and judging, which frame and together comprise the majority of the show, all centre on the production and evaluation of the performance. The performance thus is the key element, but the *mise-en-scène* and the 'story' are different. The framing story is about the work involved in producing the performance and this is the key to both the difference from older talent quests and the distinctiveness of this grouping of reality television. These are shows about work and that applies whether or not celebrity contestants are involved.

So You Think You Can Dance, like the occasional dance item in the *Got Talent* format, uses ordinary people as competitors, but those people are highly trained and have often already started earning money from dance. Much is made in discussion of reality television about how it produces (short-term) celebrities from the untalented and those with little to offer other than bad behaviour,[3] but it is rare for those without musical training to succeed in the singing competitions and not possible for ordinary people without dance training to get through the auditions for the dancing ones. The biographical

[2] Misha Kavka, *Reality Television, Affect and Immediacy: Reality Matters* (Basingstoke: Palgrave Macmillan, 2008), 17 (her emphasis).
[3] This is more often a popular pundit position than a scholarly one, but see also Richard Huff, *Reality Television* (Westport, CT: Praeger, 2006).

backstory provided on *So you Think* insistently details the long process acquiring the proficiency necessary to dance both within the special field under which dancers qualified for the competition and the range of alternative modes in which they are required to dance each week. Versatility and willingness to extend their capabilities is essential for the contestants and the judges' assessments draw on the professional language of many dance styles, educating viewers as they do so.

Dancing with the Stars' format ensures that any analysis of the programme will need to engage with celebrity, and I have done this elsewhere,[4] noting the rarity of celebrity reality shows which have no ordinary analogue (as *Celebrity Apprentice* and *Celebrity Masterchef* both do). *I'm a Celebrity... Get Me Out of Here!*, which also has no ordinary analogue, is predicated on finding out how much humiliation people are willing to undergo to regain fame.[5] The *Strictly/Dancing* format though, by some measures the world's most popular programme,[6] is primarily polite and respectful and provides positive publicity for the celebrities far in excess of the chances for poor coverage. Of course it always includes at least one celebrity to give an 'edge', a target for negativity, gossip and increased ratings; in 2010–11, the principal period under discussion here, Chaz Bono, Ann Widdicombe and Brynne Edelstein provided this in the US, UK and Australia respectively. The focus here though will be on celebrity only inasmuch as is needed to explicate the particulars of presentation and their aesthetic consequences.

Most reality talent shows are studio based, although they may move to an iconic venue – the Sydney Opera House or Blackpool Tower – for a special show near or at the final. The studio, complete with studio audience, is where the performance, the pre-performance chat and the evaluation of it all occur. The stage area is available for the presenters and the competitors, but is marked out as a performance space by lighting. During the performance, the lighting is theatrically inflected and there are neither cutaways for reaction shots to the judges or the studio audience, nor comments in voice-over. The non-performance components, whether they are in the studio, archival film or rehearsal footage, have standard studio-style naturalistic lighting, are highly edited and replete with reaction shots and voice-overs. The performance though is the spectacle at the heart of the format and is presented as the subject of scrutiny equally for the judges and the viewers. Judges' comments

---

[4] Forthcoming from *Celebrity Studies*.

[5] On this see Su Holmes, 'It's a Jungle out there!: Playing the Game of Fame in Celebrity Reality TV', in *Framing Celebrity: New Directions in Celebrity Culture* ed. Su Holmes and Sean Redmond (London: Routledge, 2006), 45–65.

[6] 'The greatest shows on Earth', *Television Business International* (October/November 2008): 63–4, 66, 68–9.

afterwards may guide viewers' responses and votes, although the occasional exasperated comment as viewers 'save' less proficient dancers indicate such guidance may not be followed.

The *Dancing with the Stars* format, developed from the British programme, *Strictly Come Dancing*, had several precursors which contributed both to those elements available for formatting and its national inflections. They are particularly salient to my two main examples, the British and Australian versions. The earliest is the British television programme *Come Dancing*, a ballroom dancing show in which ordinary people danced competitively in teams representing regions. It ran intermittently and with various presenters from 1949 to 1998. John Fiske and John Hartley analyzed it in their 1978 study as combining codes of ritualised social conflict (the competition) and ritualised social coherence (the dance).[7] The team aspect, which intensified the social coherence, is no longer very evident, although the occasional production number by the professional dancers alone provides something reminiscent of it.

The next text, both chronologically and in terms of obvious influence, is the film *Strictly Ballroom* (1992), Baz Luhrman's first feature as a director. Generically it mixed romcom and mockumentary in a narrative set in the world of competitive ballroom dancing. An ugly duckling story with a multi-cultural theme, it was a great success domestically and internationally. Many professional and semi-professional dancers took part and its domestic success led to increased Australian public interest in ballroom dancing. Given how frequently it is talked of in general studies of ballroom dancing,[8] it appears that this transfer was not restricted to Australia.

Domestically however, the increased popularity of such dance contributed to the development of an Australian Broadcasting Corporation show called *Strictly Dancing* where amateur and semi-professional pairs competed in a glittery studio set with a stand-up comedian host, Paul McDermott, a resident band and three judges drawn from a panel of seven. The competitors and judges often provided evidence of the multicultural appeal of dance, so central to the film, though without the film's agonistic setting. There was no viewer voting and the show ran from February 2004 to 2006.

The format of this show was marketed and one episode of the Australian original showed footage of an Indian version and made reference to the BBC having bought the rights. Whether or not this latter was actually the case, the BBC did not make a programme to the format. What the BBC did

---

[7] John Fiske and John Hartley, *Reading Television* (London: Methuen, 1978), 129.
[8] For example, in Juliet McMains, *Glamour Addiction: Inside the American Ballroom Dance Industry* (Middletown, CT: Wesleyan University Press, 2006).

instead was to hybridise the Australian products with their own no longer running programme. First broadcast in May 2004, the most striking evidence of this was the otherwise nonsensical title *Strictly Come Dancing*. The title is meaningless in territories not having screened *Come Dancing*, so the mundane, but self-explanatory *Dancing with the Stars* became the title under which it was licensed. Elements of the set and the use of a comedian-presenter were also incorporated, though as I have recently argued a very large proportion of presenters are (male) stand-up comedians anyway.[9] The chosen lead presenter was Bruce Forsyth, long-time television quiz and variety host, accompanied by ex-model Tess Daly.

The format was taken back to Australia, as *Dancing with the Stars*, by the commercial Seven Network in October 2004 which made no reference to its British title, presumably because for the first couple of series, the ABC show *Strictly Dancing* was still screening. It did, however, reference the film very strongly by employing some of its actors: the co-host, Sonia Kruger and two of the judges, Todd McKenny and the film's lead Paul Mercurio. Kruger was initially paired with Darryl Somers, whose previous variety show host role echoed Forsyth's. (Kruger left the show at the end of 2011, while Mercurio had lasted only a few seasons, so McKenny is the sole remaining such trace of the film, but the programme had established its own identity quite quickly.)

In what follows, I will refer to the format as *Dancing with the Stars*, the British show as *Strictly*, which is how it is popularly referred to in its home territory, and the Australian show as *Dancing*. These are my main examples because I have lived through whole seasons of them in the originating country and thus am able to comment on the reception context in ways more extensive than relying on the programme's website. I will occasionally refer to the US show, but as I am reliant on YouTube for my exposure to it, I will not be depending on it to develop my argument.

The show involves a competition between celebrities – 8–14 of them dependent on the national version – dancing with professionals and judged by a panel of ex-dancers. Each week the couples perform routines they have learnt in the previous week, moving on as the number of competitors reduce, from one each to two routines a week. Couples are voted off by a combination of judges' and viewers' votes. The format requires heterosexual display, even by non-heterosexual celebrities, which may be why the very 'out' actor John Barrowman only appeared on a one-off BBC Christmas special rather than dance with a woman for a whole series.[10]

---

[9]Frances Bonner, *Personality Presenters: Television's Intermediaries with Viewers*. (Farnham: Ashgate, 2011).

[10] *Strictly Dancing* had included occasional same-sex pairs among the competitors and occasional

The presenting duo and their interactions with the judges are important elements of the format and provide the starting point for my examination of the gender dynamics of the format. It is characteristic for the male presenter to remain anchored on the studio dance floor, set in front of the band with the judges seated as a panel along the left hand side. The female presenter starts the show beside the male, but then adopts something of a 'roving reporter' role, going backstage into the green room to talk to contestants about their performances, their reactions to the judges' comments and any issues that may have arisen since the previous programme, including media responses to the shows and its celebrities. She thus has more airtime than the male, provides more information for the viewer about what is happening and, in the Australian case of Sonia Kruger, generates more of the fun elements. She was certainly more closely identified with the show than the second male presenter, the actor Daniel McPherson, so his dominance in the show's dynamics seems to result from a combination of his gender, stasis in the studio and interchanges with the judges. Leaving the studio floor signifies subordination in the same way that lead presenters of other programmes stay in the home set, while reporters are sent on assignment. In the British version women have greater prominence due in part to the age of the male presenter, Bruce Forsyth, who now only presents one of the weekend shows, being replaced on the other by Claudia Winkelman, the 2010 female presenter of the weekday spin-off chat show *It Takes Two*, herself now replaced in that role by ex-contestant, Zoe Ball.

As well as masculinity and a single location, Forsyth has televisual longevity underpinning his prominence; he has well over fifty years' experience on screen, nearly all of it in prime time. (In contrast the American host, Tom Bergeron, was previously a daytime personality, but his position has been bolstered by his continuation through three changes of co-presenter.)

Gender and the mobility of the programme's labour force interact in ways which are distinctive to this format. Instead of each version of the format being sealed off from others, there is regular interchange. Several male judges move between versions: Len Goodman and Bruno Tonioli do the British and American shows almost simultaneously, Craig Revel Horwood did the British and the New Zealand ones, while Mercurio did the Australian and New Zealand ones for the period in which his appearance on both overlapped – he left after a few years and the New Zealand format ceased in 2009. The male judges do not get replaced because they are judged too old, as the British Arlene Philips was, although Horwood's face lift and the jokes made

---

rumours about the possibility of a same-sex couple competing on *Strictly* itself have been aired in recent years.

about it, even by presenter Tess Daly, are useful counterweights here. Female ex-contestants can be recalled in other roles. As well as Ball coming back as a presenter, Philips' replacement was an ex-contestant, the singer Alesha Dixon (now left for *Britain's Got Talent* and replaced by ex-ballerina Darcy Bussell). Professional dancers of both genders move between versions. Adding to the impression of a *Dancing with the Stars* 'family' is the way that contestants from one series retain that as part of their career identity, for example by returning to a current series to comment from their experience and demonstrating ostensibly that they remain involved, as loyal viewers do.

The presenters, however, really do 'anchor' the individual versions in the national particular. Forsyth's long light entertainment career ensures *Strictly* remains ineffably British. Kruger was key to the Australianness of *Dancing* and her replacement by ex-Spice Girl Mel B, who seems to be developing a presence on Australian reality talent shows (she is a judge on *The X Factor*), shifts the national emphasis elsewhere. She does, however, testify further to the existence of a *Dancing with the Stars* 'family', having been the runner-up in the fifth US series. Much promotion of *Dancing* 2012 has been done by the highest profile competitor, long-term daytime personality Kerri-Anne Kennerley, but her ability to project the distinctive mode of brash Australian public femininity that Kruger did, was comparatively short term since she did not remain long in competition.

The nomenclature used in the world of dance is confusing and apparently inconsistent, especially that centred on the word 'ballroom' itself. The dancing engaged in on *Dancing with the Stars* is competitive, referred to at times as 'international' style, and comprised of ballroom and Latin dances. While much of competitive dance is organized around the term 'DanceSport', adopted to help in the push to make ballroom dancing an Olympic competition, this is not a term used in the television programme, I suspect for copyright reasons. 'Social' refers to dances that have the same names as those used competitively, as well as many others which are not, but this is the version people engage in for pleasure. During the 2011 Australian series, a celebrity newsreader was being kept in the show long into its run by viewer votes despite the judges' disapproval of her performances. One week the judges pointed out to her very firmly that what the programme required was not the social dancing she was delivering, but proper competitive dancing. She was chastened and trained harder the next week. It was one of the many occasions in which viewers were instructed about distinctions and terminology.

Competitive (ballroom) dancing is organized around gender difference. Men and women dressed differently and performing different though complementary steps dance together in restrictive formalised ways. The conventional gendering of competitive dance, carried into the television format, is present in the rhetoric of leading and following, of 'gentlemen' and 'ladies', and especially in the costuming. The dominant male and the passive female are performed in routine after routine. But in opposition to this conservatism in competitive dance, both members of the couple are athletes and both must display athleticism even if they need to mask it by grace. Gendering is performed, both in Judith Butler's and the more popular way of considering it, but how fully is the lead/follow really embodied? George Uba notes: 'while the female partner may willingly dress in a costume defining her along the historical lines of the "lady", in the course of the dance itself her motions seldom if ever appear submissive'.[11] Both Uba and Caroline Jean Picart, speaking as practitioner scholars and not referring to the television programme, rephrase the lead/follow relation. Uba notes that 'the reality is that the man (that is, the male dancer position) serves more as a "cue-er" than as a leader'.[12] While Picart in talking of her own practice in both roles, observes:

> I am particularly interested in what it means to communicate clear bodily cues, such that the person I am dancing with can easily adjust to these (which is what leading entails), or to be sensitively attuned, every muscle and nerve alert, for the slightest cue, so that two separate bodies may move in unison (which is what following requires).[13]

This separation of lead and follow from male and female will be important throughout the analysis.

But the binary that provides the fissure to open up understanding of the show and the contradictions of its gendering is the division between professional and amateur. Half of the people competing at any one time are professional and at the beginning they are almost always in equal numbers of men and women. These people not only train the celebrities but they choreograph their routines. Juliet McMains, speaking of the American ballroom dance industry, points out that the professionals are teachers as well as choreographers and because the industry runs largely on pro-am competitions, the professionals 'know not only how to coach a neophyte dancer to performance level, but are also experienced in crafting choreography that allows the professional to do 90 per cent of the work, enabling the students

---

[11] George Uba, 'From Signifying to Performance: International Ballroom Dance and the Choreographies of Transnationalism,' *Journal of Asian American Studies* 10:2 (2007): 150.
[12] Uba, 'From Signifying to Performance'.
[13] Caroline Jean S. Picart, *From Ballroom to DanceSport: Aesthetics, Athletics and Body Culture* (Albany: State University of New York Press, 2006), 8.

to appear much more skilled than they really are'.[14] The international character of competitive dance makes this observation applicable beyond the US. And this provides another modulation of the lead/follow rhetoric and reality, since the professional even within the female/follow role is likely to be providing more of the cues. At the beginning 50 per cent of the professionals are in this role. So, while the British title *Strictly Come Dancing*, is more distinctive, *Dancing with the Stars* is a more descriptive title for the format because it describes the pro–am combination around which all is organized.

The professional partner/choreographer is where the apparent conservative gendering of the format is challenged since control and direction is divided not by gender but by experience and training. Those knowledgeable about pro–am contests may be especially admiring of the skills of the female professionals, who need to appear simultaneously to be being led while cueing. Given the greater frequency with which male celebrities win the competition, the skills of the female professionals are all the more substantial.

There is one other aspect of gender within the pro–am binary that deserves consideration for its contribution to the previously discussed spectacle. This relates to the dance move known as the 'lift'. Lifts are moves which always result in studio applause when successful. They are the punctuation of the routines, the display of bodies and costumes, and they are usually performed by men of women. Changes in ballet, musical, and contemporary dance concerned to capitalize on the female dancers' strength and various dynamic forces allowing greater equality of movement have transferred into the programme to mean that on occasion the female celebrity lifts her male partner. If it becomes possible for a female celebrity to perform a lift of a male professional this is foregrounded in advance, during the performance and after the show. Pamela Stephenson Connolly competing in 2010 *Strictly* performed one late in the season on which she came third. In addition to the gender aspect here, Stephenson Connolly was one of the older celebrities, which intensified the achievement. Nevertheless, her femininity was repeatedly recuperated by reference to her husband and his opinions of her work, but such is the national fondness for the comedian Billy Connolly, producers would have been remiss to do otherwise. Like Stephenson Connolly's, all female lifts are performed within a comic mode. Given that her prior television work had been as a comedian, this was well situated in expectations of her, but such a set-up in the previous career is not required; women lifting men seems ipso facto comic. Perhaps in consequence, lifts

---

[14] Juliet McMains, 'Reality Check; *Dancing with the Stars* and the American Dream', in *Routledge Dance Studies Reader* ed. Alexandra Carter and Janet O'Shea (Florence, KY: Routledge, 2010), 284.

are not equally available to all women capable of them. They are rare for female professionals (perhaps too obviously revealing the 'real' state of play) and if they do perform them are never foregrounded within the programme. Furthermore, such moves are not engaged in by the young, very feminine celebrity women who are likely, as actor Kara Tointon was in 2010's *Strictly*, to be the female type to win the competition.

Focusing on the pro–am division also brings in another aspect of reality television, that which I have long investigated under the term 'ordinary'. One of the key features of reality TV is its use of ordinary people, but what happens when the people involved occupy the two terms 'celebrity' and 'professional', especially when many of the professionals start edging into the other category? Those that persist in the show season after season may begin to achieve their own degree of celebrity and are referred to familiarly by fans. When professional Artem Chigvintsev injured his back on the 2011 *Strictly*, his health became one of the lead items on the website's home page. Gossip items from celebrity 'hot spots' like the British Ivy report the activities of certain high-profile professionals like Anton du Beke no differently from the items on those competing as celebrities. In this confusing situation, I want to suggest that ordinariness is both thinned and doubled. The ordinary people are both the professionals and the celebrities. In the programme's logic, the professionals are ordinary since they start from a position of public anonymity; they are unknowns. Yet their training and skill mean that even at the start of their televisual exposure they are not actually like (most of) us. The celebrities are not like us because they are known, but in their amateurishness they are similar to most viewers. Dancing is not their metier, indeed if it were it would disqualify them from competing. When the Australian TV gardener Jamie Durie competed in *Dancing*, there was much debate about his adult career having included a stint as a male strip show dancer. Despite his repeatedly pointing out that the discipline was totally different, the possibility of unfair advantage was felt to have contributed to his early elimination. Celebrities present their ordinary abilities to be modelled into a semblance of competence in ways very similar to the ordinary people who compete in shows like *Faking It* (UK, Channel 4, 2000–4) where intensive training transforms the ordinary subject. There is a parallel to the non-celebrity talent shows where the rhetoric and reception is that anyone can make it, but the reality is that anyone with years of training can use a reality talent show as an additional audition space for the breakthrough to a professional career, or to take a nascent career to a higher level. As noted above, dance is even more emphatic than singing here because the latter has high-profile exceptions like Susan Boyle. *Dancing*'s celebrities are able to 'fake it' not only because of the amount of work they put into training, but also because of the professionals' experience in making amateurs look proficient.

It is useful to start examining how the programme's overall aesthetic might be termed cheerfully vulgar through examining how thoroughly the format is located within the practices and conventions of vaudeville and music hall. *Dancing with the Stars* reveals that these links, so evident and discussed in early television history, persist. They can be seen in all examined formats from the setting and costuming to the routines and the very evident playing to the (studio) audience. In *Strictly* it is even more obvious through the use of Bruce Forsyth as chief presenter, as well as the inclusion of a trip to Blackpool towards the end of a series for surviving contestants to perform in the Ballroom there. The vaudeville past is even more present in the post-show tour, Strictly Live. This is less evident in Australia where there is not a related live show and where the host for the last few years has been an actor with no career link to vaudeville/musical hall, but a live post-show tour is an aspect of the format's activities in the US.

Dance routines were common components of vaudeville/musical hall shows and also of the early television variety shows which drew so many of their performers from those circuits. Among the comic dance routines and the chorus-line numbers, were occasional spectacular pairs dances, most particularly the so-called 'apache' dances, drawn, so English-speaking audiences were assured, from the seedier nightclubs of Paris. Traces of these melodramatic enactments of passion and possessiveness with their theatrically overstated sexual politics are readily seen in *Dancing*'s routines, especially in the format's fondness for the paso doble. This particular 'Latin' dance is a great favourite with producers and judges, who repeatedly inform viewers that the female role is as the cape to the male's bullfighter. No other dance is so insistently metaphorised, or so redolent of variety and vaudeville forebears.

Variety is also evident in the vocal performances of musical guest celebrities which become more common as the number of contestants reduce while the running time needs to be retained. Additionally, it is evoked in the judging segments where judges play out their assigned roles (as the 'heavy', the encouraging one, or the voice of authority for instance). This may include making occasional jokes or instigating studio audience booing by marking down a popular favourite. Dana Heller refers to their producing 'spectacles of merciless rejection' alternating with 'jubilant authorisation to advance to the next stage'.[15] The presenters enact the master/mistress of ceremonies role,

---

[15] Dana Heller, '"Calling out around the World": the Global Appeal of Reality Dance Formats', in *Global Television Formats: Understanding Television across Borders*, ed. Tasha Oren and Sharon Sharaf (London: Routledge, 2011), 40.

including, in Forsyth's case, characteristic lame jokes and trademark catch-phrases. In each British series there is at least one routine using paraphernalia from circus or pantomime which requires a celebrity contestant to 'fly' (on wires attached to a harness). Ann Widdicombe flew in 2010, Russell Grant did so in 2011 in a human cannonball effect, Victoria Pendleton flew on a bicycle in 2012. This transmutation of the variety show and its vaudeville/musical forbears, through its hybridising with the talent quest and reality television is not restricted to the dancing variants of reality talent shows. It is to be found in all of them, perhaps even more clearly in the *Got Talent* format with its greater range of skills in competition.

The vaudeville/music hall heritage and the emphasis on visual components that watching dancing requires provide a starting point for a discussion of the format's aesthetic as 'cheerful vulgarity', but there are obvious problems in choosing to talk of almost anything as vulgar. The usual defence is to refer to etymological linkages to 'the common people' or 'the working class', and the considerable popularity of the programme would support this, but my hope is that by using the modifier 'cheerful' and locating the programme in the popular tradition of music hall, my identification of a vulgar aesthetic is not read as dismissive or condemnatory. It certainly is not intended that way. Nor do I intend to rest my ascription of vulgarity in the emphasis dance places on the human body. The disciplining of the dancing body as it performs according to highly formalised competitive rules in a designated space and in time to an allocated piece of music mitigates the likelihood of such a simple equation. Jane Desmond has noted the 'rhetorical linkage [of] nondominant races, classes, gender and nationalities with "the body" to physicality instead of mentality'.[16] While this could be followed further here, especially through consideration of the professionals' backgrounds, there seems no benefit when a programme centred on dance and dance training is necessarily and properly concerned with the body and physicality. 'The body' is the ultimate locus of the costumes and lighting that are key to my consideration of vulgarity. But the devising and memorising of the routines requires considerable mentation.

Uba, Picart and McMains all stress the upper class referents of ballroom dancing, but in the UK and Australia at least, these are very distant. Social and competitive dance are both mass activities, perhaps most firmly located in the lower middle class but available to all able to afford instruction. Fiske and Hartley's discussion of *Come Dancing* still has considerable pertinence. They comment on the elements of self-deception by which the 'courtesy

---

[16] Jane Desmond, 'Embodying Difference: Issues in Dance and Cultural Studies', *Cultural Critique* 26 (Winter 1993/4): 35.

of the Edwardian upper class' is aped in the hand and leg movements of the dancers, 'but we know, and the dancers know, that they are ordinary people from today's subordinate class'.[17] They comment on how the women's dresses reveal a fantasy of class mobility by 'a brash "vulgarity in the quantity of petticoats and sequins and in the stridency of the colours"'.[18] The shift to celebrities and the previously noted dispersal of ordinariness across both types of dancers in the contemporary descendants of the programme may have changed the character of the fantasy somewhat, but the vulgarity of the costumes (now often the men's as well as women's) and the colours on-screen persist.

While Fiske and Hartley named the vulgarity 'brash', I think 'cheerful' more accurately describes the good-humour and inclusiveness of the newer format. The high popularity of *Dancing with the Stars* requires that it have a broad appeal, as is evident in the UK by the extent to which discussion of events during each year's series can be found across the range of daily newspapers, from the *Daily Telegraph* to the *Sun* (not excluding *The Guardian* and the *Daily Mail*). Celebrities are chosen from widely popular fields, not niche ones, with the television actors coming largely from soaps. The class specificities of the participants in the series or of their appeal are very difficult to unravel, especially given the complications brought by celebrity. Fans of Felicity Kendall competing in *Strictly* in 2010 are unlikely to have been similarly located to those of fellow competitor, Destiny's Child singer Michelle Williams.

So how is the vulgarity and cheerfulness made manifest now? There is no place for subtlety; judges fulfil their allocated roles and together with the presenters direct viewers to preferred readings. Costumes now are revealingly tight and/or skimpy and brightly coloured far more often than they display quantities of petticoats. Their sequins and other decorative embellishments reflect the light which is deployed melodramatically to underpin both the emotions on display and the themes being played to. Familiarity is desired and provided in the first instance by the long run of the show (heading towards its eleventh series in the UK), and also in the elements of the format which may be tweaked from series to series, but are rarely much altered. The music is well known though sometimes seems to be ill-matched to the dance. The celebrities, of course, have the familiarity their celebrity mandates.

The dancers' costumes are designed to enhance movement and reveal well-toned bodies; they add to the spectacle, but they also add to production costs. Combined with scheduling details they reveal differences between

---

[17] Fiske and Hartley, *Reading* Television, 131.
[18] Fiske and Hartley, *Reading* Television, 131.

the British and Australian versions. *Strictly* is a BBC flagship programme. It is an important piece of the schedule in the lead-up to Christmas and the two weekend shows together with the weekday spin-off means it is stripped across the week. If its aesthetic is vulgar it is not by chance. The Australian show in contrast screens only once a week even though it is one of the most popular shows on air during its run, which usually starts just after Easter. In the early episodes when there are many celebrities to dress, the costuming is visibly cheaper, verging on the tawdry in fabric colour and design. The difference between the celebrities and the professionals, who may be wearing their own much more expensive performance costumes, is substantial and incongruous, but this disappears as the programme continues and the number of celebrities to be dressed each week reduces. Such disparity is not to be seen in the British format.

Costumes emphasize any story or character that the choreography or the week's theme provides and they do so in overstated, stereotypical ways. Not only does their design ensure that they draw attention, but presenters and judges direct attention to them, as does paratextual commentary. Exposed flesh operates similarly. Both judges' and viewers' comments have suggested that the British professional Ola Johnson calibrates the skimpiness of her costume to compensate for the (lack of) proficiency of her partner. During 2011, Australian judges said that professional Carmello Pizzino would do well to cover his bare chest more. Such comments are not made of the celebrities and the appearance of a nicely defined male celebrity chest is an anticipated part of each series, regarded as increasing the celebrity's chance of success.

Further attention is given to costumes in the British version by the regular segment in the Friday edition of *It Takes Two* of a preview and discussion of a couple of the costumes to be seen in the weekend's shows. Technical terms for costume construction are used, with viewers instructed for instance about what a godet is and why it would be used. Like the references to steps and arm movements, such discussion creates and caters to an audience heavily invested in the programme beyond the spectacle, the revelation of celebrity ordinariness and the sniping of the judges, but in the materiality and corpo-reality of the performances themselves. The lighting during the performance segments, with its washes of lemon, pink and lavender focuses attention on the composition and the movement of fabric and any beading or embroidery on it. As such a palette indicates, the theatrical inflection of the lighting, mentioned earlier, encourages a light-hearted enjoyment of the spectacle, again reminiscent of circus conventions.

So potent and pervasive is discussion of *Strictly* on and off television that it can be considered a recurrent feature in the annual passage of the British popular imagination: part of the build-up to Christmas. Despite the demands it makes on its celebrity contestants' time and energies, it has little difficulty finding a new group each year because it is usually so beneficial to their reputations. Rather than provide consolatory viewing, to use Ellis's term for the programmes we watch when there is nothing more engaging available,[19] it is actively awaited and eagerly watched by large segments of the population as providing guaranteed pleasure. And despite the lower budget, limited airtime and absence of a culmination with a seasonal celebration, the Australian version does a muted version of the same.

I have argued that the appeal of the show lies in its cheerfully vulgar spectacle where the performances present well-known personalities in overstated costumes and theatrical lighting acting out mini-narratives of gendered courtship in dance form. The form means that the gender dynamics are nearly always quite playful, exaggerated in keeping with the costuming and the mock-seriousness of the judges' score paddles. There is no real courtship intended (though it may eventuate and become an additional publicity theme) and, as demonstrated above, the gendered picture may involve some sleight of hand, but the whole show centres on the one or two minutes when all other elements pause for the display of talent. The professional–amateur division obscures the real gender hierarchies in those couples where the celebrity is male and ensures that all the celebrity amateurs appear to have become more proficient than is usually the case.

The spectacle, though, is embedded in a different narrative that tells of the importance of work to achievement. The work narrative is never so obtrusive as to impinge on the pleasure of viewing and no matter how forceful the judges' comments about the greater importance of training, discipline and application, viewers can still disregard it and vote on popularity.[20] The contestants cannot foreground the work too much, instead they must present themselves as enjoying themselves despite the work involved and the harsh judgements made of their skills. The costuming and comportment may be far from their preferred style, but they need to maintain the upbeat tone which is the programme's hallmark. Above all, these joyous spectacles of rhythmic corporeal mastery draw viewers to share a common experience at the same time, a rarity in these days of fragmented viewing.

---

[19] John Ellis, *TV FAQ: Uncommon Answers to Common Questions about TV* (London: I. B.Tauris, 2007), 13–14.
[20] On an instance of this in the *Strictly* 2008 season see Gunn Sara Enli, 'Mass Communication Tapping into Participatory Culture: Exploring *Strictly Come Dancing* and *Britain's Got Talent*,' *European Journal of Communication* 24:4 (2009): 481–93.

Bibliography

Bonner, Frances. *Personality Presenters: Television's Intermediaries with Viewers*. Farnham: Ashgate, 2011.

Desmond, Jane. 'Embodying Difference: Issues in Dance and Cultural Studies.' *Cultural Critique* 26 (Winter 1993/4): 33–63.

Ellis, John. *TV FAQ: Uncommon Answers to Common Questions about TV.* London: I. B. Tauris, 2007.

Enli, Gunn Sara 'Mass Communication Tapping into Participatory Culture: Exploring *Strictly Come Dancing* and *Britain's Got Talent.*' *European Journal of Communication* 24:4 (2009): 481–93.

Fiske, John, and John Hartley. *Reading Television*. London: Methuen, 1978.

Fung, Anthony. 'Coping, Cloning and Copying: Hong Kong in the Global Television Business.' In *Television across Asia: Television Industries, Programme Formats and Globalization*, edited by Albert Moran and Michael Keane, 74–87. London: Routledge, 2011.

Heller, Dana. '"Calling out around the World": the Global Appeal of Reality Dance Formats'. In *Global Television Formats: Understanding Television across Borders* edited by Tasha Oren and Sharon Sharaf, 39–55. London: Routledge, 2011.

Holmes, Su. 'It's a Jungle out there!: Playing the Game of Fame in Celebrity Reality TV.' In *Framing Celebrity: New Directions in Celebrity Culture* ed. Su Holmes and Sean Redmond, 45–65. London: Routledge, 2006.

Huff, Richard. *Reality Television*. Westport, CT: Praeger, 2006.

Kavka, Misha, *Reality Television, Affect and Immediacy: Reality Matters*. Basingstoke: Palgrave Macmillan, 2008.

McMains, Juliet. *Glamour Addiction: Inside the American Ballroom Dance Industry*. Middletown, CT: Wesleyan University Press, 2006.

—'Reality Check; *Dancing with the Stars* and the American Dream.' In *Routledge Dance Studies Reader*, edited by Alexandra Carter and Janet O'Shea, 280–91. Florence, KY: Routledge, 2010.

Moran, Albert. *New Flows in Global TV*. Bristol: Intellect, 2009.

Picart, Caroline Jean S. *From Ballroom to DanceSport: Aesthetics, Athletics and Body Culture*. Albany: State University of New York Press, 2006.

Uba, George. 'From Signifying to Performance: International Ballroom Dance and the Choreographies of Transnationalism.' *Journal of Asian American Studies* 10:2 (2007): 41–67.

(No author) 'The greatest shows on Earth.' *Television Business International* (October/November 2008): 63–4, 66, 68–9.

20

Television sublime: The experimental television of Lithuanian CAC TV

Linus Andersson

In 1961, FCC-chairman Newton Minnow famously imagined American television as a 'vast wasteland'.[1] The metaphor still lingers on and I believe that its endurance partly is due to its ability to capture a *sublime* aspect of the experience of television. Definitions and meanings of the sublime are manifold; for the purposes of this chapter, I draw on the understanding of the sublime as an aesthetic category simply referring to that which is too overwhelming. The sublime could be described as a sense of awe: 'whenever the power of an object or event is such that words fail and points of comparison disappear, then we resort to the feeling of the sublime'.[2] Important to note is that this awe is free from ordinary judgements on value or taste, and my point is that this feeling can be invoked by contemporary television: it is impossible to grasp the sheer 'vastness' and variety of the output, from the simplest commercials to high end drama, and still it all comes together in the mundane and familiar phenomenon called 'television'. Roger Silverstone has noted how the experience of television is so integrated in everyday life that it 'escapes' from us even noticing it.[3] It is part of an everyday aesthetics that receives little attention, and when television is

---

[1] Erik Barnouw, *Tube of Plenty: The Evolution of American Television*, second edn (New York, Oxford: Oxford University Press, 1975/90), 299.
[2] Philip Shaw, *The Sublime* (New York: Routledge, 2006), 2.
[3] Roger Silverstone, *Television and Everyday Life* (London: Routledge, 1994), 2.

approached as an art-form it is done so by distinguishing it from the vast wasteland.[4]

In what follows I will elaborate on this and discuss television as an aesthetic object, drawing on encounters with an unusual television programme: *Contemporary Art Center TV* (*CAC TV*), a Lithuanian experimental television show that was produced by CAC, an art centre in Vilnius, and aired on the commercial, national channel TV1 between 2004 and 2007. My line of inquiry is to explore what ideas about television this experiment articulated, and the associated implications for understanding aesthetic apprehensions of television as an art-form. The argument is that CAC TV, through its unique position of producing a specific kind of art in a commercial mass media context, was able to explore ideas and notions of television in a way that not only concerns the world of modern art, but also informs television and media theory. I will discuss this by concentrating on two episodes of the show and a slogan that was used by CAC TV.

While television underwent considerable transformations in the early 2000s,[5] various experiments and reconsiderations of the medium took place across Europe. In Italy *Telestreet*-channels[6] challenged a corrupt media system through pirate transmissions. In Amsterdam the *Institute for Unstable Media* gathered TV artists and activists in a workshop called 'Exploding Television' in 2006; in the winter of 2010 two art institutions hosted exhibitions that addressed television: 'Are You Ready for TV?' at MACBA, Barcelona and 'Changing Channels: Art and Television 1963–1987' at MUMOK, Vienna.

Another example of this blend of contemporary art and television was *CAC TV*.[7] In 2004 a new TV channel, TV1, approached the Contemporary Art Center in Vilnius with an unusual suggestion. The station offered the centre a weekly 30-minute slot for producing their own television show, with no restrictions concerning content. Hence *Contemporary Art Center TV* (*CAC TV*) was born. Initially it presented itself as a 'TV program about the making of a TV

---

[4] Christopher Anderson, 'Producing an Aristocracy of Culture in American Television', in Gary Edgerton and Jeffrey Jones, (eds) *The Essential HBO Reader* (Lexington: University Press of Kentucky, 2008), 23–41.

[5] Primarily in terms of digitalisation and introduction of view-on-demand services, cf. Amanda Lotz, *Television Will be Revolutionized* (New York: New York University Press, 2007).

[6] Telestreet was a movement of local pirate TV-transmissions in Italian cities, e.g. Bologna (see Matteo Pasquinelli, 'Manifesto of Urban Televisions', *Subsol* (2003), http://subsol.c3.hu/subsol_2/contributors3/pasquinellitext.html [accessed 4 April 2012], See also Michaela Ardizzoni, 'Neighborhood Television Channels in Italy: The Case of Telestreet', in Michaela Ardizzoni and C. Ferrari, (eds) *Beyond Monopoly: Globalization and Contemporary Italian Media* (Plymouth: Lexington Press, 2010), 171–84.

[7] The original title in Lithuanian reads *Šiuolaikinio Meno Centro Televizija* (*ŠMC TV*), but the English translation and abbreviation (*CAC TV*) was often used.

program' where curators and artists explored the phenomenon of television and aimed at 'reinventing' the medium. Usually the show consisted of quasi-documentary occurrences, spontaneous meetings and conversations. In an interview with art journal *Frieze*, the curator of *CAC TV*, Raimundas Malašauskas mentioned some of the intentions of the series:

> I hope linguists will not mind me appropriating their terminology to say that TV has become a global language and that, in this era of user-generated content, it is quite logical that various sub-dialects are being invented at the same time as its technical possibilities are being developed. We never wanted to show artworks on CAC TV; our idea was to produce a TV program using art as its operating system. We saw art as a complex organism that afforded the means and methods of rearticulating all other possible subjects (including banality and self-reflexivity) in a different way on TV.[8]

Discriminating between a programme *about* art and a programme that *is* art was central to what CAC TV wished to pursue. This is a difference of phenomenological significance: between representation and being. Most aesthetically oriented studies of television have dealt with the representational aspect (what television 'shows' rather than what it *is*), either defined in terms of 'quality narratives';[9] as a certain articulation of semiotic resources, e.g. the 'aesthetisation' of news or suffering;[10] or aesthetics as formalist and compositional aspects.[11] But the aesthetics of CAC TV is perhaps better understood through what has been called a 'media sensitive' approach.[12]

Philosopher Tanya Di Tommaso[13] argues that much of the literature on television aesthetics simply regards TV as a vehicle for transmitting narratives, and that the medium itself has not sufficiently been the focus for aesthetic consideration. She suggests a distinction between an *instrumental* and an *aesthetic* approach to television. The distinction allows for an appreciation of the sublime experience of television: the aesthetic approach care

---

[8] Aron Schuster, 'Broadcast News', *Frieze* 106 (2007), 23–41.

[9] Jeffrey Sconce, 'What if? Charting Television's New Textual Boundaries', in Lynn Spigel and Jan Olsson, (eds) *Television after TV* (Durham, NC: Duke University Press, 2004), 93–112.

[10] Cf. John Thornton Caldwell, *Televisuality: Style, Crisis and Authority in American Television* (New Brunswick, NJ: Rutgers University Press, 1995), and Lilie Chouliaraki, *The Spectatorship of Suffering* (London: Sage, 2008).

[11] Cf. Nikos Metallinos, *Television Aesthetics: Perceptual, Cognitive, and Compositional Bases* (Mahwah, NJ: Lawrence Erlbaum Associates, 1996), and Jeremy Butler, *Television Style* (London: Routledge, 2010).

[12] Liv Hausken, *Medieestetikk* [Media Aesthetics] (Oslo: Scandinavian Academic Press, 2009).

[13] Tanya Di Tommaso, 'The Aesthetics of Television', *Crossings* 3 (2003): 66–98.

less about what content is being transmitted than about the medium itself. A similar point has been made by Liv Hausken who suggests that artistic explorations might inform media theory.[14] Taken as point of departure it encourages us to ask not only what media theory can say about CAC TV, but what can we learn from CAC TV?

Some stylistics of CAC TV resemble those associated with art cinema, where the illusory spectacle of narrative conventions are disrupted – sometimes referred to as 'narrative intransitivity'[15] – a technique characterized by gaps and interruptions, episodic construction and undigested digression. Originally intended to emancipate and activate the critical faculties of the spectators, much of what was developed as counter strategies in drama and film have become integral parts of mainstream television.[16] Butler, for instance, draws parallels between Brecht's epic theatre and today's TV commercials.[17]

It has been suggested that television is too commercial to allow for narrative experiments similar to modernism in literature and European cinema.[18] This poses a potential challenge for alternative and experimental television: is it possible to contest television from the perspective of television? Some would argue that the rise of 'quality TV' in recent years have proved television's capacity to deliver strong and complex works.[19] But much of what is labelled 'quality' television (e.g. highly acclaimed drama series) is likely to be appreciated in the guise of a DVD box set instead of as part of the scheduled flow. HBO – emblematic for this development – notably maintains that 'It's not TV.'

So what then is TV? A vast wasteland? Two examples of CAC TV's engagement with this sublime aspect that I will pursue here are 'television as dream' and 'television as reality'. Starting with dream: In the opening frames of the episode titled 'For a Sleeping Audience' (2007, n.d.), the following text travels across the screen:

A DREAM ABOUT A TELEVISION PROGRAM broadcast for the sleeping audience

There is an obvious absurdity in transmitting a television programme for a sleeping audience, as sleeping people cannot follow it. And what about us who are awake and watching, who are we? Perhaps what they are suggesting is a show for those who fall asleep in front of their television sets,

---

[14] Hausken, *Medieestetikk*, 14.
[15] Peter Wollen, *Semiotic Counter Strategies: Readings and Writings* (London: Verso, 1982), 80.
[16] Caldwell, *Televisuality*.
[17] Butler, *Television Style*, 109.
[18] Nick Lacey, *Narrative and Genre: Key Concepts in Media Studies* (New York: Palgrave, 2000), 121.
[19] Anderson, 'Producing an Aristocracy of Culture in American Television'.

or is it meant to be metaphorically sleeping (and thus a programme to wake people from their slumber)?

One possible interpretation is the resemblance between psychoanalytical theories about the function of dreams and the way television works. An example of this could be found in Wood,[20] who discusses television as a means to handle cultural trauma. On the opposite side to that argument there is the claim that television is in fact *reversed* psychoanalysis.[21] The psychoanalytical aspect finds support in a quote from curator Malašauskas:

I am sure if Sigmund Freud had lived in the second half of the 20th century he would have had his own TV show. [...] The ratings for his show would have been higher than for those presented by Adorno or Aristotle! I think Freudian psychoanalysis has become part of the fabric of television. Everybody is a psychoanalyst these days and, as we stated in our first manifesto, 'everybody is a TV producer'.[22]

Apart from the psychoanalytical interpretation of TV as dream, there is the implication of what could be described as the 'dream kitsch' argument, drawing on early twentieth-century critique of mass culture.[23] In that tradition the sleeping audience is one that ought to be awakened, i.e. emancipated from its subordination. The episode itself supports both these interpretations as it is set in places that could be described as dream worlds: first a park collecting old Soviet monuments (a dream to reconcile a trauma of the past), then a shopping mall (commercial dream kitsch).

Turning from the world of dreams to that of reality, philosopher Germina Nagat[24] has suggested that the main aesthetic feature of television is realism. Realism in television culture took a new turn in the early 2000s with the popularity of 'reality TV'.[25] At the moment of CAC TV's inception, reality television was a pervasive format in international mainstream television (and

---

[20] Peter H. Wood, 'Television as Dream', in Richard Adler, ed. *Understanding Television: Essays on Television as a Social and Cultural Force* (New York: Praeger, 1976/81), 55.

[21] Theodor W. Adorno, 'How to Look at Television', *The Quarterly of Film and Television* 3 (1954): 213–35.

[22] Schuster, 'Broadcast News'.

[23] Susan Buck-Morss, *Dreamworld and Catastrophe: Mass Utopia in East and West* (Boston: MIT Press, 2000).

[24] Germina Nagat, 'Aesthetics of the Image-Wired World', in Ruth Lorand, ed. *Television: Aesthetic Reflections* (New York: Peter Lang, 2003), 31–44.

[25] Reality TV has generated an extensive literature. For an overview of analytical perspectives, see Susan Murray and Laurie Ouellette, (eds) *Reality TV: Remaking Television Culture* (New York: New York University Press, 2009).

Lithuania was no exception).[26] CAC TV tapped into that trend by defining their show as a 'reality meta show'. The objective of the reality meta show was to make a programme about the making of a television programme. Its definition of reality is more philosophical than the one assumed by the format 'reality TV'. Reality TV as a generic term, like realism, refers to a set of conventional representational tools. The reality that intrigues CAC TV is rather the possibility of (the idea of) television to make things real. This is especially evident in the episode 'The Hesdalen Phenomena' (2006, n.d.). It portrays a road trip to a small Norwegian village, Hesdalen, which has attracted the attention of global mass media due to numerous UFO sightings. CAC TV goes there to look for UFOs but instead of documenting paranormal activities the episode develops into an exploration of television's truth claims. One such truth claim would be to prove by showing, transforming the TV-audience into a witness.[27] In the beginning of the episode the crew explains that the only way to get to Hesdalen is to drive a car wearing a blindfold. 'Television', Malašauskas says, 'is going to prove that it is possible. Television proves many things, especially the truth' (2:50–3:00).

Another way to conceptualize television's sublime feature is through CAC TVs slogan that read 'Every program is a pilot; every program is the final episode', a slogan that implies that CAC TV's shows are elevated from the everyday flow of the ordinary schedule.

An established term for the first draft for a TV-show, the pilot is something else than the actual show itself. The pilot is the expression of an idea, a sketch (a dream about a television programme?). By appropriating this notion and claiming every programme as a pilot, CAC TV aims at the unfixed character of an experimental try-out. If the pilot is a dream, then the finale could be described as the ultimate realisation of that dream. The notion of the final episode has developed into something of an event in contemporary television culture. The final episodes of, for instance, *Seinfeld* (1998) and *The Sopranos* (2007) received much attention[28] and became media events in themselves. By connecting to these terms in their slogan, CAC TV presents itself as an extraordinary exception. It is interesting to compare the implications of this slogan with that of HBO. What is CAC TV according to its slogan? The

---

[26] Bjorn P. Ingvoldstadt, 'Post-Socialism, Globalization and Popular Culture: 21st Century Lithuanian Media and Media Audiences', PhD diss., Indiana University, 2006.

[27] See Daniel Dayan and Elihu Katz, *Media Events: The Live Broadcasting of History* (Cambridge, MA: Harvard University Press, 1992).

[28] On *Seinfeld*'s finale, see David Lavery and Sara Lewis Dunne, (eds) *Seinfeld, Master of its Domain: Revisiting Television's Greatest Sitcom* (New York: Continuum, 2006). For *The Sopranos*, see David Lavery, Douglas L. Howard, and Paul Levinson, (eds) *The Essential Sopranos Reader* (Lexington: University Press of Kentucky, 2011).

simultaneous pilot/finale suggests instability, a moment of the undecided that promotes an aesthetic, media sensitive perspective on the medium of television. If HBO urges its viewers to enjoy the show and forget that they are watching television, CAC TV's attitude is 'Don't mind that there is a show, enjoy television.'

The opposition between art and mass culture is familiar to scholars of media and cultural studies. Despite frequent attempts to bridge the gap (e.g. elevating the status of popular texts), an institutional separation between the two persists. CAC TV was unique in working on both arenas and the outcome of that experiment might perhaps tell us something not only about the show in itself, but about the ideas about television that shaped it.

So, what ideas were expressed, and what implications for understanding aesthetic apprehensions about television as an art-form could be derived from CAC TV? First, the level on which CAC TV operated was an idealist one, where the fascination with television as a phenomenon was primary. The examples above touched on a sublime aspect of television: awe before the ability to create dream worlds and to construct reality in a banal setting.

Secondly, if HBO turned television into art, did CAC TV turn art into television? Through their slogan they relativised the relation between show and medium, privileging an aesthetic sensitivity where television is more interesting than what it transmits. This preoccupation with the medium is perhaps what CAC TV brought from the art world into television, and is one that could inspire to a more media sensitive take on the overwhelming experience of watching television.

Bibliography

Adorno, Theodor W. 'How to Look at Television'. *The Quarterly of Film and Television* 3 (1954): 213–35.

Anderson, Christopher. 'Producing an Aristocracy of Culture in American Television.' In *The Essential HBO Reader*. Edited by Gary Edgerton and Jeffrey Jones, 23–41. Lexington: University Press of Kentucky, 2008.

Ardizzoni, Michaela. 'Neighborhood Television Channels in Italy: The Case of Telestreet.' In *Beyond Monopoly: Globalization and Contemporary Italian Media*, edited by Michaela Ardizzoni, and C. Ferrari, 171–84. Plymouth: Lexington, 2010.

Barnouw, Erik. *Tube of Plenty: The Evolution of American Television*, second edn. New York and Oxford: Oxford University Press, 1975/90.

Buck-Morss, Susan. *Dreamworld and Catastrophe: Mass Utopia in East and West*. Boston: MIT Press, 2000.

Butler, Jeremy G. *Television Style*. London: Routledge, 2010.

Caldwell, John Thornton. *Televisuality: Style, Crisis and Authority in American Television*. New Brunswick, NJ: Rutgers University Press, 1995.

Chouliaraki, Lilie. *The Spectatorship of Suffering*. London: Sage, 2008.

Dayan, Daniel, and Elihu Katz. *Media Events: The Live Broadcasting of History*. Cambridge, MA: Harvard University Press, 1992.

Di Tommaso, Tanya. 'The Aesthetics of Television.' *Crossings* 3 (2003): 66–98.

Hausken, Liv. *Medieestetikk* [Media Aesthetics]. Oslo: Scandinavian Academic Press, 2009.

Ingvoldstadt, Bjorn P. 'Post-Socialism, Globalization and Popular Culture: 21st Century Lithuanian Media and Media Audiences.' PhD diss., Indiana University, 2006.

Lacey, Nick. *Narrative and Genre: Key Concepts in Media Studies*. New York: Palgrave, 2000.

Lavery, David, and Sara Lewis Dunne, (eds) *Seinfeld, Master of its Domain: Revisiting Television's Greatest Sitcom*. New York: Continuum, 2006.

Lavery, David, Douglas L. Howard, and Paul Levinson, (eds) *The Essential Sopranos Reader*. Lexington: University Press of Kentucky, 2011.

Leverette, Marc, Brian Ott, and Cara Louise Buckley, (eds) *It's not TV: Watching HBO in the Post-Television Era*. New York: Routledge, 2008.

Lotz, Amanda. *Television Will be Revolutionized*. New York: New York University Press, 2007.

Metallinos, Nikos. *Television Aesthetics: Perceptual, Cognitive, and Compositional Bases*. Mahwah, NJ: Lawrence Erlbaum Associates, 1996.

Murray, Susan, and Laurie Ouellette, (eds) *Reality TV: Remaking Television Culture*. New York: New York University Press, 2009.

Nagat, Germina. 'Aesthetics of the Image-Wired World.' In *Television: Aesthetic Reflections*, edited by Ruth Lorand, 31–44. New York: Peter Lang, 2003.

Pasquinelli, Matteo. 'Manifesto of Urban Televisions.' *Subsol*. (2003). http://subsol.c3.hu/subsol_2/contributors3/pasquinellitext.html [accessed 4 April 2012].

Schuster, Aron. 'Broadcast News.' *Frieze* 106 (2007).

Sconce, Jeffrey. 'What if? Charting Television's New Textual Boundaries.' In *Television after TV*, edited by Lynn Spigel and Jan Olsson, 93–112. Durham, NC: Duke University Press, 2004.

Shaw, Philip. *The Sublime*. New York: Routledge, 2006.

Silverstone, Roger. *Television and Everyday Life*. London: Routledge, 1994.

Wollen, Peter. *Semiotic Counter Strategies: Readings and Writings*. London: Verso, 1982.

Wood, Peter H. 'Television as Dream.' In *Understanding Television: Essays on Television as a Social and Cultural Force*, edited by Richard Adler, 55–73. New York: Praeger, 1976/81.

21

Closer to the action: Post-war American television and the zoom shot

Nick Hall

The rise of the zoom shot in post-war American television, and its subsequent impact on American film style, is a neglected area of the history of moving image media. Historical accounts of the zoom lens are scarce, and the most comprehensive overviews have been given by film historians.[1] Where these accounts refer to television, they have generally referenced Erik Barnouw, whose remarks about the zoom are limited to its use in baseball coverage.[2] John Belton has linked zooming to American television drama, arguing that a group of directors who later became prominent in Hollywood rehearsed zoom techniques on the small screen.[3] This view has appeared in more recent film textbooks,[4] but directors of live and filmed television drama were neither homogeneous nor simultaneous in their adoption of zoom techniques, and the complexity and variety within these broad examples has not been fully explored. As this chapter will explain, in the years between 1946 and 1960, the zoom became widespread in the television industry and was used in both studio-based and outside-broadcast, or 'remote', contexts. For directors of

---

[1] Paul Joannides, 'Aesthetics of the Zoom Lens', *Sight and Sound* 40:1 (Winter 1970/1): 40–2. Stuart M Kaminsky, 'The Use and Abuse of the Zoom Lens', *Filmmakers Newsletter* 5:12 (October 1972): 20–3. John Belton, 'The Bionic Eye: Zoom Esthetics', *Cineaste* 11:1 (Winter 1980/1): 20–7. Barry Salt, *Film Style and Technology* (London: Starword, 1992).
[2] Erik Barnouw, *Tube Of Plenty* (New York: Oxford University Press, 1975), 102.
[3] Belton, 'The Bionic Eye', 25.
[4] David A. Cook, *Lost Illusions* (Berkeley: California University Press, 2000), 361.

live news and sports, the zoom lens was an ideal tool to maintain continuity while keeping action on the screen at all times. For dramas shot in cramped television studios, the zoom offered compositional flexibility, while providing adventurous directors with new visual effects.

To understand the place of the zoom shot in American television, the technology must be situated in the proper historical context. Forms of zoom shot have been noted in lantern shows dating to the late eighteenth century,[5] and the technology to produce a variable focal length telescope was patented as early as 1890. A very early motion picture zoom lens was patented in 1901,[6] but there is no record of any surviving films in which it was used, and the earliest extant zoom shots are found in Paramount features dating from 1926.[7] Despite economic depression and approaching conflict, zoom lens development continued throughout the 1930s and into the Second World War: Paramount, Kodak and the C-Lens Corporation were among the American firms that continued to develop the technology.[8] Indeed, the war did much to catalyse the development of what became early postwar American television's most significant zoom lens. The United States Signal Corps, requiring a zoom-type viewfinder for the Bell and Howell cameras used by their propaganda cameraman and finding major manufacturers unable to provide a suitable design, turned to an Austrian-born mechanical engineer named Frank Back. Dr Back was an optical specialist who had travelled to America from Paris in 1939, having left the country of his birth the previous year. After a few years working as an engineering consultant in the New York area, he set up his own workshop and began to work on solving problems for the Signal Corps. By 1945, Back had contributed two inventions to the war effort: a viewfinder for the Signal Corps, and elements of a device designed to improve flight trainers used by US Navy aviators. Zoom lens technology was central to both.[9]

When the war ended, Back adapted the technology in these devices

[5] Mervyn Heard, *Phantasmagoria: The Secret Life of the Magic Lantern* (Hastings: Projection Box, 2006), 97.

[6] Rudolf Kingslake, *History of the Photographic Lens* (London: Academic Press, 1989), 155.

[7] Salt, *Film Style and Technology*, 185.

[8] John G. Capstaff and Oran E. Miller, 'Photographic Objective'. US Patent 2,165,341 filed 28 July 1936 and issued 11 July 1939; Lodewyk J. R. Holst, William Mayer, and Harry R. Menefee, 'Lens System'. US Patent 2,130,347 filed 22 September 1934 and issued 20 September 1938; Lewis L. Mellor and Arthur Zaugg, 'Variable Equivalent Focal Length Lens'. US Patent 2,159,394 filed 9 June 1936 and issued 23 May 1939.

[9] Frank G. Back, 'A Positive Vari-focal View-finder for Motion Picture Cameras', *Journal of the Society of Motion Picture Engineers* 45:6 (December 1945): 466–71; 'Non-intermittent Motion Picture Projector With Variable Magnification', *Journal of the Society of Motion Picture Engineers* 47:3 (September 1946): 248–53. See also *Frank Back Papers*, MSS 0568, Mandeville Special Collections Library, University of California, San Diego: Folders 1–2.

to create a film camera zoom lens, which he named the 'Zoomar'. The name, he later claimed, was borrowed from aviation, because 'zooming in a flying airplane produces the same feeling as looking at the zooming motion pictures'.[10] Back introduced the lens to film and television technicians at a meeting of the Society of Motion Picture Engineers in Hollywood on 25 October 1946, predicting that the Zoomar would revolutionise filmmaking in the fields of documentary, education, sports, news, advertisements and medical productions. He concluded his presentation with the ambitious claim that: 'It is no exaggeration if we say that the close-up, this powerful means of expression given to the motion picture industry by D. W. Griffith, has really come into its own by the introduction of the zoom shot.'[11]

Paramount Newsreel was the first major purchaser of the Zoomar lens, but Back – along with business partners Jerry Fairbanks and Jack Pegler – recognized that the newly reborn American television industry would be more lucrative in the long run. He redesigned the Zoomar lens to make it compatible with Image Orthicon cameras, and the trio embarked upon an energetic marketing campaign designed to sell Zoomar lenses to the many television stations opening in American cities. Back, Pegler and Fairbanks were hands-on salesman, travelling personally to stations in order to demonstrate the lens to technicians and executives. By November 1947, orders had been received from stations in Los Angeles, New York, Philadelphia, Washington DC, Chicago and Baltimore.[12] Meanwhile Pegler negotiated with NBC in New York, persuading the network to buy Zoomar lenses for themselves.[13] By the end of 1949, at least 31 stations and network centres had purchased Zoomar lenses,[14] and by 1957, Pegler boasted of having sold lenses to over half of the television stations in the United States, as well as to broadcasters in a number of other countries.[15]

When Paramount Newsreel pioneered the Zoomar in 1947, their aim had been to improve baseball coverage. Studio publicity highlighted rave reviews of the lens's effects, including a clipping from the Washington DC *Evening Star*, which remarked that: 'Zoomar audiences are close enough to touch Johnny Lujack when he drops back for a pass. Spectator gets the feeling he

---

[10] Frank G. Back, 'The History and Present of the Zoom Lens', *Frank Back Papers* MSS 0568, Mandeville Special Collections Library, University of California, San Diego: FB/352/05.

[11] Frank G. Back, 'The Physical Properties and the Practical Application of the Zoomar Lens', *Journal of the Society of Motion Picture Engineers* 49:1 (July 1947): 62–3.

[12] 'Songwriter to Make 16mm For Nontheatrical Use', *Boxoffice*, November 22 1947, 64.

[13] *National Broadcasting Company Records*, Wisconsin Historical Society: Box 596, Folder 32.

[14] 'Zoomar Lens – Six More TV Outlets Buy', *Broadcasting-Telecasting*, August 29 1949: 65.

[15] 'Zoomar, Inc vs. Paillard Products, Inc', *Irving R. Kaufman Papers*. Library of Congress, Special Collections Department, Washington, DC. Box 9, Folder 1: 331.

might be spiked or trampled. Just about impossible to beat for excitement.'[16] It was perhaps natural, therefore, that when television stations acquired Zoomar lenses, baseball was among the first, and most notable, uses found for them. Between 1947 and 1952, trade press reviews of baseball coverage frequently gave special mention to Zoomar techniques, though their reviews were not always complimentary. In 1948 *Billboard* complained that action outpaced the flexibility of the lens, adding that:

> Zoomar is okay when used to increase size of players – when the lens 'zooms' forward, in other words, but when it 'zooms' backward so that size of players on screen is reduced, the effect was disappointing and made the viewer feel as if he had been taken away from the activity.[17]

Despite criticisms such as these, by the mid-1950s television networks and stations had fallen into what *Variety* described as a 'fixed pattern' when covering baseball, which included at least one, and increasingly two, Zoomar lenses.[18] Beyond baseball, the lens augmented coverage of sports including horse- and boat-racing, American football, and boxing.

As Belton notes, zoom lenses were also used in television news coverage and in the more broadly defined arena of current affairs. One of NBC's first tests of the Zoomar lens was on coverage of the Macy's Thanksgiving Day parade in 1947,[19] and as the technology spread, local stations used the lens to economically provide coverage of nearby events. In November 1948, Chicago station WBKB mounted 'the simplest remote in video history' by pointing a Zoomar-equipped studio camera towards the State Street Bridge, which was to be lowered for the first time.[20] Parades and presidential inaugurations also benefited from the flexibility of Zoomar lenses. In a review of the televising of General Macarthur's return from Japan in 1951, *Billboard* highlighted the 'particularly impressive [...] Zoomar views of the general during the parade'.[21] Similar coverage brought viewers close to the inauguration of President Eisenhower in January 1953. *Variety* remarked: 'There was no shortage of

---

[16] 'Paramount Publicity Material', *NBC Company Records*. Wisconsin State Historical Society: Box 596, Folder 32.

[17] Cy Wagner, 'Tele's Baseball Coverage All Right But Lacks Interest', *Billboard*, April 24 1948, 15.

[18] Herm, 'Tele Still On the Ball in B.B. Coverage; Cameras On the Spot for Openers', *Variety*, April 23, 1952, 23ff..

[19] T. C. Wilbur, 'Letter to R E Shelby', December 19, 1947, *NBC Company Records*, Box 596, Folder 32.

[20] 'Simple TV Remote', *Broadcasting-Telecasting*, 15 November 1948, 106.

[21] June Bundy, 'Industry Hits All Time High On Tough MacArthur Assignment', *Billboard*, 28 April 1951, 3, 47.

good vantage points for the image orthicons. [...] And where they couldn't get within point-blank range, telescopic and Zoomar lenses bridged the gap.'[22]

It was particularly appropriate that Zoomar lenses should be used in coverage of the Eisenhower inauguration, for as Mary Ann Watson has noted, zoom lenses were one of a number of new technologies which transformed television coverage of the national political conventions that took place in the United States in 1952.[23] That year's conventions were the first that would be televised for a mass audience: while television cameras had been present in 1948, only six stations were able to carry live coverage. In 1952, convention proceedings would be broadcast to 104 stations in 68 cities.[24] The conventions were an opportunity for television networks to prove themselves as a source of serious journalism, alongside newsreel and the printed press. Television networks were eager to provide entertaining and immediate coverage, and the significance of zoom lenses in helping the networks to meet these aspirations should not be underestimated. As Watson notes, the networks developed portable cameras designed to enable them to show live footage from the conference floor. However, this technology proved problematic. Networks struggled to persuade politicians to allow live cameras on the conference floor, and when they were used, poor image quality limited their usefulness. One report noted that 'portable equipment did not prove satisfactory, giving at best a murky picture. In the Republican convention the networks found it preferable to cover floor events by combining a radio signal from walkie-talkies carried by roving reporters on the floor with video provided by long-range lens cameras from the booths.'[25] While some of these were fixed telephoto devices, footage confirms that in many cases zoom lenses were used for this purpose. The power of the device can be seen in footage of a physical fight during a speech by Senator Everett Dirksen during the Republican convention. The camera operator zooms from a wide shot of the milling crowd to a closer shot which shows – albeit murkily, because of the number of optical elements inside the lens barrel – the confrontation taking place between individual delegates and security staff. This reframing takes place as a commentator describes the fracas, promptly showing home viewers what they could otherwise only have been told.[26] At other times,

[22] Bert Briller, 'Iconoscopes Invade Ike Inaugural, Capturing Color, Capers, Camera-derie', *Variety*, 21 January 1953, 33.

[23] Mary Ann Watson, 'Television and the Presidency', in *Columbia History of American Television*, ed. Gary R. Edgerton (New York: Columbia University Press, 2007), 210.

[24] Gardner Soule, 'How TV Will Take You to Conventions', *Popular Science* (June 1952): 139.

[25] Charles A.H. Thomson, *Television and Presidential Politics* (Washington, DC: Brookings Institution, 1956), 37.

[26] *1952 Floor Fight On Seating Of GA Delegates*. First broadcast 6 July 1952. C-SPAN, http://www.c-spanvideo.org/program/3987–1 [accessed 10 November 2011].

zoom lenses were used to quickly provide well-framed shots for cutaways from lengthy, static speeches. The advantages of zoom-augmented television coverage were explicitly referenced in positive reviews after the events: *Life* magazine reported that

> television made the Republican convention the most widely-viewed event in history. Its [*sic*] astonishing Zoomar lens, operating from high in the cavernous amphitheatre, sucked up the distance to bring millions of viewers face to face with a single screaming delegate among the hysterical thousands far below.[27]

Beyond news and sport, the zoom also exerted a strong influence over the visual style of entertainment and drama programming. From the outset, Zoomar lenses were used on studio cameras as well as on outside broadcast/ remote units. An early example was the puppet show *Kukla, Fran and Ollie*, which enjoyed a prominent position in NBC's early evening schedules between 1948 and 1952 and was popular with both children and adults.[28] The show's producers, WBKB in Chicago, did not, however, make a creative choice to use a zoom lens. Finding that they were unable to locate two camera tubes which produced satisfactorily matching images, they decided to use just one, with a Zoomar lens installed.[29] Yet while the reasons behind the station's decision to use such a lens were ostensibly pragmatic, the aesthetic consequences were highly significant. An examination of an early episode of *Kukla...* ('Lemonade') demonstrates that the show played out entirely in a setting of minimal depth, with the camera positioned almost straight-on to the performers, and panning limited to about 20 degrees to the left or right. The camera did not track, dolly, or crane, and set decoration was minimal, limited to a stylised proscenium arch and an unseen stage surface onto which necessary props could be placed.[30]

Upon this austere canvas, *Kukla...* creates two distinct but physically related environments, corresponding with the show's child and adult audiences. One performance space is that which exists when the camera tightly frames the stage and its arch, creating an on-screen environment inhabited solely by puppets. In early episodes, the puppets inhabit their own diegetic world, and there is no insistence on playing directly to home viewers. In the episode

[27] 'Television Showed The Floor To History's Biggest Audience', *Life*, 21 July 1952, 18.
[28] Susan Gibberman, 'Kukla Fran and Ollie' in *Encyclopedia of Television* (vol. 1), ed. Horace Newcombe, (Chicago: Fitzroy Dearborn, 2004), 1289–91.
[29] Victor Ford, 'How Zoomar Aids TV Photography', *American Cinematographer* 30:6: 202ff.
[30] 'Lemonade', *Kukla, Fran and Ollie: The First Episodes* (1949–54, Chicago, IL: Burr Tillstrom Copyright Trust, 2010), DVD.

'Lemonade', for example, over eight minutes pass until a line of dialogue is uttered, with the time filled by the 'business' of a puppet squeezing lemons and setting up a stand to sell lemonade. In scenes such as these, by gradually zooming into closer shots which contain only the puppet characters and exclude the sides of the stage, the *Kukla...* camera operator excludes almost entirely the 'adult world'. As sparely furnished as the set is, the viewer might be transported into the world of the puppets. However, when a human character appears, the camera gradually zooms out, and pans slightly, to alter the setting, reintroducing the physical bounds of the puppet performance space, and accommodating the physically larger human character. The broader performance space includes human players: often Fran Allison alone, joined occasionally in some episodes by other members of the crew. This environment is differently constituted, being both more self-referential than that puppet diegesis, and more directly addressed to the audience. It is in the flexibility of transition between these two performance spaces that the zoom proves valuable. Rather than breaking the physical space, the transition between the two is accomplished smoothly and gradually via the zoom lens, in a manner that is barely perceptible to the audience. Crucially, for a show that intentionally appeals to a dual audience, both the child-friendly puppets and the more adult-targeted Fran are maintained constantly in frame.

By the mid-1950s, the zoom lens was well established in the television industry. In addition to Zoomar lenses and the less-popular RCA Electra-zoom, new designs, such as the French Pan-Cinor, were introduced during the decade. These were applied to studio-filmed shows such as *Night Court USA*, where the zoom shot was one technique used to persuade viewers that they were watching the unpredictable proceedings of a real urban courtroom. *Night Court USA* was shot with three cameras in a small studio, and a zoom lens mounted on one increased the variety of compositions available to the show's director, creating a more 'mobile' aesthetic than would otherwise have been possible.[31] In addition to enabling greater compositional flexibility, the zoom was also used to create a sense of spontaneity. In one episode, for example, a disturbance in the public gallery is captured via a zoom shot which shifts the frame from a witness's testimony to a protesting spectator: a technique familiar from the (genuinely unpredictable) political conventions described above.[32]

As zoom lenses designed for film cameras became increasingly available, directors of anthology and serial drama gradually began to incorporate the

[31] Joseph V. Mascelli, 'Filming Courtroom Dramas For Television', *American Cinematographer* 40:1 (January 1959): 32–3.
[32] Episode 3, *Night Court USA, Vol. 2*, 1958, Banner Films.

technique into their own productions. It is important to note that the directors referred to here were not a homogenous group working at the same time, in the same place, or on the same sorts of shows. The television careers of John Frankenheimer and Robert Altman, for example, overlapped by only a few years, and while Frankenheimer worked largely in anthology drama, Altman's work was more focused on serials. Extant copies of television drama directed by Frankenheimer, Altman, Robert Mulligan, Sydney Pollack, Blake Edwards and others provide an impression of how the zoom developed in American television drama between 1954 and 1963.

Zoom shots appear to have been relatively scarce in anthology drama produced by Mulligan and Frankenheimer. Mulligan uses the zoom in an episode of *Philco Television Playhouse* to emphasize the intimacy of an embracing couple on a railway platform,[33] while Frankenheimer zooms – once only – in order to centre and enlarge a distressed Evelyn Rudie halfway through a *Playhouse 90* production of Kay Thompson's *Eloise* series of books.[34] These appear to have been isolated and fairly reserved examples, whereas Edwards and Altman, working a few years later, were more adventurous. In a 1959 episode of *Peter Gunn*, Edwards zooms to depict the point-of-view of a comic in the grip of paranoid delusions. As the comic performs his act, we see the audience from his perspective, settling on two people who appear to be talking to one another. Whispers, imagined by the comic, flood the soundtrack, while a zoom-in provides an extreme close-up on the conversing pair.[35]

Altman, too, uses the full range of the zoom lens to communicate information that will be important later in an episode. In an early scene from a 1961 episode of the drama series *Bus Stop*, for example, a young man shoots dead a shop owner. A rapid zoom shows that the bullet exited the victim and lodged itself in an alarm clock, which becomes an important artefact later on, as police officers attempt to solve the crime.[36] Altman further develops his use of the zoom in 'Once Upon A Savage Night', a *Kraft Suspense Theatre* episode first broadcast in 1964. Instead of occasional, isolated zooms at moments of high tension, such shots appear throughout the episode, and are used for a variety of reasons – some more motivated than others. Altman zooms to emphasize the shock on the face of a woman as she is strangled; to depict the killer's gaze as he apparently chooses his next victim; for more

[33] Robert Mulligan, 'Time Of Delivery', *Philco Television Playhouse* . 31 October 1954, NBC Television.

[34] John Frankenheimer, 'Eloise', *Playhouse 90*. 22 November 1956, CBS Television.

[35] Blake Edwards, 'The Comic', *Peter Gunn*. 12 October 1959, NBC Television/Spartan Productions.

[36] Robert Altman, 'A Lion Walks Among Us', *Bus Stop*. 3 December 1961, ABC Television/Twentieth-Century Fox.

prosaic reasons – simply to alter framing, or to emphasize the speed of a police car; and in one case, at the very beginning of the episode, abstractly into the leafless branches of a tree.[37]

In television drama, we can note a chronological progression in the manner in which the zoom was used, from reserved and rather cautious applications in the 1950s to more extensive and adventurous examples in the 1960s. While the role of directors should not be underestimated, gradual techno-logical developments which applied equally to television and film were also a significant factor. The zoom shot was a well-established element of television style by the mid-1950s, and it seems likely that this would have influenced the cinema with or without the 'TV generation' directors. Indeed, from the mid-1960s, there was a marked increase in the use of the zoom shot in both American film and television. In 1965 the NBC comedy-drama *I Spy* broke ground with extensive use of location filming, coupled with frequent zooms, often rapid and dramatic. From *Planet of the Apes* (Franklin J. Schaffner, 1968) to *McCabe and Mrs Miller* (Robert Altman, 1971), zooms became more prominent and noticeable in feature films, increasingly fulfilling the function of the dolly or tracking shot. These ways of use were matched in television series such as *Marcus Welby, MD* and *Owen Marshall, Counsellor-at-Law*.[38] Critics quickly recognized the trend: a discussion of *mise-en-scène* in a 1975 edition of *Movie* is dominated by debates around the zoom.[39] However, a full understanding of the role of television in the zoom's development has been slow to develop. Zoom shots appear in film and television to this day, yet they are often historicised as a peculiarity of the Hollywood cinema of the 1960s and 1970s, and frequently associated with flashy, self-conscious, or low budget approaches. These interpretations may be valid, but the zoom's complex history beyond the cinema also deserves detailed consideration.

Bibliography

Back, Frank G. 'A Positive Vari-focal View-finder for Motion Picture Cameras.' *Journal of the Society of Motion Picture Engineers* 45:6 (December 1945): 466–71.

—'Nonintermittent Motion Picture Projector with Variable Magnification.' *Journal of the Society of Motion Picture Engineers* 47:3 (September 1946): 248–53.

---

[37] Robert Altman, 'Once Upon A Savage Night', *Kraft Suspense Theatre*. 24 April 1964, NBC Television.

[38] Robert V. Kerns, 'Using The Zoom Lens Creatively', *American Cinematographer* 52:3 (1971), 226–8. See also Belton, 'The Bionic Eye', 25.

[39] Ian Cameron *et al.*, 'The Return of Movie', *Movie* 20:1 (1975): 4–9.

—'The Physical Properties and the Practical Application of the Zoomar Lens.' *Journal of the Society of Motion Picture Engineers* 49:1 (July 1947): 57–63.

—'The History and Present of the Zoom Lens.' 1980. *Frank Back Papers*, UCSD. FB35205.

Barnouw, Erik. *Tube Of Plenty*. New York: Oxford University Press, 1975.

Belton, John. 'The Bionic Eye: Zoom Esthetics.' *Cineaste* 11:1 (1980/1): 20–7.

National Broadcasting Company Records. Box 596, Folder 32. Wisconsin Historical Society, Madison, WI.

Briller, Bert. 'Iconoscopes Invade Ike Inaugural, Capturing Color, Capers, Camera-derie.' *Variety*, 21 January 1953: 33.

Bundy, June. 'Industry Hits All Time High On Tough MacArthur Assignment.' *Billboard*, 28 April 1951: 3, 47.

Cameron, Ian *et al.* 'The Return of Movie'. *Movie* 20:1 (1975): 1–26.

Capstaff, John G. and Oran E. Miller. 'Photographic Objective.' US Patent 2,165,341 filed July 28, 1936 and issued 11 July 1939.

Cook, David A. *Lost Illusions*. Berkeley: California University Press, 2000.

Ford, Victor. 'How Zoomar Aids TV Photography.' *American Cinematographer* 30:6 (June 1949): 202.

Frank Back Papers. MSS 0568, Mandeville Special Collections Library, Geisel Library, University of California, San Diego.

Gibberman, Susan. 'Kukla Fran and Ollie.' In *Encyclopedia of Television* (vol. 1), 1289–91. Edited by Horace Newcombe. Chicago: Fitzroy Dearborn, 2004.

Heard, Mervyn. *Phantasmagoria: The Secret Life of the Magic Lantern*. Hastings: Projection Box, 2006.

Herm. 'Tele Still On the Ball in B.B. Coverage; Cameras On the Spot for Openers.' *Variety*, 23 April 1952: 23.

Holst, Lodewyk J. R., William Mayer, and Harry R. Menefee. *Lens System*. US Patent 2,130,347 filed 22 September 1934 and issued 20 September 1938.

Joannides, Paul. 'Aesthetics of the Zoom Lens.' *Sight and Sound* 40:1 (1970/1): 40–2.

Kaminsky, Stuart M. 'The Use and Abuse of the Zoom Lens.' *Filmmakers Newsletter* 5:12 (1972): 20–3.

Kerns, Robert V. 'Using The Zoom Lens Creatively.' *American Cinematographer* 52:3 (1971): 226–8.

Kingslake, Rudolf. *History of the Photographic Lens*. London: Academic Press, 1989.

Kukla, Fran and Ollie: The First Episodes. DVD. Burr Tillstrom Copyright Trust, 2010.

Mascelli, Joseph V. 'Filming Courtroom Dramas For Television.' *American Cinematographer* 40:1 (January 1959): 32–3.

Mellor, Lewis L., and Arthur Zaugg. 'Variable Equivalent Focal Length Lens'. US Patent 2,159,394 filed 9 June 1936 and issued 23 May 1939.

Salt, Barry. *Film Style and Technology*, second edn. London: Starword, 1992.

'Simple TV Remote.' *Broadcasting-Telecasting*, 15 November 1948: 106.

'Songwriter to Make 16mm For Nontheatrical Use.' *Boxoffice*, 22 November 1947: 64.

Soule, Gardner. 'How TV Will Take You to Conventions.' *Popular Science*, June 1952: 137–41.

'Television Showed The Floor To History's Biggest Audience.' *Life*, 21 July 1952: 18–19.

Thomson, Charles A. H. *Television and Presidential Politics*. Washington, DC: Brookings Institution, 1956.

Wagner, Cy. 'Tele's Baseball Coverage All Right But Lacks Interest.' *Billboard*, 24 April 1948: 15.

Watson, Mary Ann. 'Television and the Presidency.' In *Columbia History of American Television*, 205–34. Edited by Gary Edgerton. New York: Columbia University Press, 2007.

'Zoomar Lens – Six More TV Outlets Buy.' *Broadcasting-Telecasting*, 29 August 1949: 65.

'Zoomar, Inc vs. Paillard Products, Inc.' *Irving R. Kaufman Papers*. Boxes 8–9. Library of Congress, Special Collections Department, Washington, DC.

22

Think-tape: The aesthetics of montage in the post-war television documentary

Ieuan Franklin

Introduction

The creative aesthetics of British TV documentary were first elaborated in the late fifties and early sixties. Essentially they were the work of one man and his immediate co-operators: Denis Mitchell ... worthwhile films were being made by others too, but it was Mitchell's qualities that spoke loudest, seemed most attuned to television's potential.[1]

Before we examine Denis Mitchell's intervention in television aesthetics in this period, it is necessary to firstly understand the formative influence of his own background in radio, a pre-eminent example of the cross-migration in personnel and practices from radio to TV during the 1950s that provided pointers to television's potential. This will allow us to posit some historical explanations for the brief resurgence in the poetic or impressionistic documentary that Mitchell's work heralded.

In general, this chapter will be greatly concerned with sound, which may at first appear strange, given that it appears in a collection about television aesthetics and style. The creative uses of sound, however, are underdeveloped in contemporary television aesthetics, and are also underrepresented

---

[1]Christopher Williams, 'Arts in Society: The Petrification Effect', *New Society*, 30 October 1969, 697.

in television studies, especially given the crucial role of sound in maintaining attention during television viewing. Sound typically exists in a subordinate relation to image both at the level of practice and of criticism. As Kevin Donnelly has observed: 'Considerations of television still suffer from ocular-centric assumptions that prioritize the image despite the fact that television has always been an audio-visual medium, often having a close relationship with its cousin, the radio.'[2]

As a pioneering experimenter with soundtracks, Mitchell is likewise a somewhat neglected figure. Despite having long been critically lauded as a kind of television auteur, Mitchell's considerable legacy has received very little scholarly attention, with notable if infrequent exceptions.[3] The filmmaker Michael Darlow believes that 'it is a measure of the continuing low esteem in which television is held as an art form' that there are so few sustained assessments of Mitchell's remarkable body of work: 'Had he made his films for the cinema it is a fair bet that the true successor of John Grierson and Humphrey Jennings would, in a career spanning more than thirty years and one hundred programmes, have had numerous books and analytical articles devoted to him.'[4]

This can also, at least partly, be attributed to the inaccessibility of post-war television documentary, as we will see. In recent years Mitchell's best-known film *Morning in the Streets* (BBC, 1959) has been not only retransmitted but also repurposed (as archive footage), and we will later assess this re-emergence from the archives. Mitchell was concerned to draw attention to the *inner lives*, as well as the social lives, of the people he recorded and filmed, and hence the problem and paradox of how to render interiority in aesthetic terms will be tackled in further discussion of *Morning in the Streets*. This 'social impressionism' was also characteristic of other exponents of the 'personal documentary', a type of documentary which will be briefly outlined and revisited. After chronicling the personal documentary we will explore how the development of editing technologies facilitated the use of impressionistic montage, and enabled filmmakers to free themselves from the confines of scripting and dramatic re-enactment. Finally, this chapter will conclude by suggesting that the period of documentary history that Mitchell dominated

[2] K. J. Donnelly, 'Experimental Music Video and Television', in *Experimental British Television*, ed. Jamie Sexton and Laura Mulvey (Manchester: Manchester University Press, 2007), 166.

[3] Karel Reisz, 'On The Outside Looking In: Denis Mitchell's Television Films', in *International Film Annual*, ed. William Whitebait, No. 3 (London: John Calder, 1959), 50–4; Philip Purser, 'Think-Tape: A Profile of Denis Mitchell', *Contrast* (Winter 1961), 108–14; Stuart Hall and Paddy Whannel, *The Popular Arts* (London: Hutchinson, 1964), 65–6; John Corner, 'Documentary Voices', in *Popular Television in Britain*, ed. John Corner (London: BFI, 1991), 42–9.

[4] Michael Darlow, 'Denis Mitchell 1st August 1911–1st October 1990. A Celebration of His Life and Work' (National Film Theatre Programme, London Southbank, 1990), unpaginated.

can be regarded as a *formative* period in which documentary auteurs prevailed, who often managed, like Mitchell, to combine formal innovation with social critique.

Radio roots/routes

The roots of British factual television in radio broadcasting have often either been overlooked or actively critiqued as a hindrance to its development. Early television was often perceived as 'radio with pictures', and there is a residual folk memory of television's over-reliance on the programming and techniques of its older cousin.[5] Certainly the assumption persists that television's debt to radio journalism retarded formal innovation in documentary work, or at least caused a rupture in the continuity of the documentary tradition.[6] During the 1950s, however, there was a migration of BBC radio personnel over to television, which in limited cases helped to foster innovation and to develop working practices that had originated in radio, especially in the BBC Regions. This aspect of the Corporation's history has received very little scrutiny, but a consolidation of this kind undoubtedly occurred in the area of what was often termed the 'actuality documentary' or the 'personal documentary' (the term 'actuality' referring here to sound or footage recorded 'on location'). During the late 1950s and early 1960s a new generation of documentarians in radio *and* television sought to escape the confines of the studio environment and gain direct access to hitherto obscure people and places. In doing so they were not motivated by the need to seek evidence for a journalistic brief or investigative thesis, but instead by a curiosity about the hidden occurrences of everyday life.

The origins of the actuality documentary can be traced back to experimentation with radio drama and features at the BBC North Region (Manchester) during the 1930s, the place where Mitchell was to craft his ground-breaking radio features and television documentaries during the 1950s. In the inter-war period the station manager Archie Harding recruited left-leaning writers, musicians and producers such as D.G. 'Geoffrey' Bridson, Olive Shapley, Ewan MacColl and Joan Littlewood to combine poetic, musical and journalistic styles of writing and production. Similarly, Laurence Gilliam of the BBC Features Department in London (where Mitchell worked between 1949

---

[5]For example, from 1946 until 1954 television news as such was simply a relay of the late-evening radio news accompanied by a still image of a clock.
[6]Patrick Russell and James Taylor, *Shadows of Progress: Documentary Film in Post-War Britain* (London: BFI, 2010), 7.

and 1950) encouraged amongst feature makers an approach to radio which paralleled John Grierson's notion of documentary as 'the creative treatment of actuality'.[7] Writer-producers such as W. R. 'Bertie' Rodgers and David Thomson roamed the Celtic fringes of Britain during the 1940s, recording folk-tales verbatim on acetate discs in villages and islands remote from the spectre of war. Despite the literary pedigree of these producers, their work chose to embrace radio's status as an oral medium, circumventing the institutional protocols which favoured scripting and studio-based production (it was no coincidence that programming made in accordance with such protocols could be more easily vetted by BBC management).[8]

It was the arrival of the mobile tape recorder in the early- to mid-1950s, however, that was to provide the decisive break with outmoded and restrictive practices, and it was to prove of inestimable value to BBC producers working in the post-war period who had an interest in 'giving voice to the voiceless'. The influential *Radio Ballads* (made by Charles Parker, Ewan MacColl and Peggy Seeger) tapped into a rich oral tradition, linking – through sound montage – vernacular voices with folk songs, both of which functioned as narration (in place of scripted commentary). The work of this group was to provide a model for television documentarians keen to create what (to quote Chris Gehman on Michel Brault's achievements in the context of Canadian and Quebecois documentary) many documentarists were striving for throughout the 1950s: 'a form of documentary not reliant on scripts, dramatic re-creations, staged events, and literary devices, but deriving its form from material gathered in contact with the real events and people portrayed'.[9]

In British television this tradition has developed through the work of Michael Croucher, Charlie Squires, Harold Williamson, Mike Grigsby, Edward Mirzoeff, Paul Watson and Philippa Lowthorpe, amongst others.[10] Philip Donnellan is another key example, a prodigious documentary filmmaker (making some 70 films for the BBC between the mid-1950s and early 1980s) whose television practice was built upon his own background in radio features and his close

---

[7] John Grierson (1898–1972) was a pioneering documentary film-maker, theorist and animateur who is often regarded as the father of the British and Canadian documentary film traditions. Grierson founded the British 'documentary movement', a loose collective of filmmakers who made documentaries with a pedagogic remit, often advocating social change, with sponsorship from industrial, commercial and governmental sources.

[8] Ieuan Franklin, 'Folkways and Airwaves: Oral History, Community & Vernacular Radio' (PhD thesis, Bournemouth University, 2009).

[9] Chris Gehman, 'The Wide-Angle Cinema of Michel Brault', *University of California, Berkeley Art Museum & Pacific Film Archive*, 2006, http://www.bampfa.berkeley.edu/filmseries/wideangle [accessed 12 March 2012].

[10] Incidentally, several of these filmmakers pioneered styles of documentary that anticipate elements of what we now call reality TV.

working relationship with Charles Parker, his colleague at the BBC Midlands Region in Birmingham. Parker collaborated with Donnellan on a number of television documentaries during the 1960s and 1970s, and Donnellan also adapted many of the *Radio Ballads* for television. In his unpublished memoirs Donnellan explained how the tape editing he conducted as a radio producer prepared him for working with film: 'With the coming of the tape recorder, we were more and more structuring radio programmes in a filmic form ... because we were using very similar plastic materials, cutting them together, and, whether we knew it or not, starting to handle things in the form of a montage.'[11]

The real pioneer in this area, however, was Denis Mitchell, who was firmly embedded in the 'actuality' tradition, having recorded African farm-workers using wire-recorders for the South African Broadcasting Corporation during the late 1940s, and having pioneered the use of the portable tape recorder at the BBC North Region in Manchester during the mid-1950s. During the latter period Mitchell tirelessly roamed and frequented the streets, pubs, homes and boarding houses of Northern cities, recording stories and testimony. After conducting this fieldwork, Mitchell exploited the creative possibilities of montage tape editing, weaving together actuality and ambient sound to create impressionistic 'sound portraits' of subcultures and the hidden occurrences of everyday life for a series entitled *People Talking* (1955–8).

After being trained in factual television production Mitchell spent the rest of the 1950s both making BBC radio features and adapting them – *In Prison* and *Night in the City* (both 1957); *On Tour* (1958); *Morning in the Streets* and *Soho Story* (both 1959) – into television documentaries. In doing so Mitchell developed his preferred modus operandi for his television work, which can be summarized as follows: (1) forming the thematic nucleus of the programme and the bulk of its soundtrack by editing together speech recorded on as much as 40 hours of magnetic tape; (2) filming on location, revisiting the people and places chronicled in the original fieldwork; and (3) editing sound and vision together, mounting images with the separately recorded 'wildtrack'. Thus the sound would be edited (without recourse to the inclusion of interview questions or narrative commentary), to a series of pictures not necessarily in a literal or diegetic relationship with the soundtrack.

As the late Sir Denis Forman has observed, Denis Mitchell brought from radio to television the sort of virtuosity in handling soundtracks that Stewart McAllister had applied to the films of Humphrey Jennings.[12] Mitchell had

---

[11] Quoted in Lance Pettitt, 'Philip Donnellan, Ireland and Dissident Documentary', *Historical Journal of Film, Radio and Television* 20:3 (2001): 354.
[12] Denis Forman, *Persona Granada: Memories of Sidney Bernstein and the Early Years of*

been in South Africa during the War, and was only introduced to the work of Jennings retrospectively, by Karel Reisz in the mid-1950s.[13] Yet it was, in fact, largely through the work of Denis Mitchell that the disjunctive style of Jennings (utilizing disjuncture or counterpoint between sound and image) was brought into television. It is somewhat surprising, as Dai Vaughan has noted, that 'the extension and elaboration of the disjunctive manner of Jennings', which had 'always been regarded within the documentary movement as a somewhat esoteric form', was 'the option settled upon by the supposedly "popular" new medium'.[14] This preference for the disjunctive, poetic 'mode' even managed to surmount the burgeoning cine vérité style, which had permeated television broadcasting in America. A certain continuity of influence can be detected here, as the Jennings style had recently been 'invested with a fresh acerbity' by the Free Cinema documentaries, many of which shared Mitchell's interest in working-class life and his predilection for impressionistic montage.[15] As Dai Vaughan has noted:

> From the film-makers' point of view, as opposed to that of the television establishment, a major factor in the preference for this sort of documentary was that the alternative in people's minds was still, at that time, not a leap into the untried possibilities of vérité but a reversion to the heavyweight re-enactments and commentary-dependency which had rewarded with respect bordering upon sycophancy the bureaucratic institutions from whom Grierson had sought sponsorship.[16]

Although it is important to highlight Mitchell's affinities with the Free Cinema filmmakers and with the remarkable work of Humphrey Jennings, it should also be emphasized that Mitchell's break with the orthodox methods of television documentary production was the result of casual impulse rather than design. As the television critic Philip Purser has noted, 'Mitchell drifted

---

Independent Television (London: Andre Deustch, 1997), 190.

[13] Corner, 'Documentary Voices', 53.

[14] Dai Vaughan, *Television Documentary Usage* (London: BFI, 1976), 3.

[15] For an introduction to Free Cinema, see inter alia Alan Lovell and Jim Hillier, *Studies in Documentary* (London: Secker & Warburg, 1972); Jack C. Ellis, *The Documentary Idea: A Critical History of English Language Documentary Film and Video* (Englewood Cliffs, NJ: Prentice Hall, 1989); Richard M. Barsam, *Non-Fiction Film: A Critical History* (Indianapolis: Indiana University Press, 1992); Eric Barnouw, *Documentary: A History of the Non-Fiction Film* (Oxford: Oxford University Press, 1980). The BFI has created a bibliography of Free Cinema at http://webarchive. nationalarchives.gov.uk/20090104191600/http://bfi.org.uk/features/freecinema/bibliography.html [accessed 15 June 2012].

[16] Vaughan, *Television Documentary Usage*, 4.

into film-making with a uniquely open mind',[17] and the inconsistent but startlingly vivid qualities of his early documentary aesthetic owe much to his unstudied and spontaneous approach. Although some television documentary of this period may have suffered from the lack of a direct inheritance of the 'tradition of craftsmanship' from the earlier sponsored documentary,[18] it is important to note that some television documentarians broke new ground through sheer ignorance of this tradition, or by drawing upon the alternative tradition of what we might term vernacular radio (as sketched above). It is easy to underestimate the impact on television documentary of a technique which offered an alternative to the conjunction of word and image (the two saying exactly the same thing) which had been increasingly determined and codified by institutional protocols (such as shot/reverse-shot). As David Russell has observed:

> The idea that what is seen must always conform to, and not digress from or contradict what is said, is not only a central feature of the televisual form, it is what makes the whole notion of 'truthful' television possible. For if there is no dissonance…, if the rhetoric of the image is identical to the rhetoric of the word, then a televisual truth, which resembles a documentary truth is achieved. Not matter than in this process the visual is no more than a doubling of the verbal, a tautology…[19]

In discussing the determining factors which created a brief resurgence of the poetic documentary (we will also examine other technological and historical determinants later in this chapter), we must not forget the social and ethical dimensions of such work. In many examples of the Griersonian documentary the working classes were celebrated for their hard work but rarely allowed to speak for themselves. If marginal subjects did appear, it was typically as victims of a social problem requiring a specific solution (e.g. the occupants of slum housing in Edgar Anstey and Arthur Elton's Housing Problems of 1935), and not as individuals possessing a distinct way of life. In marked contrast, the work of Mitchell and some of his contemporaries embodied a respect for the uniqueness of individuals, places and communities, and sympathy for the marginalised and downtrodden. As we will see, through an examination of Mitchell's landmark documentary Morning in the Streets, such work challenged the tendency in documentary whereby the underprivileged are defined by their material conditions rather than their beliefs, wants, aspirations or culture.

---

[17] Purser, 'Think-Tape: A Profile of Denis Mitchell', 109.
[18] Russell and Taylor, Shadows of Progress, 6.
[19] David Russell, 'A World in Action', Sight and Sound 59:3 (Summer 1990): 175–6.

Television, the archive and aesthetics

During its long 'infancy' television has suffered from an inferiority complex, and whilst it has developed its own grammar, it has often failed to accommodate the remedial attempts of those who have attempted to expand its vocabulary. Mitchell's major contribution was to revolutionise the use of sound in television, rejecting the prevailing conformity represented by synch-sound, in-view presenters and talking head interviews, in favour of vernacular voices and 'wildtrack' sound (separately recorded and 'mounted' sound). Mitchell developed a demotic style of documentary which gave voice to the voiceless and privileged intimacy and interiority. *Morning in the Streets* was the epitome of this style: a hand-crafted work of art, with each element of a complex montage soundtrack carefully married to each shot to create a disjunctive and creative relationship between sound and image.

Before we further explore the impact of Mitchell's 'wildtrack' sound on television aesthetics and its technological basis, we can briefly consider the notion that the formative era of the television documentary that Mitchell dominated has itself slipped from popular memory. Reflecting on obscured aspects of documentary history, Michael Chanan has noted a 'particular kind of historical unfolding' in which influential films fade from public memory and fall out of circulation, leading to the absence of the kind of canon one finds in other artistic fields. He has argued that this effect was exacerbated by the coming of television whereby documentary became 'part of the evanescent flow of programmes, as ephemeral as journalism and [again] rapidly disappearing into the big black hole of the archives, from which very few are beginning, very selectively, to emerge'.[20] Amongst the innovative and influential British filmmakers lost to posterity in this way he singles out Denis Mitchell and Philip Donnellan.

Morning in the Streets is one of those select films that *has* emerged from the archive – the BBC now showcases the film in its entirety as part of an online archive on working-class Britain, and it has been broadcast several times in recent years.[21] Recently scenes from *Morning* have also been extensively utilized as archive footage; for example, substantial sequences featured in Terence Davies' elegiac documentary about Liverpool *Of Time and the City* (2008). The imagery of children playing street games in *Morning* was also

---

[20] Michael Chanan, *The Politics of Documentary* (London: BFI, 2007), 25.
[21] See http://www.bbc.co.uk/archive/working/189.shtml [accessed 22 March 2012]. The film has been shown on BBC4 several times, for example in 2008 as part of the *Liverpool on the Box* season to coincide with the city being awarded European Capital of Culture.

used in the three-part series *Hop Skip and Jump: the Story of Children's Play*, produced by Steve Humphries and first shown on BBC4 in 2009.

Morning in the Streets is a rare social document of working-class life in Northern England during the late 1950s (the city we see is never actually identified; the film was shot in Salford, Manchester and Stockport, as well as Liverpool). It is especially valuable in its portrayal of the activities and concerns of several generations, from children's street games to the grief and thrift of an elderly generation whose lives are marked by both World Wars. This cross-generational and intimate focus was something lacking from the majority of the Free Cinema documentaries of the period.[22]

The 'repurposing' of *Morning* as archive footage in Davies' recent film essay *Of Time and the City* is at times ingenious but it is also problematic. In *Of Time and the City* much of *Morning*'s evocative imagery (for example, the 'establishing shot' of the cityscape; the majestic slow tracking shot along a terrace street; the rag and bone man; the woman emerging from the washroom with her laundry bunched up on her head) and sounds (the children's songs, some snatches of testimony) retain some of their poignancy but at the cost of being subsumed within the director's highly personal and subjective 'memoryscape'[23] of a Liverpool upbringing. In some ways the usage is creative – Les Roberts has recently drawn attention to Davies' use of musical counterpoint (juxtaposing Mitchell's footage of children playing and singing with Gheorge Popescu-Branesti's hymn *Watch and Play*) to convey an acute sense of longing, with Mitchell's contemporaneous actuality now serving as an evocation of time passed.[24] However, *Of Time and the City* includes very little of the humour of *Morning*, or of its exposure of social conditions (for example, the slum housing), which prompted the television critic Peter Black to write at the time that 'poverty and a soul-bleaching ugliness of surroundings are still besieging human spirits'.[25] The curiosity and empathy that led the original filmmaker to focus on an originating constituency (a street, a family, or a community), and which still infuses the original film, is missing. The displacement of long sections of *Morning* from

---

[22]The most celebrated Free Cinema documentaries of the period sought to give voice and representation to the social life of youthful, dynamic and discrete communities of interest (such as jazz devotees, teenagers and market traders), and were predominantly filmed in London and the South. One exception is John Fletcher's *The Saturday Men* (1962), about West Bromwich Albion football club, which was scripted by Denis Mitchell.

[23]See Julia Hallam and Les Roberts, 'Mapping, Memory and the City: Archives, Databases and Film Historiography', *European Journal of Cultural Studies* 14:3 (1 June 2011): 355–72.

[24]Les Roberts, *Film, Mobility and Urban Space: A Cinematic Geography of Liverpool* (Liverpool: Liverpool University Press, 2012), 193.

[25]Peter Black, 'Teleview', *Daily Mail* (London, March 1959). Thanks to Linda Mitchell for this (undated) clipping.

their context and soundtrack also aligns them decisively with the 'observer consciousness'[26] manifest in Davies' voice-over narration. Consequently this entails the loss of the 'respect for people's individuality without which one cannot hope to make universal social statements'[27] that was characteristic of Denis Mitchell. In the words of Mitchell, the filmmaker's 'task is to imply his own view of life (he can never openly state it by any form of editorialising) without distorting the truth that is the lives of the people he has chosen'.[28]

More generally, in most instances of its usage as archival footage only the visual iconography of *Morning* is retained, not the complex soundtrack which accompanied it, which means that only the documenting function of the filmmaker is honoured, and not his artistic expression. This is a tendency which can be more widely attributed to the privileging of the indexical aspect of film and photography.

The crucial element that made *Morning* so original and distinctive is therefore missing when repurposed in this manner: the film's ability to evoke emotion in the viewer by providing points of access to individual subjectivities, in the form of tape-recorded thoughts and feelings reproduced on the soundtrack. As Roy Peters has observed of documentary photography, 'the documentary "real" might be considered in terms of emotional authenticity as much as or as opposed to verisimilitude'.[29] Mitchell's technique inflects our feelings towards the people who feature within the film, and establishes a contrast between the sombre ruminations of the isolated members of an older generation (captured via wildtrack) and the communal playground songs of the children (captured in the 'present tense' of synch-sound, one of the few instances where synch-sound is used in the film).

Keith Evans described this technique as the 'counter-pointing of an Émile Zola type realism on the screen, with a James Joyce stream of consciousness on the sound-track',[30] and he argued that it was television's major contribution to the aesthetics of the visual media. It prefigured the later rejection by some avant-garde and independent filmmakers in the early 1970s of the 'seamless editing' and the 'tyranny of synch-sound' that has consistently dominated television documentary (although the influence here was typically Godard rather than Mitchell). Mitchell's method of counter-pointing became known in the industry as 'think-tape', and a similar technique was also evident in

---

[26] John Corner, *The Art of Record: a Critical Introduction to Documentary* (Manchester: Manchester University Press, 1996), 87.

[27] Colin Moffat, 'Birmingham Revival', *Contrast Television Quarterly* 4:3 (Spring 1965): 85.

[28] Norman Swallow, *Factual Television* (London: Focal Press, 1966), 178.

[29] Roy Peters, 'Half Truths', *Ten.8* (1979): 13.

[30] Keith Evans, 'Television as a Popular Medium', in *Mass Communications: Selected Readings for Librarians* (London: Clive Bingley, 1972), 98.

Ken Loach's classic 1966 drama documentary *Cathy Come Home*, whose use of wildtrack sound matches John Corner's description of the mode of documentary that *Morning* epitomises: 'In this mode, places, people and social actions are viewed within the framing given by the speech of uniden-tified and often unseen participants, whose apparently unsolicited recounting of anecdotes and opinions provides a rich, informational address, grounding the film in "subject" rather than "observer" consciousness.'[31]

The first example of this technique in *Morning* occurs at 02:09, during a shot in which the camera tracks back through an empty street of crowded terrace houses. A middle-aged woman recalls a recent trip to Shrewsbury with the Bootle Evening Townswomen's Guild: '...Oh it was *beautiful*. There was every shade of green, I didn't know there were so many shades of green. And the little lambs...'. This is (or, at least, this is intended to represent) the voice of a woman who lives in one of these houses, so the viewer has a sense of eavesdropping on thoughts, or on a private conversation. In addition we gain the first sense of a disjuncture between sound and image, in this case both the absence of the speaker and the contrast between the 'shades of green' spoken of with the monochrome of the terraced street. More specifically, it can be regarded as an example of the interplay between medium-specific codes and channel-specific codes. The aural channel consists of recorded speech (with a musical score faded underneath it), and the semantic content of this channel (the description of the vivid variety of 'greens') is in ironic juxtaposition with the urban and uniform aesthetic that constitutes the visual channel, and the medium-specific constraints under which it occurs (grainy, black-and-white 16mm stock for a low-definition television screen). As Ed Buscombe has demonstrated, examining the use of such codes in televised football, while the technical constraints of the medium define the range of possible uses open to each code, the actual, specific use made of them is determined by the culture of the broadcasters (or in this specific case, the intentions of the filmmakers).[32]

Social impressionism

Despite its impressionism, *Morning in the Streets* is also one of the few televisual social 'documents' of its era that fully gives the lie to the myth of affluence that abounded at this time; the myth that an increasing prosperity was erasing class boundaries, that 'we've never had it so good'. Peter Black

---

[31] Corner, *The Art of Record*, 87.
[32] Quoted in John Fiske, *Introduction to Communication Studies* (London: Methuen, 1982), 21–2.

asserted that it 'made one wonder again just where the Welfare State ends'.[33] Another reviewer remarked, 'This is the other side of *Coronation Street* with a vengeance.'[34] *Morning in the Streets* is not a 'social problem' film in the traditional sense of the term; the viewer receives no facts or statistics about the socio-economic conditions of modern life. As John Berger wrote about Lindsay Anderson's Free Cinema documentary *Every Day Except Christmas* (1957): 'The squalor of our society today – as distinct from the 'thirties – is revealed more sharply in the values it breeds than in plain economic facts. And this demands a far more subtle approach from the social commentator.'[35]

Although it exposed the horrors of slum housing in vivid detail, the real achievement of *Morning in the Streets* was to reveal *in human terms* and through personal testimony how working-class communities are atomised by poverty, unemployment, class stratification and war. With the erosion of working-class industries and collectivism, unemployment had begun to become a personal tragedy for people, rather than a public scandal. [36] As Berger implied, the site of working-class struggle had relocated to a less accessible place – the inner landscape of the mind – which filmmakers could not hope to convey by traditional forms of reportage.

Mitchell had a fondness for the continuous filming of people listening whilst people are talking to them out of shot (the exact opposite of the shot/reverse shot formula which dominated television), in order to 'reveal thoughts, actions and feelings which are *unsaid*'.[37] Mitchell's achievement was therefore to convey the noetic and imaginary as well as the physical worlds inhabited by the people that he filmed and recorded, and this is crucial to an understanding of his impact on television aesthetics. Richard Hoggart, in an open letter to Karel Reisz about Reisz' Free Cinema documentary *We are the Lambeth Boys* (1959), questioned how far that film had moved beyond the presentation of exteriors; and asked that such 'essays' should develop by becoming 'much more subjective...to encompass the inner life'.[38] The answer lay in *Morning in the Streets*, which was transmitted in the same year. Mitchell had found, through symbolic montage, a way to organize sequences according to the flow and logic of affect and inner feeling rather than effect and physical causation. Symbolic montage, which has typically been

[33] Black, 'Teleview'.

[34] Michael Gowers, 'Mitchell's Poem of Bricks', *Daily Mail* (London, 1962).

[35] John Berger, 'Look at Britain!', *Sight and Sound* 21:1 (1957): 13.

[36] See Jeremy Seabrook, 'The Changing Face of Unemployment', *Ten.8, No. 11* (1983).

[37] Russell, 'A World in Action', 175, describing a similar technique by Eric Rohmer.

[38] Quoted in Stuart Laing, *Representations of Working-Class Life, 1957–1964* (Oxford: Macmillan, 1986), 115.

associated with fictional, dramatic or avant-garde modes of expression,[39] can in this way be distinguished from continuity editing, which maintains the spatial and temporal continuity of observation.

The personal documentary

Despite the experimental aesthetic of *Morning in the Streets*, it remains a highly accessible 'text'; if there is a challenge it is to the assumptions, conventions and stereotypes which dominated the representation of 'social issues' (or the conception of what is 'socially useful') in broadcasting at that time. Mitchell's experimental aesthetic and focus on interior lives was highly influential in helping to usher in a new form of documentary, the 'personal documentary', which marked something of a regional renaissance in BBC documentary. Aside from *Morning*, other examples of the personal documentary cited by Mitchell's colleague and fellow filmmaker Norman Swallow in *Factual Television*[40] are *Joe the Chainsmith* and *The Crystal Makers* (Philip Donnellan, 1958 and 1961), *Citizen '63* (John Boorman, 1963) and *Borrowed Pasture* (John Ormond, 1960). During this period Denis Mitchell was based in Manchester, Philip Donnellan in Birmingham, John Boorman and Michael Croucher in Bristol, and John Ormond in Cardiff. These experiments in 'televérité' were paralleled by landmark documentaries made about artists and classical composers for the BBC's *Monitor* programme by the John Read and Ken Russell, respectively.[41] Television documentary was refining its role, becoming intimate and personalized, and loosening its institutional attachments to the public spheres of journalism (current affairs) and spectacle (the outside broadcast). In these films the producers and/ or directors, through the 'creative treatment of actuality' (to use Grierson's famous phrase), expressed their attitude not only to the immediate subject-matter (an individual, a way of life, a place or community) but also to the world and times in which they lived.

---

[39] David Hogarth, *Documentary Television in Canada: From National Public Service to Global Marketplace* (Montreal: McGill-Queen's University Press, 2003), 66.

[40] Swallow, *Factual Television*, 176–84.

[41] Of course I do not want to suggest that the personal documentary was solely the preserve of the BBC. We should not forget, for example, ground-breaking documentaries such as Peter Morley's *Black Marries White – The Last Barrier* (1964), made for ATV (the ITV contractor for the English Midlands), and Denis Mitchell and Norman Swallow's work for Granada in the early to mid-1960s.

The Mitchell style and the role of technology

Many instances of the personal documentary can also be characterized by a rebellion against the subordination of *mise-en-scène* to script. Mitchell, in particular, rejected the documentary mode whereby signification is arbitrarily imposed through the use of commentary, and instead showcased the unique prosody of vernacular speech. Mitchell noted on many occasions that he had very seldom used a script in making television documentaries – instead he used a tape recorder to collect testimony, the core of which formed the basis of a treatment and a shooting script. Thus his work was rooted in oral tradition and communal exchange.

Mitchell liked to edit tape at home, cutting up sections of quarter-inch tape and hanging them up on a wall, ready to be incorporated into sequences of sound montage. This aptitude with editing magnetic tape continued into his career into television and later gave Mitchell the confidence to edit film with the same verve and innovation. Throughout his career there can be witnessed a developing confidence in the use of editing as a means of creating counterpoint: both in enabling creative disjuncture between sound and image, and in creating associative and dialectical connections between whole sequences in documentaries such as *Main Street Africa* (BBC, 1960) and *Chicago* (BBC/ABC-WBKB, 1961). In the latter film the editing style was synonymous with Mitchell's poetic and pathological attention to modern urban life. To quote a contemporary review of the film:

> Mitchell's method, like that of many a modern poet, is to juxtapose images for their ironic significance, and so he cuts back and forth from the high-livers to the low-lifers, from the delirious pool-side party at Hugh Hefner's swank playboy diggings on the North State Parkway, to the stuporous ghosts in the Skid Row saloons, from colored kids in a school playground to rich kids promenading at a society fashion show.[42]

As Stuart Hall and Paddy Whannel observed in 1964; 'In his later work [...] we see Mitchell beginning to compose and create more directly, to shape and to impress connections upon his material, with greater freedom'.[43] It is important to emphasize here the important role played by gifted film editors such as Leonard Trumm and Mac Errington – as noted earlier, parallels can be drawn with the collaborative working relationship between Humphrey

---

[42] Anon., 'Chi Crix On That TV Documentary: What's The Big Fuss All About?', *Variety*, September 30, 1961.
[43] Hall and Whannel, *The Popular Arts*, 258.

Jennings and the film editor Stewart McAllister.[44] Mitchell's predilection, like Jennings', was for a poetic style of documentary that freed the image from the constraints of synchronous sound, the tyranny of real time and the onus of narrative development. This gave a good deal of creative licence to Mitchell and his editors to juggle shots more freely and impressionistically. Mitchell admitted that he found filming rather boring and that, in his opinion, the real creative work began in the editing stage. Like fellow television documentarian John Ormond, Mitchell 'bargained on the lucky accident which, when viewed in the cutting room, chimed in with the initial notion of the treatment'. Like a poet (Ormond *was* actually a poet) he 'depended on telling imagery or a cadence of speech to work on the eye and the ear', what Ormond referred to as 'a kind of gentle branding'.[45]

There were several essential technical developments that encouraged filmmakers like Mitchell to pursue the 'dangerous art' of montage, and to break from documentary's previous reliance on unwieldy equipment and the monotonous rehearsal and performance of everyday activities. The initial developments, as Dai Vaughan has pointed out, were the introduction of magnetic sound stock and the tape-joiner.[46] Magnetic sound stock could be cut and rearranged in a way that optical could not, and so 'opened up the possibilities for disjunctive editing of sound and picture'.[47] The development of film joiners that used sticky tape instead of film cement further removed inhibitions against editing, as the tape joiner makes a 'butt-join', which does not entail the loss of frames. Experiments with editing tape or sound stock in this way were thus extended to the picture 'track'. As Vaughan, who was himself an experienced documentary editor, has noted, 'We could try out any idea, however unpromising, knowing that if we did not like it we could try something else. With the invention of the tape joiner, documentary became truly an editor's medium.'[48]

Conclusion: The era of the documentary artist

Mitchell's approach to documentary filmmaking heralded a brief era in which documentary filmmakers were not necessarily required to deliver a script as a condition of their project being approved. Instead they were

---

[44] See Dai Vaughan, *Portrait of an Invisible Man: The Working Life of Stewart McAllister, Film Editor* (London: BFI, 1983).

[45] David Berry, *Wales and Cinema: The First Hundred Years* (Cardiff: University of Wales Press, 1996), 291.

[46] Dai Vaughan, 'The Space Between Shots', *Screen* 15:1 (1974): 75.

[47] Ibid.

[48] Ibid.

effectively commissioned by the BBC to create documentaries with their own imprimatur.[49]The Mitchell style was the highpoint of a formative and experimental era of television documentary; at this time the documentary format was not so constricted by stipulations about audience comprehension (note the subsequent prominence of anchormen and presenters such as Dan Farson and Richard Dimbleby), narrative structure or journalistic thesis. Poetic documentaries also received a boost because of the BBC's efforts to maintain the kind of programmes that (the relatively new) ITV shied away from.[50]

More generally, the growing distaste for the expository style of documentary reflected the changing political and economic conditions that created the post-war consensus; there was less call for the kind of social 'propaganda' that the Griersonian approach had offered.[51] In these circumstances, public service broadcasting was left to assume some of the social and pedagogical responsibility that had been fundamental to the sponsored documentary, whilst being able to exercise greater editorial independence in this area of factual television.

With television's deep-rooted attachment to the journalist thesis or the 'well-made play', there has often been a corresponding absence of texts which are 'open to tension, contradiction and the unconscious'.[52] The frequent disruptions and disjointed modes of address that characterized 'the Mitchell style' give the lie to the notion of the passive reception of realist texts. Mitchell's early documentaries, like the *Radio Ballads* (which drew upon both Ewan MacColl's background in radical theatre and Mitchell's own work with MacColl in radio features), utilized the Brechtian concept of 'collision montage', in which the viewer or listener's interpretative faculties are mobilized through 'a montage clash of discourses'.[53] Documentarians like Mitchell might be said to have briefly acquired the freedoms usually reserved for novelists, playwrights and poets in developing introspection, allusion and symbolism through montage.

Returning to the notion of this era of documentary slipping from memory, the rise of the personal documentary during this period counters the prevailing notion that the filmed essay has been in terminal decline since the rise of television and reportage. British television has often been characterized by a

---

[49]See Richard Cawston, 'Editing, Cinévérité Style', *Journal of the Society of Film and Television Arts*, no. 26, 'Editing: Film and Television' (Winter 1966/7): 12–16.

[50]John Ellis, *Seeing Things: Television in the Age of Uncertainty* (London: I. B. Tauris, 2000), 56.

[51]Sunil Manghani, 'Television Documentary: Overview', in *Encyclopedia of the Documentary Film*, vol. 3 (Oxford: Routledge, 2006), 1304.

[52]John Caughie, 'Rhetoric, Pleasure and "Art Television" – Dreams of Leaving', *Screen* 22: 4 (1 December 1981): 17.

[53]Derek Paget, *Trues Stories: Documentary Drama on Radio, Screen and Stage* (Manchester: Manchester University Press, 1990), 47.

tension between wishing to break free of its constraints in order to become art, and the reality of being a highly industrial production process.[54] In this chapter I hope to have demonstrated that, albeit briefly, the growth of the 'personal documentary' raised the possibilities of a convergence between 'art (the most obdurately personal area of human activity) and television (the most public, at least in outward organization)';[55] two areas of activity which until then had very little in common.

Bibliography

Anon. 'Chi Crix On That TV Documentary: What's The Big Fuss All About?' *Variety*, 30 September 1961.

Barnouw, Eric. *Documentary: A History of the Non-Fiction Film*. Oxford: Oxford University Press, 1980.

Barsam, Richard M. *Non-Fiction Film: A Critical History*. Indianapolis: Indiana University Press, 1992.

Berger, John. 'Look at Britain!' *Sight and Sound* 21:1 (1957):12–14.

Berry, David. *Wales and Cinema: The First Hundred Years*. Cardiff: University of Wales Press, 1996.

Black, Peter. 'Teleview'. *Daily Mail*. London, March 1959.

Caughie, John. 'Rhetoric, Pleasure and 'Art Television' – Dreams of Leaving'. *Screen* 22:4 (1 December 1981): 9 –31.

Cawston, Richard. 'Editing, Cinévérité Style'. *Journal of the Society of Film and Television Arts*, no. 26, 'Editing: Film and Television' (Winter 1966/7): 12–16.

Chanan, Michael. *The Politics of Documentary*. London: BFI, 2007.

Corner, John. 'Documentary Voices'. In *Popular Television in Britain*, edited by John Corner. London: BFI, 1991.

—*The Art of Record: a Critical Introduction to Documentary*. Manchester: Manchester University Press, 1996.

Darlow, Michael. 'Denis Mitchell 1 August 1911 – 1 October 1990. A Celebration of His Life and Work'. National Film Theatre Programme, London Southbank, 1990.

Donnelly, K. J. 'Experimental Music Video and Television'. In *Experimental British Television*, edited by Jamie Sexton and Laura Mulvey. Manchester: Manchester University Press, 2007.

Ellis, Jack C. *The Documentary Idea: A Critical History of English Language Documentary Film and Video*. Englewood Cliffs, NJ: Prentice Hall, 1989.

Ellis, John. *Seeing Things: Television in the Age of Uncertainty*. London: I. B. Tauris, 2000.

---

[54] See Geoff Mulgan, 'Television's Holy Grail: Seven Types of Quality', in *The Question of Quality*, ed. Geoff Mulgan, The Broadcasting Debate (London: BFI, 1990).

[55] Allison Simmons, 'Television and Art: A Historical Primer for an Improbable Alliance', in *The New Television: A Public/Private Art* (Cambridge, MA: MIT Press, 1977), 15.

Evans, Keith. 'Television as a Popular Medium'. In *Mass Communications: Selected Readings for Librarians*. London: Clive Bingley, 1972.

Fiske, John. *Introduction to Communication Studies*. London: Methuen, 1982.

Forman, Denis. *Persona Granada: Memories of Sidney Bernstein and the Early Years of Independent Television*. London: Andre Deustch, 1997.

Franklin, Ieuan. 'Folkways and Airwaves: Oral History, Community & Vernacular Radio'. PhD thesis, Bournemouth University, 2009.

Gehman, Chris. 'The Wide-Angle Cinema of Michel Brault'. *University of California, Berkeley Art Museum & Pacific Film Archive*, 2006. http://www.bampfa.berkeley.edu/filmseries/wideangle

Gowers, Michael. 'Mitchell's Poem of Bricks'. *Daily Mail*. London, 1962.

Hall, Stuart, and Paddy Whannel. *The Popular Arts*. London: Hutchinson, 1964.

Hallam, Julia, and Les Roberts. 'Mapping, Memory and the City: Archives, Databases and Film Historiography'. *European Journal of Cultural Studies* 14:3 (June 1, 2011): 355–72.

Hogarth, David. *Documentary Television in Canada: From National Public Service to Global Marketplace*. Montreal: McGill-Queen's University Press, 2003.

Laing, Stuart. *Representations of Working-class Life, 1957–1964*. Oxford: Macmillan, 1986.

Lovell, Alan, and Jim Hillier. *Studies in Documentary*. London: Secker & Warburg, 1972.

Manghani, Sunil. 'Television Documentary: Overview'. In *Encyclopedia of the Documentary Film*, 3:1303–8. Oxford: Routledge, 2006.

Moffat, Colin. 'Birmingham Revival'. *Contrast Television Quarterly* 4:3 (Spring 1965): 84–5.

Mulgan, Geoff. 'Television's Holy Grail: Seven Types of Quality'. In *The Question of Quality*, edited by Geoff Mulgan. The Broadcasting Debate. London: BFI, 1990.

Paget, Derek. *Trues Stories: Documentary Drama on Radio, Screen and Stage*. Manchester: Manchester University Press, 1990.

Peters, Roy. 'Half Truths'. *Ten.8* (1979).

Pettitt, Lance. 'Philip Donnellan, Ireland and Dissident Documentary'. *Historical Journal of Film, Radio and Television* 20:3 (2001): 351–65.

Purser, Philip. 'Think-Tape: A Profile of Denis Mitchell'. *Contrast* (Winter 1961).

Reisz, Karel. 'On The Outside Looking In: Denis Mitchell's Television Films'. In *International Film Annual*, edited by William Whitebait, 50–4. No. 3. London: John Calder, 1959.

Roberts, Les. *Film, Mobility and Urban Space: A Cinematic Geography of Liverpool*. Liverpool: Liverpool University Press, 2012.

Russell, David. 'A World in Action'. *Sight and Sound* 59:3 (Summer 1990): 174–9.

Russell, Patrick, and James Taylor. *Shadows of Progress: Documentary Film in Post-War Britain*. London: BFI, 2010.

Seabrook, Jeremy. 'The Changing Face of Unemployment'. *Ten.8, No. 11* (1983).

Simmons, Allison. 'Television and Art: A Historical Primer for an Improbable Alliance'. In *The New Television: A Public/Private Art*, 2–15. Cambridge, MA: MIT Press, 1977.

Swallow, Norman. *Factual Television*. London: Focal Press, 1966.

Vaughan, Dai. 'The Space Between Shots'. *Screen* 15:1 (1974): 73–86.

—*Television Documentary Usage.* London: BFI, 1976.
—*Portrait of an Invisible Man: The Working Life of Stewart McAllister, Film Editor.* London: BFI, 1983.
Williams, Christopher. 'Arts in Society: The Petrification Effect'. *New Society*, 30 October 1969.

23

What FUIs can do: The promises of computing in contemporary television series

Cormac Deane

If, as Friedrich Kittler says, 'media determine our situation',[1] any description that we make of our situation is also necessarily a description of our media. This recursive twist is in turn found in the very media that we examine here in an attempt to describe our situation. Kittler's phrase is deliberately vague in its potential application across the field of media theory, so the comments in this chapter are based on a specific premise: our media screens are increasingly proliferating with their own, inner screens, and this is a particularly noticeable aesthetic feature of certain contemporary television series. When we watch the series under examination in this chapter, we spend a significant amount of time looking at the screens of computers and other devices, and hearing the sounds they make, within the narrative. The observations made here are based on a sample of the many hundred episodes combined of *CSI [Las Vegas]* (US, 2000–12), *Investigator Mariko* (Japan, 1999–2012), *Spooks* (UK, 2002–11) and *24* (US, 2001–10).

The user interfaces (UIs) found in these narratives are best described as FUIs (pronounced 'phooeys'), which stands for fantasy (or fake, or fictional, or faux) user interfaces. These screens do not, in other words, feature UIs that we may recognize from real-world experience, but they do provide the

[1] Friedrich Kittler, *Gramophone, Film, Typewriter* (Stanford: Stanford University Press, 1999), xxxix.

impression of computing environments being manipulated by characters on screen. This impression is achieved in large part by the audio output of the FUI, and this is a point that I will revisit in the later part of this chapter. The contemporary FUI provides a scientific, or scientific-seeming, gaze which visualizes features of an environment that are often otherwise invisible or inaccessible (infra-red, microscopic, CCTV, etc.). The FUI can transparentise bodies, objects and buildings, and produce schematic images of them which can sometimes be rotated on several axes. Indeed, these images are often rotated or manipulated in some other way for no apparent reason other than to give the sense that the computational work is live and busily ongoing as we watch.

In *24*, reams of numbers will appear in the FUI to indicate vast data sets that refer to concepts such as geographical location and vital life signs, and which are somehow derived from or applied to video or photographic images. Grids and other indicators of measurement and coordinates are also prominent features, as is a high degree of redundancy in the information being conveyed, where spoken dialogue and images on the monitor deliver the same information. For example, at 11.55 a.m. in Season 5 of *24*, two CTU agents in separate locations watch a satellite image of a car. At first, the FUI displays the information clearly, and the dialogue mirrors this: 'Valerie, the feed should be coming through to your laptop now'. But then the image quality deteriorates: 'Something's wrong. The feed's breaking up'. The same thing happens on the other screen: 'We're experiencing the same problem with our signal'. Finally, one CTU operator finds the source of the problem: 'I'm tracing the corruption [keyboard is tapped for 3 seconds]… it's the server'. The map/satellite images in this sequence (and often in others) are always accompanied by a smaller screen window where the same infor- mation in computer 'code' is displayed, i.e. incomprehensible alphanumeric 'content' that scrolls down like a credit sequence. The repetition of the same information as screen text, as screen image and as dialogue arises from the challenge of ensuring that the viewer does not get lost in the complications of plot development, and possibly also from the pleasure afforded by a kind of computational aesthetic. This repetition is also an instance of redundancy, a term I use in a non-pejorative information-theory sense, which means that there is a high degree of informational inefficiency in evidence in these narra- tives, a theme which we will return to.[2]

This description of the FUI concentrates on its visual appearance, but as we shall see, the distinctive sounds that are made by FUIs – hissing, fizzing,

---

[2] See James Gleick, *The Information: A History, a Theory, a Flood* (London: Fourth Estate, 2011), 219–31.

clicking, buzzing, trilling, bleeping and beeping – are key to understanding the status of the embedded computer monitor and of the events that take place in it. That status is addressed here under the rubric of TVIII, i.e. the current era of digital screen media where traditional points of difference between cinema and television, such as audiovisual quality, production values, viewing conditions, star actors and so on, are flattening out.[3] Among the distinctive texts of TVIII are high-concept global brands such as those under discussion here. Not only are the differences between cinema and television breaking down in TVIII, but the screens on all kinds of other devices (laptops, phones, etc.) are being absorbed into television technology, and are absorbing more and more of viewers' attention, even to the point of being the primary point of contact with screen culture as a whole.[4]

The four TV shows under examination here are all internationally successful multi-season series which place FUIs centre-stage, even if only for relatively brief periods in each episode. In keeping with the spirit of TVIII, the trend for FUIs is also strong in feature films,[5] particularly in top-grossing action movies, such as *Déjà Vu* (Scott, 2006), *The Bourne Ultimatum* (Greengrass, 2007) and *Iron Man 2* (Favreau, 2010). Thus the FUI is a persistent, international phenomenon that links disparate texts and is evidence of a set of aesthetic, narrative and even ontological concerns that is shared across a global media marketplace. In this context, when computer monitors are so prominent, it becomes clear that fundamental 'film studies' concepts – for instance, spectatorship, enunciation and seamlessness – need to be reassessed. Not only that, but new problematics (at least, new to the discipline of screen studies) now force themselves onto the agenda, e.g. information, cybernetics, interactivity and user interfaces. The relation of screens that are embedded within other screens has of course already been addressed by several authors as their frequency ebbs and flows in television and in cinema. The appearance of one screen within another is treated by Charles Barr, for

---

[3]See Robin Nelson, *State of Play: Contemporary 'High-End' TV Drama* (Manchester: Manchester University Press, 2007), 7; Catherine Johnson, 'Tele-branding in TVIII', *New Review of Film and Television Studies* 5:1 (2007): 5–24; and Matt Hills 'From the Box in the Corner to the Box Set on the Shelf', *New Review of Film and Television Studies* 5:1 (2007): 41–60.

[4]See Mike Reynolds, 'Study: One-Third of U.S. Households Watch TV Video via Internet', *Multichannel News*, 17 February 2012, http://www.multichannel.com/article/480725-Study_One_Third_of_U_S_Households_Watch_TV_Video_via_Internet.php [accessed 10 December 2012]; Brian Stelter, 'Youths Are Watching, but Less Often on TV', *New York Times*, 8 February 2012, B1; Todd Spangler, 'Half Of Americans Watch Online Video: Nielsen' *Multichannel News*, 20 October 2011, http://www.multichannel.com/article/475509-Half_Of_Americans_Watch_Online_Video_Nielsen.php [accessed 10 December 2012]

[5]Cormac Deane, 'From THX to FUI to C4I to HUD: The Special Effects of the Control Room, 1971–2012', in *Special Effects: New Histories, Theories, Contexts*, ed. Bob Rehak *et al.* (London: BFI/Palgrave Macmillan, forthcoming).

example, as evidence of a kind of inter-medium commentary at the critical moment in the 1950s/1960s when television started to eclipse cinema.[6] In a longer study, Christian Metz examines films within films and frames within frames as an extension of his more well-known investigations of enunciation and spectatorship.[7] The issues that arise in both these cases and in others[8] are of a different order to those that we are concerned with here, however, because the degree of remediation, that is, the process in 'which one medium is itself incorporated or represented in another medium'[9] is significantly higher in the sample of shows under discussion, both because of the proliferation of computer screens in cultural products in general and more specifically because of the increasing centrality of computing in the genres in question.

CSI and Investigator Mariko are forensic police dramas, with each episode centering on a murder and the physical traces that are left behind. The challenge in each case is to observe the scene in such a way that certain physical phenomena are correctly identified as important, i.e. informational, and then, as they habitually say in CSI, 'processed' appropriately. In other words, the challenge is to filter out what we might call the noise of non-information. Spooks and 24 are spy/action thrillers featuring the efforts of secret services to counter threats to, respectively, the United Kingdom and the United States. In most episodes, the challenge is to data-mine valuable information from undifferentiated data drawn from CCTV footage, satellites, credit card records, fingerprint databases and so on.[10]

The common threat in all of these is from an excess of data, from what Scott Lash calls the 'information overload'[11] that comes with living in an information society. Anxiety about this threat and our ability to overcome it may or may not be well grounded, but what is important for our purposes is that

---

[6]Charles Barr, 'Broadcasting and Cinema: Screens within Screens', in All Our Yesterdays: 90 Years of British Cinema, ed. Charles Barr (London: BFI, 1986), 206–24.

[7]Christian Metz, L'énonciation impersonnelle, ou le site du film (Paris: Méridiens-Klincksieck), and Cormac Deane, 'Introduction to Christian Metz's Impersonal Enunciation, or the Place of Film', New Review of Film and Television Studies 8:4 (2010): 343–7.

[8]Bernard Leconte, Images abymées: Essais sur la réflexivité iconique (Paris: L'Harmattan, 2000); Bernard Leconte, L'écran dans l'écran et autres rectangles scopiques (Paris: L'Harmattan, 2004); and Sébastien Févry, La mise en abyme filmique: Essai de typologie (Liège: Céfal, 2000).

[9]Jay David Bolter and Richard Grusin, Remediation: Understanding New Media (Cambridge, MA: MIT Press, 1999), 45.

[10]See K.A. Taipale, 'Data Mining and Domestic Security: Connecting the Dots to Make Sense of Data', Columbia Science and Technology Law Review V (2003): 1–83; United States Government Accountability Office, Data Mining: Early Attention to Privacy in Developing a Key DHS Program Could Reduce Risks, Report to the Chairman, Committee on Appropriations, House of Representatives, GAO-07–293, February 2007.

[11]Scott Lash, Critique of Information (London: Sage, 2002), 49.

there is an often fearful perception of informational overload. This problem of excess, where the sheer number of shows and the proliferation of modes of watching them (regardless of schedules, geography and so on), has an effect in some recent television criticism that Jason Jacobs describes as a 'pervasive sense of a crisis of authority in the face of a dangerously prolif-erating medium';[12] television is threatening to become 'an object of study which has simply been overwhelmed by too many texts – too many texts for the discipline of television studies to discipline; too many texts and too many carriers of texts'.[13]

That the same challenge arises both inside these narratives and in the media which bring these narratives to us is an indicator of the recursive tendencies, the feedback loops, that are at the heart of digital media. Not only is television becoming confusingly diffuse (though it is arguable that it was always thus), but now it transmits narratives featuring further screens which themselves are inundated by wave upon wave of data. This is not to assert a simply reflective theory that these shows mirror the real world, or illustrate it, rather it is to make a broader claim about the mutual interplay between what Kittler calls 'our situation' and our cultural products and technologies. In other words, this analysis of the aesthetic of screen embeddedness, which is everywhere in contemporary culture, and especially prominent in many TV series, is an updating of Fredric Jameson's observation in relation to experi-mental video art, that 'every age is dominated by a privileged form, or genre, which seems by its structure the fittest to express its secret truths'.[14] This means that the emergence of a new television style or aesthetic, such as embedded screens and/or the shows that they feature heavily in, ought to be regarded not simply as a new object of study but as a symptom of a more general ontological/technological shift.

We might say that there are too many outputs in the current media environment, in the sense that too many screens and speakers are producing information that is in turn being absorbed as inputs into the system. However, such feedback loops are narratively desirable in the dramas under discussion. Consider episode 8 p.m.–9 p.m. of Season 4 of *24*, where Chloe has her computer cross-reference two databases of video imagery and then finds what she calls 'the right frame' to pick out the fuzzy image of the registration plate of a suspect vehicle, which is rendered legible thanks to the bleeping processing power of her machine. This output is instantly relayed to her boss

---

[12] Jason Jacobs, 'The Medium in Crisis: Caughie, Brunsdon and the Problem of US Television', *Screen* 52:4 (2011): 503.

[13] John Caughie, 'Mourning Television: The Other Screen', *Screen* 51:4 (2010): 411.

[14] Fredric Jameson, *Postmodernism or, The Cultural Logic of Late Capitalism* (London: Verso, 1991), 67.

Tony, who instantly sends out an order for 'inter-agency support on setting up a grid' to find the van – in other words, the computer screen's output becomes an input into the narrative as a whole and into the other computer systems within it. These in turn produce their own outputs, and in the hyper-active enframing and reframing that occurs particularly in *24* and *Spooks*, the effect expands exponentially.

These narratives present deluges of information as threats only to tackle them using the weapon of computation. Significant pieces of information are identified or isolated and meaningful action is then taken by Jack in *24*, Harry Pearce in *Spooks*, Grissom in *CSI* and Mariko in *Investigator Mariko*. Correspondingly, there is a subset of characters in these series whose function it is to operate the computers in such a way that the correct infor-mation is yielded – respectively, this subset includes (among others) Chloe O'Brian, Tariq Masood, David Hodges and Kenji Inui. The technical challenge that these characters face may be expressed in terms of signal-to-noise ratio. That is, any flow of data contains a part that is important (the signal) as well as a part that is unwanted (noise), and a good ratio keeps the signal high and the noise low. The concept of noise as I use it here is both figurative (as in information theory) and literal (as in auditory content). In sound recording for film and television, noise comes from the machinery that is used to make the recording in the first place. Particularly in the first few decades of sound film, innovations came thick and fast to muffle camera and other machinic noise and to control microphones more accurately in order to enable synchronised sound recording.[15] Why, then, are FUIs always accompanied by sound effects which are not only unnecessary for the plot, but seem to add noise where it is easily avoided? In the second half of this chapter, I will examine the function of sound in FUI scenes as a way of identifying the capacities of computing that the FUI promises in contemporary TV drama.

The sound of computation

Television is traditionally a more sound- rather than image-oriented medium. There are several possible reasons for this: because ongoing direct address to the viewer is an aspect of television's distinctive liveness, because television

---

[15] See Rick Altman, 'The Evolution of Sound Technology', in *Film Sound: Theory and Practice* (New York: Columbia University Press, 1985), ed. Elisabeth Weis *et al.*, 37–43; John Belton, 'Technology and Aesthetics of Film Sound', in Weis, *Film Sound*, 63–72; Mary Ann Doane, 'Ideology and the Practice of Sound Editing and Mixing', in Weis, *Film Sound*, 54–62; and Barry Salt, 'Film Style and Technology in the Thirties: Sound', in Weis, *Film Sound*, 37–42.

has to compete for attention in domestic viewing situations, because television sets traditionally have poorer sound output than cinema.[16] In all of these, television aims to achieve a higher signal-to-noise ratio by filling the sound channel with as much content as possible. This goes some way towards explaining why in the shows under discussion so many sounds are called on to perform the difficult task of conveying the soundless activity of computation. But these reasons for television's taste for more rather than less sound are not as valid in the era of TVIII, and the shows under consideration here are typical of that era. FUI sounds are not only hard to justify in these terms, but they are totally non-realistic, in the sense that user interfaces in the real world rarely make any sounds at all and efforts to introduce sounds, such as Apple's SonicFinder project of the 1980s, have been quietly shelved.[17] Normal computing activity is almost totally silent compared to FUIs such as those we find in *Spooks*, for example. In episode 1 of Season 10, the dialogue of the three characters scanning CCTV footage is interspersed with the low-level, high-speed electronic chatter that accompanies the streams of data as they flow across the screen, ending in a pulsing alarm bleep indicating a 'Match'.

I suggest that the sounds that accompany FUIs in contemporary TV drama present us with a way of understanding how the emergent properties of digital media, a category which itself includes TVIII, are imagined. An emergent property is one that arises spontaneously within a complex system from a set of relatively simple starting points. In these dramas, computation appears to have emergent characteristics to the extent that FUIs display features that are more normally associated with living entities. Emitting noise is one of these features. Once again, I use 'noise' in its informational and auditory meanings. That is, the strange soundtrack of the FUI is also informational noise which, as Michel Serres observes, is an integral, necessary component of any system of communication: 'In the system, noise and message exchange roles according to the position of the observer and the action of the actor'.[18]

What precisely is the connection between the on-screen activity of a FUI and the sounds that accompany it? FUI sounds may be unsynchronised with on-screen movement, indeed computer sounds are at times heard 'off',

[16] Bernadette Casey *et al.*, (eds) *Television Studies: The Key Concepts* (London: Routledge: 2008), 112–13; John Ellis, *Visible Fictions: Cinema, Television, Video* (London: Routledge, 1992), 127–39 and 160–71; and Karen Lury, *Interpreting Television* (London: Hodder Arnold, 2005), 57–9.

[17] See W. W. Gaver, 'The SonicFinder, a Prototype Interface that Uses Auditory Icons', *Human Computer Interaction* 4 (1989): 67–94; Bill Moggridge, *Designing Interactions* (Cambridge, MA: MIT Press, 2007), 575–8.

[18] Michel Serres, *The Parasite* (Baltimore: Johns Hopkins University Press, 1982), 66.

i.e. without us being able to see the corresponding moving images on the monitor at all. But in many instances, the activity of computation is conveyed by using isomorphic sync-points, which are moments when an on-screen action correlates precisely with a sound effect.[19] Thus, in numerous episodes of *Investigator Mariko*, when the FUI has finished a calculation aimed at correlating a piece of evidence with a database, a written message in Japanese and English flashes in red at a regular rate and is rhythmically echoed by a soft yet urgent bleep.

In her examination of short animated cinema advertisements which foreground the capacities of Dolby sound systems, Vivian Sobchack notes that 'the desire to mark sound as visible rather than the visible as sounding provides the main impetus for and function of the Dolby trailers. In all but the most recent of them, sound originates, dominates, and shapes the image, rather than the image dominating and grounding (or anchoring) the sound'.[20] This is a reversal of the normal situation in film and television, where the image is prior and the soundtrack provides a sense of fullness, a situation that Christian Metz calls 'primitive substantialism'.[21] This 'stabilising function of sound', as Steven Connor calls it,[22] is part of an ideological system which uses sound in a highly controlled and controlling fashion in order to accentuate the suturing effect of the classical cinematic experience.[23] But the FUI that is embedded inside a television show is a much less coherently closed screen, as it gives no coherent answer to the question of whether the sound or the image is prior, a question which correlates to the (un)identifiability of the true site of computation. The activity of computation takes place on neither of these perceptual levels, but it manifests itself intermittently and inconsistently on one or both of them. At times, the FUI sound effect seems to be a rendering of the image, as in an Oramics machine, while at others, the image seems to be a rendering of the sound of computation, rather like an oscilloscope; once again, inputs become outputs and outputs inputs. This uncanny combination is reminiscent of Chladni patterns, where the vibration of a string coincides with the self-formation of grains on an adjoining plate into snowflake-like symmetries, 'as though the arbitrary symbolic code of phonetic script is suddenly thrown into an authentic and true connection with

---

[19] Scott Curtis, 'Early Warner Bros. Cartoons', in *Sound Theory Sound Practice*, ed. Rick Altman (London: Routledge/AFI, 1992), 201.

[20] Vivian Sobchack, 'When the Ear Dreams: Dolby Digital and the Imagination of Sound', *Film Quarterly* 58:4 (Summer 2005): 4.

[21] Christian Metz, 'Aural Objects', in Weis, *Film Sound*, 156.

[22] Steven Connor, 'Sounding Out Film', 2000, http://www.stevenconnor.com/soundingout/ [accessed 5 March 2013].

[23] See Mary Ann Doane, 'The Voice in the Cinema: The Articulation of Body and Space', in Weis, *Film Sound*, 162–76.

its signifier. The utterance and its written manifestation are one, the note and its notation are uniquely formed at the same time'.[24]

Of course, the net effect of combining sound with FUIs is not to confuse or to unbalance the signal-to-noise ratio. In all of these instances, the intended significance of the sound and/or vision is clear, yet we are still at pains to rationalise why the sound is there. Given this, we should also consider the FUI and its sound effects as a display of technological mastery and wizardry, in other words, a version of what is elsewhere called the 'cinema of attractions'.[25] This is very much in keeping with the concept of TVIII, where spectacle and high production values are no longer the exclusive purview of cinema. The sound effects are not added for verisimilitude, rather the opposite. The FUI is more science fiction than science, and once again this chimes with the imaginative freedom with which scientific reality and human technological capacities are treated in, particularly, *CSI* and *24*.

So the screens in these narratives show us what cannot be done by computers in reality, but only in fiction. That is, the FUI offers what it cannot provide. It enables us to see that the very activity that embedded screens purportedly enable – seeing the imperceptible – is precisely what the medium is unable to do. That is, TV shows with extreme degrees of embedded screens attempt to distract the viewer from the thing they cannot do by seeming to achieve it. The FUI is a window onto a virtual world; so the split screens of *Spooks* and *24* are windows onto many worlds at once, while the re-enactment CGI scenes in *Investigator Mariko* enable us to witness events that by definition have not been witnessed, and so-called 'CSI-shots'[26] follow impossible-to-follow bullet trajectories through bone and flesh.

Anne Friedberg, writing in 2006, argues:

> ... only in the last two decades – markedly with the advent of digital imaging technologies and new technologies of display – did the media 'window' [begin] to include multiple perspectives within a single frame. And as a coincident development, the interface of computer display made this 'new' multiple-'window'/multiple-screen format a daily lens,

---

[24] Aura Satz, 'Shapes with the Sound of Their Own Making', *Cabinet* 44 (Winter 2011/12): 33–4.

[25] Tom Gunning, 'The Cinema of Attraction: Early Film, Its Spectator, and the Avant-Garde', *Wide Angle* 8:3–4 (Fall 1986): 1–14; Tom Gunning, '"Now You See It, Now You Don't": The Temporality of the Cinema of Attractions', *The Velvet Light Trap* 32 (Fall 1993): 3–12.

[26] See Karen Lury, '*CSI* and Sound', in *Reading CSI: Crime TV Under the Microscope*, ed. Michael Allen (London: I. B. Tauris, 2007), 107–21; Silke Panse, 'The Bullets Confirm the Story Told by the Potato: Materials without Motives in *CSI Crime Scene Investigation*', in Allen, *Reading CSI*, 153–66; Mark J. P. Wolf, 'Subjunctive Documentary: Computer Imaging and Simulation', in *Collecting Visual Evidence* ed. Jane Gaines *et al.* (Minneapolis: University of Minnesota Press, 1999), 274–91.

a vernacular system of visuality. This remade visual vernacular requires new descriptors for its fractured, multiple, simultaneous, time-shiftable sense of space and time. Philosophies and critical theories that address the subject as a nodal point in a communicational matrix have failed to consider this important paradigm shift in visual address.[27]

The crisis in visual address described here expresses itself in various symptoms, one of which arguably is TVIII itself as a general phenomenon. More specifically, I suggest here that the introduction of sound is another such symptom. Faced with an entirely silent yet moving image (i.e. a normal computer user interface), sound is introduced to counter anxiety about the source of enunciation and as a way to acknowledge the seams between simultaneous sites of enunciation and to aid our identification with the proxy screen-viewer whom we watch as she or he watches a monitor inside our monitor.

Visions of artificial life in screen narratives have always evoked anxiety concerning the relation between humans and machines, but in the pre-FUI era, i.e. the era before that defined above by Friedman, artificial life either used to be silent (cf. the arrays of silent console displays in *Star Trek*) or it would speak with some degree of intelligibility – cf. HAL in *2001: A Space Odyssey* (Kubrick, 1968), Joshua in *WarGames* (Badham, 1983), Kitt in *Knight Rider* (Larson, 1982–6), C-3PO and even R2-D2 in *Star Wars* (Lucas, 1977).[28] But the introduction into screen narratives of the embedded screen as a site of disembodied computation and as a familiar part of our lived experiences in the eras of the PC and of TVIII more generally, has brought unintended, unforeseen and emergent consequences. The closed feedback loops of classical sound editing, where the Foley artist provides a whumpf to accompany a closing car door, still exist to be sure. But the encroachment of the FUI mentality into many screen experiences – for example, when the captions for a televised sports event audibly and visually whizz onto and off the screen – leaves open countless feedback loops whose effects potentially exceed the promises made by the FUI.

---

[27] Anne Friedberg, *The Virtual Window: From Alberti to Microsoft* (Cambridge, MA: MIT Press, 2006), 3.

[28] On computer-speech, see Michel Chion, *Film: A Sound Art* (New York: Columbia University Press, 2009), 331–7.

Bibliography

Altman, Rick. 'The Evolution of Sound Technology.' In *Film Sound: Theory and Practice*, ed. Elisabeth Weis *et al.*, 37–43. New York: Columbia University Press, 1985.

Barr, Charles. 'Broadcasting and Cinema: Screens within Screens.' In *All Our Yesterdays: 90 Years of British Cinema*, ed. Charles Barr, 206–24. London: BFI, 1986.

Belton, John. 'Technology and Aesthetics of Film Sound.' In *Film Sound: Theory and Practice*, ed. Elisabeth Weis *et al.*, 63–72. New York: Columbia University Press, 1985.

Bolter, Jay David and Richard Grusin, *Remediation: Understanding New Media*. Cambridge, MA: MIT Press, 1999.

Casey, Bernadette, Neil Casey, Ben Calvert, Liam French and Justin Lewis, eds. *Television Studies: The Key Concepts*. London: Routledge, 2008.

Caughie, John (2010) 'Mourning Television: The Other Screen.' *Screen* 51:4 (2010): 410–21.

Chion, Michel. *Film: A Sound Art*. New York: Columbia University Press, 2009.

Connor, Steven. 'Sounding Out Film.' 2000, http://www.stevenconnor.com/soundingout/ [accessed 5 March 2013].

Curtis, Scott. 'Early Warner Bros. Cartoons.' In *Sound Theory Sound Practice*, ed. Rick Altman, 191–203. London: Routledge/AFI, 1992.

Deane, Cormac. 'Introduction to Christian Metz's *Impersonal Enunciation, or the Place of Film*.' *New Review of Film and Television Studies* 8:4 (2010): 343–7.

—'From THX to FUI to C4I to HUD: The Special Effects of the Control Room, 1971–2012.' In *Special Effects: New Histories, Theories, Contexts*, ed. Bob Rehak, Dan North, and Michael S. Duffy. London: BFI/Palgrave Macmillan, forthcoming.

Doane, Mary Ann. 'Ideology and the Practice of Sound Editing and Mixing.' In *Film Sound: Theory and Practice*, ed. Elisabeth Weis *et al.*, 54–62. New York: Columbia University Press, 1985.

—'The Voice in the Cinema: The Articulation of Body and Space.' In *Film Sound: Theory and Practice*, ed. Elisabeth Weis *et al.*, 162–76. New York: Columbia University Press, 1985.

Ellis, John. *Visible Fictions: Cinema, Television, Video*. London: Routledge, 1992.

Févry, Sébastien. *La mise en abyme filmique: Essai de typologie*. Liège: Céfal, 2000.

Friedberg, Anne. *The Virtual Window: From Alberti to Microsoft*. Cambridge, MA: MIT Press, 2006.

Gaver, W. W. 'The SonicFinder, a Prototype Interface that Uses Auditory Icons.' *Human Computer Interaction* 4 (1989): 67–94.

Gleick, James. *The Information: A History, a Theory, a Flood*. London: Fourth Estate, 2011.

Gunning, Tom. ''Now You See It, Now You Don't': The Temporality of the Cinema of Attractions.' *The Velvet Light Trap* 32 (Fall 1993): 3–12.

Gunning, Tom. 'The Cinema of Attraction: Early Film, Its Spectator, and the Avant-Garde.' *Wide Angle* 8:3–4 (Fall 1986), 1–14.

Hills, Matt. 'From the Box in the Corner to the Box Set on the Shelf.' *New Review of Film and Television Studies* 5:1 (2007): 41–60.

Jacobs, Jason. 'The Medium in Crisis: Caughie, Brunsdon and the Problem of US Television.' *Screen* 52:4 (2011): 503–11.

Jameson, Fredric. *Postmodernism or, The Cultural Logic of Late Capitalism*. London: Verso, 1991.

Johnson, Catherine. 'Tele-branding in TVIII.' *New Review of Film and Television Studies* 5:1 (2007): 5–24.

Kittler, Friedrich. *Gramophone, Film, Typewriter*. Stanford: Stanford University Press, 1999.

Lash, Scott. *Critique of Information*. London: Sage, 2002.

Leconte, Bernard. *Images abymées: Essais sur la réflexivité iconique*. Paris: L'Harmattan, 2000.

—*L'écran dans l'écran et autres rectangles scopiques*. Paris: L'Harmattan, 2004.

Lury, Karen. *Interpreting Television*. London: Hodder Arnold, 2005.

—'*CSI* and Sound.' In *Reading CSI: Crime TV Under the Microscope*, ed. Michael Allen, 107–21. London: I. B. Tauris, 2007.

Metz, Christian. 'Aural Objects.' In *Film Sound: Theory and Practice*, ed. Elisabeth Weis *et al.*, 154–61. New York: Columbia University Press, 1985.

—*L'énonciation impersonnelle, ou le site du film*. Paris: Méridiens-Klincksieck, 1991.

Moggridge, Bill. *Designing Interactions*. Cambridge, MA: MIT Press, 2007.

Nelson, Robin. *State of Play: Contemporary 'High-End' TV Drama*. Manchester: Manchester University Press, 2007.

Panse, Silke. 'The Bullets Confirm the Story Told by the Potato: Materials without Motives in *CSI Crime Scene Investigation*.' In *Reading CSI: Crime TV Under the Microscope*, ed. Michael Allen, 153–66. London: I. B. Tauris, 2007.

Reynolds, Mike. 'Study: One-Third of U.S. Households Watch TV Video via Internet.' *Multichannel News*, last modified 17 February 2012; http://tinyurl.com/8fbn7sp [accessed 12 October 2012].

Salt, Barry. 'Film Style and Technology in the Thirties: Sound.' In *Film Sound: Theory and Practice*, ed. Elisabeth Weis *et al.*, 37–42. New York: Columbia University Press, 1985.

Satz, Aura. 'Shapes with the Sound of Their Own Making.' *Cabinet* 44 (Winter 2011/12): 33–9.

Serres, Michel. *The Parasite*. Baltimore: Johns Hopkins University Press, 1982.

Sobchack, Vivian. 'When the Ear Dreams: Dolby Digital and the Imagination of Sound.' *Film Quarterly* 58: 4 (Summer 2005): 2–15.

Spangler, Todd, 'Half Of Americans Watch Online Video: Nielsen' *Multichannel News*, last modified 20 October 2011, http://tinyurl.com/3fo7bg3

Stelter, Brian. 'Youths Are Watching, but Less Often on TV.' *New York Times*, 8 February 2012, B1.

Taipale, K.A. 'Data Mining and Domestic Security: Connecting the Dots to Make Sense of Data.' *Columbia Science and Technology Law Review* V (2003): 1–83.

United States Government Accountability Office. 'Data Mining: Early Attention to Privacy in Developing a Key DHS Program Could Reduce Risks.' GAO-07–293, February 2007.

Wolf, Mark J.P. 'Subjunctive Documentary: Computer Imaging and Simulation.' In *Collecting Visual Evidence*, ed. Jane Gaines *et al.*, 274–91. Minneapolis: University of Minnesota Press, 1999.

Index

24 6, 46, 213, 309–14, 317
2001: A Space Odyssey 318

Abbott, Paul 236
Abbott, Stacey 1, 232, 236
Abrams, J. J 1
Absalom, Absalom! 169
Adam's Rib 181
Affron, Charles 211, 216
Aherne, Caroline 114, 126–7
Airline 115
Akass, Kim 73, 103
Albrecht, Chris 186
Alias 1–2, 8
All in the Family 73
Allison, Fran 283
Altman, Robert 284–5
American Horror Story 6
Anderson, Lindsay 300
Andersson, Linus 18
Andrews, Eamonn 244–7
Anstey, Edgar 295
Apsion, Annabelle 230
Aqua Teen Hunger Force 136
Archer 16, 135–43
Aristotle 100, 273
Arnett, Will 106
Arnold, Matthew 188
Arrested Development 16, 103–12
art 25–42, 47, 68–73
At Last the 1948 Show 79–80
audience 10, 16, 25–27, 58–60, 64,
    69, 73, 86–8, 105–10, 113–18, 122,
    128, 136, 142, 160–2, 171, 186,
    193–5, 201–6, 220, 228, 231–5,
    236–7, 244–65, 272–4, 279–84,
    304
authorship 10, 189
Awful Truth, The 181

Bachchan, Amitabh 252
Back, Frank 278–9
Baker, Tom 234
Baldwin, Thalia 1
Ball, Alan 73, 189
Ball, Zoe 257–8
Barnouw, Erik 277
Baron-Cohen, Sacha 130
Barr, Charles 18, 311
Barrowman, John 256
Barry, Raymond 181
Barrymore, John 178
Barton, Mischa 200
Bateman, Jason 106
Battlestar Galactica 213
Bay, Michael 2
Bazin, André 247–9
beauty 15, 29–31, 40, 67, 74, 169, 177,
    204
Bell, Clive 33, 41
Bellow, George Wesley 194
Belton, John 277, 280
Bennett, Alan 119
Berger, John 300
Bergeron, Tom 257
Bergson, Henri 100
Bignell, Jonathan 10–11, 210
Black, Peter 297, 299
Boardwalk Empire 17, 185–96
Bonner, Frances 18, 62
Bono, Chaz 254
Boorman, John 301
Bordwell, David 60–1, 94
Borrowed Pasture 301
Bourne Ultimatum, The 311
Bourdieu, Pierre 47
Bowie, David 232
Boyle, Susan 261
Branco, Sérgio Dias 16–17

Brault, Michel 292
Breaking Bad 6, 15–17, 47–55, 67, 73, 187, 219–26
Brecht, Bertolt 132, 272, 304
Bridson, D. G. 291
Bringing Up Baby 16, 181
Britain's Got Talent 258
Brody, Adam 200
Brooke-Taylor, Tim 79–80, 89
Brunsdon, Charlotte 14, 64
Brydon, Rob 16, 115–23
Buchan, John 138
Buckley, Jeff 204–6
Burch, Noel 162
Bus Stop 284
Buscemi, Steve 187
Buscombe, Edward 299
Bussell, Darcy 258
Butler, Jeremy 10, 71, 74, 94–95, 105, 211, 272
Butler, Judith 259
Butterflies 15
Byrne, Gabriel 8

Caine, Michael 116
Caldwell, John T. 60–2, 70–1, 188
camera 4, 9, 15–16, 48, 58, 61, 71–3, 84, 91, 94–101, 105–14, 121, 127, 131, 155, 161, 170, 173, 177–80, 193, 202–4, 209–16, 224–6, 241–8, 278–83, 299, 314
canon 25, 37–8, 55, 70, 123, 190, 296
Cardwell, Sarah 2, 14, 119
Carmen, Sally 230
Carnivàle 57
Carroll, Noël 29–33, 37, 72
Carter, Joelle 176, 179–80
Cash, Craig 126–7
Casino 190
Cathy Come Home 299
Caughie, John 14, 125–9
Cavell, Benjamin 181
Cavell, Stanley 16–17, 79, 89–92, 178, 181
Cera, Michael 109
Chanan, Michael 296
Chaplin, Charlie 90, 155
Chapman, Graham 79–80, 84, 89

characterisation 25, 33, 49, 52–4, 94, 136
Chase, David 189
Chatman, Seymour 107
Cheers 16, 95–101
Chicago 302
Chigvintsev, Artem 261
Chiklis, Michael 212
Citizen '63 301
Clayton, Alex 13, 16
Cleese, John 79–80, 84–5, 89
Clift, Montgomery 162
Close Encounters of the Third Kind 231
Cochran, Tanya R. 5
Cock and Bull Story, A 116
Cohen, Leonard 204
Cohen, Ted 17
coherence 7, 37, 41, 46–7, 142, 255
Colasanto, Nicholas 97
Collingwood, R. G. 29–36
colour 2, 18, 38, 71, 83, 139, 154, 185, 195, 233–4, 242, 264–5
Come Dancing 255–6, 263
Community 6, 105–10
complexity 4, 14, 45–55, 69, 73, 118, 139–41, 205, 212, 221, 227
Connor, Steven 316
Contemporary Art Centre TV 270–5
Coogan, Steve 16, 115–22
Cooke, Lez 227
Cooke, Rachel 116
Corner, John 26, 36, 60, 299
Coronation Street 63, 243, 300
Cotton Club, The 194
Coppola, Francis Ford 192, 195
Coulthard, Lisa 220
Cranston, Bryan 53, 219
Creeber, Glen 63, 227–8
criteria 3, 29–31, 38–41, 54
criticism 2–5, 9–17, 30, 36–41, 45–6, 55, 79, 95, 128, 132, 214, 290, 313
Cross, David 106
Croucher, Michael 292, 301
Crudele, Frank 191
Cruz, Raymond 222
Crystal Makers, The 301
C. S. I 57–8, 73, 210, 309, 312–17

Cumberbatch, Benedict 7
Curb Your Enthusiasm 105, 110, 115–16

Daly, Tess 256
Damages 187
Dancing with the Stars 251, 254–6, 258, 260, 262, 264
Danson, Ted 96
Darlow, Michael 290
Dasgupta, Sudeep 9
Davies, Terence 296–8
Deadwood 175, 178, 186, 189, 195
Deane, Cormac 18
Déjà Vu 311
Deleuze, Gilles 25
Deming, Caren 71
De Niro, Robert 191
De Palma, Brian 191
De Rossi, Portia 106
Desmond, Jane 263
Dexter 187
dialogue 4, 28, 41, 84, 88, 126, 136–43, 175, 185, 193, 230, 234, 282, 310, 315
Dick Van Dyke Show, The 46
Dickie, George 41
Dimbleby, Richard 304
Dinnerladies 114
Dirksen, Everett 281
Di Tommaso, Tanya 271
Dixon, Alesha 258
Doctor Who 116, 233–5
Donaghy, James 236
Donaldson, Lucy Fife 17
Donnellan, Philip 292–3, 296, 301
Donnelly, Kevin 290
Dreyfus, Richard 231
Driving School 115
Du Beke, Anton 261
Dunleavy, Trisha 62
Durie, Jamie 261
Dynasty 200

Eastenders 63
Eastwood, Clint 52
Eaton, Marcia Muelder 38
Edelstein, Brynne 254

editing 12, 48, 58–61, 63, 70, 73, 84, 94, 100, 105–9, 120, 140–1, 152, 92, 212–13, 243–8, 290, 293, 298, 303, 318
Edwards, Blake 284
Edwards, Gareth 104
Ellis, John 86, 266
Elton, Arthur 295
Empson, William 12
Errington, Mac 302
evaluation 2–5, 10, 14, 23, 27, 35–41, 45–47, 54–5, 117, 149, 219–20
Evans, Keith 298
Every Day Except Christmas 300
Everybody Loves Raymond 46

Fairbanks, Jerry 279
Faking It 261
Family Guy 136
Farson, Daniel 304
Feldman, Marty 79–80, 84, 89
Fennick, W. E. 41
Feuer, Jane 60
Firefly 5, 9–10
Fish, Stanley 46
Fiske, John 255, 263–4
Fitzgerald, F. Scott 168
Flaherty, Robert 248
FlashForward 46
Forbrydelsen (The Killing) 214
Forman, Denis 293
Forsyth, Bruce 256–8, 262–3
Foucault, Michel 195
Frankenheimer, John 284
Franklin, Ieuan 18
Frasier 95–101
Friedberg, Anne 317–18
Friends 95
Frye, Northrop 147
Fung, Anthony 252

Gallagher, Peter 200
Gangs of New York 190
Garner, Jennifer 1
Garwood, Ian 201
Gatiss, Mark 7
Gehman, Chris 292
genre 2, 6, 10, 30, 48, 60–3, 70–3,

95, 105, 113–18, 135–143, 181, 187–93, 210, 229, 235, 312–13

Gervais, Ricky 114–15

Get Smart 137

Gibbs, John 4–5, 10–12

Gilliam, Laurence 291

Gilligan, Vince 48, 50

Gitlin, Todd 74

Glitter, Gary 235

Godard, Jean-Luc 298

Godfather, The 192

Goggins, Walton 176, 178–9, 212

Goodfellas 190

Goodman, Len 257

Gorbman, Claudia 202, 204

Gråbøl, Sophie 214

Grammer, Kelsey 96

Grant, Cary 178, 181

Grant, Russell 263

Grice, H. P. 127

Grierson, John 290, 292, 294, 301

Griffith, D. W. 279

Grigsby, Mike 292

Groundhog Day 16

Guffey, Cary 231

Haigh, Peter 244

Hall, Nick 18

Hale, Tony 109

Hall, Stuart 302

Hallam, Julia 15

Hamm, Jon 163

Hancock's Half-Hour 113

Handley, Taylor 201

Harlan County, USA 182

Harrelson, Woody 98

Harrison, Mark 136

Hartley, John 255, 263–4

Harvey Birdman, Attorney at Law 137

Hausken, Liv 272

Haynes, Todd 189

HBO 48, 57, 60, 68–71, 104–5, 115–16, 171, 185–96, 272, 275

Heidegger, Martin 96, 126, 131

Heller, Dana 262

Hemingway, Ernest 153

Heyerdahl, Thor 247

Hill Street Blues 74, 210

Hill, John 230

Hill, Walter 189

Hills, Matt 24–39

His Girl Friday 178, 181

Hitchcock, Alfred 182, 248

Hoffman, Dustin 189

Hoggart, Richard 300

Holmes, Su 63

Homicide: Life on the Street 48, 210

Hop Skip and Jump: the Story of Children's Play 297

Horton, Peter 209

Horwood, Craig 257

Hospers, John 32–3

Housing Problems 295

Huhne, Chris 241–2, 248

Humphries, Steve 297

immediacy 11, 14, 210–11

I Dream of Jeannie 140

I Spy 137

I'm a Celebrity... Get Me Out of Here! 254

In Prison 293

In Treatment 8–9, 73

Ingarden, Roman 37

interpretation 3–5, 10–11, 27, 35, 38–9, 201, 219–20, 273, 285

Investigator Mariko 309, 312, 314, 316–17

Iron Man 2 311

It Happened One Night 181

It Takes Two 257, 265

Jackson, Rosemary 229, 236

Jacobs, Jason 61, 188, 230, 313

Jameson, Fredric 313

Jennings, Humphrey 290, 293–4, 303

Jermyn, Deborah 58

Jessop, T. E. 39

Joe the Chainsmith 301

John Adams 186, 195

Johnson, Beth 17

Johnson, Catherine 229

Johnson, Ola 265

Jordan, Marion 227–8

Joyce, James 298

judgement 2–5, 14, 34, 38–39, 45–8, 55, 62, 71, 74, 148, 151, 161, 214, 253, 266, 269
Justified 17, 175–83

Kant, Immanuel 32–4, 39, 70, 85
Karnes, Jay 211
Kavka, Misha 252
Keaton, Buster 90
Kennerley, Kerri-Anne 258
Kerr, Walter 155
Khan, Irrfan 8
Kieran, Matthew 36
Kill Bill Vol. 2 6
Kittler, Friedrich 309, 313
Kleinecke-Bates, Iris 126
Klevan, Andrew 5–6, 16–17, 99, 117–18
Kneale, Nigel 248
Knight Rider 318
Knox, Simone 138
Kopple, Barbara 182
Kraft Suspense Theatre 284
Kruger, Sonia 256–8
Kukla, Fran and Ollie 282–3

L Word, The 187
Laciura, Anthony 191
Lady Eve, The 181
Larry Sanders Show, The 115
Lash, Scott 312
L'Atalante 185
Leavis, F. R. 11
Lee, Stewart 104
Leeves, Jane 98
Leigh, Adèle 245
Leonard, Elmore 175–6, 178
Leone, Sergio 48, 192
Les 400 Coups 248
Levine, Elana 68
Little, Ralf 129
Littlewood, Joan 291
liveness 7, 68–72, 91, 253, 314
Loach, Ken 299
Logan, Elliott 17
Long, Shelley 97
Lost 3–5, 63, 68, 221
Lotz, Amanda 186

Louie 73
Lowthorpe, Philippa 292
Luck 189
Luhrman, Baz 255
Lury, Karen 58–9, 130, 199
Lyas, Colin 35, 37

Macbeth 12
MacColl, Ewan 291–2, 304
MacDonald, Kelly 191
Mad Men 6, 11–13, 17, 48, 67, 104, 147–56, 187
Mahoney, John 98
Main Street Africa 302
Maio, Barbara 5
Malašauskas, Raimundas 271, 273–4
Maltese Falcon, The 176
Man from U.N.C.L.E., The 137–8
Mann, Michael 189
Marcus Welby, MD 285
Margolis, Joseph 34
Marion and Geoff 116
Martindale, Margo 178
Mary Tyler Moore Show, The 73
M*A*S*H 73
Maslin, Janet 175
Masterchef 252
McAllister, Stewart 293, 303
McCabe, Janet 17, 59, 73, 103, 185
McCabe and Mrs Miller 285
McCormack, Eric 93
McDermott, Paul 255
McG 2
McGregor, Ewan 230
McKenny, Todd 256
McKenzie, Ben 200
McLynn, Pauline 231
McMains, Juliet 259, 263
McPherson, Daniel 257
Mean Streets 190
Medea 182
Medhurst, Andy 129
Mel B 258
Merchant, Stephen 114
Mercurio, Paul 256
Messing, Debra 93
Metz, Christian 312, 316
Miami Vice 10, 210

Mildred Pierce 189
Miller, Arthur 155
Milligan, Spike 247
Mills, Brett 15, 105
Minnow, Newton 269
Miranda 115
Mirzoeff, Edward 292
mise-en-scène 4, 9–11, 96, 253, 285, 302
Misfits 6
Mitchell, Denis 289–91, 293–8, 300–4
Mitchum, Robert 182
Mitias, Michael H. 35
Mittell, Jason 3–5, 10–11, 14–15, 45, 103, 220–1
Moffat, Steven 7
Monitor 301
Monty Python's Flying Circus 79
Moore, Roger 119, 121
Moran, Albert 252
Morning in the Streets 290, 293, 295–7, 299–301
Moseley, Rachel 118
Moyes, Peter 142
Mulligan, Robert 284
Munsters, The 16
Munt, Sally 236
music 18, 48, 70, 80, 85–8, 141, 149, 191–2, 199–207, 232–5, 243, 253, 262, 291

Nanook of the North 248
Nayat, Germina 273
Nelson, Robin 9, 57–64, 68, 103
Newcomb, Horace 14, 68–70
Night Court USA 283
Night in the City 293
Night of the Hunter, The 6
Nip/Tuck 187
North by Northwest 178
Nurse Jackie 187
NYPD Blue 10, 210

O. C, The 17, 199–207
O'Connor, Flannery 182
Of Time and the City 296–7
Office, The 114–16

Ogden Stiers, David 100
Olyphant, Timothy 175, 177
On Tour 293
Once Upon A Time in America 192
Ormond, John 301, 303
Out of the Past 182
Owen Marshall, Counsellor-at-Law 285

Paisley, Brad 182
Palladino, Aleksa 194
Panorama 243
Parker, Charles 292–3
Parks and Recreation 105
Pateman, Matthew 9
Patsavas. Alexandra 200
Paul, Aaron 220
Peacock, Steven 1–3, 26, 101, 116
Pearson, Roberta 3, 59, 68
Peeping Tom 249
Pegler, Jack 279
Pendleton, Victoria 263
People Talking 293
Perkins, V. F. 6
Perlman, Rhea 97
Peter Gunn 284
Peters, Roy 298
Phil Silvers Show, The 16, 113
Philadelphia Story, The 181
Philco Television Playhouse 284
Philips, Arlene 257–8
philosophy 24–31, 36–40, 95, 172
Picart, Caroline Jean 259, 263
Pierce, David Hyde 100
Pitt, Michael 192
Pizzino, Carmello 265
Planet of the Apes, The 285
Playhouse 90 284
Poliakoff, Stephen 119
Pollack, Sydney 284
Popescu-Branesti, Gheorge 297
Powell, Michael 249
Pounder, CCH 211
Preston, John 117
Psycho 248
Public Enemy, The 194
Purser, Philip 294
Pye, Douglas 4–5, 10, 12

'Quality television' 1, 9, 15, 18, 37, 42, 46, 59–60, 62–4, 72, 103, 119, 127–9, 185–96, 201, 204, 207, 211–15, 232–3, 251–2, 271–2, 281, 310–11
Quatermass and the Pit 248
Queer as Folk 187

radio 18, 31, 61, 68, 91, 98, 104, 131, 232, 281, 289–4
Radio Ballads 292–3, 304
Ragsdale, Gary 180
Randell, Arthur J. 16
Randell-Moon, Holly 16
Randolph, Jeanne 172
Rawat, Navi 205
Ray Valdez, Jeremy 214
Read, John 301
realism 50–1, 166, 190, 194–5, 200–3, 210, 227–9, 273–4, 298
Red River 162
Redmond, Sean 235
Reisz, Karel 294, 300
Renoir, Jean 247–8
Rescue Me 187
Reynolds, Burt 137
Roberts, Les 297
Rodgers, W. R. 292
Rose, Gillian 166–7
Rossellini, Roberto 247–8
Rothman, William 6, 13, 17
Rowan, Kelly 203
Royle Family, The 16, 114–16, 125–32
Rudie, Evelyn 284
Russell, David 295
Russell, Ken 301

Savile, Jimmy 116
Savorelli, Antonio 105
Scannell, Paddy 126, 131
Schor, Naomi 128
Scorsese, Martin 186, 189–93
Scrubs 95, 105
Scruton, Roger 34
Sealab 2020 137
Sealab 2021 137
Searcy, Nick 176, 178

Secombe, Harry 243–6, 248–9
Seeger, Peggy 292
Seidelman, Susan 189
Seinfeld 274
Serres, Michel 315
Sesame Street 137
Sex and the City 189
Shameless 17, 227–7
Shapley, Olive 291
Shawkat, Alia 107
Sherlock 7–8
Shield, The 17, 187, 209–17
Shklovsky, Victor 132
Shone, Tom 192
Shopping City 130
Shooting the Past 57
Sibley, Frank 37
Sikora, Joseph 191
Silverstone, Roger 269
Simpsons, The 136, 138–9
Simon, David 48, 51, 189
sitcom 16, 71–3, 85–7, 93–101, 103–10, 113–18, 130, 211
Six Feet Under 73, 194
Smith, Jeff 202, 206
Smith, Liz 127
So You Think You Can Dance? 251, 253
Sobchack, Vivian 213, 316
Soho Story 293
Somers, Darryl 256
Sons of Anarchy 6
Sopranos, The 48, 57–8, 63, 67, 186–7, 274
sound 18, 38, 48–49, 57–8, 67–72, 88–91, 94, 116, 130, 142, 150, 163, 192, 199–206, 233–5, 242–3, 247, 289–305, 309, 314–18
South Park 136
Sparks, Paul 193
spectacle 18, 62, 70, 138–9, 191, 221, 230–3, 251–4, 260–6, 272, 301, 317
Spielberg, Steven 7, 231, 233–4
Spooks 6, 309, 312–17
Squires, Charlie 292
Stabile, Carol A. 136
Staiger, Janet 72

Stanley, Alessandra 187
Star Trek 59, 233, 318
Star Wars 138
Stephenson Connolly, Pamela 260
Stilley, Margo 121
Stolnitz, Jerome 34
storytelling 45–55, 125, 191, 199–206, 221
Strictly Ballroom 255
Strictly Come Dancing 251, 255–6, 260, 265
Strictly Dancing 255
subtlety 41, 46, 264
Swallow, Norman 301
Sykes, Eric 247

Tambor, Jeffrey 106
taste 25, 29, 34, 37–42, 71, 186, 190, 253, 269, 315
technology 5, 18, 58–63, 70, 86, 103, 138, 195, 243–9, 278–81, 302, 311
texture 58, 63, 83, 89, 117, 125, 141, 185, 195, 245
This is Your Life 18, 241–50
Thomson, David 292
Thompson, Kay 284
Thompson, Kristin 131
Thorburn, David 14
Threlfall, David 228
Tointon, Kara 261
Toles, George 11, 12, 13, 17
Tomlinson, Ricky 127
Tonioli, Bruno 257
Top Gun 138
Tourneur, Jacques 182
Trainspotting 230
Trip, The 16, 113–23
Truffaut, Francois 248
Trumm, Leonard 302
Twentieth Century 178
Twitter 7
Two and a Half Men 105, 115

Uba, George 259, 263
Unforgiven 52
Untouchables, The 191
Urmson, J. O. 31, 38

value 2–6, 14, 24–42, 46–8, 54, 59, 64, 69, 83, 129, 137, 150–1, 187–90, 233–41, 269, 292, 300, 311, 317
Van Pelt, Tamise 234
Vaughan, Dai 294, 303
Vermeulen, Thomas 16
Vertigo 248
Vigo, Jean 185
voiceover 4, 242, 254, 298

Walden 169
Walking with Dinosaurs 58
Walsh, Steve 235
Walter, Jessica 109
Walters, James 16–17
Waltz, Christoph 121
WarGames 318
Warshow, Robert 155–6, 164–5
Watson, Mary Ann 281
Watson, Paul 292
Wayne, John 162
We are the Lambeth Boys 300
Weiner, Matt 152
Wellman, William 194
Wells, Paul 139
Wendt, George 98
West Wing, The 7, 206
Whannel, Paddy 302
Wheatley, Helen 126
Whedon, Joss 5
Whigham, Shea 194
Whitfield, James 16
Who Wants to be a Millionaire? 63, 252
Wilcox, Rhonda V. 5
Wilde, Olivia 203
Wilde, Oscar 182
Widdicombe, Ann 254, 263
Will & Grace 16, 93–4, 98, 101
Williams, Michelle 264
Williams, Raymond 86
Williamson, Harold 292
Wilson, Benji 196
Winkleman, Claudia 257
Winter, Terence 187
Wire, The 15, 47–55, 104, 186
Wilson, George 6
Woo, John 137

Wood, Peter H. 273
Wood, Victoria 114–15
Woods, Faye 17

X Factor, The 253, 258
X-Files, The 48

Yost, Graham 175, 178

YouTube 7, 104, 256

Zea, Natalie 178
Zettl, Herbert 69
Zola, Émile 298
Zoller Seitz, Matt 194
zoom shot 18, 84, 104–5, 212–13, 277–85